THE RIGHT TO LIFE, SECURITY, PRIVACY AND OWNERSHIP IN ISLAM

Mohammad Hashim Kamali

THE RIGHT TO LIFE, SECURITY, PRIVACY AND OWNERSHIP IN ISLAM

ISLAMIC TEXTS SOCIETY

This edition published 2008 by The Islamic Texts Society
35 Parkside, Cambridge CB1 1JE, U.K.

ISBN 978 1903682 548 cloth
ISBN 978 1903682 555 paper

British Library Cataloguing in Publication Data.
A catalogue record for this book is available from the British Library.

Printed in Turkey by Mega Printing.

Contents

NOTE ON THE FUNDAMENTAL RIGHTS AND LIBERTIES IN ISLAM SERIES

The present volume is the fifth in a seven volume series entitled Fundamental Rights and Liberties in Islam: Principles and Applications. The first five volumes in the series are:

Volume 1: *The Dignity of Man: an Islamic Perspective* (2002)

Volume 2: *Freedom, Equality and Justice in Islam* (2002)

Volume 3: *Equity and Fairness in Islam* (2005)

Volume 4: *Freedom of Expression in Islam* (1997)

THE REMAINING TWO VOLUMES WILL BE:

Volume 6: *The Right to Education, Work and Welfare in Islam*

Volume 7: *Freedom of Movement, Citizenship, and Accountability: An Islamic Perspective.*

The revised order in which the seven volumes are now arranged reflects their division into the two categories of General Discussions and Particular Themes. The first three volumes constitute the general ideas, while the remaining four titles address the particular themes and topics fundamental to rights and liberties. The reader might be interested to know that Freedom of Expression in Islam also includes chapters on freedom of religion, freedom of association, and a chapter on blasphemy and apostasy.

Acknowledgements

A significant portion of the research for the preparation of the present volume was carried out at the Wissenschaftskolleg zu Berlin (Institute for Advanced Study Berlin) when I spent one academic year as a Fellow of that Institute in 2000–2001. I would like to acknowledge the generous support I have received from Professor. Dr. Wolf Lepenies, the then Rector, his deputy Joachim Nettlebeck and other colleagues and fellows of the Kolleg. I was the recipient of a Gerd Bucerius Fellow der Zeit-Stiftung grant in support of my reseach on *Fundamental Rights and Liberties in Islam: Principles and Applications,* which was instrumental to the progress of my research during my stay in Berlin. I also acknowledge with thanks the help I received from Gesine Bottomly, the chief librarian, and Hans G. Lindenberg, head of the computer unit, for the efficient service they provided, especially in digging deep into Islamic sources and the inter-library loans of rare books. Islamic research is not a main feature of their work in the Kolleg, but the efforts we made together were often more successful than expected. My project presentation in one of the weekly colloquia of the Kolleg in March 2001 led to rigorous and enlightening exchanges with the fellows, and some of the subjects we discussed remained the subject of continued communication between us. I recall vividly the discussions and correspondence on matters of mutual interest I maintained with Professors Claude Gilliot and Deborah Klimburg-Salter, who were also fellows of the Kolleg in that year. Georges Khalil, coordinator of the Islam and Modernity Group, was very helpful in lending me items of interest from his personal collection, and we frequently conversed on topical issues of the Islamic world, with special reference to Egypt.

The remaining parts of my research were conducted at the International Islamic University of Malaysia over the succeeding years. Unlike the Wissenschaftskolleg, where I was a newcomer, the IIUM environment was familiar territory for me, and the continued help I received from the library staff of the IIUM both at the Gombak campus and at the International Institute of Islamic Thought and Civilisation (ISTAC) library was instrumental to the success of this research. Mrs Salmah Ahmad of ISTAC, Mr Nirwan Syafrin, a PhD candidate who acted as my research assistant, and Diwi Abbas were all very helpful in the computer work and checking the text and corrections, and I take this opportunity to thank them warmly for their assistance.

Lastly I would like to record my heartfelt appreciation to Fatima Azzam, director of the Islamic Texts Society of Cambridge, for her unreserved support in the publication of this and the remaining volumes in the Series. I am appreciative of her meticulous attention to all aspects of the work, from funding and finance to editing, cover design, product specifications, to prompt and efficient communication between us. I have seen all of this in my previous publications with the ITS, and I remain confident that the remaining volumes in the Series will be up to the high standard of production that has become a hallmark of ITS publications.

Introduction

The four chapters of the present volume are in many ways interrelated and complementary in that they all explore various aspects of the basic rights of the individual. A person's rights to life, personal security, privacy, and ownership are the most basic of all the fundamental rights and liberties of concern to almost every legal system and tradition. To address them side by side with one another, as is attempted in the present volume, is reflective of their natural priority and significance. Except for the right of ownership, which falls under rights in *rem* (*al-ḥuqūq al-ʿayniyya*) all the other three areas of basic rights under review fall under the category of rights in *personam* (*al-ḥuqūq al-shakhṣiyya*). Rights in *rem* and rights in *personam* stand in contradistinction to rights and liberties that are called abstract or intellectual rights (*al-ḥuqūq al-maʿnawiyya*) such as the rights to freedom of speech, freedom of religion and freedom of association.

The right to personal security is an extension of the right to life simply because a person who is physically threatened and attacked tends to fear for his life. The right to life is undoubtedly the bedrock and starting point of all other rights, as rights tend to lose much of their meaning and significance in regard to deceased persons. For a living person, all his or her basic rights and liberties tend to complement one another, as none can remain unaffected in the event of the derogation and compromise of the others, and they cannot stand totally independently of one another. Even when a person's right to life is granted, to make the use of this right worthwhile, his safety against aggression and arrest, as well as respect for his privacy and what he owns, are essential to his sense of dignity and self worth.

The rights under review in this volume are of the most vulnerable to aggression and abuse, to coercive power and to the use of force. When an individual, a group of individuals, or a state plan to subjugate another party, the rights to life and personal safety are likely to be the primary targets of attack. Needless to say, these rights are also the most vulnerable to dictatorship and the vagaries of a police state. To discipline the use of coercive power and subjugate it to the rule of law and due process remain the perpetual challenge of civilization, and constitute the basic barometer of success for all forms of social organization that seek to establish normal order in society. The centrality of the rule of law and due process to the protection of basic rights and liberties can hardly be overstated. Yet the rule of law as a concept and objective needs to be articulated and expounded in respect of its essential requirements and procedures, and its refinement of detail, as well as constant supervision of its observance. Only this can substantiate the basic notion of the rule of law as a credible reality and the necessary commitment of a law-abiding government. States and constitutions often lay claim to the notion of the rule of law all too often as an abstract idea that is not reflected, or only partially reflected, in the actual conduct of government. The degree of success attained in making the rule of law a tangible reality also depends on a number of variable factors, including resource availability and finance. Yet the attitudinal question of commitment is even more important. It is not an exaggeration to say that by far the larger number of present day nation states, especially in the developing world, Muslim countries included of course, remain less than successful on the scale of the observable manifestations of the rule of law, often in the face of an unequivocal commitment in their own constitutions. The rule of law thus constitutes a more momentous challenge for Third World countries, and a basic criterion of failure and success of state organization in the era of constitutionalism.

Laws and constitutions must also be supplemented by policy measures and a pro-active attitude on the part of the law enforcement agencies if they are to nurture a culture of legality and respect for basic rights. For laws alone can be rendered meaningless if the attitude of their enforcers is confined to a mere facade of legality not reflected in the practice and conduct of the police, governor and judge. To illustrate this point, there is a certain line of distinction between the *Sharīʿah* and what is known as *siyāsah sharʿiyyah*, or *sharīʿah*-oriented policy. Whereas the former refers to established law as expounded in the text, the latter refers mainly to policy measures, pro-active decisions, and attitudes that are nurtured and designed to serve the wider purposes of good government and a meaningful implementation of the *Sharīʿah*.

This volume is a part of a larger seven-volume work on 'Fundamental Rights and Liberties in Islam: Principles and Applications,' a project that has engaged the present writer for over two decades. The first three volumes in the series addressed general themes and bore the titles *The Dignity of Man: An Islamic Perspective; Freedom, Equality and Justice in Islam*, and *Equity and Fairness in Islam*, all of which were published by the Islamic Texts Society of Cambridge, and subsequently also reprinted in Kuala Lumpur for the benefit especially of my students at the International Islamic University Malaysia, where I have been teaching the subject over a number of years. *Freedom of Expression in Islam*, which is the fourth in the series, was first published in 1997 and contains, in addition to chapters on freedom of speech and expression, which is the principal theme of this book, discussions of freedom of religion, blasphemy and apostasy, freedom of assembly and association, and a number of other themes that are subsumed by freedom of expression. These seven titles are designed to address most, if not all, the principal themes of basic rights and liberties from the Islamic perspective. This will be, to the best of the present writer's knowledge, the first work of its kind, in both the English and Arabic languages, or in any language for that matter, on the *Sharīʿah juris corpus* of basic rights and liberties. The works that have already been published were well received and found their way into the reading lists of university courses on Islamic law in many English-speaking universities worldwide. The positive feedback I have received on them have, in fact, been a motivating factor for me to extend the scope of this work to what it has become now. In the early stages of this work, I had only envisaged writing on selected themes, starting with my *Freedom of Expression in Islam*. The scope was then extended over the years to treat other relevant topics, ending with my engagement with the special themes and topics related to the subject in subsequent years of my research.

I would like to thank the Islamic Texts Society for its decision to publish the remaining three of these seven volumes simultaneously. This will help to overcome a shortage, and in certain cases a total lack, of specialized information for English readers, of basic rights and liberties in *Sharīʿah*. This work is new even for non-English readers of *Sharīʿah* in Muslim countries in that it treats the subject in a manner and style that makes it readable for a modern student of Islamic law.

The existing *fiqh* manuals, which are mainly available in Arabic, do not address the subject in the way it is presented here. The *fiqh* literature of the scholastic period was mostly written centuries before the era of constitutionalism at a time when the basic framework and approach to fundamental rights was markedly different. The *fiqh* literature in the genre of *al-aḥkām al-sulṭāniyya* (rules of government) discuss topics of concern to the institution of caliphate, justice and court procedures, crimes and punishment, duties of army leaders, governors and police and so forth. Matters of concern to basic rights are on the whole discussed not as distinctive themes and chapters in their own right, but in conjunction with other titles. Neither the treatment of basic rights nor the data of relevance to them were consolidated and given the prominence they deserve. The *fiqh* literature, moreover, does not recognise a formal distinction between constitutional law and other laws. The present work departs from that precedent in that its arrangement of data is broadly in line with the titles and themes that are addressed in the present-day constitutions of both the Muslim and non-Muslim countries. This manner of selection is also thematically more exclusive compared to the wide-ranging coverage of *al-aḥkām al-sulṭāniyya* and *siyāsah sharʿiyyah*. To consolidate the substantive aspects of the subject and the scattered data in a thematically coherent form was a significant part of that challenge. The present writer's concern was not just to give coherence and consolidation to that data, but also to give adequate scope and depth to particular subjects, some of which were not treated in a way that could be of use in this work. The present writer was faced with the task of constantly enhancing and revising his writings on the various chapters presented here because of the absence of precedent and consolidated texts. Much of the scattered data that I explored did not yield specific materials in an order or sequence. Often I came across data after having completed a chapter, and had therefore to move backwards and forwards over the years of my involvement in writing this work. What this must also imply is that I claim no finality for any part or chapter of the present volume, or for any other works in the series. What is presented here merely indicates a stage of progress in my own quest for information. There still remains scope for further research and development of the relevant data in the vast body of *fiqh* literature. Yet the fact that almost every one of the chapters presented in this work begins with a review of the source materials of the *Qurʾān* and *Sunnah*, and the work as a whole follows through the basic blueprint of the source evidence, in itself provides a measure of assurance about the overall direction of the discussion and research. Yet the present writer assumes responsibility for any errors of interpretation that may have arisen due to the absence of information or the inability to find relevant data, and remains committed even after publication of this work, to rectify and amend what needs to be corrected in the light of fresh evidence, and hopes that this will be attempted in a subsequent edition, if and when such an occasion arises in the future. As noted earlier, the right to personal security is addressed in the first two chapters on the right to life and the right to physical safety against aggression respectively. This latter aspect of personal security also extends to a discussion of pre-trial and trial procedures, and the accused person's entitlement to safe conduct under the rule of law.

Although the present work adopts what may be said to be a textbook oriented approach that is designed to provide an overall treatment of the subject, and does not primarily concern itself with issue-oriented research, it consists in reality of a combination of both approaches. This is a function, to some extent, of the nature of the topics and sub-topics that are raised and addressed. The first chapter, which addresses the right to life, for example, involves a variety of themes, some of which are treated in the manuals of Islamic law, and the writer's task concerning them was basically one of a consolidated presentation of existing information. Our coverage of the right to life includes, in addition to its conventional *fiqhī* format focusing mainly on murder, unintentional killing, just retaliation (*qiṣāṣ*), blood money (*diyyah*) and compensation for wanton miscarriage of pregnancy (*ghurrah*) in culpable homicide and bodily injuries. The manuals of Islamic law discuss these topics at great length and the information on them is also fairly consistent in the scholastic treatment of the various schools of law. Then there are aspects of the right to life in relationship to abortion, euthanasia, duelling, and even suicide, which are not text-book issues, and obtaining reliable information on them required a research-oriented approach. Information on them is either scanty or non-existent in the expected sources, and the writer was often faced with the task of locating the data, and of finding his way through a diversity of views and attitudes towards them. Certain aspects of abortion are still in need of exploratory research in Islamic law and the scholastic treatment of the subject needs to be brought a step closer and read in conjunction with advances in medical science. On occasion, one comes across issues on which earlier juristic doctrine needs to be modified and interpreted in the light of developments in science.

The insight that is gained from available scientific knowledge is often indispensable to offering *ijtihād*-based responses to issues. Mercy killing, or euthanasia, has given rise, for instance, to complex questions of relevance to science and jurisprudence. Even the basic definition of death that is connected with the cessation of breathing needs to be re-examined. The question is asked, for example, whether the brain death of a person who merely breathes through a life-supporting machine, and is otherwise certain to die, is equivalent to the conventional notion of death. Life-supporting machines can keep a person alive for long periods and the question arises of whether a deliberate removal of that machine under the difficult circumstances of exorbitant costs and scarce availability can be equated with murder. Then there are questions about whether a person's right to life also confers upon him the right to death and the right to decide on his own death with or without the help of others, including a physician. These questions have not been addressed in the existing sources and manuals of Islamic law, and what is presented concerning them in the present volume is more of a preliminary inquiry than a presentation of settled law.

Suicide is treated in the sources and manuals of *Sharīʿah,* and yet some of the more recent manifestations of suicide, such as suicide bombing, in the guise often of martyrdom and *jihād,* are not treated and what is said concerning it by a few contemporary commentators is open to further inquiry and research. What is said here also applies to some extent to our discussion of *qiṣāṣ* and *diyyah,* albeit in a slightly different capacity. Although there is basically no shortage of reliable information on these subjects in the sources of Islamic law, questions tend to arise about the suitability and relevance of the scholastic treatment of these subjects in a modern legal system that operates in a totally different framework to that of the tribal milieu of the Arabian society of earlier times. The basic idea of just retaliation is a Qur'ānic mandate predicated upon the sanctity of life and recourse to a just system of judicial relief. These are the unchangeable objectives of the law of *qiṣāṣ* which are not in dispute. Yet some of the detailed expositions of this right in the works of scholastic jurisprudence remain open to question, and it is on questions of this kind that the writer is often faced with the difficult task of providing a balanced treatment that is at once credible and also presentable to a modern reader of Islamic law.

Muslim jurists of recent times have deliberated on the issues presented here, yet many issues remain open to further enquiry and remain in need of consensus regarding matters of interpretation. The conventional classification of *qiṣāṣ* as a pure human right is one such issue that gives rise to questions. For the general public is bound to have a stake in the punishment of murder, which is hardly of concern only to the family and relatives of the victim. We note in this connection also that the juristic division of rights into the Rights of God and Rights of Man has no clear origin in the Qur'ān and *Sunnah*.

Chapter two of this volume takes up the right to personal security (*ḥaqq al-amn*) against unlawful arrest and aggression in both its physical sense of onslaught and attack as well as the right of the accused to fair treatment in pre-trial and trial proceedings. The basic principle of the rule of law here is the presumption of innocence, or of non–liability (*al-barā'ah al-aṣliyyah*) unless a person is proven guilty. A person may only be arrested on reasonable suspicion for purposes of investigation when there is a charge against him. Since arrest itself is a coercive action and entails the possibility that the person might be innocent, arrest by itself does not entitle the enforcement authorities to presume he is guilty. For all intents and purposes, the detainee should be presumed innocent and fairly treated unless there is evidence to the contrary. Innocence is a presumption rebutted by proof of guilt, and this is not for the police to decide. The police must not therefore treat the detainee as a convict and a proven criminal unless the court declares him so. Questions about the permissibility or otherwise in Islamic law of arrest and detention on grounds of suspicion lead us to address the lines of distinction between reasonable suspicion and that which originates in malice; between suspicion and accusation; and the personal record and reputation of the individual involved.

The affirmative evidence, the right to personal security presented from the sources of *Sharī'ah*, is basically in harmony with the constitutional law principle of legality, since the *Sharī'ah* too applies the parallel maxim of original non-liability or innocence (*barā'ah al-dhimmah al-aṣliyyah*). Muslim jurists have addressed many of the finer aspects of suspicion and accusation (*al-ẓann, al-tuhmah*) and the juristic discourse on them is predicated on the basic guidelines of the Qur'ān and *Sunnah*. The schools of law are in disagreement about certain issues, such as the permissibility or otherwise of preventive detention, as it consists of a premature imposition of punishment that goes against the original assumption of non-liability.

The juristic position of *Sharī'ah* on the basic principle of legality may be said to be that there is no crime and no punishment unless the law provides otherwise, which is parallel, to a large extent, with the principles of modern law and constitution. Yet the *fiqh* discourse tends to be somewhat scant on aspects of the principle of legality, and grey areas persist, because of a shortage of relevant data, differences of juristic opinion and differences in the style and framework of discourse. Many of the juristic works of *fiqh* that contain relevant details, such as that of Ibn Farhun's *Tabṣirat al-Ḥukkām*, and Ibn Qayyim al-Jawziyya's *Al-Ṭuruq al-Ḥukmiyyah* are medieval and the relevant discourse on aspects of the principle of legality is written in a different style.

There are also substantive differences of perspective between the *Sharīʿah*-based discourse and that of the modern law where notions such as the Right of God (*ḥaqq Allāh*) can only find rough parallels in modern law. This is to mention only one aspect of *Sharīʿah* criminal law. The larger part of this question is the continued validity of the divine text and its related religious norms that do not find parallel expressions in modern law. And these are not merely theoretical issues of comparative interest. The juxtaposition of the two legal systems in the spheres of criminal law and constitution is dictated by the mixed, often irreconcilable, pattern of laws that exist in many present-day Muslim countries and jurisdictions.

The researcher in *Sharīʿah* law is also faced with a certain shortage of data on the procedural aspects of trial and evidence and matters of concern to law enforcement. For the *Sharīʿah* pays by far the greatest attention to substantive law and does not provide adequate details on procedural aspects of the enforcement of law. This partially explains the fact that criminal procedure in many Muslim countries is largely borrowed from, and supplemented by, Western legal doctrines.

Yet one observes that Islamic revivalism in the latter part of twentieth century brought with it the demand that law and government in Muslim societies should be coherent with Islamic heritage and the *Sharīʿah*. The somewhat indiscriminate importation and borrowing of Western laws and constitutions came under scrutiny and criticism. Many Muslim countries consequently began to integrate more and more of the *Sharīʿah* into their applied laws and the process is continuing. But to provide an adequate response to the demand for enhancing the Islamic input of laws requires preparatory work since the gap between Islamic and Western law has grown wider over the decades, and in some cases centuries, of borrowing of foreign laws wholesale. The present work may be seen as a step in the direction of providing workable responses to the idea of enhancing the *Sharīʿah* input in modern law.

The chapter under review also discusses court procedure regarding the admissible varieties of evidence in *Sharīʿah*. The existing practice in the *Sharīʿah* courts of many Muslim countries is dominated by long-standing conventions often at variance with statutory law principles, and therefore need re-examination and review. The near-total reliance on eye-witnesses as a means of proof in *Sharīʿah* courts, for example, has been accompanied by a certain circumspection and doubt about the admissibility of other means of proof, such as circumstantial evidence, documents and scientific evidence. Yet these conventional practices are not always seen in proper perspective. In the present book I advance the view that the conventional lines of distinction between *shahādah* (testimony) and *bayyinah* (evidence in the broadest sense) need not be inflexible and rigid, and if properly interpreted and understood will help to reduce the gap between the *Sharīʿah* and modern law. This analysis is now generally accepted, and it tends, once again, to bring the Islamic and Western legal systems closer to one another in an important area of court proceedings. Some Muslim countries, including Malaysia, have taken up the idea of enhancing and then introducing the *Sharīʿah* law of evidence not only in *Sharīʿah* courts but also the civil courts as well, and the tendency now is for the two types of courts to admit *Sharīʿah*-based evidence equally. Documentation, circumstantial evidence, photography, sound recording and laboratory evidence should all be in principle acceptable in both the *Sharīʿah* and civil courts.

Confession is an accepted means of proof in both systems and care is taken in this area by the source evidence of *Sharīʿah* to preclude and disqualify confessions obtained through coercion, espionage and doubtful methods of data gathering. The *Sharīʿah* even takes a step further to entitle the accused and even the convict in the more serious (*ḥudūd*) crimes to withdraw his confession at any stage prior to the execution of punishment. Confession obtained under duress is most likely to be disqualified in both systems. The right to counsel is also recognised for the defendant in both legal systems, yet there are manifest differences in the world of practice between Muslim countries, both in relationship to one another, and by comparison with their Western counterparts. The affordability of legal aid is inadequate in many Muslim countries, but there need be no differences of principle between Islamic and Western jurisdictions in this area.

A certain discourse has developed—for example in the *fiqh* writing of the Ḥanbalī and Mālikī schools, about the permissibility of beating an accused person charged with a grave offence, such as theft, in order to obtain a confession. The advocates of this view maintain that given the nature of theft and the secrecy that normally surrounds it, it would be difficult to prove it by eyewitnesses. Unless the accused person is otherwise a man of good reputation, he may be beaten to obtain a confession if this is the only way left to protect the rights of the victim. This argument may not be totally unfounded and may have seemed plausible at a time when law enforcement agencies did not have access to the modern means of crime detection. Yet when judged by the more objective standards of impartiality and procedural correctness, substantiated by a careful reading of the relevant evidence in the sources of *Sharīʿah,* a confession obtained under duress is worthless, and this is the litmus test that has to be applied. Beating the accused may secure a self-incriminating confession. The more important question about the value of that confession remains, however, which is why the majority of *fiqh* scholars do not validate beating the accused during interrogation, nor indeed at any stage, regardless of the type of offence or the personality of the accused.

The right to privacy (*ḥaqq al-khuṣūsiyyah*), which is the subject of chapter three, is mainly concerned with the privacy of one's home, confidential correspondence, and immunity against invasion of privacy in the forms of espionage and other violations. Certain aspects of the right of privacy have been highlighted in the Qur'ān, whereas other themes of relevance to it have been addressed in the *Sunnah.* Yet the *fiqh* literature on many aspects of the right of privacy has remained generally unconsolidated and under-developed. With the exception of a few recent works, the present writer was unable to find an exclusive treatment of this right in the *fiqh* sources, and the information obtained from many places has generally been unsystematic and piecemeal. The Qur'ān is emphatic on the sanctity of the home against unsolicited intrusion and viewing without the permission of its inhabitants. The discourse on privacy also extends to the right of the female inhabitants of private dwellings to seclusion, and protection from intrusive structures, neighbors and strangers. This latter aspect of the right of privacy is depicted in the Qur'ān and Sunna through actual case situations of how the Bedouin Arabs and others during the time of the Prophet did not observe the privacy of his home, and disregarded the limitations of time and place in the encounters they had with the Prophet and the members of his family. As such the Qur'ān also provides a degree of insight into the lifestyles and practices of Arab society at that time. In many ways the Qur'ān sought to reform Arab Bedouin practices that were predicated on the desert lifestyle of a borderless environment which left much to be desired for a more settled lifestyle and environment of Madina. The Bedouin lifestyle could barely provide for personal privacy and the sanctity of the home. Tents were not surrounded by protective barriers, and a sense of personal insecurity must have accompanied the absence of physical demarcation between the private dwelling and public domain as the tent itself often stood on, and surrounded by, public territory.

The *ḥadīth* literature on the subject sometimes brings to light episodes that convey a certain shift in the physical features of private dwellings in Madina. Instances that contain a description of real life situations often provide an insight into the housing conditions of Madina. Thus it is stated in a *ḥadīth*, for example, that the Companions used to knock at the door of the Prophet's house with their fingernails, or else that some unscrupulous individuals peeped through the door cracks thereof. Reports of this kind are consistent enough to suggest that Madinan society in those days had already experienced a settled lifestyle and changes in the physical features of the home. Yet it is also understood that the front door was neither solid nor provided an effective barrier against intrusion. Some of the Qur'ānic verses on the subject also confirm this when it states, for example, that it is not proper to enter houses through the back door instead of using the front entrance, and then when doing so the visitor must greet the inmates and introduce himself. It would appear that the Madinan years of the Prophet's 23-year long mission marked a rapid transformation to settled patterns of residence. Thus, it is suggested that instances of irregularity and violation of the privacy of homes must have been frequent. It is also significant that after migrating to Madina in the 13th year of his ministry, the Prophet changed the name of Yathrib to Madina, which literally means 'a city', and is related to the Arabic word for civilisation (*madaniyyah*). The physical shift was only one aspect of the matter, but the concern to reform some of the entrenched practices and attitudes of Arab society has often provoked an exceedingly forceful manner of address in the Qur'ān and *ḥadīth*.

A more intimate aspect of privacy addressed by Islam was in its definition of the concept of ʿ*awrah*, that is, the parts of the human body that were deemed to be private and were not to be exposed in ritual prayer and in the presence of others. Much of this was addressed through specification of the desired dress form and appearance in public for men and women respectively. This was done within the rubric of *satr al-ʿawrāt* (concealment of privacies) wherein ʿ*awrāt* in its plural form signifies the multi-dimensional aspects of privacy, not only in the physical sense but also in the many intangible ways by which the integrity of this concept could be violated. *Satr al-ʿawrāt*, which is the title of a section of this work, features more prominently in the *ḥadīth*, which tend to elaborate the basic guidelines of the Qur'ān on the subject. Another subtitle of this chapter is *kitmān al-sirr* (concealing confidential information), which supplements *satr al-ʿawrāt*, even though the former is almost exclusively concerned with the confidentiality of what transpires between individuals who confide in one another in an atmosphere of trust. These are further substantiated by emphatic exhortation in the Qur'ān and *ḥadīth* on the avoidance of suspicion and mistrust (*sū' al-ẓann*), which often lies at the root of the violation of privacy, including of course, the explicit Qur'ānic prohibition of espionage (*al-tajassus*). Some of these tend to combine moral advice and legal ruling but tend on the whole to present the reader with aspects of privacy that cross between law and morality, and so drawing clear lines of distinction between them is somewhat difficult. The discussion here is also a reflection of the inherent complexity of the concept of privacy, which hardly yields itself to a clear definition. To this may be added the fact that the concept and scope of privacy tend to vary from culture to culture and in relationship to the evolution of society from pre-modern to modern and to advanced technological settings. Ambiguity about some of the basic components of privacy remain, even in other jurisdictions, including the English and American common law traditions, where the basic recognition of the right to privacy remains open to question.

Whether one speaks of the avoidance of suspicion and mistrust concerning others, or of *kitman al-sirr* and *satr al-ʿawrāt*, the prohibition in each case rests on human fraternity and fraternity among the community of believers (the *ummah*). The Islamic concept of *ukhuwwah* (fraternity) is often thought to be confined to Muslims, yet there is little evidence in the sources to support the notion that the basic concept of privacy or its various manifestations are exclusively addressed to Muslims. For the rules of privacy are conveyed almost entirely in broad and general terms that are inclusive of both Muslims and non-Muslims, men and women, almost regardless of any level of distinction between them. The exception is espionage; the prohibitive rules of the Qur'ān and *ḥadīth* on espionage do not extend to an enemy during war, but apart from this context of open hostility the basic guidelines of Islam on the right to privacy extend to all human beings.

Moreover, the right of privacy in Islam is not confined to the living but extends, *mutatis mutandis*, to deceased persons, whose nakedness and failings (*ʿawrah*) and all confidential information about them are treated under the same rules that apply to the living. The *Sunnah* contains emphatic guidelines that render an attack on the privacy of the dead and revealing their weaknesses even more heinous than doing so to the living, for the simple reason that they are not there to defend themselves, and ill-conceived exposure would be sure to offend their living relatives.

The latter part of this chapter discusses restrictions on the right to privacy in respect of certain individuals and situations. A witness in court, a personal doctor, or even a religious scholar who gives a *fatwā* may be unable to serve the cause of truth and justice, or protect and promote the common good (*maṣlaḥah*), if they were to observe the rules of privacy strictly. Hence the *Sharīʿah* makes suitable but qualified exceptions in their favour.

The right of ownership (*ḥaqq al-milkiyyah*), the last chapter of the present volume, is one of the best-established and widely recognised of all basic rights in *Sharīʿah*, as it is in most other legal traditions also. This chapter looks at four aspects of ownership, beginning with a review of affirmative evidence in the Qur'ān and *Sunnah*, then the types of ownership that are recognised in *Sharīʿah*, followed by an exposition of the legitimate means to acquire ownership, and ending with the restrictions that the *Sharīʿah* imposes on the exercise of this right.

Private ownership is the prototype of ownership that features prominently in the Qur'ān and *Sunnah*, although other varieties of ownership have also been recognised either explicitly or by inference. Our review of the source evidence in this chapter also draws attention to an aspect of ownership unique to Islam, and which distinguishes Islam's perspective on ownership from that of other legal traditions. This is the Qur'ānic doctrine of the vicegerency of man (*istikhlāf*), which designates him as God's trustee and vicegerent in the earth. God Most High declares His exalted self as the real and eternal owner of the heavens and the earth. Man's ownership is, by comparison, delegated and secondary, so that the human owner of property is a custodian and trustee who must observe the basic terms of that responsibility in the use and exercise of this right. The vicegerency of mankind tends to add at least two important dimensions to ownership, one of which is the spiritual dimension manifested in the recognition of God's sovereign authority, and which demands God-consciousness in the exercise of the right of ownership.

The other dimension of vicegerency is manifested in the accountability of the owner, who stands answerable to the community of believers entrusted with the authority to rule. The individual owner thus remains accountable to the community in the faithful exercise of his rights. Although both the community and the individual are vicegerents (*khalāʾif*) of God in the earth in their respective capacities, it is the community that is vested with the authority to govern and is therefore to ensure the correct observance of responsible ownership by individual members. This aspect of vicegerency also means that the community has a stake in private ownership, which is in turn manifested in the imposition of a number of restrictions and levies, such as *zakāh*, that must duly be observed. When this is done, it leaves the human owner the effective master of his property.

It is most probably the unqualified and universal character of vicegerency as a trusteeship of the whole of mankind in the earth that the *Sharīʿah* has envisaged, a near-total egalitarian regime of legal rules applicable to all human beings, Muslim and non-Muslim alike. The *Sharīʿah* does not recognise any line of discrimination in the basic terms of the right of ownership between Muslims and non-Muslims. Except for non-Muslims who are at war with Muslims, anyone who acquires property through the recognised means of ownership becomes the lawful owner, and also becomes subject to the restrictions that the *Sharīʿah* imposes on the exercise of this right. Several types of ownership are thus recognised, including individual and collective ownership, private and public ownership and the state of ownership of unowned lands. Ownership can also be either complete, which includes ownership of both of the corpus (*ʿayn*) and the usufruct (*manfaʿa*), or it can be partial, which includes ownership of either the corpus or the usufruct, but not both. Ownership can also be of movable or of immovable property, of tangible property, or of intangible assets in the form of a right, or of intellectual property that is abstract and intangible, and they all tend to be regulated, in varying degrees, by their own rules.

The *Sharīʿah* recognises a variety of ways and means for acquisition, disposition and transfer of ownership, including labour (*ʿamal*), which is the most pervasive of recognised means of ownership in that nearly all other means of acquisition of ownership expounded in this book involve some measure of labour. This is true, for example, of hunting, reclamation of barren land, ownership of mineral wealth and treasure troves, land grants (*iqṭaʿ*) by the state, *zakāh* and other levies, inheritance and bequest. As can be seen only the last two, and also receiving the *zakāh,* do not involve labour, whereas all the other types do to varying degrees. The law in this section regulates the manner in which mineral wealth may be owned, and provides guidelines for the proper operation of inheritance and bequest. The public or the community alone can own certain types of assets that are essential for public welfare, such as roads, rivers, grazing lands, forests and other public amenities, whereas ownership of mosques and *waqf* properties belongs to God Most High, and is therefore normally precluded from the scope of private ownership. These are not transferable through sale, gift, and inheritance etc., but the state is authorised to regulate their proper use and maintenance.

To ensure the valid exercise of the right of ownership, the *Sharīʿah* imposes a number of restrictions. The rules of *Sharīʿah* on the prevention of harm to others, considerations of public interest (*maṣlaḥah*) and rules that pertain to necessity (*ḍarūrah*) are among the principal restraints on ownership. Nearly all types of ownership recognized by the law are subject to some kind of restriction. Yet these last three mentioned types of restrictions, though distinguishable from one another, tend to be at least partially convergent in that what is deemed to be in the public interest may also be a necessity and prevent harm. Text book writers have nevertheless discussed them separately, since they do tend to differ in their details. Other restrictions on the right of ownership are manifested in the *Sharīʿah* regulations on taxation, land utilisation, pre-emption (*shufʿ*), inheritance and bequest.

The *zakāh* and other levies represent restrictions on ownership in the sense that the owner can be compelled to pay them. Similarly, barren land that has no lawful owner may be owned by individuals who cultivate it, but it may be taken away from them if they fail to reclaim it within a period of time. The *Sharīʿah* also entitles legal heirs to assigned portions in the estate of their deceased relative. These rights reflect the fact that the deceased person must observe, during his lifetime, the rules of inheritance and may not disinherit any of his close relatives. The owner's rights are also restricted by the rules of bequest, as he or she may not bequeath more than one third of his or her estate to a stranger, or indeed to one of the legal heirs on grounds of favouritism and discrimination. Pre-emption (*shufʿ*) is of a limited application, but it represents a restriction in that the owner of a joint or neighbouring property must give priority, when he wishes to sell his landed property, to the joint owner and neighbour as a mark of friendship that the *Sharīʿah* expects in those situations. Yet it may finally be said that, restrictions notwithstanding, the owner remains the master of his property since the *Sharīʿah* restrictions are nearly all formulated to avoid unwarranted interference in the right of the owner to what he lawfully owns. The restrictions imposed are all qualified and carefully regulated, and premised upon the basic sanctity of ownership. A *ḍarar* (harm), for example, that the owner's use of his property may cause to another party, is usually ignored unless it becomes exorbitant (*fāḥish*) and intolerable, in which case it may constitute a valid basis for legal action by the injured party. Other similar qualifications exist in respect of almost every restriction imposed on the right of ownership.

CHAPTER ONE

The Right to Life (*Ḥaqq al-ḥayāt*)

I. Introductory Remarks

The right to life is the starting point and foundation of almost all other basic rights and liberties. For they exist when life exists and most of them terminate when life comes to an end. The rights to privacy, ownership, the freedom of speech and expression, freedom of movement, and the like, are meaningful only in relation to living persons and almost worthless in relation to the deceased. In this sense the right to life stands on a unique footing since all other rights are derivable from this right. It is a primary right in the sense that no civilization can flourish without protecting and guaranteeing the right to life of its members. This would explain why jurists and philosophers have generally treated the right to life as the most non-negotiable. It is an inherent right of every human being because it pre-exists the state and any social order preceding it. It is inherent because it derives from the very fact of being human. A corollary of this is that the right to life is enforceable against everyone almost without exception.

Although the right to life is generally recognised as the inherent right of every human being under the *Sharīʿah*, man is not the creator of life, and life is, in this sense, deemed to be a God-given gift and a manifestation of His divine grace. For God alone is the creator of life and it is by virtue of His express will and command that the *Sharīʿah* proclaims every aggression against it a crime and a violation both of the Right of God (*ḥaqq Allāh*) and that of the human being (*ḥaqq al-Ādamī*). Life is sacrosanct and the *Sharīʿah* seeks to protect it through the law of just retaliation (*qiṣāṣ*), which makes its hostile destruction punishable by death, and, in cases of unintentional slaying, makes the killer liable to the payment of blood money (*diyyah*) to the family of the deceased.

The *Sharīʿah* also contains a variety of other provisions designed to protect human life. These are reviewed and summarised in the following pages. The discussion that follows is presented in twelve sections, beginning with a review of some of the general provisions of the Qurʾān and *Sunnah* in relation to the sanctity of life, and the grave view that is taken of all acts of violence that seek to destroy it. This also involves a brief discussion of the right to self-defence, which entitles every person to repel aggression and protect himself against attack. This is followed, in the succeeding two sections, by an overview of the *Sharīʿah* provisions on just retaliation and blood money (*qiṣāṣ* and *diyyah*), as well as the supplementary punishment of barring the killer from receiving any benefit from the estate of his victim. We then briefly review the *Sharīʿah* position on the death penalty. Suicide is discussed in the section after, and section five addresses the subject of abortion. The two sections that follow are devoted to a discussion of euthanasia, and *laqīṭ,* or the abandoned child, whose life is exposed to the threat of destruction. This is followed, in turn, by a review of the rules of warfare that need to be observed before war and during the conduct of war, with a view to preventing unnecessary brutality and destruction. The last section offers a brief discussion of the *Sharīʿah* concessions (*rukhṣah sharʿiyyah*) granted in situations of necessity and hardship in order to limit exposure to life-threatening situations.

Some of these subjects, such as *qiṣāṣ* and *diyyah*, are addressed in the *fiqh* sources in considerable detail, whereas others are covered in brief outline, and the information found on them is not always relevant to our concerns. My purpose here is not to present an exhaustive treatment of any of these topics but to address them from the perspective of constitutional law, which emphasises the sanctity of life, and the commitment of *Sharīʿah* to protection against aggression. Since the *fiqh* texts that contain information on these subjects do not normally distinguish constitutional law from other legal themes, one often needs to be selective in the choice of data as well as in the tone of language used.

II. The Sanctity of Life

To outline the sanctity of human life, the Qurʾān contains numerous verses and unequivocal warnings to those who deliberately kill. The text is equally emphatic that the killer calls upon himself the curse and condemnation of God in the hereafter, in addition to the temporal punishment the killer must suffer. To quote the Qur'ān:

ومن يقتل مؤمنا متعمدا فجزاؤه جهنم خالدا فيها وغضب الله عليه ولعنه وأعد له عذابا عظيما.

And one who deliberately kills a believer, his punishment will be permanent abode in Hell, God's wrath and curse, and a great punishment (in the hereafter) (4:93).

In a *ḥadīth* recorded by both Bukhārī and Muslim, the Prophet said:

إن أول الناس يقضى عليه يوم القيامة رجل استشهد، فأتى فعرّفه نعمته فعرفها، فقال: ماعملت فيها؟ قال: قاتلت فيك حتى استشهدت، قال: كذبت ولكنك قاتلت لأن يقال: جرئ، فقد قيل، ثم أمر به فسحب على وجهه حتى ألقي فى النار.

The first person who will be taken into account on the Day of Resurrection will be the one who desired martyrdom for himself... He will be asked...: What did you do to the favor granted to you? He says: I fought in your cause until I was martyred. Allāh says: You lie. No, you fought so that you would be known for bravery...He is ordered to be taken away...until he is thrown into fire.[1]

One who kills another human being deliberately is forever precluded from God's forgiveness. On numerous instances, the Qur'ān reminds sinners and transgressors that God forgives them if they repent and wish to correct themselves. This is not, however, granted to murderers, a message clearly conveyed in the emphatic tone of the verse just quoted. According to a *ḥadīth* narrated by al-Barā' b. ʿĀdhib, the Prophet is reported to have said in figurative language:

لزوال الدنيا أهون على الله من قتل مؤمن بغير حق.

The perishing of the entire world is lighter in the eyes of God than the unjust killing of a believer.[2]

Abu Dardā' has reported that he heard the Prophet say:

كل ذنب عسى الله أن يغفره إلا من مات مشركا أو مؤمن قتل مؤمنا متعمداً.

God grants forgiveness to every sin (a person commits) except for one who dies as an associator (*mushrik*) or a believer who deliberately kills another believer.[3]

In another *hadīth* also reported by Abū Dardā', the Prophet declared:

لايزال المؤمن معنقا صالحا مالم يصب دماً حراماً ، فإذا أصاب دما حراما بلح.

A Muslim remains a Muslim and upright until he has shed blood that is *harām*; when he does that, his link (with Islam) is severed.[4]

'Ubāda Ibn al-Āmit has also reported that the Prophet said:

من قتل مؤمنا فاعتبط بقتله لم يقبل الله منه صرفا ولاعدلا.

One who has killed a believer without just cause, God will not accept any of his good deeds, whether obligatory or supererogatory.[5]

Further, on the sanctity of human life, God Most High declares:

من أجـل ذلك كتبنا على بنى اسرآئيل أنه من قتل نفسا بغير نفس أو فساد فى الأرض فكأنما قتل الناس جميعا ومن أحياها فكأنما أحيا الناس جميعا.

We prescribed for the children of Israel that truly one who kills another human being without the latter being guilty of murder and corruption in the land, it would be as if he has killed the whole of humankind, and one who gives life to one person, it would be as if he gives life to the whole of humankind (5:32).

The reference to the laws of the Torah in this verse is indicative of continuity of values between revealed laws in the Torah and Bible and in the Qur'ān. The text is also worded in the broadest of terms in that it refers to the destruction of human life without any further qualification regarding the race, religion, age or gender of the killer or his victim. The conclusion is thus drawn that a Muslim may be executed for killing a non-Muslim, a woman or a child, a sane or insane person alike. It is a general and absolute (*ʿāmm, muṭlaq*) ruling, which applies to all cases to which it could possibly apply.[6]

Two of the early Meccan Qur'ānic verses on the sanctity of life which will be discussed in some details are:

ولاتقتلوا النفس التى حرم الله إلا بالحق، ومن قتل مظلوما فقد جعلنا لوليه سلطانا فلايسرف فى القتل إنه كان منصورا.

Slay not the life which God has made sacrosanct unless it be in the cause of justice. Whoever is wrongly slain, We have given power to his near kin, but let him not indulge in excess. He (the near kin) will certainly be helped (to seek redress) (17:33).

The second verse declares the following people to be virtuous:

والذين لايدعون مع الله إلها آخر ولايقتلون النفس التى حرم الله إلا بالحق.

Those who do not associate any other deity with God, nor slay the life which He has made sacrosanct unless it be in the course of justice (25:68).

The order of priority set forth in this latter verse makes the protection of human life clearly the next most important value after belief in God and dedication to justice.

Both these verses were revealed in Mecca and both consist of general provisions focused on unlawful killing of another human being without further qualification or reference to any of the qualities of the deceased person.[7] The fact that these passages were revealed in Mecca, where Muslims had no government or law enforcement power of their own, might help to explain the near total reliance on private methods of punishing homicide: the entitlement to retaliation (*qiṣāṣ*) of the near kin and a promise to help them obtain justice. The law of *qiṣāṣ* was subsequently confirmed after the Prophet's migration to Madina, when the Muslims established a government of their own. This is shown by the fact that the two Qur'ānic verses (2:178–179) on this subject, as quoted below in the context of *qiṣāṣ*, begin with the typical address 'O believers,' a phrase typical of the Madinese portions of the Qur'ān. It is interesting to note that the Madinese verses on *qiṣāṣ* lay special emphasis, not so much on retaliation, but on forgiveness. Thus, it appears that the law of *qiṣāṣ* was revealed in two stages. In its Makki stage, the prohibition of killing was espoused with moral guidance in which those who avoided killing were praised and the near kin and family of the deceased were advised to avoid excess in retaliation. Respect for equality and avoidance of excess in *qiṣāṣ* as well as the subject of forgiveness (*ʿafw*) were later developed in the Madinese legislation.[8] But before discussing the Madinese legislation further, certain points of interpretation in the two verses under review need to be highlighted.

Firstly, the Qur'ānic phrase *illā bi'l-ḥaqq* ('unless it be in the course of justice') occurs in both the verses just quoted, which has in turn given rise to detailed interpretations. The following three situations will be discussed:

a) Killing in Lieu of a Right: Killing another human can only be justified in pursuit of an established right. The Qur'ān grants the nearest kin (*walī al-dam*) of the murder victim the right to seek just retaliation, which he may enforce by a judicial order. The leading schools of law are in agreement that the *walī al-dam* may not retaliate without obtaining a court order first. Retaliation in intentional homicide combines the right of God (*ḥaqq Allāh*) and the right of man (*ḥaqq al-ādami*) in which the right of man is, however, predominant, and as such, it can be waived, or substituted for blood-money, if the heirs of the deceased so wish. The question arises as to whether another person, a stranger in this case, can actually take the law unto his own hands and kill a murderer on the assumption that the Qur'ān has validated killing him in pursuit of justice. The answer to this question is in the negative simply because the right to retaliation that the Qur'ān grants is for the *walī al-dam* only and the stranger in this case cannot justify his action under the Qur'ānic provision of *illā bi'l-ḥaqq*. Since the stranger will have acted outside the framework of 'an established right,' he would be liable to retaliation himself.[9]

A related question is whether forgiveness that might have been granted by the murder victim prior to his demise is valid, and whether it replaces the right of the nearest kin in respect of retaliation. Most jurists have also answered this question in the negative to say that retaliation is a right of the family, and not of the murder victim himself, and that the near kin will still be entitled to seek retaliation. Some other jurists have, on the other hand, held that forgiveness by the victim is taken into account, which must mean that the near kin is no longer entitled to *qiṣāṣ*. It is thus stated that a pardon of this kind is also likely to quench the urge of the near relative for *qiṣāṣ*. Whether *qiṣāṣ* is demanded by the near relatives, or even when they waive it and grant a pardon, or when waived by the victim himself, in all these cases, the government as society's representative is entitled to impose a deterrent punishment as a matter of judicious policy (*siyāsah sharʿiyyah*), in order to protect society against criminality and aggression.[10]

The community also has a right to kill in the course of crime prevention, such as killing a terrorist and a highway robber, for whom the Qur'ān has prescribed a threefold punishment, including the death sentence. This is a public right issue and falls under the Qur'ānic stipulation of killing in pursuit of an established right. The state is also authorised to bring to justice and execute criminals in order to protect the community from their evil.[11]

b)   Execution of a Court Order: Killing in the course of justice naturally includes the execution of an obligatory court order. When the lawful authority, the ruler and the judge (*ūlu'l-amr*), issue orders for someone to be executed, and this command is in conformity with the *Sharīʿah*, it will be in the course of justice. If the command itself is unlawful, and if the person to whom it is addressed knows it to be so, then it does not qualify for the Qur'ānic stipulation of *illā bi'l-ḥaqq* and may consequently be disobeyed. This is also the purport of the *ḥadīth* proclaiming that 'There is no obedience in transgression; obedience is only required in righteousness,' and the *ḥadīth* which similarly declares that 'No creature may be obeyed in what amounts to disobedience of the Creator.' If the person to whom the unlawful order to kill another person is issued is able to disobey it, he is under an obligation to do so, but if he is not able to defy the order in question, it may amount to a situation resembling duress, a matter which the jurists have discussed in detail.

c)   Right to Self-defence: Killing in the course of justice also entitles the individual to the right of self-defence, which may necessitate killing the attacker (*al-ṣā'il*) in the course of safeguarding one's own life or that of another innocent person. A person threatened with, say, a knife or gun, is entitled by the express authority of the Qur'ān and *hadīth* to defend himself and prevent aggression by any means at his disposal. This is implied in the phrase '*illā bi'l ḥaqq*' But the right to self-defence is also addressed in at least two other Qur'ānic passages as follows:

فمـن اعتدى عليكم فاعتـدوا عليه بمثل مـا اعتدى عليكـم واتقوا الله واعلموا أن الله مع المتقين.

When someone is aggressive towards you, you may retaliate in proportion to the pain inflicted on you, but fear God and know that God is with those who restrain themselves (2:194).

ولمن انتصر بعد ظلمه فأولئك ما عليهم من سبيل. إنما السبيل على الذين يظلمون الناس ويبغون فى الأرض بغير الحق أولئك لهم عذاب أليم.

And whoso defends himself after he has suffered oppression, there shall be no blame on him. Blame is only on those who oppress the people and resort to acts of rebellion and lawlessness without just cause. (42:41–42).

Elsewhere the Qur'ān simply praises those 'who defend themselves against aggression.' (29:22), as it is indicative of courage to stand for one's rights and curb aggression. Muslim jurists are in agreement that defending oneself against aggression is an obligation when one is able to do so, especially in the event where the attack violates one's personal honour or that of one's spouse. The Ḥanbalīs have held that when the attack threatens but does not violate personal honour (*al-ʿirḍ*), defending oneself against it is permissible only. These two positions obviously provide different answers to the question of whether one actually incurs a sin by not defending oneself.[12] The Prophet is reported to have said in a *hadīth*:

مـن قتـل دون دينـه فهـو شهيـد، ومـن قتـل دون دمـه فهـو شهيـد، ومن قتل دون ماله فهو شهيد، ومن قتل دون أهله فهو شهيد.

One who is killed in defending his faith is a martyr; one who is killed in defending his own life is a martyr; one who is killed in defending his property is a martyr; and one who is killed in defending his family is a martyr.[13]

In another *ḥadīth*, Abū Hurayra has reported that:

عـن أبى هريرة رضـي الله عنـه قال: جاء رجـل إلى رسـول الله صلى الله عليه وسلم فقال: يا رسول الله: أرأيت إن جاء رجـل يريـد أخـذ مالي؟ فقال: فلا تعطـه مالـك، أرأيت إن قاتلنـى؟ قال: قاتلـه ، قـال: أرأيت إن قتلنى ؟ قال: فأنـت شهيد، قال: أرأيت إن قتلته ؟ قال: هو فى النار.

A man came to the Prophet and asked: 'O Messenger of God, what would you say concerning a person who wants to take my property,' to which the Prophet replied: 'Do not give it.' The man asked again: 'What if he fights me?' to which the Prophet replied, 'You fight back.' The man asked again: 'What if he kills me?' The Prophet's response to this was: 'You will be a martyr.' The man asked again: 'What if I kill him?' and the answer came: 'He will be in Hell.'[14]

In yet another *ḥadīth*, the Prophet is reported to have said:

من حمل علينا السلاح فليس منا.

One who unleashes his weapon on us is not one of us.[15]

The wording of the first *ḥadīth* indicates that repelling aggression is not only lawful but becomes a duty in certain circumstances, and it matters little whether the attack takes place during the day or night, within residential areas or outside. Whenever a person is able to repel an attack, he should do so.

The right to self-defence also extends to attacks by a child, the insane and animals, although some have argued that an attack by an animal does not qualify as a crime and the one who defends himself against this is acting out of necessity rather than self-defence.[16]

In the light of these guidelines, the right to defence has generally been defined as 'repelling unlawful aggression against human life, honour and property.'[17] This is a broad definition that tends to encapsulate lawful defence in all its verities, and extends the scope of this right to the defence of one's honour and property as well. When a thief breaks into someone's house at night, the inhabitant is entitled to defend his property by any means at his disposal, including the ultimate measure of killing the invader.[18] ʿAbd Allāh Ibn ʿUmar has thus reported a *ḥadīth* that 'one who defends his property against unlawful attack and fights for it and dies as a result dies as a martyr.'[19]

من قتل دون ماله فهو شهيد

According to an alternative definition, legal defence is the 'obligation of everyone to protect one's own life and property, or the life and property of another human being, against an unlawful attack, by recourse to the use of force if necessary in order to repel that attack.'[20] The first of these two definitions is considered to be preferable because it is comprehensive and does not render self-defence an obligation in all cases. The majority of jurists have held that defending one's property against attack by an assailant is permissible, which means that it is a right only, and not an obligation as such. The owner is thus at liberty not to protect his property, in which case, he will not be violating a duty. According to an alternative opinion, defending one's property is an obligation if it consists of a living being but not otherwise.[21]

As shown in these definitions, the right to self-defence is not confined to oneself but extends to others whose life may be vulnerable to destruction. This is the purport of a *ḥadīth* which directs the Muslim to:

أنصر أخاك ظالما أو مظلوما، فقال رجل: يا رسول الله أنصره إذا كان مظلوما، ارأيت إن كان ظالما كيف أنصره؟ قال: تحجزه تمنعه من الظلم فإن ذلك نصره.

Help your brother, whether an oppressor or oppressed. The Companions asked: 'How do we do that?' The Prophet replied: 'Help the oppressor to stop being oppressive and help the oppressed to defend himself.'[22]

The Prophet declared in another *ḥadīth*:

كل المسلم على المسلم حرام ، دمه، وعرضه، وماله.

Everything that belongs to a Muslim is forbidden to his fellow Muslim: his blood, his property, and his honour.[23]

Notwithstanding the use of the word 'Muslim', the purport of this and the preceding *ḥadīth* is not necessarily confined to Muslims since the sanctity of life and property are upheld in the Qur'ān and *Sunnah* for everyone. The Prophet mentioned the Muslims in his familiar style of addressing his community. The tone of his address and the general evidence of *Sharīʿah* relating to it do not confine the substance of his statement to Muslims alone. The Prophet reiterated the same message in his farewell pilgrimage to an audience in the sanctuary of the *Kaʿbah*:

إن دماءكم وأموالكم وأعراضكم حرام عليكم كحرمة يومكم هذا فى شهركم هذا وفى بلدكم هذا.

Your lives, your honour and your property are forbidden unto one another like the sanctity of this day, in this month and in this city.[24]

The three objects mentioned in this *ḥadīth* are among the holiest places, months and days in Islam, and reference to them in the *ḥadīth* is evidently for added emphasis on the sanctity of human life.

According to another *ḥadīth*:

ذكر رسول الله صلى الله عليه وسلم الكبائر أو سئل عن الكبائر، فقال: الشرك بالله، وقتل النفس، وعقوق الوالدين، فقال ألا أنبئكم بأكثر الكبائر؟ قال: قول الزور وشهادة الزور، قال شعبة: أكثر ظنى أنه قال: شهادة الزور.

The Messenger of God mentioned the gravest of all sins as he was asked about them and he said: To join partners in worship with God, to slay a soul [which God has forbidden], and to be unkind to one's parents. The Prophet then added that one of the greatest of all sins is to give false testimony, or tell a deliberate lie. Shu'ba (the narrator of this *ḥadīth*) said: Most probably the Prophet said: 'false testimony.'[25]

III. Just Retaliation and Blood Money (*Qiṣāṣ wa Diyyah*)

Literally, '*qiṣāṣ*' means 'equivalence'. It implies that a person who has committed a given crime will be punished in the same way, in the same proportion, and by the same means that he used in harming his victim. *Qiṣāṣ* thus means that the punishment should be equal to the crime. A person may not, therefore, inflict a greater harm than that which has been inflicted on him. *Qiṣāṣ* under Islamic law applies to whoever causes death with the intention of causing death, or with the intention of causing such bodily injury as is likely to cause death. The use of a weapon or lethal instrument in homicide cases is often indicative of the intention to cause death on the part of its user.

Qiṣāṣ is the principal punishment for murder (*qatl al-ʿamd*), whereas payment of blood money (*diyyah*) is the principal punishment in unintentional killing, and inculpable homicide that resembles murder and represents an intermediate category between intentional and unintentional killing. *Diyyah* is also paid in murder cases in which the relatives of the victim waive their right to *qiṣāṣ* and choose to receive a compensation. An intensified *diyyah* (*diyyah mughallaẓah*) is payable to the heirs of the deceased in culpable homicide not amounting to murder. As a general rule, the *diyyah* is payable by the criminal himself, or his agnate legal heirs (ʿ*āqilah*).[26]

The Qur'ān provides the basic authority for *qiṣāṣ*, as in the following passage:

وكتبنا عليهم فيها أن النفس بالنفس والعين بالعين والانف بالأنف والأذن بالأذن والسنّ بالسن والجروح قصاص فمن تصدق به فهو كفارة له ومن لم يحكم بما أنزل الله فأولئك هم الظالمون.

And We prescribed to them (the Jews in the Torah) that life is for life, and eye for eye, and nose for nose, and ear for ear, and tooth for tooth, and retaliation for wounds. But he who grants a pardon, it shall be an expiation for him (5:45).

The Qur'ānic law of *qiṣāṣ* is thus a continuation of the Jewish-Christian teachings on the law of an eye for an eye and a tooth for a tooth. Jewish law provided for *qiṣāṣ* but not for *diyyah,* whereas Christianity emphasized *diyyah.* Islam validates both. The purpose in all the three traditions is to limit the punishment and harm exacted against the offender, and also to curb vindictive violence.

'Life for life' is the essence of the law of retaliation here and the words of the text do not envisage any qualification of the kind that could form the basis of discrimination. Scholastic jurisprudence is, however, not as categorical on this point. According to Imams Mālik and Shāfiʿī, a Muslim may not be executed by *qiṣāṣ* for killing a non-Muslim, on the basis apparently of a *ḥadīth* which says just that: 'A Muslim is not killed for killing a non-Muslim'. The Ḥanafīs have disagreed and cited in support the abovementioned verse which clearly does not admit any discrimination. They have understood the *ḥadīth* to be applicable only to a belligerent non-Muslim (*ḥarbī*) who is at war with the Muslims.[27] Muhammad al-Ghazālī and his commentator, Yūsuf al-Qaraḍāwī, have gone on record to say that the *ḥadīth* at issue is not only an *āḥād ḥadīth* (solitary) but also that it is in conflict with the clear text of the Qur'ān (i.e.5:45). The Qur'ān lays down the basic principle on the subject of *qiṣāṣ* and it is in greater harmony with the fundamental right of every human being to life, regardless of colour, race and creed. Qaraḍāwī added that al-Shaʿbī and al-Nakhāʿī had held this view even before Imam Abū Ḥanīfa, and it represents the authoritative position of *Sharīʿah* on the subject.[28]

A certain ambiguity in the understanding of the text under review arose during the time of the second caliph ʿUmar b. al-Khaṭṭāb. There was a case of murder in the Yemen in which seven individuals from Ṣanʿā had colluded in the murder of one person. The issue was whether executing several persons for the killing of one could be validated within the given terms of the verse above. The phrase 'life for life,' in this verse was initially understood to mean one life for one life, but after consultation with the Companions, the caliph ʿUmar decided to execute them all if they took an equal part in the crime. The caliph is widely quoted to have made a resolute and dramatic statement on that occasion as follows: 'If the population of Ṣan'ā had colluded, he would not hesitate to execute all of them.' This was a correct decision and now represents settled law. Muslim jurists have elaborated that murder is rarely committed by one person and that it is often planned and carried out through collaboration. If the Qur'ānic provision of *qiṣāṣ* were to be confined to one person only, people's lives could not be protected against aggression. The fourth caliph ʿAli is similarly reported to have executed three persons who had colluded in the murder of a man, and the position here is said to have been upheld by general consensus (*ijmāʿ*).[29]

In addition to just retaliation, the *Shariʿa* has provided a supplementary punishment for murder when it is committed among close relatives, which is the exclusion of the offender from the estate of his victim. A person cannot therefore kill a close relative and then inherit his assets. Execution by *qiṣāṣ* of a pregnant woman is to be postponed until the birth of the child. If the child has no one to support it, the execution of punishment on the mother is delayed until he or she is weaned, during which period the mother may be released on bail or kept in light custody.[30]

The Qur'ān also underscores the rationale of the law of retaliation in the following verse:

ولكم فى القصاص حياة يأولى الألباب لعلكم تتقون .

And there is life for you in retaliation, O people of understanding—so that you protect yourselves against aggression (2:179).

Qiṣāṣ saves life in the sense that vendettas are appeased by it, and it acts in the meantime as a deterrent for others. It also seeks to deter further hostility between the parties and helps peace and security prevail in the community. The victim's family must cease hostility after *qiṣāṣ*. It is also noted that *qiṣāṣ* is only a right, it is not an obligation, and the heirs of the deceased are entitled, indeed advised, not to insist on it. The Qur'ān further provides:

يأيها الذين آمنوا كتب عليكم القصاص فى القتلى الحر بالحر
والعبد بالعبد والأنثى بالأنثى فمن عفى له من أخيه شيئ فاتباع
بالمعروف وأدآء إليه بإحسان ذلك تخفيف من ربكم ورحمة
فمن اعتدى بعد ذلك فله عذاب أليم .

O you who believe, retaliation is prescribed for you in all cases of murder: the free for the free, and the slave for the slave, and the female for the female. But if remission is made to one by his (aggrieved) brother, prosecution (for blood-wit) should be according to usage and payment in fairness. This is an alleviation from your Lord and a mercy from Him, but anyone who becomes aggressive after that shall bring upon himself a painful chastisement (2:178–179).

The law of retaliation is premised on the notion of total equality between the life of the slayer and the slain. The only factor that determines the application of *qiṣāṣ* is the destruction of an innocent human life. The law of *qiṣāṣ* thus applies when the victim is a child, insane, elderly or ill. None of these are taken into account and the principle of life for life is the essence of equality in *qiṣāṣ*.[31]

Maḥmūd Shaltūt has quoted Ibn al-ʿArabī's *Aḥkām al-Qurʾān* concerning a certain debate that arose over between a Ḥanafī jurist the above verse, known as al-Zuzani, and his Shāfiʿī counterpart, ʿAṭāʾ al-Maqdisī, in the sanctuary of the Prophet's mausoleum in Medina in 487 AH (c.1128 AD). The debate took place in the presence of a number of the scholars of Medina. Zuzani was asked whether a Muslim may face retaliation for killing a non-Muslim, to which he replied in the affirmative. Then he was asked for the grounds of his response and Zuzani cited the above verse.

His opponent al-Maqdisī objected to say that equality was a prerequisite of *qiṣāṣ* and there was no such equality between a Muslim and a disbeliever. To this it was added that the verse itself stipulates equality as a pre-condition when it states 'the free for the free, the slave for the slave…*et seq.*' And lastly, the verse recommends remission or pardon by one's brother, and there is no such fraternity between a Muslim and a disbeliever.

Zuzani replied that the claim of inequality in respect of *qiṣāṣ* between a Muslim and a disbeliever is incorrect. For they are equal in respect of the sanctity of their lives. Suppose a Muslim steals the property of a *dhimmī*, the *ḥadd* of theft would apply to the Muslim. This means that the *dhimmī's* property is protected in the same way as that of the Muslim, and so is his life—both are equally protected.

As for the suggestion that the beginning of the verse is qualified by its latter portion, this too is incorrect. The verse begins with a general (*ʿāmm*) declaration and ends with a particular (*khāṣṣ*) provision; the two remain as they are and there is no conflict. The verse begins with a general pronouncement of equality between all human beings and ends by reference to a specific aspect of that equality, namely the payment of *diyyah* as a substitute for *qiṣāṣ*.

As for the reference to remission among brethren in the faith that the text validates, Zuzani says about it that 'Your statement about fraternity among the believers is correct' but it is relevant to the subject of remission (*ʿafw*) in the verse and not to the provision on *qiṣāṣ*. There is a general declaration on *qiṣāṣ* and a particular one on remission, and the latter does not affect the general application of *qiṣāṣ*.[32]

Two further points have been added to this analysis, one of which concerns remission or pardon, to which a reference is made in this verse, not by way of exclusion but by way of encouragement. The text should not therefore be read to mean that difference of religion is a barrier to forgiveness. The other point which Shaltūt has clarified concerns the scope of fraternity. Here it is stated that the fraternity mentioned in the text is not confined to fraternity in the faith but may be understood in all its possible applications, which would include one's real brother by blood, brother in faith and brother in humanity. The correct understanding of *qiṣāṣ* therefore remains applicable in relation to both Muslims and non-Muslims.

Although *qiṣāṣ* was not unfamiliar to the pre-Islamic Arabs, they often violated the essential equality of this concept through exaggeration in revenge. When hostile Arab tribes threatened to avenge the opponent party by *qiṣāṣ,* they often swore to kill a free man of the enemy for the murder of a slave, or a male for the murder of a female. It was with reference to such practices that the Qur'ān verses above were worded 'the free for the free, the slave for the slave, and the female for the female.' The purpose here was 'to emphasise the mendacity of previous practice, and not as it were, to confine the scope of *qiṣāṣ* itself.' This is understood from the general terms of the law of *qiṣāṣ* as found in the phrases 'life for life—*al-nafsu bi'l-nafs*,' and 'requited is prescribed for you in all murder cases.' *Qiṣāṣ* therefore applies in all directions, which means that the male is retaliated for killing a female and a Muslim for killing a non-Muslim and so forth.[33]

Discriminatory practices in homicide cases were also encountered among the Jews. Ibn ʿAbbās has thus reported, concerning the two Jewish tribes of Madina, Banu al-Naḍīr, and Banu Qurayẓa, that the former discriminated against the latter. When a man of Banu Qurayẓa killed one of Banu Naḍīr, the latter would retaliate by killing one of Banu Qurayẓa, but if a member of Banu Naḍīr killed one of Banu Qurayẓa, the former gave one hundred *wasaqs* (camel load) of dates in compensation. On one such occasion, when a man of Banu Naḍīr had killed someone of the Banu Qurayẓa, the latter brought the case for adjudication to the Prophet. It was concerning this case that a Qur'ānic verse was revealed addressing the Prophet:

وإن حكمت فاحكم بينهم بالقسط، إن الله يحب المقسطين.

And if they (non-Muslims) ask you to adjudicate, then judge among them with justice (*bi'l-qisṭ*) (5:42).

والقسط النفس بالنفس.

'*Bi'l-qisṭ*' in this context means just retaliation without any discrimination.[34]

Should there be mitigating circumstances which call for leniency, the murderer may be exempted from *qiṣāṣ* and made, as the text under review provides, to pay blood money (*diyyah*) to the family of the victim.

The relatives of the victim may choose to forgo the *diyyah* altogether as *diyyah* is their right but not an obligation. They are, in fact, encouraged not to punish but to forgive. If only one of the heirs of the deceased pardons the culprit, or settles on receiving blood money from the victim's side, there will remain no right of retaliation for the remaining heirs. Another exception to the rule of *qiṣāṣ* is when a person kills his own descendant, such as the father who kills his son. For him, there would be no retaliation but a deterrent punishment (*taʿzīr*). If there are several culprits and one of them is exempted from *qiṣāṣ*, the rest are also exonerated from *qiṣāṣ*, although they may still be punished and given deterrent sentences under *taʿzīr*.

The Qur'ān also permits retaliation in certain types of bodily injuries. If a person willfully cuts off the hand of another, his hand is to be cut off in retaliation, and if a person strikes out the tooth of another, he is also liable to retaliation. But *qiṣāṣ* may not be inflicted in the case of the breaking of any other bones than the teeth, as it is impossible to observe equality in other fractures. *Qiṣāṣ* for parts of the body also holds good between a Muslim and a non-Muslim, since both are equal with respect to the consequences of their offences. According to a *ḥadīth* on the authority of Anas b. Mālik 'No case of *qiṣāṣ* came before the Prophet wherein he did not advise the grant of forgiveness.'[35]

ما رأيت النبي صلى الله عليه وسلم رفع إليه شيئ فيه قصاص إلا أمر فيه العفو.

In another *ḥadīth* reported by Abū Hurayra:

ما زاد الله عبدا بعفو إلا عزا.

When a man grants pardon (to an act of injustice he suffered), God Most High increases him in honour.[36]

In yet another *ḥadīth* it is provided that:

ومن قتل له قتيل فهو بخير النظرين إما أن يودي وإما أن يقاد .

The slain (or his family) has a choice of two things, either to take a *diyyah* or to retaliate.[37]

Thus, it is either *qiṣāṣ* or *diyyah* in the sense of the one or the other, but the two do not combine in the same case, especially when the family of the deceased has granted a pardon, or waived their right to *qiṣāṣ* and opted for a *diyyah*. The heirs of the deceased, in a murder case, include those who are entitled to a share in the estate of the deceased, whether male or female, according to the majority. But according to Imam Mālik, the heirs of the deceased for the purposes of *qiṣāṣ* and *diyyah* are his male agnate heirs, such as son, father, and brother.[38] Grant of a pardon by the relatives also exonerates the offender from *qiṣāṣ*, but the relatives may accept *diyya*. This is the view of Imams Shāfiʿī and Ibn Ḥanbal, whereas Imam Abū Ḥanīfa has held that pardoning in *qiṣāṣ* means that the relatives do not take anything as this is an act of good will and *iḥsān* on the part of the relatives within the meaning of the Qurʾānic terms 'maʿrūf and iḥsān'. (2:178).[39]

I shall not elaborate here on juristic details about the different types of homicide except to say that Muslim jurists have classified homicide into three main types, namely murder (*qatl al-ʿamd*) which is punishable by *qiṣāṣ*; killing as a result of error (*qatl al-khaṭaʾ*) such as when a hunter shoots and kills a person (this is punishable by payment of blood money (*diyyah*) to the heirs of the deceased plus an expiation (*kaffārah*) that consists of charity to the poor or of atonement by fasting); and culpable homicide (*qatl shibh al-ʿamd*) such as when A strikes B with a stick without intending to kill him but his hostile act actually kills B. (This too is punishable by payment of *diyyah*).

It is provided in a *ḥadīth* that the victim of a bodily injury, or, in the event of his death, his legal heirs, may take one of the following three options:

من أصيب بدم أو خيل فهو بالخيار بين إحدى ثلاث : فإن أراد الرابعة فخذوا على يديه : بين أن يقتصّ أم يعفو، فإن أخذ من ذلك شيئا ثم عدا بعد ذلك فله النار خالدا فيها مخلدا أبداً .

One who is victim of death or injury has one of three options, and if he opts for a fourth, he must be grabbed by the hand (and stopped): To retaliate, or forgive, or take blood money. One who does other than these indulges in excess and will suffer the torment of Hell forever.[40]

Ibn Taymiyya quoted this and commented that the warning in this *hadīth* is particularly concerned with the pursuit of revenge after a grant of pardon, or acceptance of *diyyah*. As soon as one of the available options is exercised, all hostility must cease from that moment.[41]

One of the rules of *qiṣāṣ* is that it must be carried out in the least painful manner. If the offender is a minor or insane, there shall be no *qiṣāṣ* but only *diyyah,* which, according to the majority, will be payable by the family or *ʿāqila* (nearest relatives) of the offender. Others maintain that minors or the insane are not liable to *diyyah* either.[42]

As a general rule, the death of the offender himself removes all claims. *Diyyah* is also applicable as a substitute to *qiṣāṣ* in cases where the requirements of the latter cannot be fulfilled. Furthermore, reconciliation between the parties is generally recommended even before adjudication, even though the community and state retain the right to impose a *taʿzīr* punishment after reconciliation. The Imams Mālik and Abū Ḥanīfa have held that the state must impose a *taʿzīr* punishment in every case of intentional killing wherein neither the *qiṣāṣ* nor *diyyah* is implemented. The Imams Shāfiʿī and Ibn Ḥanbal have held, however, that once a victim's relatives grant pardon to a *qiṣāṣ* convict, he is exempt from all punishment. The other two Imams mention that although *taʿzīr* punishment is not compulsory in every case, it should be meted out when the public interest demands it. However, *taʿzīr* in such cases must, as a general rule, be less than the death penalty.[43]

According to the majority of opinions, excepting the Ḥanafīs, the offender in the cases of both *qiṣāṣ* and *diyyah* is liable to an expiation (*kaffārah*). *Kaffārah* in this case consists of the release of a slave (when this was possible—a suitable alternative nowadays may be to donate towards saving the life of a patient who requires a transplant or an expensive operation), feeding sixty poor persons, or two months of fasting. The Ḥanafīs have held that *kaffārah* is applicable to erroneous killings but not to cases where the murderer is subject to *qiṣāṣ*.

There is some disagreement about the manner in which retaliation is enforced. Whereas some jurists have suggested a reciprocal method of executing the murderer in the way he killed his victim, the preferred view is that the death penalty should be executed by decapitation with a sword, and supervised by the authorities. Most jurists have concurred

on the use of the sword as this is deemed to be swift, and in view of
the fact that the *Sharīʿah* does not validate maiming or torture. Since
the purpose is to apply a swift and clean method, there should be no
objection from the viewpoint of *Sharīʿah* to other methods that are
now available, such as the electric chair or lethal injection, which are
even faster and more efficient.

For *qiṣaṣ* to be implemented, the legal capacity and the intent to
kill of the killer, and the *ʿiṣmah* or innocence of the victim must be
proven. The victim is not, in other words, one of those whose life is
not legally protected, such as an enemy soldier or a rebel. Attention
is also paid to the motive of the crime, to the whereabouts of the
deceased body, and to the kind of instrument used, whether a lethal
weapon or not. Uncertainty in these proofs is likely to reduce the
murder charge (*qatl al-ʿamd*) to one of quasi-deliberate homicide (*qatl
shibh al-ʿamd*).[44] Furthermore, *qiṣāṣ* applies to murder only, and is not
applicable to mitigated cases and manslaughter that involve a mistake
or accident, since these are factors that preclude the implementation of
capital punishment.

Diyyah for the loss of life is determined at one hundred camels of a
roughly equal combination of one, two, three, and four years of age.
The monetary equivalent of this is cited, according to some reports,
as eight hundred (gold) dinars or eight thousand (silver) dirhams. It is
reported that due to price rises, the caliph ʿUmar b. al-Khaṭṭāb later
raised these monetary equivalents to one thousand dinars and twelve
thousand dirhams respectively. The current rate of *diyyah* is 40,000
riyals in Saudi Arabia. In Pakistan, too, the monetary equivalent of
diyyah currently stands at RS 40,000.[45]

The details of *diyyah* are determined mostly by the *Sunnah* which,
like the Qur'ān, does not draw distinctions on the basis of gender and
religion. Yet the juristic opinion of the *fuqaha'* has held the *diyyah* of a
woman is half the *diyyah* of a man, a controversial distinction. This is
because the source evidence does not recognise any distinction of the
sort and the Qur'ān has provided an egalitarian formula on the inherent value of human life. I may recount here the combined account of
Muhammad al-Ghazālī and his commentator, Yūsuf al-Qaraḍāwī, on
this issue. The latter has endorsed the former's position to the effect
that 'the *diyyah* of a woman is equal to that of a man, the reason being
that the Qur'ān has not differentiated between them. The assumption
then that a woman's life is cheaper (*arkhaṣ*) than that of man, or that
her right is of lesser value, is a false assumption (*zaʿm kādhib*) and it is
contrary to the noble Qur'ān. A man who kills a woman is executed,

just as is a woman who murders a man is. Their blood is equal. What, then, is the reason for inequality in their *diyyah*?'[46]

Qaraḍāwī then continues: 'The Shaykh (al-Ghazālī) could have perhaps added the *ḥadīth* that 'the *diyyah* for loss of life is one hundred camels—*fi'l-nafs mi'atun min al-ibil*' to show that the Prophet did not differentiate the *diyyah* of a man from that of a woman.[47] The claim that the *diyyah* of a woman is half that of man refers to a *ḥadīth* to that effect, but that *ḥadīth* is unsound. It has a broken *isnād* (chain of transmitters) attributed to Muʿādh b. Jabal. Al-Bayhaqī wrote that this *isnād* is certainly unreliable and there is nothing to that effect in either al-Bukhārī or Muslim. The claim about consensus (*ijmāʿ*) in support of the alleged distinction is also weak. Al-Shawkānī has recorded that at least two early scholars, Abū Bakr al-Aṣamm and Ibn ʿUlayya opposed it. More recently, Muṣṭafā al-Zarqā has also opposed it. The Qur'ān draws no distinction between one life and another, between that of an infant and an adult in his prime, a great *ʿālim* and a commoner, a man and woman—are all equally subject to the laws of *qiṣāṣ* and *diyya*. This is because the text provides 'one who kills another human being (*man qatala nafsan*), without the latter being guilty of murder and corruption in the land, it would be as if he has killed the whole of mankind.'(5:32).

من قتل نفسا بغير نفس أو فساد فى الأرض فكأنما قتل نفسا جميعا.

When a dead body is found in a locality without any sign of the killer, and all efforts to identify the killer fail, the state is responsible for paying blood money to the victim's family in place of its basic commitment and responsibility to protect the lives of its citizens.[48]

The principle of *diyyah* finds analogous expression in contemporary criminology, which often recommends decriminalisation of the act and recourse to victim compensation as an alternative to the punishment of incarceration. *Diyyah* is, however, not totally analogous with civil damages. This is because *diyyah* has a punitive component which gives it punitive characteristics. It is akin to the imposition of a fine for a particular crime with the proviso that in the case of *diyyah* the fine goes to the victim's family rather than the state. The rules of *diyyah* also permit the state to stand as a substitute for the victim's family in order to secure the *diyyah* from the perpetrator, and to provide the victim or his family with the necessary compensation. Thus, it is not necessary for the *diyyah* to be paid directly to the victim or his family. It can be paid to the state in the form of a fine provided that the state assumes the responsibility of being able to satisfy the needs of the victim's family.[49]

If the offender himself can pay the *diyyah*, he is responsible for paying it in the first place since the *ʿāqila* comes in to help with the payment only when the offender is unable to pay. This is also implied in the Qur'ānic text on the subject of *diyyah* (*al-Nisā'*, 4:92) as quoted above. Since this verse does not make any reference to the *ʿāqila*, it is understood that *diyyah* is payable by the offender himself. The *ʿāqila* provision in Islamic law represented a departure from the basic principle of the personal responsibility of the offender on grounds of cooperation in unintentional crime. The purpose was also to make security and crime prevention a direct concern of the family and tribe. During the time of the second caliph, ʿUmar b. al-Khaṭṭāb, the colleagues at the work-place of the offender (*ahl al-dīwān*) were included in his *ʿāqila*, and this marked an early shift in the locus of *ʿāqila*, a provision which was altogether characteristic of tribal society and its particular set of conditions.[50]

In response to the question of whether the rules of *ʿāqila* can be meaningfully applied at the present time, difficulties do arise, both because of weaker tribal ties, and because of the tension that exists between the rules of *ʿāqila* and the constitutional principle of legality. In this connection, Maḥmūd Shaltūt has rightly observed, quoting Ibn ʿĀbidin in support of his view, that the *ʿāqila* provision in the *Sunnah* represents a temporary legislation (*tashrīʿ zamani*) that was meaningful in the tribal setting of earlier times, but no longer applies.[51] One may add that though the *ʿāqila* provision is no longer applicable, the basic idea of the payment of some kind of financial compensation to the family of the victim in crimes of violence still holds good. The offender himself should be required to pay the whole of the *diyyah*, or, failing that (especially when the offender is unable to pay it), it should be the responsibility of the state. In the event where the offender can pay a part of the *diyyah*, the state may bear responsibility for the rest. Pension regulations, especially relating to the state pension, and the question of the deceased person's entitlement to a state pension or a life insurance cover, are additional factors likely to be taken into consideration by a court in the determination of *diyyah* or its equivalent compensation for a crime.

There is another provision in the *Sunnah* concerning homicide in obscure circumstances, or when a dead body is found and the case cannot be solved, even after strenuous efforts. Recourse may be had, in that situation, to the principle of *qasāma*, or taking oaths from all the people who might be suspected in the incident or who live in the locality. This entails that fifty men of the nearest vicinity, who are identified by the family of the deceased, must take solemn oaths that they have neither killed nor have any knowledge of the killer. Once they take such an oath, they are absolved of *qiṣāṣ*, but are still collectively liable to pay a *diyyah* to the family of the deceased for their negligence in ensuring safety within the area under their supervision and control.[52]

Qasāma is premised on the rationale that the *Sharī'ah* does not accept the notion that human blood could be shed in vain, or that there could be a killing for which no one is accountable. Basic authority for *qasāma* is provided in a *ḥadīth*, narrated by Ziyād b. Abi Maryam, which may be summarised as follows:

A man came to the Prophet, peace be on him, and informed him that he had found the dead body of his brother amidst such and such a tribe. The Prophet told him to bring together fifty persons among them who must swear by God that they had neither killed nor known the killer. The man then asked if this was all that was to be done, to which the Prophet replied that he was also entitled to one hundred camels (as *diyyah*).[553]

Even when the parties reach an agreement to convert *qiṣāṣ* into the payment of *diyyah*, the government authorities are entitled to impose a punishment on the offender. For payment of *diyyah* only settles the Right of Man aspect of the crime, whereas crimes of violence are also crimes against society, and the state, representing society, may grant pardon or impose a punishment, if it deems either to be in the public interest (*maṣlaḥa*).[554]

IV. Modern Law and Practice on *Qiṣāṣ* and *Diyyah*

With reference to its contemporary application, it may be noted that the right to *diyyah* has been utilised in Saudi Arabia, where the state plays an increasingly prominent role in cases of murder, assault and damage to property. In the interests of public order and internal security, 'the state is not content with private settlement of disputes through the payment of blood money (*diyyah*). Although in *Sharī'ah diyyah* is preferable to *qiṣāṣ* as a way of settling disputes, as it is closer to clemency, it is no longer sufficient to terminate a dispute through payment of *diyyah,* and the assailant is therefore held liable to a state-imposed sanction.'[55] The traffic regulations of Saudi Arabia also prescribe that someone who knocks down and kills a person in a traffic accident is liable to pay *diyyah* to his legal heirs and, in addition, is liable to imprisonment.[56]

One or two points of general interest may be made here briefly, one of which is that *diyyah,* whether for loss of life or of limb, should not be seen to be putting a price tag on human life and limb. Rather, its focus is on the plight of the family that has suffered, the potential loss of income that results and so forth. The purpose of *diyyah* in the Qur'ān is, after all, the alleviation of suffering and the showing of compassion, and it is not a rigid imposition unrelated to the conditions of the offence and its victim. Another point that may have a bearing on the assessment of a suitable *diyyah* is reference to prevailing custom and the conditions of employment, cost of living, life insurance indicators and the like.

The *Sharīʿah* provisions on *diyyah* are on the whole applied in Saudi Arabia and relative factors that affect the value of money, in cases involving people from other countries, and changes in the rate of currency and the desire to curb excessive demands for blood money are all taken into account. Blood money for non-Muslims in Saudi Arabia is equal to that of a Muslim. A combination of statutory legislation and Islamic criminal law is also applied in regard to labour relations and motor vehicles. The rates of compensation for work accidents are fixed by a special committee, which on the whole relies on Islamic law. In motor vehicle accidents, the police determine the guilty parties, while the *Sharīʿah* court fixes the amount of blood money.[57]

Qiṣāṣ is also contained in the applied law of Saudi Arabia. One particular case for which it gained international publicity was the Gilford case. Frank Gilford, from South Australia, had to decide whether to insist on death by *qiṣāṣ* or to accept *diyyah* in connection with the death of his sister, Yvonne Gilford. The case was tried in Riyadh, where two nurses were charged with killing the deceased. In the end, the brother of the deceased chose to accept *diyyah,* which he in turn donated to a hospital in memory of his sister. The two nurses were consequently released.

Another case of the conversion of *qiṣāṣ* to *diyyah* was that of Sarah Balabagan in 1995. A fifteen year-old Muslim from the Philippines was sentenced to death by *qiṣāṣ* in the United Arab Emirates. She was found guilty of killing her employer, Almas Mohammed al-Baloushi, by stabbing him 34 times. She pleaded self-defence as the employer had tried to rape her. The trial court had earlier confirmed that Balabagan was a victim of rape, but she was also found guilty of manslaughter. She was sentenced to seven years' imprisonment and was ordered to pay 150,000 dirhams to the victim's relatives. The sentence was contested and appealed against and the appeal court imposed a death sentence by firing squad. The Philippines authorities intervened and later the victim's family was persuaded to grant a pardon from *qiṣāṣ* and instead accepted 150,000 dirhams as *diyyah*. Balabagan's sentence was also reduced to imprisonment for a year and a hundred lashes.[58]

Iran and Pakistan have also adopted the *Sharīʿah* provisions on *qiṣāṣ* and *diyyah* in their respective laws. The Iranian Law of *Ḥudud* and *Qiṣāṣ* 1982 (sections 62-68) and also the Law of *Taʿzīr* 1983 regulated *ḥudūd, taʿzīr, qiṣāṣ, diyyah* and *kaffārah* in accordance with the Ithna ʿAshari Imamiyya School, and with that almost codified the law in respect of the offences of murder, homicide, bodily injury, sexual offences and offences against property, such as theft and robbery. These laws were later revised and partially amended in 1996. The amended laws, which were approved by Parliament, tend to emphasise accuracy in the enforcement of *qiṣāṣ* so that the victim is not exposed to pain in excess of the magnitude of the offence. *Qiṣāṣ* for bodily injuries under Iranian law may not be implemented in conditions where inflicting injury by way of *qiṣāṣ* was likely to become infectious.[59]

In Pakistan, the Criminal Laws (Amendment) Ordinance 1991 amended the Penal Code and the Criminal Procedure Code to enable *qiṣāṣ* and *diyat* to be applied. The punishments of *qiṣāṣ, diyat* and *arsh* (compensation for injury) are added to the range of punishments provided in the codes. The offences of murder and bodily injuries can be dealt with through *ṣulḥ* or mutual agreement and can be settled by payment of *diyat* or *arsh*. Because of this, even intentional murder is not liable to the mandatory sentence of death. Homicide caused by negligence or an accident is liable only to the payment of *diyat, arsh* and or *taʿzīr* punishment. Offences of bodily injury are also dealt with by these methods. Thus, these offences are treated both as crimes and as torts. But the position here differs with civil law in that *diyat* and *arsh* mainly determined by law and not by the assessment of the court.[60]

In the Sudan, a number of laws were enacted in 1987 with a view to bringing the country's laws into conformity with the *Sharīʿah*. Included in these were the Penal Code 1983, and Criminal Procedure Code 1983. The Penal Code went into force on 8 September 1983 and introduced the *hudud* and *qiṣāṣ* laws. The Criminal Procedure Code regulated criminal investigation, prosecution and trial in conformity with the *Sharīʿah*.[61]

In Malaysia, two northern provinces, Kelantan and Terengganu, have proposed to enforce the *ḥudūd, qiṣāṣ* and *diyyat* laws in their respective Enactments. The Syariah Criminal code II Bill 1993 of Kelantan deals with *qiṣāṣ* offences in part II (sections 24–38) and makes wilful killing (*qat al-ʿamd*) punishable with death by *qiṣāṣ*, if the next of kin does not grant pardon, and if a pardon is granted, *diyyat* will be payable to the victim's relatives, or in some cases the offence may be punished by *taʿzīr*. The Bill also makes provisions for bodily injuries and circumstances where *qiṣāṣ* may not be enforced. It also addresses issues of proof and evidence in part II (see p. 39–48). The attached schedules (II & III) to this Bill specify the types of injuries and the amounts of *diyat* or *irsh* that they carry.

Section 28 the Hudud Bill of Kelantan provides:

> The *wali* (guardian, next of kin) may at any time before the punishment of death as the *qiṣāṣ* punishment is executed, pardon the offender either with or without a *diyat;* and if the pardon is with a *diyat,* this shall be paid either in a lump sum or by instalments, within a period of three years from the date of final judgment, and if in the meantime the offender dies, the *diyat* shall be recoverable from his estate.

Section 35 provides:

> Whoever causes bodily injury to a person shall be punished with *qiṣāṣ* punishment, that is, with similar bodily injury as that which he has inflicted upon his victim, and where *qiṣāṣ* punishment cannot be imposed or executed because the conditions required by the Syariah law are not fulfilled, the offender shall pay *irsh* to his victim and may be liable to a *taʿzīr* punishment of imprisonment.

Terengganu introduced its Syariah Criminal Enactment on *Ḥudūd* and *Qiṣāṣ* 2002 in (74) sections, and has closely followed the provisions of the Hudud Bill of Kelatan. Its sections on *qiṣāṣ* and *diyat* are identical to those of the Kelantan Bill.

As of writing, neither of these Enactments are being enforced and both remain as proposed Bills. The Terengganu Bill was proposed by the State Legislature Assembly in July 2002, whereas the Hudud Bill of Kelantan was ratified by the State Legislative and assented to by the Sultan of Kelantan in 1993. The Hudud Bill of Kelantan has remained in suspense due to conflict of jurisdiction, as it does not conform to the terms of the Federal Constitution and its provisions as spelt out in the

9th Schedule, List 2. It also exceeds the terms of the Muslim Courts (Criminal Jurisdiction) Act 1965 as amended in 1984. Under this Act, the Syariah Courts may deal with offences punishable with imprisonment for up to three years, or fines of up to RM5,000, or whipping up to six strokes, or a combination of all these. The *ḥudūd* punishments and death by *qiṣāṣ* exceed these limits, which is why the Hudud Bill of Kelantan 1993 still remains in abeyance.

In March 2004, the Islamic party (PAS) suffered major losses in the general elections and lost Terengganu, which came once again under the control of the ruling party of Malaysia, the United Malay National Organisation (UMNO). Within weeks of the UMNO victory, the Chief Minister of Terengganu, Idris Jusoh, announced that the disputed Hudud Bill 2002 would be revised and amended.

V. The Killer Does Not Inherit

This title is a literal translation of at least one version of several *ḥadīths* that, worded, differently, convey the same meaning. The ruling of the *ḥadīth* on this matter is self-evident in its basic message that when a person kills another, the killer cannot inherit from the victim. But jurists have differed widely on the detailed implications of this ruling as to whether the bar here applies to erroneous killing and culpable homicide in the same way as it does to murder, and whether or not direct and personal involvement, as opposed to indirect involvement, is a factor to be taken into account.

Briefly, the Mālikī school has confined the application of the *ḥadīth* 'the slayer does not inherit—*lā yarith al-qātil*,' to deliberate killing which precludes unintentional homicide, regardless of the direct or indirect involvement (*mubāsharah wa tasabbub*) of its perpetrator in the offence. Erroneous killing does not therefore constitute a bar to inheritance in the Mālikī school, but it does constitute a bar to *diyyah* in that the killer may not inherit back the *diyyah* which he has paid as a result of his unintentional killing. The Mālikīs apply their ruling on this exclusion from inheritance to all persons, including children and the insane.

Imam Abū Ḥanīfa has held, on the other hand, that killing debars the killer from inheritance provided it is direct (*bi'l-mabāshir*) and hostile, regardless of the type of killing, but that the ruling here does not apply to children or the insane.

The Shāfiʿīs and the Ḥanbalīs apply the principle of protected life, that is, life which the *Sharīʿah* regards as protected and sacrosanct (*maḍ mūn*), as opposed to that of an enemy warrior, for example. One who destroys a protected life is barred from the inheritance of his victim regardless of the manner or type of killing. This includes both intentional and erroneous killing, whether direct or indirect, and even where the killer is a child or insane. All are barred from inheritance. But one who destroys an unprotected life, for example a person sentenced to execution by a court of law, or an assailant who has killed in self-defence, the killer in such cases is still entitled to inherit from his victim. This is probably the most wide-ranging position in that it covers nearly all instances of homicide, and a ruling of this nature is deemed to be necessary so that property and inheritance are not seen as incentives to killing among relatives and associates.[62]

The next question that arises is whether or not the killer is also barred from a bequest that his victim might have made in his favour. The Mālikīs who only consider intentional killing a bar to inheritance, maintain that unintentional killing does not preclude the killer from a bequest even if the deceased person had known his killer; but if he had known the identity of his killer and still made a bequest in his favour, the killer may be allowed to receive the bequest. Imam Abū Ḥanīfa has held that all hostile killing in which the killer is directly involved constitutes a bar to bequest, but that the killer may be allowed to receive the bequest with the consent of the legal heirs. The Shāfi'īs have recorded two different views on this, one of which precludes the killer from bequest in all cases, even if the heirs give consent, and the contrary view entitles the killer to bequest in all cases without any need for consent by the legal heirs.[63]

Without entering into further details, it may briefly be mentioned that the Sharī'a also imposes an atonement (*kaffārah*) on the killer in all unintentional homicide. This may consist of freeing a slave, feeding sixty poor persons, or fasting for two months. Since the first of these no longer applies because of the termination of slavery, the rough equivalent of it may be given in charity to a good cause, especially one that saves lives. And lastly *kaffārah* is not a substitute to *diyyah,* which means that both are payable in cases of unintentional homicide.[64]

VI. Could the Death Penalty Be Based on *Ta'zīr?*

In response to this question, Muslim jurists have suggested that criminal acts that seriously harm the public interest ought to be ultimately punishable by death in order to protect society against dangerous and incorrigible criminals. For example, the death penalty, based on *taʿzīr*, may be imposed in cases of espionage and blasphemy, and could also be imposed on habitual criminals who pose a serious danger to society. But rehabilitation and deterrence, which constitute the overall purpose of *taʿzīr*, should be kept in mind as a preferable alternative.

The judge's discretionary powers in *taʿzīr* normally do not extend to the imposition of the death penalty, which the law has basically confined to *qiṣāṣ* and also some cases of *ḥudūd*. The head of state has some authority nevertheless to determine criminal acts that are punishable by death, but only if absolutely necessary. For example, the death penalty is proper in the case of the incorrigible criminal only when it is indispensable to protecting society against his menace.

Ḥanafī writers consider the death penalty on the basis of *taʿzīr* a necessary measure to ensure political order and government. Thus, they determine that the death penalty can be inflicted, but only with great restraint.

The *ḥudūd* crimes that carry the death penalty in the established *fiqh* are *zinā* by a married person (*muḥṣan*), highway robbery (*ḥirāba*) and also apostasy (*ridda*). The penalty for *ḥirāba* and terrorism involving bloodshed is founded in the clear text of the Qur'ān (5:32–33), as is *qiṣāṣ* for intentional killing as discussed above. The death penalty for *zinā* and also *ridda* have, on the other hand, been stipulated in *ḥadīth*. The Qur'ān only provides a punishment of one hundred lashes for all cases of *zinā* without any reference marital status. A similar situation obtains concerning the death punishment for apostasy, which is stipulated in a *ḥadīth* but on which the Qur'ān is silent altogether, and many scholars have gone on record to say that apostasy carries a deterrent *taʿzīr* punishment only. The issue is open to interpretation, but falls outside our immediate concern here.[65]

VII. Suicide (*al-Intiḥār*)

Suicide falls under the Qur'ānic provision of killing without just cause (*illā bi'l-ḥaqq*) simply because a person does not have the right to take his own life.[66] Since life is a God-given gift and His prized creation, it may not be subject to destruction and abuse even by oneself. This is why the *Sharīʿah* forbids suicide and recognises no exception whatsoever to its prohibition. It is a heinous sin, for which the perpetrator is liable, in the event of an unsuccessful attempt, to a deterrent penalty of *taʿzīr*. If the attempt succeeds, the person is still liable to an expiation (*kaffārah*) which may be taken from his property, according to the Shāfiʿīs and some Ḥanbalīs, whereas Imams Abū Ḥanīfa and Mālik do not make *kaffārah* a requirement.[67] The Qurʾānic authority on this is the prohibitive text which addresses the people:

ولا تقتلوا أنفسكم، إن الله كان بكم رحيما.

Kill yourselves not, for God is truly Merciful to you. (4:29).

People who are driven to despair are thus reminded to have faith in God's mercy in the hope that He will relieve them. The prohibition of suicide by this clear text means that it is a violation of the *Sharīʿah* and that anyone who facilitates or collaborates in the act of suicide is also liable to a deterrent (*taʿzīr*) punishment.[68]

Al-ʿIbādī has quoted early commentators on the interpretation of this verse (4:29) and has drawn attention to the following five points:

1) The obvious meaning is that God Most High has forbidden suicide.
2) It also means that 'you may not kill one another.' This interpretation is attributed to Ibn ʿAbbās, Saʿīd b. Jubayr, ʿIkrima and others.
3) One may not undertake a task which is likely to cause one's own death, even if it is religious obligation. In support of this, the episode wherein the Companion ʿAmr b. al-ʿĀṣ, in the battle of Dhāt al-Salāsil, had a wet dream but prayed in congregation with others without ablution or bathing due to cold weather is cited. When the Prophet was informed of this he mentioned it to ʿAmr, who is said to have quoted this Qurʾānic verse in response—and the Prophet is said to have laughed but did not object otherwise.
4) No one should deprive himself of the enjoyments of life; to do this would be tantamount to acting contrary to this verse.
5) Lastly, the verse means 'do not kill yourselves by indulgence in self-destruction including crime [and consumption of lethal substances]'.[69]

The Qurʾān also forbids believers from courting danger and inviting death and destruction upon themselves, as in the following verse:

ولا تلقوا بأيديكم إلى التهلكة.

Throw not (yourselves) into the (mouth of) danger by your own hands. (2:195)

The momentous decision to commit suicide is most likely to be taken by those who are driven to despondency and despair. The Qur'ānic advice to such people is as follows:

قل يعبادى الذين أسرفوا على أنفسهم لاتقنطوا من رحمة الله إن الله يغفر الذنوب جميعا.

O My servants who have indulged in excess concerning themselves! Do not despair of the mercy of God. For God forgives all sins (39:53).

To let oneself be driven to a state of utter despair is equated to misguidance, which should be avoided. This is also the subject of another verse that follows:

ومن يقنط من رحمة ربه إلا الضآلون.

And who will despair of the mercy of God except those who are misguided? (15:56).

The Prophet has spoken strongly in condemnation of suicide, as in the following *ḥadīth*:

من تردّى من جبل فقتل نفسه فهو فى نار جهنم يتردى فيها خالدا مخلدا فيها أبدا ومن تحسّى سمّا فقتل نفسه، فسمّه فى يده يتحساه فى نار جهنم خالدا مخلدا فيها ومن قتل نفسه بحديد فحديدته فى يده يتوجّا بها فى بطنه فى نار جهنم خالدا مخلدا فيها.

The one who throws himself off a mountain cliff and kills himself will be doing the same to himself perpetually in Hell. The one who takes poison and kills himself shall be holding the same in his hand and permanently taking it in Hell, and the one who kills himself with a weapon will be piercing his body with it perpetually in Hell.[70]

A similar *ḥadīth* proclaims that the 'one who kills himself with something in this life will also be tortured by it on the Day of Resurrection.'[71]

ومن قتل نفسه بشيئ فى الدنيا عذّب به يوم القيامة.

Life is a divine trust (*amāna*) in the hands of its bearer, who is expected to safeguard and cherish it with a sense of responsibility and care. As for those who undergo painful experiences that they cannot tolerate, the Qur'ānic guidance to them is that life is a testing ground and many will face hardship, but patience, perseverance and hope in the face of adversity build the inner resources of the individual, and may also bring great spiritual rewards.[72]

Al-Bukhārī has recorded a *hadīth* to the effect that the Prophet looked at a man, in a battle against the pagans, and he was by all accounts one of the most capable of Muslim warriors. But the Prophet said concerning him:

من أحبَّ أن ينظر إلى رجل من إهل النار فلينظر إلى هذا. فتبعه رجــل فلـم يزل على ذلك حتى جرح فاستعجـل الموت، فقام بذبابة سيفه فوضعه بيـن ثديه فتحامل عليه حتى خرج مـن بين كتفيه، فقال النبى صلى الله عليه وسلم: إن العبد ليعمـل فيما يرى الناس عملَ أهـل الجنـة وإنه لمـن أهـل النار، ويعمـل فيـما يرى الناس عمل أهل النار وهـو من أهـل الجنـة، وإنمـا الأعمال بخواتمها.

One who wants to look at someone from the inhabitants of Hell—let him look at this man.' Another man followed him and kept on following him until the fighter was injured, and in a wish to die quickly, he placed the tip of his sword on his breast and leaned over it until it passed through his shoulders (and killed himself). The Prophet added: 'A person may do deeds that seem like the deeds of the people of Paradise while, in fact, he is from the dwellers of Hell. Similarly, a person may do deeds that look like the deeds of the people of Hell while he is, in fact, from the dwellers of Paradise. Verily the deeds of Man are judged by their consequences.[73]

In Common Law, suicide in which a legally competent person voluntarily kills himself by stabbing, poison or any other way, commits a felony and was punishable by forfeiture of his goods and chattels and an ignominious burial of his body by the highway. This was, however, abrogated in the U.K. Suicide Act 1961 (Sec.1), and suicide is not a crime under this Act. However, by virtue of section 2(1) of this Act, a person who aids, abets, counsels or procures the suicide or attempted suicide of another is guilty of a statutory offence.

In some jurisdictions in the United States, suicide is still an offence involving moral turpitude and may involve criminal prosecution. In other jurisdictions, suicide itself is not a crime but is regarded a grave public wrong and an act involving moral turpitude.

In India, suicide is not a crime, although the attempt to commit suicide is an offence under section (309) of the Indian Penal Code 1860. The logic of making the attempt at suicide an offence was probably to provide a deterrent against it.[74]

The *fiqh* texts are silent on the issue of suicide bombing, which has become a tragic and disturbing phenomenon of the Israeli-Palestinian conflict, especially since Israel unleashed a new wave of aggression on the street processions of the Palestinian youth in 2000–2001. The upsurge in suicide bombing as the preferred tactic of groups claiming to be Islamic warriors has brought mixed responses from Muslim scholars. Most scholars of standing have not hesitated in condemning this, and the September 11 (2001) attacks on the United States, as contrary to Islamic principles.

It is simplistic to lump together the Palestinian suicide bombings with al-Qaeda terrorist activities, as few would deny the genuine suffering of the Palestinian people or the legitimacy of their demand for a homeland and state. It is equally simplistic to equate suicide bombing with martyrdom as many have claimed. This is because suicide bombing challenges two fundamental principles of Islam: the prohibition against suicide and the deliberate killing of non-combatants. In the context of war, the line between suicide and combat is often very fine and easily crossed. The Prophet Muhammad clearly sought to draw a line separating martyrdom in battle from suicide. According to the *ḥadīth*, reviewed above the Prophet repudiated and denounced those who deliberately took their own lives in the course of battle, even by a warrior suffering from severe wounds. The Muslim fighter enters the battle not with the intention of dying, but with the conviction that if he should die, it would be for reasons beyond his control. Martyrdom does not begin with a suicidal intention, let alone the linkage of that intention with the killing of non-combatants. Suicide bombers intentionally set out to kill themselves and other civilians and thus violate the norms of Islamic law and ethics.

In September 2003, the former Malaysian Prime Minister, Dr. Mahathir, denounced Palestinian suicide bombing and said that suicide bombing was unacceptable in Islam. Mahathir, himself a strong supporter of the Palestinians, added that they resorted to suicide bombing because they did not have proper weapons in their fight for an independent homeland. 'Nevertheless, it is wrong to commit suicide bombing because it causes loss of innocent lives. Fighting is one thing, but if you go onboard a school bus and kill all the school children, I don't think it is a brave move.'

Dr. Mahathir made these remarks in response to a statement of Abdul Hadi Awang, leader of the opposition Islamic Party, PAS, who had said that Islam permitted suicide bombing in the fight against oppression. He added that his party supported the Palestinian militant group Hamas and considered suicide bombings as acts of martyrdom. Mahathir added in his response to these remarks that the root cause of the Palestinian problem was not religion but territory, and unless this issue was resolved it would be difficult to persuade Hamas not to take up violence.[75]

In November 2003, the Arab states condemned the suicide car bombing in Riyadh that killed 17 and wounded more that a hundred persons, mainly Arabs. The 22-member Arab League denounced the attack as a 'terrorist and criminal' act, while Saudi Arabia and its five neighbours in the Gulf Cooperation Council condemned it as 'cowardly and terrorist.'

The Arab League secretary-general, Amar Musa, said such acts 'only aim to destabilise...terrify and kill' innocent people. The Egyptian President Husni Mubarak condemned it as a 'criminal act,' and the foreign minister of Iran, Kamal Kharazi, said 'killing defenceless women and children in the holy month of Ramadan...is against Islamic values and human ethics.'[76]

Those who have raised the issue of 'collateral damage' in this context are mistaken, because non-combatants are chosen as the direct target of suicide bombing. They are neither collateral nor incidental. Even if the cause of fighting the Israeli aggression is a valid one, it does not justify killing non-combatants.

The argument of reciprocity that some scholars have advocated is also questionable. The Shaykh of Azhar Muhammad al-Ṭanṭāwī has validated suicide bombing if the enemy targets the civilian population, in which case he thought the response in the form of suicide bombing falls under *jihād,* and becomes a personal duty of every one under attack. For death in this case is for an honourable cause.[77]

The late Hamas leader, Sheikh Aḥmad Yasin, who fell victim to Israeli target bombing, has also been quoted as saying 'As long as they target our civilians we will target their civilians.'[78] Israeli aggression has undoubtedly inflicted atrocities both through direct targeting of civilians as well as through the disproportionate use of force, such as sending tanks against boys throwing stones or sending helicopter gunships to assassinate Palestinian leaders. Yet the justification of suicide bombing as retaliation or as a form of *jihād* is questionable as it begins on an erroneous premise that goes against the ethics of both just retaliation and justified violence. What drives the bombers—often impressionable teenagers—on their suicidal missions are promises of a martyr's reward by the so-called religious scholars, who fuel the frustration and volatility of tender emotions with their misguided instructions.

VIII. Duelling and Permission to Kill

The *Sharīʿah* forbids the individual from giving permission to be killed. For no-one is entitled to grant such a permission. Muslim jurists are generally in agreement that no human agency has either the ability to create or the authority to terminate human life. Muslim jurists have consequently held that if a person permits another to mutilate a limb or a part of his body, this would suspend retaliation, but the offender is still liable to a *taʿzīr* punishment. If a person gives permission to be killed, and this is carried out, this will not, according to the majority of jurists, save the killer from death punishment by *qiṣāṣ*. Only the Ḥanafīs have held that the permission to kill here operates as a doubt (*shubha*) and this suspends the death punishment by *qiṣāṣ* but not a deterrent punishment (*taʿzīr*) or *diyyah* that may still be imposed by the judge. This is because permission does not detract from the enormity of killing, and it is as such of no value. According to a minority Ḥanafī opinion, *qiṣāṣ* is still applied and the permission is ignored. The Mālikīs have held that the permission in question is of no value as it is wrong in the first place, and fails, therefore, to count as a valid *shubha*. A permission of this kind is, in any case, premature, as it is granted prior to the right of *qiṣāṣ* having materialised. Hence the killer is liable to the death punishment by way of retaliation.[79] If the victim grants a pardon before he dies while still in possession of his faculties, this absolves the killer, according to the majority, excepting the Mālikīs, from both *qiṣāṣ* and *diyyah,* and no action is taken. This is said to be the purpose of the Qurʾānic text which provides, concerning *qiṣāṣ* and *diyyah,* that: فمن تصدق به فهو كفارة له 'One who makes a charity of it, it shall be counted as expiation (*kaffārah*) for him,' (5:45). A minority Mālikī opinion exonerates the killer in this case from both *qiṣāṣ* and *diyyah* but a *taʿzīr* punishment may still be imposed.[80]

As a corollary of the principle that life is sacrosanct and its inviolability cannot be compromised by any agreement or permission to kill, the *Sharīʿah* also forbids duelling, in which two people challenge one another to a fight to death, usually to vindicate honour, or prevent humiliation. Duelling may be on the basis of a prior agreement or a mere willingness to hurt or kill one another. The opponent either uses a lethal weapon, such as a sword and firearm, or fight without any weapon. What is important is that both sides encourage one another to hurt and to kill. Whatever the motive may be, if the duel leads to the killing of one, the killer will be liable to the death penalty, and the killing will qualify as murder if he intended to kill. If the intention was only to inflict injury and it led to death, this will also qualify as intentional killing. In the absence of an intention to kill, the killing is likely to be classified as quasi-intentional (*shibh al-ʿamd*). Criminal responsibility would in all cases be attributed to the one who has agreed to duel. The only situation where the *Sharīʿah* permits duelling is in the battlefield and also against a lawless rebel (*bāghi*). There are reports that the Prophet had permitted warriors in the battles of Badr and Uḥud to enter a duel and entertained one such challenge himself. But even so, the Ḥanafīs maintain that one should not volunteer to it but may only respond to a challenge.[81] Should one of two duellers receive an injury which subsequently leads to death, it will count as intentional killing and no credibility whatsoever is given to the agreement that permits the combatants to shed each other's blood. The basic guideline here is laid down in the following *hadīth*, recorded by both Bukhārī and Muslim:

إذا التقى المسلمان حمل أحدهما على أخيه السلاح فهما فى جرف جهنم، فإذا قتل أحدهما صاحبه، دخلاها جميعا. وفى رواية عنه قال: إذا التقى المسلمان بسيفهما، فالقاتل والمقتول فى النار، قلت: هذا القاتل؛ فماالمقتول؟ قال: إنه كان حريصا على قتل صاحبه.

When two Muslims unleash their swords against one another, the killer and the killed will both land in Hell. The Companions then asked: What is the victim's guilt in this case, O Messenger of God? To this, the Prophet responded: He was eager to kill his opponent.[82]

IX. Abortion (*Isqāṭ al-Janīn*)

Abortion is generally defined as 'the deliberate termination of pregnancy.'[83] It is the expulsion of a foetus from the uterus, which may either be before it has reached the state of viability or after that stage. A more detailed definition of abortion (*isqāṭ al-jaīin, Ijihāḍ*) is formulated by the Pakistan Council of Islamic Ideology as follows:

> Whoever causes a woman to miscarry a child whose limbs or organs have been fully or partially formed, commits abortion, if such miscarriage is not caused in good faith for the purpose of saving the life of the woman. If the woman causes herself to miscarry, she may also be guilty of abortion.[84]

Abortion that results in the death of the foetus may either be spontaneous or induced. A spontaneous abortion, also known as miscarriage, occurs as a result of injury, internal disorder or natural causes and the foetus passes from the woman's body. Induced abortion (*isqāṭ al-ḥaml*) may be inflicted by another person on a woman with a child whose organs or limbs have not been formed, and she miscarries as a result. If the miscarriage is not caused in good faith for the purpose of saving the life of the mother, it is *isqāṭ al-ḥaml*. This too can be caused by the woman herself.[85] The foetus may be removed artificially with medical means, in which case several methods are used to carry out abortion. The physician may use a vacuum to suck out the contents of the uterus, usually at the early stages. Next is the dilation and evacuation method, known as D & E, whereby the foetus is dismembered in the uterus and then removed. Another method is that of injecting a solution which kills the foetus and causes it to pass from the woman's body.[86]

Science maintains that human life goes through stages in a continuum from the time of conception to death. There are four such stages in the pre-natal development of a human. The first is in the fallopian tube where the fertilised ovum remains for about three days. Cell division begins during this time. The next stage begins with implantation in the uterus, where rapid cell division continues. The embryo stage begins two weeks after conception. At this time, there is organ differentiation. All the internal organs one will ever have are present in rudimentary form by the end of the sixth week. The foetus stage begins from eight weeks to birth, in which there is continuous growth but nothing new is added. A foetus is thus in possession of all necessary human characteristics.

The foetus is alive and can develop into a human being, yet on average sixty per cent of all conceptions end in early miscarriage, sometimes even before a woman is aware of her pregnancy. This suggests that the foetus is a potential human being, not an actual person. Automatic miscarriage occurs because of over-exertion, or an internal disorder which makes the body unable to cope with the process.[87]

Literally, *janīn*, the Arabic equivalent of foetus, means something that is veiled or covered. It could, in this sense, apply to anything that develops inside the mother's womb. This is how the term occurs in the Qur'ān (53:32): 'God knows you well when He brings you out of the earth and when you are hidden in your mothers' wombs—*ajinnatun* (pl. of *janīn*).'

وهـو أعلم بكـم إذ أنشأكـم مـن الأرض وإذ أنتـم أجنـة فى بطون أمهاتكم.

In another passage, the Qur'ān expounds the various stages of the growth of *janīn*:

ولقد خلقنا الإنسان من سلالة من طين ثم جعلنه نطفة فى قرار مكيـن ثـم خلقنـا النطفـة علقـة فخلقنـا العلقـة مضغـة فخلقنـا المضغة عظاما فكسونا العظام لحما ثم أنشأنه خلقا أخر...

We created man from the essence of clay. Then We placed him as a drop of sperm (*nuṭfah*) in a place of rest (the womb). Then We made the sperm a clot of congealed blood (*ʿalaqah*). Then We made it a chewed lump (*muḍghah*). Then We made of that lump bones, and clothed the bones with flesh. Then We developed another creature out of it. (23:13).

The last segment of this verse marks a point of departure when it says that 'another creature' is developed. According to commentators, the term refers to 'ensoulment' and the beginning of a different stage of development marked by the vesting of human characteristics therein.[88] Muslim scholars are divided on the precise signification of these Qur'rānic terms. According to Imam al-Shāfiʿī, it would appear that the stage of foetus begins when the stages of al-ʿalaqah (congealed blood) and al-muḍghah (chewed lump) are completed, and the foetus develops clear human features such as fingers, eyes etc. According to an alternative interpretation, *janīn* signifies that which exists in the womb after ensoulment. Yūsuf al-Qaraḍāwī wrote that 'all Muslim jurists hold abortion after the ensoulment of the foetus to be *ḥarām* and a crime against a living and fully formed human being.'[89] A certain ambiguity has remained, however, about the precise time of ensoulment. According to a *ḥadīth* that Muslim has recorded: 'After the lapse of forty two nights of *nuṭfah* (drop of sperm) in the womb, God sends an angel that shapes it into human form and equips it with the faculties of hearing and sight, and its bones are covered with flesh and skin.' The *ḥadīth* continues to point out that the gender of the foetus and its course of destiny in life are also determined from that time.[90] The implication is that ensoulment occurs after six weeks.

Some jurists take the view that each of the three stages, *nuṭfah*, *ʿalaqah* and *muḍghah*, is 40 days long. This is in fact indicated in a *ḥadīth* on the authority of ʿAbd Allāh b. Masʿūd wherein the Prophet said 'for each of you, creation in the womb of your mother takes 40 days, then it takes the same length of time to develop into *ʿalaqah,* and again it takes similar time to turn into *muḍghah*. Then God Most High sends an angel who breathes spirit into it...'[91]

إن أحدكم يُجمع خلقه فى بطن أمه أربعين يوما، ثم يكون فى ذلك علقة مثل ذلك، ثم يكون فى ذلك مضغة مثل ذلك ثم يرسل الله الملك فينفخ فيه الروح...

According to an alternative interpretation, all the three stages are completed in 40 days. In response to the question of whether the foetus has perception and movement prior to receiving a soul, it is suggested that the movement it possesses is like that of a growing plant. Its movements and perceptions are not voluntary. But when the soul is breathed into the body, the movements and perceptions become voluntary.[92] According to al-Ghazālī, abortion is prohibited after the completion of *muḍgha*, since after this stage ensoulment occurs, but there are different views on this as the text does not specify the precise timing of ensoulment.[93]

One of the basic questions that has dominated the debate about the legality or otherwise of abortion is the role the mother's well-being and her consent may play. Another argument is about the extent to which the law should protect the unborn. Those who argue for prohibition or strict legal restrictions on abortion describe themselves as pro-life, whereas those who emphasise the woman's right to have an abortion describe themselves as pro-choice and maintain that abortion should be allowed if a woman's life or health is endangered by her pregnancy. Others have argued that abortion should be allowed if there is a danger that the child will be born with a serious mental or physical defect. They also approve of abortion if the pregnancy resulted from incest or rape. This view proceeds on the assumption that foetuses are not persons and are not therefore entitled to rights normally given to persons, and that birth alone marks the beginning of personhood.[94]

In a 1996 resolution of the Islamic Fiqh Academy of India, the following was decided: 'If a woman suffering from AIDS becomes pregnant and a qualified doctor confirms that in all likelihood, the foetus will also develop AIDS, in that case, 'prior to the life coming in the embryo during the period which the Muslim jurists have fixed at 120 days, permission for abortion can be given.'[95]

Whereas the Islamic view of life focuses on ensoulment, an alternative medical view highlights brain function, and maintains that humanity does not begin with the fact of conception. A functioning brain is essential for a person to be alive. The beginning of brain function also indicates a radical change in the development of the foetus. Since a person is regarded dead when his brain ceases to operate, an unborn child would similarly be considered a human being once its brain begins to function.[96]

Abortion is forbidden after the inception of life in the foetus. If the foetus is miscarried due to a criminal act or aggression towards its mother and the foetus is stillborn, the offender is liable to a punishment. But if the foetus comes out alive and then dies as a result of aggression inflicted on the mother, the offender is liable to a heavier punishment. The important factor in both cases that affects the quantitative aspect of punishment is the condition of the mother, and whether the abortion is by her consent or by an act of aggression against her.

Abortion with the consent of the mother and prior to the inception of life has provoked different responses from Muslim jurists. The Shāfiʿīs have allowed it in the first forty days of pregnancy provided that the spouses are in agreement, and it is not harmful to the mother. Abortion is forbidden after forty days, which is believed to be the starting point of life in the foetus.[97] Al-Ghazālī, himself a Shāfiʿī, and some other Shāfiʿī jurists have held, on the contrary, that abortion is forbidden absolutely, even at the early stages of pregnancy when the foetus might only consist of a blood clot and tissue. Aborting a foetus at any stage is an offence as it destroys its right to life. The heinousness of that 'offence increases after the inception of life and it is criminality and aggression at its utmost when the foetus actually emerges alive.'[98]A Shāfiʿī jurist, Abū Bakr b. Abi al-Saʿīd al-Qarafi, held abortion to be permissible at the *nuṭfa* and *ʿalaqa* stages, but that it is an offence at the subsequent stage of *muḍgha* and the offence increases in gravity after the inception of life (*nafkh al-rūḥ*) therein.[99] The Mālikīs have disallowed abortion at any stage of pregnancy on the analysis that the foetus has the potential to develop and live to maturity, and have forbidden abortion completely after the foetus becomes a living organism upon completion of forty days.[100] The Ḥanafīs and Ḥanbalīs are less rigorous and have held abortion to be permissible prior to the inception of life in the foetus within the first one hundred and twenty days of pregnancy, which to them marks the *nafkh al-rūḥ*, or ensoulment. But it is generally considered reprehensible and sinful if it is without a valid ground. An example of a valid reason is when the woman's milk dries up because of the pregnancy and she has a breast-feeding child, while the father cannot afford to hire a wet nurse, or when the mother is too weak to withstand the strains of pregnancy and birth. Both schools have held abortion to be forbidden after one hundred and twenty days.[101] Abortion to them is the lesser of the two evils. If a mother's life is endangered such that an abortion becomes necessary, the life of the mother should not be sacrificed for the sake of saving the foetus.[102] The Shīʿa Jaʿfariyya have held the perpetrator of abortion to be liable to *kaffārah* even prior to ensoulment provided that it is caused by direct action (*bil-mubāshara*) as opposed to indirect causation. It thus appears that the schools of law are generally in agreement on the prohibition of abortion after ensoulment, but have held different views on it prior to that stage.

An infant's right to life is established from the moment he or she is born alive. To kill or destroy it is murder in the full sense. To be born alive means the emergence of the infant alive, or even a part thereof, from its mother. Killing the infant at this time, even prior to the severance of the umbilical cord, is murder provided that signs of life are observed. If a foetus is miscarried before birth as a result of aggression against the mother, the perpetrator commits a crime, although it is not classified as murder for want of proof that it had commenced its life in the womb of its mother and would certainly have been born alive. Even so, the perpetrator is liable to punishment as well as payment of compensation to the mother, known as *ghurra*, which is a portion of *diyyah* as explained below.

Abortion caused by a criminal act against the mother has given rise to a certain difference of opinion about whether it should be viewed as an offence against both the mother and the foetus, or against the foetus in its own right. Any act inflicted on the mother which causes the death of the foetus is classified as homicide if it is established that the foetus emerged alive and then died as a direct result of the criminal act. But it is an offence of lower degree if the foetus emerges without any sign of life. The crucial question here is about the commencement of life. For as long as the foetus is hidden in its mother's womb, it is considered a part of the mother, but it is treated as a living human as of the moment it is known to have commenced life. It is as of this moment that the foetus acquires a legal personality (*dhimmah*) and becomes capable of receiving rights, such as inheritance and bequest, but cannot incur an obligation until it is born alive.[103] Abortion without the mother's consent, which is a result of violence or inducement inflicted on the mother, is thus a crime. Whether it is a crime against two persons, the foetus and the mother, or only the mother herself, are among the questions that the *fuqaha'* have addressed.

In the event where violence against the mother causes the death of the mother and foetus in her womb and it is not known whether the foetus died by the death of the mother or directly by the criminal act against her, the law imposes two separate punishments, one for the mother which is a full *diyyah* and the other for the foetus consisting of a *ghurrah*, which is five per cent of *diyyah,* that is payable on account of the death of the foetus.

Abortion as an offence is the induced detachment of the foetus from her mother's womb, and the offence takes place regardless of whether the foetus emerges alive or dead, although this factor has a bearing on the punitive consequences that the perpetrator faces. The offence can be caused by an act, whether violent or otherwise, that even threatening words that can cause anguish and then abortion are enough to indicate the offence.

An incident that occurred during the time of the caliph ʿUmar b. al-Khaṭṭāb has influenced Muslim juristic writings on abortion. It is reported that the caliph summoned a woman because of some adverse information he had received against her. When the caliph's messenger delivered the message to her, she was struck with fear and on her way to the caliph's court, she panicked and miscarried her pregnancy. The infant 'cried once or twice and then died.' The caliph consulted the Companions about this and many responded that he was not responsible, and that as a leader, it was a part of his duties to discipline or admonish unruly behaviour that came to his notice. ʿAlī b. Abī Ṭālib took an exception and held the view that the caliph was liable to the payment of *diyyah*, for 'you caused her the anguish and she aborted.' The caliph accepted this and paid the *diyyah* to the woman.[104]

Abortion does not occur unless the foetus has actually exited from the womb of its mother. If someone strikes the mother on the stomach or induces her to take medicine to abort or kill the foetus in her womb, these acts are punishable by a deterrent *taʿzīr* punishment. Unless they actually lead to the exit of the foetus, doubt about the life or death of the foetus persists, and abortion may be difficult to establish. Having said this, advances in medicine may make it possible to establish the facts more accurately than was previously possible. If it can be determined that the foetus died as a result of the criminal act inflicted on the mother, this should be enough, and it may not be necessary for the foetus to actually depart from its mother. The fact that scholastic jurisprudence made the foetus's exit a precondition of abortion was simply because of the persistent difficulty of determining the timing of its death, and what caused it. If this could be determined, with the aid of modern medical facilities, then it can safely be assumed that the new position would essentially conform to the spirit, if not the letter, of the scholastic discourse of jurists, and the actual exit of the foetus from the womb of its mother may not be necessary to determine that a violation of the right to life has taken place.[105]

The question of what is considered a foetus (*janīn*) whose abortion constitutes an offence has also been variously answered. Further to what has already been said on the views of the *madhāhib,* the Imams Abū Ḥanīfa, Shāfiʿī and Ibn Ḥanbal held that the foetus should have the appearance of a human being, even if partially-formed. If it is a mere clot without formation, it will fail to be called a *janīn,* but they added that seriously doubtful cases should be referred to expert opinion. Imam Mālik held, on the other hand, that the offence is punishable, even if what is aborted consists of a clot, or even congealed blood, and that actual formation and the appearance of a human form are not a requirement.[106]

Abortion that is punishable by just retaliation (*qiṣāṣ*) or by the payment of blood money (*diyyah*) refers to a living foetus that emerges from her mother's womb and shows sign of life. If it is established that a living foetus was intentionally killed, *qiṣāṣ* applies. All that is required is to ascertain whether the foetus exited his or her mother while alive, even for a short time, and then died. For just retaliation to be applied as a punishment in this case, it is also necessary that the foetus exits the mother's body while the mother is still alive, as it is otherwise difficult to know whether the death of the foetus was caused by the death of the mother or by the criminal act inflicted on her. Once again, in the light of advances in modern medicine, the juristic ruling on this may also be liable to change. If modern medicine can actually determine the precise cause of death of a foetus, then suitable sanctions can be determined on that basis. ʿAwdah has observed in this connection that changing the rules of *fiqh* in line with modern scientific knowledge is harmonious with the spirit of scholastic jurisprudence if not with its letter.[107]

The following three situations are envisaged in determining liability for punishment in abortion:

1) When the foetus is detached from its mother alive as a result of the act of violence inflicted on her, and subsequently dies because of that act, the offender is liable to just retaliation (*qiṣāṣ*), in the case of intentional killing of the foetus, according to those who recognise the existence of an intention to kill in that situation, and it is a full *diyyah* in all other cases. For those who do not recognise an intention to kill the foetus while still in the womb, the punishment in all cases is a full *diyyah*. One of the subsidiary consequences of the distinction between intentional killing and manslaughter in this situation is that the *diyyah* of intentional killing is payable by the killer, whereas it is payable by his relatives and associates, that is his *ʿāqila*, in unintentional killing. The *diyyah* is also multiplied in proportion to the number of infants. Two *diyyahs* are thus payable for two infants, and three separate *diyyahs* for three infants and so on. If the mother also dies due to that act of violence, a separate *diyyah* will be payable, and this does not amalgamate with the *diyyah* of the foetuses, regardless of the number of foetuses involved.[108]

2) In the event where the foetus is detached from its mother and emerges stillborn, the punishment for this is a *ghurra* (compensation), which is payable in the case of the destruction of an embryo, or a formed child stillborn, as a result of assault suffered by the mother during pregnancy. The person responsible for the destruction of the child in embryo is liable to pay the *ghurra* over and above any liability he may bear for injury to the mother. All the Sunni Schools regard this money as belonging to the child itself, and therefore transferable to its legal heirs. If the abortion is caused by a relative, say by the father, he cannot inherit according to the ruling of the *ḥadīth* which precludes the killer from inheritance.

   If the mother herself causes the abortion, for example by taking a drug known to cause abortion, she is also liable to a *ghurra* that is inherited by the child's relatives other than herself—provided that the human form is distinguishable in the foetus. If the foetus is aborted alive and then dies, a *diyyah* will be payable by the male relatives (*ʿāqila*) of the child. The jurists have debated the issue of the emergence of human form in the foetus. Many are of the view, especially in the Ḥanbalī and Mālikī schools, that abortion is prohibited at the stage of *mudgha* even before distinctive human formation and the emergence of such parts of the body as hands, ears and eyes. There is much diversity of juristic opinion on details among the schools, and even within one and the same school of law. The majority consider ensoulment a requirement of prohibition, *ghurra* and *diyyah,* whereas a minority consider earlier stages, such as the emergence of the human form, or *mudgha* formation that signifies the beginning of the emergence of limbs, as criteria for the application of these rules. The Mālikīs and Imam al-Ghazālī have held abortion to be prohibited from the moment of conception.

Ghurra as a punishment is authorised by the *ḥadīth* wherein it is reported that two women from the clan of Ibn Hudhayl fought, and one struck the other with a rock, which killed both the victim and the foetus in her womb. The case was brought to the attention of the Prophet, in which he ruled that the *diyyah* of her foetus was a *ghurra* payable to the legal heirs of the child. A full *diyyah* was also imposed for the life of the mother, to be paid by the *ʿāqila* of the killer.[109] It is further reported that the caliph ʿUmar b. al-Khaṭṭāb consulted the Companions about the punishment of abortion and Mughīra b. Shuʿba reported that the Prophet had imposed a *ghurra*. The caliph asked if Mughīra's report could be verified, and Muhammad b. Maslama confirmed Mughīra's report.[110]

Ghurra for male and female infants is the same, and it is imposed in the same amount both in intentional and unintentional inducement of the foetus. *Ghurrah* is also multiplied in accordance with the number of foetuses aborted.[111]

3) When injury is inflicted on the mother and the foetus is lost first, and the mother dies subsequently, a full *diyyah* is payable on account of the death of the mother and a *ghurrah* for the foetus. This will apply to the case where a person gives the mother medicine, for example, for the purpose of aborting the foetus she carries, but not to kill her, and she actually dies after the abortion of the foetus. In the event where the mother dies

after the abortion of a living foetus and the latter also dies afterwards, two separate *diyyas* will be imposed on the offender, one for the mother and the other for the foetus.

When a person strikes a pregnant woman with a knife or sword with the intention to kill, and the woman dies together with two foetuses, one of which emerges dead with a mark of the injury, and the other emerges alive and then dies, the killer is liable to three punishments: *qiṣāṣ* for the murder of the mother, a full *diyyah* for the foetus that emerged alive, and a *ghurra* for the foetus that emerged dead.[112]

There is also a supplementary punishment of atonement (*kaffārah*) for the abortion of a foetus by the offender regardless of whether the foetus emerges alive or dead, and whether the abortion is self-inflicted by the mother or by another person. If several people collaborated in the abortion, each one is liable to a *kaffārah* as a supplementary punishment. If more than one foetus is aborted, the amount of *kaffārah* is also multiplied by that number according to the Imams Shāfiʿī and Aḥmad b. Ḥanbal. Imam Abu Ḥanīfa has held, on the other hand, that *kaffārah* is payable only in cases where the foetus emerges alive and then dies.[113]

Abortion is an offence under the Malaysian Penal Code, which provides that the act of causing miscarriage with or without the consent of the woman constitutes an offence (section 312). The subsequent two sections, however, provide that the punishment will be more severe if abortion is carried without the woman's consent, or if it later causes her death.

A ruling of *ijtihād* on abortion issued by the *fatwa* committee of Kuwait has been highly acclaimed by Qaraḍāwī, who considers it an example of innovative *ijtihād* that combines the *Sharīʿah* position with scientific knowledge. The *fatwa* was issued in September 1984 and is as follows:

It is prohibited for a physician to attempt abortion on a pregnant woman after the expiration of 120 days from the date of *ʿulūq,* that is, when the *janīn* turns into a congealed blood clot unless abortion would save the life of the mother.

Abortion is permissible with the agreement of the spouses before the completion of forty days of *ʿulūq.*

Abortion is not permissible between forty and one hundred and twenty days of pregnancy except in two situations: first, when continued pregnancy would substantially harm the mother's health, and second, when it is established that the foetus would be invalid or permanently deficient and the deficiency is incurable.

Barring situations of urgent necessity, all abortions must be carried out in Government approved hospitals. Abortion after the expiry of 40 days may not be carried out unless it is approved by a committee of specialist physicians, at least one of whom specialises in gynaecology. The decision must have the approval of at least two Muslim physicians of upright character.[114]

Among modern scholars, ʿAbd al-Salām Madkūr, Wahba al-Zuḥaylī, and Jamīl Ibn al-Mubārak have also held that abortion is forbidden, before and after ensoulment, unless it is dictated by necessity and on valid grounds.[115]

X. Euthanasia (*Qatl al-Marḥamah*)

Originally a Greek word, Euthanasia means 'a good and honourable death', and also 'a happy death.' Medical dictionaries refer to it as a 'quiet, painless death.' It is defined as procuring the painless death of a person to end his suffering due to compassion especially in cases of incurable and painful diseases.[116] This is an altogether new subject in fiqh in the sense that it has not been addressed separately in its juristic literature, but it has been addressed by juristic works of recent origin.

Euthanasia is of two types, voluntary, and involuntary:

a) Voluntary Euthanasia: This occurs when a patient expresses a wish to die. It may include taking active steps to procure death, such as by administering lethal drugs (active euthanasia) or by withdrawal of life support treatment (passive euthanasia). When a person specifically requests his or her life to be ended, it is regarded as voluntary euthanasia. In non-voluntary euthanasia, the patient gives no consent nor makes any request as he or she may be incapable of giving it. The basic question that arises is the state of mind of the patient and the doubt about whether a patient wishing to die is capable of making a sound decision at all. The next question arising in this connection is whether the right to live also confers upon its bearer the right to die.

In active euthanasia, the doctor is actively involved in the termination of the life of the patient for whatever reason, hence the emphasis is on the doctor's act itself. Had it not been for the doctor's intervention, in other words, death might not have occurred. In the case of passive euthanasia, more emphasis is placed upon the cause of death than on the doctor's negative act, such as the termination of a life support system at the patient's request. The doctor has full knowledge of the patient's condition, but neither he nor his act is the immediate cause of death.

Despite what has been said, it is often difficult to draw a clear line of distinction to characterise the doctor's act as active or passive. These are the wet sands of euthanasia and the same may be said with regard to the patient's state of mind and disposition.[117]

    (b) Involuntary Euthanasia: Involuntary euthanasia is described as that in which the act that accelerates death or the death itself is not rooted in the wish of the subject but originates in the wish of a close relative or guardian. The patient may be comatose and unable to communicate his or her, wish and the responsibility of deciding to terminate his or her life rests with another person. The case of involuntary euthanasia is complex and raises interesting ethical questions. One of these is whether a third person is competent to decide on another person's life or death, even if he is a guardian. Guardianship, it is added, is created for the benefit of a person so that the one who is unable to guard his own right may be protected by his guardian. It is questionable whether that purpose is being achieved in the case at hand.

The view that physician-assisted death must be resisted is based on the inalienability of the right to life. No-one may violate it, and that includes the individual himself, and the physician. It is said that individuals do not own their bodies and may not make decisions on terminating their own lives. The sanctity and inviolability of life is compromised if it can be terminated on the sole basis of the consent of a person himself, or the professional judgment of a physician.

The recognition of the right to die has on the other hand the scope to create a sense of autonomy on the part of the patient in regard to his own life and death. From a jurisprudential viewpoint, the right to life may be incomplete unless a person enjoys complete control as to his person, and this includes the right to die. This may be deduced from an analogy with the right of property, which is incomplete unless the right to destroy it, without harm to others, is also recognised. Although this may be a discrepant analogy because life and property are not alike, in recent years, organ donation and the trade in human organs seem to have brought the right to life a step closer to the right to property and ownership. It is still open to debate whether a fundamental right also applies in the negative sense, such as the destruction of one's right to live. For even in the case of property, the right to destroy it is not a recognised right in the absolute sense that would admit no restriction. A man who owns a factory, for example, where some persons are employed, certainly has proprietary rights over it, yet he is not permitted to set fire to it as this will affect the livelihood of others and jeopardise their rights. 'All fundamental human rights are similarly placed, including the right to live.' Individuals do not live on islands, so to speak, and their lives are of concern to their relatives and loved ones, to whom they owe certain obligations, one of which is to avoid, as far as possible, inflicting suffering on them.[118]

The New Jersey Court in America ruled in *re Quinlan's*[119] case, where it reasonably appeared that a comatose patient would not return to the cognitive state of life, that it was permissible that doctors hold off the life support system from the patient. This decision of the court was followed by a volley of other cases seeking court permission to terminate medical care. But in a number of other cases the courts ruled contrary to *re Quinlan* precedent. For example, a Californian court aptly rejected the plea of a patient seeking the doctor's assistance to die, seemingly on the simple ground that the assistance to die is available, but limited to a request for passive euthanasia. Where a patient sought premortem cryogenic suspension of his body, the court ruled that he had no constitutional right to assisted death. From the case law so far, it appears that the right to die may be claimed by a terminally ill patient because he is in an absolute vegetative state of health and is unlikely to return to normal life. It is also held that competent patients have no right to compel unwilling doctors to withdraw their life support treatment. The courts in America have so far been cautious, and do not grant any request that involves the doctor's active participation to help a patient end his life.[120] The American Medical Association has not only questioned the patient's right to claim a doctor's assistance to die, but has condemned it and held that any assistance rendered by the physician in this regard is tantamount to intentional killing.[121]

The fact that the *Sharīʿah* forbids suicide implies that the right to life cannot be claimed negatively, and the right to die is clearly not recognised. This is conveyed explicitly in the Qurʾān, which enjoins the faithful not to take their own lives.[122] The same is confirmed in the *ḥadīth* which we earlier reviewed in conjunction with suicide. Two separate incidents have also been reported in which two Companions received injuries so painful that they killed themselves. Both incidents drew disapproving remarks from the Prophet to the effect that both men wiped out their good deeds by that single act of suicide. A person's consent, whether granted to a medical doctor or anyone else, that his life may be terminated is therefore of no account. This position also extends to consent given by a guardian or relative of the patient to a third party, or to a medical practitioner. Since the patient himself is not authorised to give a valid consent, a third party is even less able to do so in this case, and consent given by such a person cannot be of any merit. Consent by a relative can only be regarded as evidence to endorse the case, for example, of a passive decision by a medical specialist not to continue the prolonged use of a life support system for a comatose patient.

Qaraḍāwī gives the following examples of passive euthanasia (*taysir al-mawt al-munfaʿil*) and then offers some analysis. Suppose that a terminal cancer patient, or one with severe head injuries, will certainly die if his treatment is discontinued. There is no hope of any cure-only prolongation of his condition. To discontinue treatment speeds up death and puts and end to the suffering of the patient and his family. It also means that the natural course of events is left unmediated and the law of causation takes its course.

The ʿulamā have generally subscribed to the view that seeking treatment for one's illness is not obligatory; it is only permissible (*mubāḥ*). According to a minority opinion held by the followers of Imams Shāfiʿī and Aḥmad b. Ḥanbal, to seek treatment for one's illness is recommendable (*mustaḥab*). Some have even debated the question of which is the preferable course: treatment, or being patient with an illness untreated? In a chapter on *al-Tawakkul* (trust in God's will) al-Ghazālī refuted the assertion that abandonment of medication was recommendable in all cases. According to yet another minority opinion, to seek treatment for one's ailment is obligatory (*wājib*). Qaraḍāwī supports a combination of these two views in which seeking treatment is either recommendable or obligatory, but adds that specific decisions can best be made in the light of particular contexts.

The fact that the Prophet encouraged his Companions on many occasions to seek treatment when they suffered illness supports the conclusion that it is recommendable to do just that. But it is said that the encouragement given was related to hopeful cases. As for terminal illness and conditions that inflict great pain and suffering on the patient and his family, and all that medication can possibly achieve is to extend that condition with no hope for recovery—treatment in these situations is neither obligatory nor recommendable. Provided the physician does not actively engage in putting an end to a patient's life, his inaction to 'let nature take its course' is neither reprehensible nor forbidden, which means that it is permissible. The physician may abandon medication or discontinue a life support facility to a patient who is in an absolutely vegetative condition, is perpetually comatose, or is medically classified as brain dead. To keep such a person alive at exorbitant costs for a long period that could be many years, only inflicts suffering on the relatives, and depletes their financial resources.[123] Qaraḍāwī added that he discussed his views with experts in both medicine and *fiqh* in conferences in which he had participated, and his views were met with general approval.[124]

As for cases of active euthanasia where the physician takes measures, such as administering a greater quantity of a dangerous drug, or poison with the intention to kill a patient who is not in an absolutely hopeless situation and the possibility remains of improvement with medication and life support system-this is absolutely forbidden and qualifies as murder, even if the physician acts compassionately in order to put an end to the patient's suffering.[125]

One may add to this that the availability of more advanced evaluation methods nowadays may significantly help the doctor to assess the prospects of recovery and survival more accurately. There is a scoring system known as the Apache Score which accurately predicts overall mortality for critically ill patients. Similarly, there is the Glasgow Coma Scale, which also aids the doctor in his judgment. If the probability of survival is high, then a life support machine may be used to sustain life and assist recovery. Intensive care is very costly and is not advisable in cases where there are extremely low chances of survival. After all, the purpose of life support equipment is not to prolong the patient's agony but to aid recovery and a return to normal life.[126]

In conclusion, it may be said that destruction of life in all forms is forbidden in Islam, and this also applies to euthanasia. In the event, however, where medical evidence conclusively declares a patient's state to be beyond recovery and there remains no prospect of survival, euthanasia may be permissible strictly on a case by case basis. Since it is difficult to draw a clear distinction between active euthanasia and passive euthanasia, the case by case approach is recommended and the evidence in each case would need to be examined and careful conclusions drawn while assuming that every case is governed by the general principle of the sanctity of life. Only when continuation of a vegetative life amounts to what may be deemed as decidedly harmful, one may be able to make a decision in the light of the *ḥadīth* which declares that 'harm may neither be inflicted nor reciprocated—*lā ḍarara wa la ḍirāra fi'l-Islām.*'

XI. The Abandoned Child (*al–Laqīṭ*)

Laqīṭ normally refers to a lost child or a child abandoned by its parents on the street, or some such place, and found by someone who has no knowledge of the name, identity, parentage, religion or domicile of the child. It is an 'infant abandoned by its relatives due to penury or shame. One who abandons and neglects it is a transgressor, and one who protects the abandoned infant is rewarded, and bringing it to safety is a collective obligation—*farḍ kifā'ī* of the community.'[127] To save the life of the *laqīṭ* is an act of great merit, in conformity with the Qur'ānic declaration:

$$\text{ومن أحياها فكأنما أحيا الناس جميعا.}$$

'One who saves the life of one, it is as if he saves the life of all people,' (5:32).

The origin, religion and identity of the abandoned infant, and whether it is born to a married couple or an offspring of an illicit relationship, are all immaterial to the duty that the Sharīʿa imposes on everyone to save its life.[128]

Anyone who causes the death of an abandoned infant, or leaves it unattended until it dies of starvation, exposure to cold or attack by animals is liable for murder.[129] There is disagreement among Muslim jurists as to the right to custody and guardianship of the *laqīṭ*, as well as responsibility for its protection and care—whether it belongs to the government, or to the person who finds and brings the infant to safety in the first place. The preferred view on this seems to be that the person who secures the life of the *laqīṭ* has prior claim to its custody if he or she is fit to take care of it, failing which it is the responsibility of the state, which is authorised to place the infant in the custody of upright persons who may wish to undertake the task.[130] Should any assets be found with the *laqīṭ*, they belong to the infant; if he or she were tied to a riding animal (or found in a vehicle), for example, the animal or vehicle would be treated as the property of the *laqīṭ* and may be sold for the child's upkeep by the person who finds him. The *laqīṭ's* property is expended on its upkeep first, and only thereafter, his maintenance becomes the responsibility of the *bayt al-māl*. The power of guardianship over the *laqīṭ* belongs to the state in accordance with the purport of a *ḥadīth* that 'the Sultan is the guardian of one who has no guardian—*al-Sulṭānu waliyyun li-man lā waliyya lahu*.' The person who finds and saves the *laqīṭ* does not automatically have the power of guardianship due to the absence of a legitimate reason, which is either a blood tie (*qarāba*) or lawful authority (*sulṭa*), but he may act in certain ways that are beneficial to the *laqīṭ*, such as receiving a gift or donation on his or her behalf.[131] To act in this capacity is a form of assistance that is required of all Muslims, in accordance with the Qur'ānic address to the believers to 'Cooperate with one another in good work and in righteousness, and do not cooperate in hostility and sin.' (5:2).

وتعاونوا على البر والتقوى ولاتعاونوا على الأثم والعدوان .

The effort of the person who saves the *laqīṭ* is analogous to the one who saves a drowning person; both partake of *farḍ kifā'ī* and are acts of spiritual merit. In the event where no-one else is expected to know about or be able to bring the *laqīṭ* to safety, the *farḍ kifā'ī* is elevated to a personal duty (*farḍ ʿaynī*) that falls on the person who is able to protect the *laqīṭ* against destruction. To say that bringing the *laqīṭ* to safety is a collective duty of the community means that if some people fulfill it, the whole community is absolved of it, but if no-one does it, all fall into sin and are held responsible. The spiritual reward for the performance of this duty belongs to the person, or persons, who actually perform it and save the life of the *laqīṭ*.[132]

XII. Warfare

With a view to protecting innocent life against aggression, the *Sharīʿah* lays down certain guidelines on warfare which may be summarised under three headings as follow:

1   The grounds for war.
2   Measures that must be taken before war.
3   Rules that must be observed during war.
1)   Grounds for war: With regard to the grounds that justify warfare, the Qur'ān stipulates three such, namely defence, breach of treaty and the prevention of oppression (*fitna*). The subject of defence is addressed in the following text addressed to the believers:

وقاتلوا فى سبيل الله الذين يقاتلونكم ولاتعتدوا إن الله لا يحب المعتدين.

And fight in the way of God those who wage war on you and do not be aggressive, for God loves not the aggressors (2:190).

The substance of this directive is upheld in at least two other passages as follow:

لاينهاكم الله عن الذين لم يقاتلوكم فى الدين ولم يخرجوكم من دياركم أن تبروهم وتقسطوا إليهم إن الله يحب المقسطين، إنما ينهاكم الله عن الذين قاتلوكم فى الدين وأخرجوكم من دياركم وظاهروا على إخراجكم أن تولوهم.

God does not forbid you from being fair and just to those who do not wage war on you concerning your faith and do not expel you from your homes. God loves those who are just. He only forbids you concerning those who fought you over your religion and expelled you from your homes... (60:8–9).

فمن اعتدى عليكم فاعتدوا عليه بمثل مااعتدى عليكم واتقوا الله واعلموا أن الله مع المتقين.

You may repel the aggression of the one who is aggressive toward you, by its equivalent, and fear God, for God is truly with those who are conscious of Him (2:194).

This second passage clearly validates reciprocal treatment in matters of war and peace. The occasion of revelation of this verse, which was revealed in the sixth year of the *hijrah* before the treaty of Hudaybiyya appears to have contemplated the possibility of war occurring during a holy month (i.e. of Dhi'l-Qaʿda), but this factor was ignored and reciprocal treatment was validated even during that month and at all times.[133] In another verse, it is provided that:

فإن اعتزلوكم فلم يقاتلوكم وألقوا إليكم السلم فما جعل الله لكم عليهم سبيلا.

If they (enemy forces) withdraw and do not fight you and make an offer of peace to you, then God has opened no way for you (to fight against them). (4:90).

And then again:

وإن جنحوا للسلم فاجنح لها وتوكل على الله

If they (the enemy forces) incline towards peace, then you should incline towards peace too and place your trust in God. (8:61).

The second ground for war that Islam validates is the breach of a treaty and the betrayal of trust. This is the subject of at least two Qur'ānic verses as follows:

وإما تخافن من قوم خيانة فانبذ إليهم على سواء إن الله لايحب الخائنين.

If you fear treachery from a people, throw back their covenant to them so as to be on equal terms. For God loves not the treacherous (8:58).

وإن نكثوا أيمانهم من بعد عهدهم وطعنوا في دينكم فقاتلوا أئمة الكفر إنهم لا أيمان لهم لعلهم ينتهون.

If they violate their oaths after their covenant, and taunt you for your faith, then fight the bandleaders of infidelity. For their oaths are nothing to them, that they may thus be restrained (9:12).

The third ground for war is to protect the freedom of religion, and prevent the outbreak of oppression and *fitna* that seeks to deprive the faithful of the freedom to practice their religion. The Qur'ān thus proclaims:

$$وقاتلوهـــم حتـــى لاتكون فتنـــة ويكون الـــدين لله فإن انتهوا فلا عدوان إلا على الظالمين.$$

And fight them until *fitna* is no more and God's religion is established. If they end fighting then there shall be no hostility except against the oppressors (2:193).

There were instances in the early days of Islam where Muslims were persecuted and physically tortured to compel them to renounce their faith and turn their back on Islam. The Qur'ān consequently allowed the Muslims to defend themselves against that sort of oppression.

2) Measures that must be taken before war: Since war is only permitted for a righteous cause, there must be no treacherous or underhand tactics. In every war, there is a distinct possibility of bloodshed and loss of life, and this necessitates that due care is taken to remove misunderstanding and error in the outbreak of violence. Even when there are valid grounds for war, war may not begin, as far as the Muslim party is concerned, without a clear warning and a declaration of war. This is the subject of the verse already quoted, wherein the Muslims are told that if they fear treachery and breach of treaty, then they should 'throw back their (enemy) covenant,' to the agent of treachery and fight it so that treachery does not become triumphant. To throw back the covenant here means, 'informing them clearly of their breach of treaty and betrayal so that they are not taken by surprise.'[134] The subsequent portion of the same text which reads that 'God loves not the treacherous,' confirms this conclusion. Qur'ān commentators have specified that treachery is not permitted even against disbelievers. The verse in question tells the believers to throw back their covenant and tell their enemies that they shall fight them so that both parties are equally informed of this. Treachery occurs when one party trusts that there is a peace treaty in force and the other resorts to an undeclared war. This must be avoided.

There is also evidence in the Qur'ān that encourages Muslims to grant a respite that would enable the restoration and the revival of a broken covenant, so that peace is given a better chance to prevail and bloodshed is averted. The truce that is allowed as a cooling off period should not, however, be indefinite. It is in this context that the Qur'ān validates immunity and truce for a period of four months, especially in a war with disbelievers who had a peace treaty with the Muslims (cf., 9:1–5). During this time there should be no hostility or violence, and peace should be maintained as far as possible. Writers of early history have provided detailed information about how these Qur'ānic directives were followed by the Prophet himself and the early Muslims in the many encounters and military engagements that took place with the Jews following the Prophet's migration from Mecca to Madina.[135]

3) Rules that must be observed during war: In the course of war, Muslims are prohibited from killing civilians, women and children, the elderly, religious leaders and monks who are not involved in war. In several *ḥadīths* (some of which are reviewed below), the Prophet gave detailed instructions to individual military commanders to avoid unnecessary brutality and violence, not only against civilians, but also against livestock, buildings and vegetation. Muslim commanders were also encouraged to grant safe conduct (*amān*) to individuals and groups from among the enemy forces who might wish to disengage from fighting. Once an *amān* is granted, no aggression may take place, and the individuals granted safe conduct also cannot be taken as war prisoners. The incentives to peace are enhanced further by the ruling that entitles every Muslim, not just army commanders, to grant safe conduct to the warriors, whether one or more, of the enemy forces. The procedure of granting *amān* is not a formal one. As soon as a Muslim utters a word, whether direct or indirect, to a belligerent party, which is indicative of peace, safe conduct is granted and must henceforth be observed by all Muslims.[136]

Two Companions, Samura b. Jundub, and 'Imrān b. Ḥaṣīn have both confirmed that 'the Prophet, peace be on him, used to encourage us to give charity and forbade us from maiming (war casualties).'[137]

كان النبى صلى الله عليه وسلم يحثنا على الصدقة وينهانا عن المثلة.

In another *ḥadīth* which Abū Dāwūd has recorded in a section on 'the Prohibition of Maiming,' ʿAbd Allāh b. Masʿūd reported that the Prophet said:

أعف الناس قتلة أهل الإيمان.

The most compassionate of all people in battle are the ones who observe their commitments (i.e. avoid maiming).[138]

In another *ḥadīth*, ʿAbd Allāh b. ʿUmar reported that 'the Prophet condemned killing women and children in battle.'[139]

عـن نافع، عن عبد الله أن أمرأة وجدت فى بعض مغازى رسول الله صلى الله عليه وسلم مقتولة، فأنكـر رسـول الله صلى الله عليه وسلم قتل النساء والصبيان.

Rabāḥ b. Rabīʿ reported another *ḥadīth* wherein 'the Prophet ordered the army commander Khālid b. al-Walīd, not to kill women, children and the elderly.'[140]

قل لخالد لايقتلنّ امرأة ولا عسيفا.

The first caliph Abu Bakr sent a letter to his army commander, Yazīd b. Abi Sufyān, in which he gave him the following instructions: '... you must not kill women, children and the elderly, nor must you cut or burn trees, whether fruit bearing or otherwise...avoid the destruction of buildings and livestock, unless it be for food.'[141]

Prisoners of war may not be killed *qua* prisoners unless it is for an identified cause. Ibn Rushd has even recorded, as Muhammad Hamidullah points out, the consent of the Companions of the Prophet to that effect. This does not, however, preclude trial and punishment of POWs for crimes they might have committed. Muslim jurists clearly recognise that a prisoner may not be held responsible for mere acts of belligerency.[142] Prisoners surrendering on conditions are treated according to the terms of their capitulation. On unconditional surrender, past acts of belligerency constitute no grounds for their execution.[143] Abū Yūsuf has recorded a minority view that POWs might be executed in the interests of Islam, but has himself shown aversion to this position and quoted other opinions to the effect that executing them is reprehensible and should be avoided.[144]

XIII. Concessions Granted to Protect Life

The *Sharīʿah* grants numerous concessions (*al-rukhaṣ al-sharʿiyya*) to the individual to enable him to protect his life when necessary and to prevent hardships that may jeopardise his safety. To protect one's own life is a *Sharīʿah* obligation (*wājib*), which is why every Muslim has a duty to take food, rest and also medicine, to ensure his or her safety and prevent self-harm. The individual is also permitted to break the normal rules in situations of necessity by being permitted, for example, to consume unlawful substances, such as the meat of a carcass, liquor and pork, if this will prevent death by starvation. This is because the Lawgiver gives priority to the preservation of life over religious duties and observances, and this is why the sick, the disabled, the traveller and the pregnant woman are all allowed to break the fast during the day in Ramadan. They are also allowed to shorten the obligatory prayers, or to perform them with easier postures than the regular method.

An elderly person who is unable to perform the *ḥajj* pilgrimage may ask someone to perform it on his or her behalf. These and other similar concessions that the *Sharīʿah* has granted are meant to protect the life and health of the individual from exposure to unbearable levels of exertion and hardship. It is generally recommended that these concessions should be taken advantage of. Hence it is not necessarily virtuous for a sick man to go on fasting on the grounds of piety or asceticism. The guideline here is clearly given in the *ḥadīth* where the Prophet is reported to have said:

إن الله يحب أن تؤتى رخصه كما يحب أن تؤتى عزائمه.

God loves to see that His concessions are utilised just as much as He loves to see His injunctions followed.[145]

The protection of life has been identified as one of the five essential values or goals (*maqāṣid*) of the *Sharīʿah*, and must be observed as a matter of priority. This implies that all measures that are taken to ensure its safety, whether by the individual, law enforcement agencies or legislative assemblies etc., are likely to be supported by the *Sharīʿah*. To recognise life as an essential interest, or an overriding objective, also means that promoting it through a comprehensive system of medical care, maternity benefits, child benefits etc., is in keeping with the objectives of Islam, and highly recommended. The same may be said of other measures that facilitate an honourable life for the individual, such as securing employment opportunities, grant of unemployment benefits, and pensions, and indeed any means that enable the elderly and the disabled an honourable life that is protected from disease and degradation. The *Sharīʿah* thus advocates both positive measures for the advancement of life as an essential goal and interest, as well as negative measures through the law of retaliation and the ultimate punishment by death of the one who violates the sanctity of life and deliberately takes the life of another human being.

Concluding Remarks

Criminal law in the vast majority of Muslim countries is governed by statutory legislation which can often be traced back either directly or indirectly to a western source, especially in the sphere of criminal procedure pertaining to investigation, prosecution and trial. This is partly due to the fact that the *Sharīʿah* itself does not regulate the substantive aspects of crimes and punishments as extensively as it does, say, matrimonial law and property. Substantive *Sharīʿah* law in this area is basically confined to prescribed penalties and retaliation, known as *ḥudūd* and *qiṣāṣ*. Muslim countries did not on the whole legislate on *ḥudūd* and *qiṣāṣ* until the later decades of 20th century. Pakistan took the unusual step when it introduced the Hudud Ordinance in 1978, and was followed only by some other countries such as the Islamic Republic of Iran, and the Sudan followed suit in the 1980s. In Malaysia, only the two northern states of Kelantan and Terengganu have attempted to introduce their versions of the *ḥudūd* and *qiṣāṣ*.

Having examined the laws of *qiṣāṣ* and *diyyah,* one is inclined to reflect on the potential of the *Sharīʿah* to be used as a means of enriching statutory legislation on homicide in present day Muslim countries. To give a role to the family of the deceased in the selection of *qiṣāṣ*, *diyyah* or grant of pardon, and the decision of whether or not to convert *qiṣāṣ* into monetary compensation, could, perhaps, be carefully regulated and advantageously utilised. Yet at the same time one would not want to see too much emphasis on the private right aspect of *qiṣāṣ*, since it could be abused by those who can afford to pay for their crime. Clearly, a certain *ijtihād*-based revision of the law in this area, that seeks to establish a balanced approach to the private and public, or the Right of Man and Right of God, aspects of these laws could prove advantageous. The *fiqh* rules pertaining to *qiṣāṣ* and *diyyah* tend to have down-played the public right components thereof, which may call for a corrective. A reform-oriented revision of the law would also help to correct and moderate the somewhat negative assessment of the *Sharīʿah* in this area that one often finds in the works of some commentators, both Orientalist and Muslim.

A substantial portion of the Qur'ānic verses and *ḥadīth* evidence on the sanctity of life that we reviewed in this chapter were revealed in Mecca at a time when the Muslims were a minority and were not in a position to provide law enforcement services for the community. Tribalist traditions were strong at the time, and although the Qur'ān expounded a new vision of justice that sought to subjugate tribal methods of retaliation and revenge to a set of objective principles, these principles were nevertheless designed to address those somewhat persistent realities, and in its attempt to reform the law concerning them, the Qur'ān has evidently not remained totally independent of them. This would explain the relatively high profile of the rules of *qiṣāṣ* and *diyyah* in the Qur'ān, and the degree of emphasis that the private rights (and also responsibilities) of the family, the agnatic relatives (*ʿāqila*), of the victim of homicide have acquired. The Qur'ānic laws tend to envisage security and protection of life as the collective responsibility of the family and community, which leaves open the possibility of their enforcement in a tribal setting, with or without a government. The Qur'ān does envisage a system of leadership which has not, however, been specified and could therefore take a variety of forms, including a tribal system of leadership that does not necessarily depend on a government as the only law enforcement authority—marked by a tendency, however, to move away from tribalism. This tendency finds support in the rules of equivalence in retaliation and the objectivity of the Qur'ānic standards of justice, the rule of law and the stress that the Qur'ān lays on personal responsibility away from tribalist laws and traditions. Thus it could equally be argued that the Qur'ān turned the page from tribal justice to justice under the rule of law, to be administered under a unified system of rule that might subjugate and even eliminate tribalism altogether.

The Qur'ānic verse which declares that the one who takes one innocent life is as if he had killed the whole of mankind, and the one who protects one life is like he who protects the life of the entire community (5:32)—can be taken to mean that homicide at that point is no longer seen as a violation, primarily, of the private right of the family and relatives of the victim, but of the right of God and the public right. To say that the safety of the whole community is endangered by the killing of one of its members is another way of saying that the right to life is a public right in which the community has a great deal at stake, even more than that of the victim's family. When this is read with the near-total emphasis that the Qur'ān places on objectivity of justice, it may be said that the Qur'ān has effectively subjugated the private right (*ḥaqq al-ādamī*) aspect of homicide to the Right of God (*ḥaqq Allāh*) or public right aspect thereof. Furthermore, when one reads in the Qur'ān the declaration that 'in *qiṣāṣ* there is protection of life for you...,' one could say that *qiṣāṣ* itself is viewed as a means of protecting the right of the community to safety and security in the first place. The family's right in the *qiṣāṣ* and *diyyah* have admittedly been recognized, but it is submitted that the public right aspect thereof is stronger and more dominant. To understand the Qur'ānic law of homicide as an expression of the concerns of private rights, and a prerogative therefore of the family and relatives of the victim, which is the prevailing perception in the relevant juristic literature on the subject, is tantamount, in the present writer's view, to neglecting an important aspect of the original Qur'ānic vision on the law of homicide.

One might add to this analysis that outside *qiṣāṣ* and *diyyah,* the evidence we have reviewed on such other themes as abortion, suicide, duelling, permission to kill, euthanasia and so forth present us with a different picture in that the rules of Islamic law on these subjects tend to move away from the private-public bifurcation of rights. The objective standards of justice and rights tend to take a higher profile in the exposition of the *Sharīʿah* rules concerning them. The emphasis on the public right or the private right aspect of the issue, as the case may be, tends to be placed on the merit of the case without necessarily finding a predicated anchor and focus in the private rights of the victim's family.

With reference to abortion, there seems to be a great deal of diversity in the views of the *Sharīʿah* scholars and schools, which suggests a need for uniformity and consolidation, if they are to be reflected in the applied law that governs the subject. Statutory legislation would thus be needed to consolidate the legal position and regulate the uses and abuses of abortion, while taking into consideration the basic concerns of the *Sharīʿah* in the formulation of applicable rules. Whereas a more restrictive attitude on abortion may be seen generally advisable, the law should not be too restrictive and should pay due attention to human factors such as the social stigma and personal sensitivities of the victims of abortion. All valid cases of abortion should be considered for proper medical care, and the law should aim for greater visibility and for more effective management and control of abortion by health service professionals.

Issues pertaining to war and peace can only be regulated and addressed by legislation and the rulings of national governments. The wider aspects of the conduct of war are determined on the grounds of military strategy and also in the light of reciprocal treatment, which fall beyond the jurisdiction and control of national governments. Yet to observe a set of basic and normative guidelines is important, and the Islamic norms in this area merit consideration. Muslim countries, indeed all countries, must comply with the set of guidelines they have ratified through bilateral and multilateral agreements and those that have been introduced and ratified by the United Nations. From the Islamic viewpoint, the vicegerency of man on the earth confers upon him the duty of trusteeship of this planet. This would effectively proscribe weapons of mass destruction as a violation of the terms of that trust, and their possession and proliferation cannot be supported from that perspective.

The *Sharīʿah* provisions on certain aspects of what we discuss in this chapter, on abortion, suicide, and euthanasia, do not on the whole impose rigid and binding laws. They are often in the nature of general guidelines that provide a perspective and framework that may merit attention. The more technical and specialized issues that they raise can best be determined on grounds of scientific evidence.

With reference to the scope of *taʿzīr* punishment, even if one accepts the *fiqhī* position that it can be extended as far as to include the death penalty, this does not mean that *taʿzīr* should necessarily be left undefined and subject to court discretion. Matters of concern to *taʿzīr* can be regulated and defined through statutory legislation that would take into consideration the requirements of the constitutional principle of legality in punishments. Most of the applied constitutions in Muslim countries uphold the principle of legality and provide that no one can be punished for an act or conduct unless the law clearly says so. Then it would follow that the death penalty under *taʿzīr* is automatically subsumed and statutory law needs to define both the conduct and the punishment it carries. This is not to say that *taʿzīr* is altogether redundant, for it can still play a useful role that merits consideration. All we are saying here is that the *Sharīʿah* principle of *taʿzīr* may be kept intact in certain areas, but may be defined and regulated in others. The substance of what is said here also applies, *mutatis mutandis*, to such other non-binding aspects of criminal law as the *ʿāqila* and *qasāma*. They provide ideas that should be kept and utilized, preferably on a selective basis when carefully defined and specified.

NOTES

1.   Muslim, Mukhtaṣar Ṣaḥīḥ Muslim, 289, ḥadīth 1089.

2.   Ibn Māja, *Sunan Ibn Māja*, II, 874, *ḥadīth* 2619; al-Muṣaylihi, *Ḥuqūq*, p. 323; Sayyid Sābiq, *Fiqh as-Sunna*, II, 429.

3.   Abū Dāwūd, *Mukhtaṣar Sunan Abi Dāwud*, ed., al–Bughā, p. 606, *ḥadīth* 4270.

4.   *Id.*, *ḥadīth* 4271.

5.   *Id.*, 606, *ḥadīth* 4271.

6.   Kāsāni, *Badā'i'*, VII, 237; Shaltūt, *al-Islām*, 339; Wāfi, *Ḥimāyat al-Islām*, 8.

7.   Cf. Shaltūt, *al-Islām*, 334.

8.   *Id.*, 33.

9.   Cf. Shaltūt, *al-Islām 'Aqīda wa Sharī'a*, 341 and 361; Muṣaylihī, *Ḥuqūq al-Insān*, 331.

10. Shaltūt, *al-Islām*, 427.

11. *Id.*, 342.

12. 'Awdah, *al-Tashri' al-Jinā'i*, I, 474–75.

13. Tabrizi, *Mishkāt*, Vol. II, *ḥadīth* 3529.

14. Muslim, *Mukhtaṣar-Ṣaḥīḥ Muslim*, Kitab al-Jihād, bab, man qutila dūna mālihi wa huwa shahīd, *ḥadīth* 1086.

15. *Id.*, Kitab al-Imāra, bab man ḥamala 'alayna as-silāḥa, *ḥadīth* 1235.

16. Shaltūt, *al-Islam*, 343; 'Awdah, *al-Tashri' al-Jinā'i*, I, 480.

17. Muṣaylihi, *Ḥuqūq al-Insān*, 295.

18. Shaltūt, *al-Islam*, 343.

19. Tabrizi, *Mishkāt*, Vol. II, *ḥadīth* 3512; 'Awdah, *al-Tashri' al-Jinā'i*, I, 473.

20. 'Awdah, *al-Tashri' al-Jinā'i*, I, 473.

21. *Id.*, I, 475.

22. Nawawi, *Riyāḍ al-Ṣāliḥīn*, *ḥadīth* 237.

23. *Id.*, *ḥadīth* 1527.

24. *Id.*, *ḥadīth* 1524; Bukhārī, *Ṣaḥīḥ al-Bukhārī* (Muhsin Khan's trans.), Vol. VIII, p. 43, *ḥadīth* 69.

25. Bukhārī, *Ṣaḥīḥ al-Bukhārī* (Muhsin Khan's trans.), VIII, 7, *ḥadīth* 8.

26. Cf. Kāsāni, *Badā'i' al-Ṣanā'i'*, VII, 237; Wāfi, *Ḥimāyat al-Islām*, 8. The intensified *diyyah*, like the normal *diyyah* for life, is one hundred camels, which consists, however, of different types and age groups of camels, cf. Bassiouni, *Criminal Justice*, 203.

27. Cf. 'Awda, *al-Tashri' al-Jina'i*, II.122.

28. Qaraḍāwī, *al-Shaykh al-Ghazālī Kamā 'Araftuhu Riḥlata Nīṣf Qarn*, 167.

29. Kāsāni, *Badā'i' al-Ṣanā'i'*, V, 238; Shaltūt, *al-Islam*, 373; Wāfi, *Ḥimāyat al-Islam*, 10.

30. Cf. Anwarullah, *The Criminal Law of Islam*, 73.

31. Cf. Ibn Taymiyya, *al-Siyāsa al-Sharʿiyya*, 143; Zuḥaylī, *al-Fiqh al-Islāmī*, VI, 218; Muṣaylihi, *Ḥuqūq al-Insān*, 327; Wāfi, *Ḥimāyat al-Islām*, 26.

32. Maḥmud Shaltūt, *al-Islam, ʿAqīda wa Sharīʿa*, 373–75.

33. Shaltūt, *al-Islam*, 396–370; Muṣaylihi, *Ḥuqūq al-Insan*, 327.

34. Abū Dāwūd, *Sunan Abī Dāwūd*, ed., al-Bughā', *Kitab al-diyyat, bab al-nafs bi'l-nafs, ḥadīth* 4494. See also Ibn Taymiyya, *al-Siyāsa*, 142.

35. Abū Dāwūd, *Muktaṣar Sunan Abi Dāwūd*, ed., by Muṣṭafā al-Bughā, 643, *ḥadīth* 4497.

36. Muslim, *Mukhtasar Sahaih Muslim*, 475, *ḥadīth* 1790.

37. Bukhārī, *Ṣaḥīḥ al-Bukhārī, kitāb al-diyyat, bab. man qutila lahu qatilun.*

38. Zuḥayli, *al-Fiqh al-Islāmī*, V, 288.

39. Qurṭubi, *Tafsīr al-Qurṭubi*, I, 255.

40. Tabrizi, *Mishkāt*, Vol. II, *ḥadīth* 3477.

41. Ibn Taymiyya, *Siyāsa*, p. 141.

42. Cf. Bassiouni, *Islamic Criminal Justice*, 209.

43. Ibn Qudāma, *Mughni*, VII, 745; ʿAwdah, *al-Tashriʿ al-Jinā'i*, I. 245(S. 198); al-Shāwi, *al-Mawsuʿa*, I, 308.

44. See for details Zuhāily, *al-Fiqh al-Islāmī*, VI, 260f, al-Hewesh 'Murder and Homicide,' in ed. Tahir Mahmood, *Criminal Law in Islam*, 158.

45. Abū Dāwūd, Sunan, ed. al-Bughā, (*ḥadīth* reported by ʿAbd Allāh b. ʿUmar), 652, *ḥadīth* 4542.

46. Qaraḍāwī, *al-Shaykh al-Ghazālī Kama ʿAraftuhu*, 166.

47. *Id.*

48. A long *ḥadīth* text and the episode of a dead body that was found in Khaybar appears in Kāsāni, *Badāʾiʿ*, VII, 286 see also Wāfi, *Ḥimāyat al-Islām*, 264.

49. Bassiouni, *Criminal Justice*, 205–207.

50. Kāsāni, *Badāʾiʿ*, VII, 256; al-Khaṭīb, *Mughni al-Muḥtāj*, IV, 95; Shaltūt, *al-Islam*, 315; ʿAwdah, *al-Tashriʿ al-Jinā'i*, I, 673ff.

51. Shaltūt, *al-Islam*, 316. Shaltūt refers to Ibn ʿĀbidin's view in his *Ḥāshiya*, Vol. V, in *Kitab al-maʿāqil.*

52. Should the deceased's body be found in between two or more villages, *qasāma* is applicable to the one that is physically closest to where the body is found. See for detail Abū Dāwūd, *Mukhtaṣar Sunan Abi Dāwūd* ed., al-Bughā, *Kitāb al-Diyyāt, bab al-Qatl bi'l-qasāma*, 647–49.

53. Kāsāni, *Badāʾiʿ al-Sanāʾiʿ*, VII, 286; Wāfi, *ḥuqūq al-Insan*, 263.

54. ʿAwdah, *al-Tashriʿ al-Jinā'i*, I,777.

55. Cf. Layish 'Saudi Arabian Legal Reform,' 282; see also Mahdi, *al-ʿUqubāt al-Sharʿiyya*, 92.

56. Layish 'Saudi Arabian Legal Reform,' 282.

57. *Id.*

58. Both these cases appeared in (2001) 1 L.M. (*Law Majalla*), International Islamic University Malaysia, 215.

59. *Id.*, 215.

60. Cf. Ahmad Ibrahim, *Administration of Islamic Law*, 637; Tanzilur Rahman, *Islamization of Pakistan Law*, 16.

61. See For details Tahir Mahmood, 'Criminal Procedure at the Sharīʿah Law,' in Tahir Mahmood, ed. *Criminal Law in Islam*, p. 320f.

62. ʿAwdah, *al-Tashri al-Jinā'ī*, I, 680–681.

63. *Id.*, 682–83.

64. *Id.*, 684.

65. Cf. Kamali, *Freedom of Expression in Islam*, chapter on blasphemy, 213–272; for a detailed exposition of death punishment in *Sharīʿah* see al-Kilānī, *ʿUqubat al-Iʿdām fi'l Sharīʿa al-Islāmiyya*.

66. Shaltut, *al-Islām*, 328.

67. ʿAwdah, *al-Tashriʿ al-Jinā'i*, I, 446; Zuhaylī, *Huqūq al-Insān*, 144; Jābiri, *Dimiqrātiyya*, 210.

68. *Id.*, I, 447.

69. Al-ʿIbādi, *Min al-Adab Wa'l-Akhlāq*, 164–65.

70. Tabrizi, *Mishkāt al-Maṣābīḥ*, Vol. II, ḥadīth no. 3453.

71. Bukhārī, *Ṣaḥīḥ al-Bukhārī, Kitāb al-adab b. ma yunha ʿanhu min al-sibāb*.

72. Cf. Shaykh Amīn, *Adab al-Ḥadīth al-Nabawī'*, 216; Wahbah al-Zuhaylī, *al-Fiqh al-Islāmī*, Vol. VI, 219.

73. Bukhārī, *Sahih al-Bukhārī* (Muhsin Khan's trans.), VIII, 330, ḥadīth 500. A slightly more detailed version of the same ḥadīth through another narrator is recorded at *idem*, 393, ḥadīth 603.

74. Cf. Badar D. Ahmad, 'Suicide and Euthanasia,' in Tahir Mahmood (ed.), *Criminal Law in Islam*, 173–74.

75. www.mpppillai.com/bwatch.php.3?op=see&lid=2024.

76. www.utusan.com.my/utusan/content.asp?y=2003&dt=1111&pub=utusan_Express.

77. Tanṭāwi's view published in *al-Ḥayāt*, 27 May 1998 as quoted in *al-Shāwi, al-Mawsuʿa al-ʿAsrriyya*, vol III, 93.

78. Quoted in Sohail Hashmi, *Washington Post*, Sunday, June 9, 2002, 38–01.

79. al-Zuhaylī, *Huqūq al-Insān*, 145; al-Shāwī, *al-Mawsuʿa al-ʿAṣrriya*, Vol. III, 79.

80. Cf. Wahba al-Zuhaylī, *al-Fiqh al-Islāmī*, VI, 292.

81. Cf. al-Shāwi, *al-Muwsuʿa al-ʿAṣriyya*, vol. III, 90.

82. Tabrizi, *Mishkāt*, Vol. II, ḥadīth 3538; Zuhaily, *huqūq al-Insān*, 145.

83. *Collins Dictionary.*

84. Government of Pakistan, Council of Islamic Ideology as quoted by Niazi, *Islamic Law of Torts*, 326.

85. *Id.*

86.   Cf. Foridul Islam 'Abortion and Euthanasia,' in *Essays on Islam*, 197; Meyers, *The Human Body and the Law*, 2.

87.   Cf. Foridul Islam, id,. P. 197; Beauchamp and Childress, *Biomedical Ethics*, p. 230.

88.   Al-Ṣābūnī, *Ṣafwat al-Tafāsir*, III, 304; see also Yusuf Ali; *The Holy Qur'ān*, Trans. and Commentary at note 2874.

89.   Qaraḍāwī, *al-Ḥalāl wa'l Ḥarām fi'l-Islām*, 169.

90.   Muslim, *Mukhtaṣar Ṣaḥīḥ Muslim*, ed., al-Albārī, 489, *ḥadīth* 1849. Kitāb al-Qadr, *Bāb akhlāq yukhlaq*.

91.   *Id., Kitāb al-Qadar, bāb fi'l-khalq yukhlaq.*

92.   Ibn Ḥazm, *Muḥallā*, II, 31.

93.   Al-Ghazālī, *Iḥyā' ʿUlūm al-Dīn*, Vol. II, 4.

94.   Cf. Foridul Islam '*Abortion and Euthanasia.*' 198.

95.   Islamic Fiqh Academy (India), *Important Fiqh Decisions*, New Delhi, 2001, 89.

96.   Brody, et el 'The Life Before Birth', in Carol Levine, ed. *Taking Sides*, 25.

97.   Cf. Zuhaylī, *al-Fiqh al-Islāmī*, III, 558.

98.   Ghazālī, *Iḥyā' ʿUlūm al-Dīn*, II, 53.

99.   Cf. Madkur, *al-Janīn*, 303.

100.   Cf. Al-Dusuqī, *Ḥāshiya al-Dusuqī*, II, 266; Muṣṭafā Zuhaylī, *Ḥuqūq al-Insān*, 146; Wahbah al-Zuhaylī, *al-Fiqh al-Islāmī*, III, 557.

101.   Ibn ʿAbidin, *Ḥāshiya Ibn ʿAbidin*, 3:176; Zuhaylī, *al-Fiqh al-Islāmī*, III, 557.

102.   Shaltūt, Fatāwa, 424; Madkūr, *al-Janīn*, 302.

103.   For details on the subject of legal capacity (*ahliyya*) see Kamali, *Jurisprudence*, pp. 450f. On the subject of criminal abortion (*jināya ʿala'l-ianīn*) see ʿAwdah, *al-Tashri ʿ al-Jinā'i*, II, 292 f.

104.   Ibn Qudama, *Mughni*, IX, 579; ʿAwdah, *al-Tashri ʿ*, II, 293.

105.   ʿAwdah, *al-Tashriʿ al-Jinā'i*, II, 294.

106.   Ibn ʿAbidin, *Ḥāshiya*, V, 518; ʿAwdah *al-Tashri ʿ al-Jinā'i*, II, 295.

107.   ʿAwdah, *al-Tashri ʿ al-Jinā'i*, II, 297.

108.   *Id.*, II, 300–301.

109.   Abū Dāwūd, *Sunan Abi Dāwūd*, ed., al-Bughā, 655, *ḥadīth* 4576. Ibn Qudama, *al-Mughi*, VII, 802; Ibn Rajab al-Ḥanbalī, *al-Qawāʿid*, 177 (qaʿida, no. 84).

110.   *Id.*, 655, *ḥadīth* 4570.

111. ʿAwdah, *al-Tashriʿ*, II, 299–300; Niazi, *Islamic Law of Tort*, 325.

112. *Id.*, II, 302.

113. Ibn ʿĀbidin, *Ḥāshiya*, V, 518; ʿAwdah, *al-Tashriʿ al-Jinā'i*, II, 302.

114. Cf. Qaraḍāwī, *al-Ijtihād al-Muʿāsir,.* 45. A substantially similar view has been held by Musṭafā al-Zarqā in *Fatāwā Musṭafā al-Zarqā*, 285–286. Zarqā held, however, that abortion prior to 40 days of pregnancy was reprehensible (*makruh*) and the *makruh* intensifies after that and reaches the degree of prohibition by the time the foetus develops. It becomes *ḥarām* after 120 days. An exception to all of this is averting danger to the life of the mother.

115. Madkur, *al-Janin*, 305; Zuḥaylī, *al-Fiqh al-Islāmī*. III, 557; Ibn Mubārak, *Naẓariyyat al-ḍarūra*, 427.

116. *The Collins Dictionary*; Qaraḍāwī, *Fatawa Muʿāsirah*, Vol II, 525.

117. Cf. Masoodi and Dhar, 'Euthanasia at Western and Islamic Legal Systems', 6–7.

118. Cf. Jalaluddin Umri, 'Suicide and Euthanasia: Islamic Viewpoint' in ed. Tahir Mahmood, *Criminal Law in Islam*, 165.

119. *Re Quinlan*, 355A 2d.647 (N.J.), Cert., 429 U.S. 922 (1976).

120. Cf. Masoodi and Dhar, 'Euthanasia', 11–13.

121. *Id.* 20.

122. Al-Nisā':4:29, and al-Baqarah, 2:195.

123. Qaraḍāwī, *Fatāwā Muʿāsira*, vol.II, 528.

124. *Id.*, II, 529.

125. *Id.*, II, 527.

126. Abia Siddiqui, '*Abortion and Euthanasia*', 178.

127. Ibn Qudāma, al-*Mughnī*, VI, 274; Musaylihī, *Ḥuqūq al-Insān*, 116.

128. Kāsani', *Badā'iʿ,,* ʿVIII, 3859; Ibn ʿĀbidin, *Ḥāshiya*, III, 323; Musaylihī, *Ḥuqūq*, 115.

129. Ibn Ḥazm, *Muhallā*, VIII, 273; Musaylihi, *Ḥuqūq al-Insān*, 116.

130. Kāsāni, *Badā'iʿ* VIII, 3861.

131. Kāsāni, *Badā'iʿ*, VIII, 3862.

132. Cf. Ibn Qudāma, *Mughni*, VI, 274.

133. Cf. Wāfi, *Ḥimāyat al-Islām*, 19. A similar factor is mentioned in another verse which provides 'Do not fight (the disbelievers) in the vicinity of the holy mosque (of the Kaʿba) until they wage war on you.' (2:191)

134. Cf. Wāfi, *Ḥimāyat al-Islām*, 26.

135. Cf. Wāfi, *Ḥimāyat al-Islām*, 26–29.

136. *Id.*, 30–32.

137. Abū Dāwūd, *Sunan Abi Dāwūd, Kitāb al-Jihād, bab fi'l-Nahy ʿan al-Muthla*, *ḥadīth* 2667.

138. *Id.*, *ḥadīth* 2666.

139. *Id.*, *ḥadīth* 2668.

140. *Id., ḥadīth* 2669.

141. Muṣaylihi, *ḥuqūq al-Insān*, p. 112 quoting the Musnad of Aḥmad b. Ḥanbal.

142. Hamidullah, *Muslim Conduct of State*, 215.

143. *Id.*

144. Abū Yūsuf, *al-Kharāj*, 121.

145. Ibn. Qayyim, *I'lām*, II, 242.

CHAPTER TWO

The Right to Personal Security
(*Ḥaqq al-amn*)

I. Introductory Remarks

Much of the discussion in the following pages is concerned with criminal investigation, pre-trial and trial procedures in Islamic law. Since it is in this area of law enforcement that the individual is exposed to the exercise of coercive power, the personal security of the individual on the street, and persons under investigation on criminal charges, are matters of concern to this chapter. Civil litigation does not feature prominently in this presentation because civil disputes normally do not involve police investigation and arrest. Even so, most of the general rules of evidence and trial, and also pre-trial procedures pertaining to the presentation and verification of claims, as well as the compliance by the judge, lawyer and litigant with the principle of legality, are applicable to both civil litigations and crimes.

Criminal procedure is generally predicated on the twin but contrasting objectives of conforming to due process and the control of crime. Due process focuses on providing the accused with various protections to minimise the possibility of unjust or arbitrary criminal convictions. It also seeks to facilitate the efficient administration of justice, which promotes objectivity and coherence in trial proceedings. Crime control, by contrast, emphasises a broader social interest in crime detection and prevention, and limits procedural protections for the accused so as to ensure an efficient prosecution and the conviction of the guilty.[1]

Islamic criminal procedure also faces this dilemma, and seeks to strike a fair balance between the interests of the accused and those of society. Specific procedural safeguards are occasionally prescribed by the Qur'ān or the *Sunnah*, but have generally been left to the discretion of the ruler or government. Under the doctrine of *siyāsah sharʿiyyah*, or *Sharīʿah*-oriented policy, the ruler is authorised to take measures and devise procedures that are in harmony with the goals and objectives of the *Sharīʿah*, and secure the public interest as best as possible. Simple and direct detection and trial procedures that were deemed adequate for earlier times may not be sufficient for more complex societies, where progress in various fields has also opened new avenues for more sophisticated levels of criminality and abuse. The integrity of a procedural system under these circumstances is tested by its openness to refinement and growth. Since procedural matters in the Islamic system of justice are open to considerations of public policy and justice under *siyāsah sharʿiyyah*, the process remains in principle open to further development and reform.

This chapter is presented in nine sections, beginning with a preliminary discussion on the definition and scope of *ḥaqq al-amn*, which is followed, in section three, by a review of the affirmative evidence in the Qur'ān and *Sunnah* and the precedent of the Pious Caliphs on this subject. Section four is devoted to an examination of the principle of legality and the extent of its application in *Sharīʿah*. Section five addresses the twin concepts of accusation (*al-tuhmah*) and suspicion (*al-ẓann*), which lead the discussion, in the next section, on arrest and detention, and the debate that has arisen among Muslim jurists about the basic permissibility of preventive detention. Section seven inquires into the permissibility or otherwise of beating the accused, in certain types of accusations, during interrogation. This is followed in the next section by a discussion of the right to counsel. The last section addresses the salient principles of *Sharīʿah* pertaining to evidence and trial. A short appendix at the end presents the text of the Resolution of the First International Conference on the Protection of Human Rights in the Islamic Criminal Justice System, held in Siracusa, Italy, at the International Institute of Higher Studies in Criminal Sciences, 28–31 May, 1979.

The depth and calibre of information available in the *fiqh* texts on these subjects, and its relevance to contemporary concerns about due process and law enforcement procedures, is somewhat uneven, as may be expected of works of medieval origin. Subjects such as the testimony of witnesses, and rules that apply to judicial decorum and the conduct of trial (*adab al-qāḍī*) are elaborately discussed in the *fiqh* texts, but the coverage in these sources of some of the issues of concern to police procedures and the treatment of the accused, the principle of legality, and right to counsel etc., are generally under-developed. The information on these themes is on the whole scattered and also in need of consolidation and development if one were to read it in the context of a modern trial. Criminal procedure in many present day Muslim countries is, in any case, governed by statutory legislation of a mixed origin.

Criminal procedure in Islamic law has lagged behind, partly due to the prevalence of modern criminal law and procedure that currently apply in the courts of general jurisdiction in Muslim countries. Most of these countries have modelled their legal systems and judiciary on Western prototypes, and the procedures they apply do not claim their origin in Islamic sources. Whether one speaks of Egypt or Pakistan, Malaysia or Indonesia, or indeed any jurisdiction in the Middle East, their court systems have undergone changes often under the influence of the Continental or Common Law doctrines, and only partially rely on Islamic principles. Except for Saudi Arabia, where *Sharīʿah* courts remain courts of general jurisdiction, in other Muslim countries, *Sharīʿah* courts may or may not exist, and in places where they do, they usually operate side by side with the national courts, and their jurisdiction is often limited to religious and personal law matters. For more than a century, criminal procedure in many Muslim countries has been heavily influenced by Western legal doctrines. Islamic criminal procedure has consequently remained underdeveloped and, in some areas, remains out of touch with modern realities. Scientific methods of crime detection and the discovery of facts represent a case in point as they are not addressed in the *fiqh* books. Yet a perusal of the substantive doctrines of the *Sharīʿah* would show that the basic concern for justice, human dignity and fair treatment of the accused feature prominently therein. Thus it would appear that modern doctrines and procedures that share the same values might be of a different origin, but would not necessarily disagree with the basic goals and objectives of the *Sharīʿah* on human dignity and justice.

The larger part of this chapter consists of a presentation of the *Sharīʿah* evidence as I have found in the sources I consulted. On certain issues where the evidence remains less than conclusive, and on matters about which the *ʿulamāʾ* are themselves in disagreement, I have advanced a certain perspective that is reflective of my own understanding of the source evidence.

II. Definition and Scope

The individual's right to personal security may be defined as his right to live a peaceful life without fear of aggression, unlawful arrest, detention and punishment. The assurance, in other words, that his personal safety is inviolable and shall not be compromised or subjected to coercion and abuse except under the law.[2] Some writers have, however, expanded the scope of this right to include not only the personal safety of the individual but also his property and honour. Thus according to an alternative definition, the right to safety (*ḥaqq al-amn*) means the safety of the person, his property and honour, against aggression, humiliation and torture by other individuals or the state.[3] Another observer has simply described *ḥaqq al-amn* as the inner assurance of the individual, and the absence of fear on his part about his personal security.[4]

Notwithstanding the likelihood that aggression against the personal property and the honour of the individual implies aggression against his person, since personal property and honour are subjects for which the law takes separate measures, it is preferable perhaps to confine the scope of *ḥaqq al-amn* to aggression against the person of the individual in the sense of physical aggression, unlawful detention and the violation of his right to due process. The right to due process relates, in turn, to the principle of the rule of law, also known as the principle of legality, which refers to the legal regime that regulates investigation and trial procedures, and protects the individual from the abuse of coercive power.

III. Affirmative Evidence

The rules of *Sharīʿah* pertaining to the right to personal security proceed from the Qurʾānic affirmation of the dignity of man, and its recognition of *homo sapiens* as the prize creation of God, who must therefore be treated with dignity and justice. The Qurʾān is replete with warnings against tyranny and persecution, which occur in no less than 299 places in the text, just as it is emphatic on the value of justice and the fair treatment of everyone without discrimination.[5] Rights and liberties in Islam are thus seen as a manifestation of the dignity of man, which is, in turn, an expression of the divine grace that God Most High has bestowed on humankind. The Qurʾān thus proclaims:

ولقـد كرمنـا بنـى آدم وحملنهـم فى البر والبحـر ورزقنهـم مـن الطيبات وفضلنهم على كثير ممن خلقنا تفضيلا.

And surely We have honoured the progeny of Adam; We carried them over the land and the sea; provided them with good things, and given them excellence over most of those whom We have created (17:70).

The reference to the dignity of man in this verse is substantiated by the rank he is given over most of God's creatures, as well as by the affirmation of his freedom of movement to traverse the land and the sea in order to utilise the resources of the earth. Other manifestations of human dignity in the Qur'ān are found in reference to the physical and spiritual attributes of man, and the divine affirmations below:

لقد خلقنا الإنسان فى أحسن تقويم.

We created man in the best of forms (95:17).

ونفخت فيه من روحى.

I breathed into him of My spirit (38:71).

More specifically, the Qur'ān entitles the individual to safety against aggression when it declares, in the broadest of terms:

فلا عدوان إلا على الظالمين

There shall be no hostility (*'udwān*) except against aggressors (*ẓālimīn*) (2:193).

The text clearly proscribes hostility (*'udwān*) of all kinds against those who have not committed acts of aggression, and permits acts of hostility only against oppressors (*ẓālimīn*). Oppression is thus recognised as the only ground that validates recourse to hostile action against an individual. The text, in other words, validates the use of force for defensive purposes both in individual circumstances and in matters pertaining to

war and peace. This is endorsed elsewhere in another verse where it is
provided that:

$$\text{والذين يؤذون المؤمنين والمؤمنـت بغير مااكتسبوا فقـد احتملوا بهتانا وإثما مبينا.}$$

Those who hurt the believing men and believing women undeservedly,
they bear the guilt of slander and manifest transgression (33:58).

The Qur'ān further specifies that a hostile response to aggression must
not exceed the limits of reciprocity and justice:

$$\text{فمـن اعتدى عليكـم فاعتدوا بمثـل مااعتدى عليكـم واتقوا الله واعلموا أن الله مع المتقين.}$$

To whoever is aggressive towards you, then your response must be
proportionate with the aggression inflicted upon you (in the first place),
and fear God, for God is with those who are conscious of His presence
(2:194).

$$\text{فمن عفا وأصلح فأجره على الله إنه لايحب الظالمين.}$$

Whoever forgives and makes peace, God will reward him for it. Verily
God does not love the transgressors (42:4).

A violation of the limits set by God, or a deliberate disregard for the
rule of law, are equated with *ẓulm*, as the Qur'ān declares:

$$\text{ومن يتعد حدود الله فأولئك هم الظالمون.}$$

Those who transgress the limits that God has laid down are indeed the
transgressors (2:229).

The Qur'ān thus envisages an orderly life in the community, which is
observant of the rule of law and just and peaceful behaviour. Unlike
the image that is often portrayed of the *Sharīʿah* as one of eagerness
to punish, there is considerable support in the Qur'ān for leniency,
forgiveness, and compassion, so much so that it makes this outlook
an integral part of the *Sharīʿah* and of government under the rule of
law. There is no question about the resolute attitude that the *Sharīʿah*

takes towards lawlessness and transgression. Yet this attitude is often tempered by its pull towards compassion and understanding of the offender, and the causes that lead him to deviant behaviour. The Qur'ān thus declares:

فمن تاب بعد ظلمه وأصلح فإن الله يتوب عليه إن الله غفور رحيم

Whoever repents after his wrongdoing (*ẓulm*), and reforms himself, God will turn to him (with mercy); surely God is Forgiving, Merciful (5:39).

The law in the meantime entitles the victim of *ẓulm* to defend himself, as the Qur'ān proclaims:

ولمن انتصر بعد ظلمه فأولئك ماعليهم من سبيل.

And whoever defends himself after having been oppressed, he is not to be blamed (42:41).

The victim of aggression is, in turn, advised in the following terms:

وإن عاقبتم فعاقبوا بمثل ماعوقبتم به ولئن صبرتم لهو خير للصابرين

And if you decide to punish, then punish with the like of that with which you were afflicted. But if you show patience! It is certainly best for those who remain patient (16:126).

The Qur'ānic rule of reciprocity and equivalence in the use of force should, in other words, be tempered by one's dedication to right cause, patience and self-restraint. The text thus recommends patience in the sense of not insisting on reprisal, but also that one should not be rash in the enforcement of penalties and allow time and opportunity for forgiveness, reconciliation and reform.

The *Sunnah* of the Prophet is also emphatic on the inviolability of the personal right to safety, as declared in this *ḥadīth*:

كل المسلم على المسلم حرام، دمه، وماله وعرضه.

All that belongs to a Muslim is forbidden to his fellow Muslim—his blood, his honour and his property.[6]

The *ḥadīth* here begins with a general reference to all the basic rights of a Muslim and declares them all to be sacrosanct; it then specifies three of these, namely life, property and honour, as being the most important. The general reference of this *ḥadīth* to 'all that belongs to a Muslim,' when read together with the universal Qur'ānic affirmation of the dignity of man, serves to show that the *Sharīʿah* takes an affirmative stand on all of the basic rights of man, specified or unspecified. Any right or liberty that is deemed complementary to human dignity is therefore protected. The substance of the above *ḥadīth* is endorsed in another *ḥadīth* as follows:

المسلم أخو المسلم لايظلمه ولايسلمه من كان فى حاجة أخيه

فإن الله فى حاجته

Muslims are brethren; no-one may commit acts of aggression against his brother, or humiliate and degrade him. The one who helps his brother in need, God will help him in his own moment of need.[7]

According to yet another *ḥadīth*:

ظهر المؤمن حمىً إلا فى حد أو حقّ.

The back (or flesh) of a believer is safe (against aggression), unless it is for a right, or a transgression of God's limit.[8]

Granting the individual safety from physical aggression, annoyance, intimidation and espionage is the explicit theme of a large number of *ḥadīth*, a perusal of which conveys the basic message that no-one may be deprived of dignity, humiliated or punished without cause. The attitude conveyed here is not merely a matter of conformity to the rules, but is about the integrity of the believer's commitment to the faith. To quote but a few of these *ḥadīth*s:

لاتؤذوا المسلمين ولاتعيّروهـم ولاتتبعوا عوراتهـم، فإنه مـن تتبـع

عورة أخيه المسلم، تتبع الله عورته.

Do not annoy (*lā tu'dhū*) the Muslims, or defame them, and do not expose their nakedness. For the one who exposes the nakedness of his Muslim brother, God will expose his own nakedness.[9]

According to another *ḥadīth*:

لا يحلّ لمسلم أن يروع مسلما.

It is not permissible for a Muslim to intimidate another Muslim.[10]

The same message has been conveyed more emphatically in another *ḥadīth* as follows:

لا تروعوا المسلم فإن روعة المسلم ظلم عظيم.

Do not intimidate a Muslim, for intimidating a Muslim is one of the gravest of all transgressions (*ẓulmun ʿaẓīm*).[11]

According to yet another *ḥadīth*:

إن الله يعذب يوم القيامة الذين يعذبون الناس فى الدنيا.

God will punish in the hereafter those who afflict others with torture in this life.[12]

The provisions of the Qur'ān and *ḥadīth* on the right to safety apply equally to all individuals, regardless of their religious, economic or social status. The Prophet has declared to this effect:

الناس سواسية كاسنان المشط، لا فضل لعربي على عجمي،
إنما الفضل بالتقوى.

Men are equal like the teeth of a comb. No Arab individual is superior to non-Arab except on grounds of righteous conduct.[13]

The law must therefore be applied equally to all individuals alike. To emphasise this point, the Prophet stated in a *ḥadīth* that even if his own daughter Fatima committed theft, she would be treated as any other offender and subjected to the prescribed punishment.[14]

والّذى نفسى بيده لو أن فاطمة فعلت ذلك لقطعت يدها .

In many of the *aḥādīth* quoted, the Prophet refers to Muslims rather than human beings in general. This may be a circumstantial feature of a basically wider address, simply because justice in the Qur'ān or in the other sources of the *Sharīʿah* is not confined to Muslims. Therefore, references in *ḥadīth* to Muslims on matters of concern to justice may thus be seen, in technical terms, a particular (*khāṣṣ*) matter that carries the purpose of the general (*ʿāmm*). This may be a function of the fact that the Prophet brought a new religion in a largely hostile environment, and his mentioning Muslims was to promote the new community and an awareness of its self-identity and image.

Another *ḥadīth* instructs the believer to 'help your brother, be he the oppressor or oppressed...' in order to manifest human fraternity. The Companions asked the Prophet the obvious question as to why and how they should help the oppressor, to which the Prophet responded: 'you should help him to stop it.'[15]

أنصر أخاك ظالمـا أو مظلومـا، فقـال رجـل: يارسـول الله أنصـره مظلوما فكيف أنصره ظالما؟ قال: تمنعه من الظلم فذاك نصرك إياه .

The address here is general and unqualified, applying to everyone, within or outside the courtroom; the accused person, the judge and prosecutor all alike. Accused persons and prisoners are therefore entitled to help not only to enable them to defend themselves against coercive power but also to empower them to have confidence in the system and to become normal members of the community again.

It is also relevant in this connection to note that all the general guidelines of the Qur'ān and *Sunnah* on respect for human dignity, and the prohibitions on causing insult, annoyance and oppression, are equally applicable to accused persons and prisoners. For these are mostly conveyed in the form of general (*ʿāmm*) provisions, which apply whenever they can be seen to apply. It is equally important to note that in honouring the humanity and personal dignity of its members, the community nurtures a dignified image of itself and complies with the Qur'ānic notion of the dignity of the 'progeny of Adam' (17:70).

From his reading of the source evidence ʿAbd al-Wahhāb Khallāf has drawn the conclusion that 'all the evidence that is found in the Book of God and the *Sunnah* of His Messenger on the prohibition of hostility, oppression (*ẓulm*), harm and annoyance to others is premised on the inviolability of the right to personal security (*ḥaqq al-amn*) and safe conduct of all human beings against all forms of aggression and abuse.'[16] Violating the individual's right to safety is, in other words, prohibited (*ḥarām*), and it is in principle a right which is not amenable to derogation or compromise.

It is reported that the caliph ʿUmar b. al-Khaṭṭāb had instituted a policy of meeting with his officials during the Ḥajj season. On one such occasion, the caliph addressed his officials and asked them to avoid insult, humiliation, physical abuse and misappropriation of people's property at all times. The caliph then pledged that he would personally see to it that the violators were met with justice. Then the governor of Egypt, ʿAmr b. al-ʿĀṣ, who was present when the caliph issued this directive, asked whether the caliph would retaliate in instances where government officials disciplined (*addaba*) members of the public. To this the caliph replied: 'By Him in whose hand the life of ʿUmar reposes, I shall indeed retaliate, for I have seen the Messenger of God even subjecting himself to retaliation.'[17]

عـن أبى فراس، قال: خطبنا عمر بن الخطاب رضى الله عنه،

فقال: إنـى لم أبعــث عمالى ليضربوا أبشاركـم، ولايأخذوا

أموالكم ، فمـن فعـل به ذلك فليرفعه إلى أقضية منه، قال عمرو

إبن العاص: لو أن رجلا أدب بعض رعيته أتقـصه منه؟ قال: إى

والذى نفسى بيده أقصه ، وقد رأيت رسول الله صلى الله عليه

وسلم أقصّ منه .

ʿUmar was probably referring to the incident when the Prophet was distributing war booty among warriors who were standing in a line, and one man stepped out of the line. 'The Prophet struck him with a stick and the man was hurt. The Prophet told him then: 'Come and retaliate,' to which the man replied 'but I have forgiven you O Messenger of God.'[18] (بل عفوت يا رسول الله)

Anas bin Mālik has reported another incident that also involved ʿAmr b. al-ʿĀṣ. It is stated that Muhammad b. ʿAmr, the son of the governor of Egypt, ʿAmr b. al-ʿĀṣ, had lashed an Egyptian for apparently no reason other than seeing him in the way of his horse racing. The man then complained to the caliph and the caliph summoned both the governor and his son, and then ordered the victim to retaliate by lashing the culprit, which he did. The caliph then asked the man to lash the governor, for 'You would not have been struck were it not for the fact that he was the governor's son.' The man then said, 'I have lashed the one who lashed me.' The caliph then said, 'I would not have intervened if you had in fact lashed the governor.' The caliph then turned to the governor and said:

متى استعبدتم الناس وقد ولدتهم أمهاتهم أحرارا.

Since when did you enslave the people when their mothers gave them birth as free individuals?'[19]

The recognition in *Sharīʿah* of life as one of the five essential values (*al-ḍarūriyyāt al-khamsa*) is a simultaneous recognition of the right of every individual to personal security and the right to live an honourable life. The *Sharīʿah* recognises this as one of its overriding values, alongside such other values as the immunity of one's right to practise one's faith, to own property, to have a family, and the right to the protection of one's intellect. In its positive sense, this last right means the right to seek knowledge and, in its negative sense, it means the right to protection against corrupt and destructive influences, such as drug abuse and the like. All measures that protect and promote these values are consequently upheld by the *Sharīʿah*.[20]

The right to personal security applies equally to pre-trial procedures involving criminal investigation and the collection of evidence against the accused. The latter is in principle entitled to safe conduct, especially when he or she is not notorious for criminality or corruption. The accused may neither be exposed to pressure, nor persecuted in order to incriminate himself. Should there be a confession by the accused, it must be free and voluntary, as any amount of pressure and coercion, which mars the integrity of a confession, is likely to lead to the suspension of punishment. This is the requirement of the *ḥadīth* which categorically declares: 'Drop the prescribed penalties in all cases of doubt.'[21] A confession obtained through pressure tactics is doubtful, and fails to serve its purpose. The caliph ʿUmar b. al-Khaṭṭāb refused to give credit to confessions made under fear, and went on record to say that 'A man is not secure enough, when he is in pain, frightened or imprisoned, to make a confession and incriminate himself.'[22] The law enforcement officer, the head of state and the judge are generally advised not to be eager in the enforcement of penalties. This is the purport of the remainder of the above *ḥadīth*, which is as follows:

ادرؤا الحدود عــن المســلمين مــا اســتطعتم فإن كان له مخرجـا فخلوا سبيله، فإن الإمام أن يخطئ فى العفو خير من أن يخطئ فى العقوبة.

Drop the prescribed penalties (*ḥudūd*) whenever you can. When you can find a way out for a Muslim, then clear his way. For if the Imam errs, it is better that he errs on the side of leniency than on the side of punishment.[23]

Abū Yūsuf, Chief Justice of the Abbasid state under Hārūn al-Rashīd, wrote that when a person is accused of the crime of theft, or any other crime, he may 'neither be beaten nor promised anything nor intimidated in order to illicit a confession from him.' Abū Yūsuf added that anyone who confesses to an offence, including murder and theft, under compulsion, 'is not liable to the prescribed punishment and his confession shall be devoid of effect.'[24] It is also reported that during the time of the Companions, someone by the name of Ṭāriq, who was accused of kidnapping a man from Syria, was beaten until he confessed. ʿAbd Allāh Ibn ʿUmar, who adjudicated the case, ruled that 'no punishment may be applied as the confession was made after the accused was beaten.' Ibn ʿUmar also added that people may not be arrested on the basis of mere accusation, and no claim of theft or murder should be admitted unless it was supported by upright witnesses or a confession free from threats and intimidation. Ibn ʿUmar added that it was unlawful to imprison a man on grounds of mere suspicion. The Prophet would not arrest people on the basis of suspicion alone. But it is proper that the claimant and defendant are brought together before the court. If there is evidence, the claim should be adjudicated, otherwise the defendant should be released or asked to give a surety.[25] 'The judge has no powers,' wrote al-Māwardī, 'to detain anyone unless it is for violation of a right that is clearly established.'[26]

Abū Yūsuf also wrote that the state must ensure that prisoners are not in dire need, and the authorities must assign to the needy among them, both men and women, a monthly payment that is sufficient for their food and clothing for summer and winter, and in the event of death, to meet their funeral expenses also. Prisoners are entitled to safe and fair treatment that precludes punishment and torture. The precedent for this, Abū Yūsuf added, was set by the Pious Caliphs, especially the fourth caliph, ʿAlī b. Abī Ṭālib, who entitled prisoners to allowances from the Public Treasury unless they were affluent, in which case he would spend on them from their own property.[27] Abū Yūsuf has also quoted, in this connection, the caliph ʿUmar Ibn ʿAbd al-ʿAzīz's letter which he sent to his officials, asking them to ensure that 'none of the Muslims in their prisons is restricted to the extent that he cannot stand upright to perform his prayer, and that no-one is restricted so much as to be unable to sleep at night, except for those who are wanted for murder. They should all be given charitable donations to improve their diet and the variety of food they eat.'[28]

I turn next to an examination of the principle of legality and the extent of its application in Islamic law.

IV. The Principle of Legality

This basically means that no one may be incriminated or punished without a legal text which specifically defines the crime and the punishment in question. It also means that the judge may not punish anyone on the basis of his own wishes without lawful evidence and proof. The legal text that is applied must have been in existence at the time the offence was committed. The law may not, in other words, be retroactively enforced. It also means that only the offender and no-one else can be held responsible for his deeds. The requirement of due process in interrogation and trial is designed to ensure that the accused is protected against the abuse of coercive power. The principle of legality is thus essentially concerned with the limitation of the power of the state, and its operation acquires special significance in the area of criminal law.[29]

Islamic constitutional theory is explicit on the principle of the limitation of the power of the state under the rule of law. The Islamic state is, accordingly, bound to administer and uphold the Sharīʿah.[30] There is no place in Islam for arbitrary rule by a single individual or a group. The basis of decision and action in an Islamic polity should not be individual whim and caprice, but the Sharīʿah.[31] The ʿulamāʾ have unanimously held that the head of state and government officials are accountable for their conduct like everyone else, and also that they are equally bound by the decisions of the courts of justice. In response to the question of how the decision of a qāḍi, who is an employee of the Imam, can bind the Imam, it is stated that the judge discharges his duty not in his capacity as an employee of the Imam, but as a representative of the community whose task it is to implement the Sharīʿah. There is consequently no recognition of special privileges for anyone in *Sharīʿah*. Equality before the law and before the courts of justice is clearly recognised for all citizens alike.[32] It is once again indicative of the high priority that Islam accords to the rule of law that it frees the citizen of the duty to obey political authority if the latter itself violates the law. This is the clear message of the *ḥadīth* which declares that 'There is no obedience in transgression; obedience is in lawful conduct only.'[33] According to another *ḥadīth*:

$$\text{لا طاعة فى معصية الله ، إنما الطاعة فى المعروف .}$$

> There is no obedience in transgression; obedience is required in righteousness.[34]

Based on unequivocal authority provided in a number of similar *ḥadīth*s, the conclusion is drawn that 'Islam confers on every citizen the right to refuse to commit a crime, should any government or administrator order him to do so.'[35] Both the right of the head of state to the obedience of his officials and the citizenry, and the latter's obligation to obey, are qualified (*muqayyad*), as opposed to absolute (*muṭlaq*) provisions. When a high ranking official issues an order to his inferior and the latter knows that acting on it is unlawful and he still carries it out, he is personally responsible and also liable to punishment.'[36] But if the official to whom an unlawful command is addressed does not actually know it is unlawful and acts on it in good faith, he is not responsible provided that the order was within the jurisdiction of the issuing officer. If the latter compels his subordinate to commit a crime, both will be held responsible, especially in cases of crimes of violence, such as homicide and bodily injury. Even duress in its full sense does not provide a valid ground of absolvement from responsibility in homicide and injury. In the event where an official claims that he was forced to kill or injure another due to compulsion and duress by his superior, his claim is unlikely to exempt him from anything. It makes no difference, once again, whether the junior officer is a soldier in the army, a police officer or civil servant.[37] Maḥmaṣṣāni has concurred with Ibn Khaldūn that the sovereignty of an Islamic state is restricted in so far as the state is under obligation to comply with the *Sharīʿah*. Hence the conclusion that when the state issues a command that violates the *Sharīʿah*, the citizen has no duty to obey it.[38]

The *Sharīʿah* safeguards rights of the citizen by laying down a set of principles that are designed to ensure due process in the administration of justice. Included in these is the presumption of original non-liability (*barā'a al-dhimma al-aṣliyya*), which simply presumes that no-one is guilty of a crime unless the contrary is proved through lawful evidence.[39]

This principle is derived from the *Sharīʿah* law doctrine of *istiṣḥāb*, or presumption of continuity, which presumes the validity of *status quo ante* when there is no evidence to suggest that it has changed. Thus according to a legal maxim, which is also derived from *istiṣḥāb*, 'The norm is that the past continues to be as it was known,' (*al-aṣlu baqā' mā kāna ʿalā ma kān*). The principle of *barā'a* is an extension of the same logic in that the individual is born free and remains free of all liability and guilt unless there is evidence to prove the opposite. Anyone who claims that the *status quo* has changed and that the individual bears a liability, or has committed an offence, must prove this by means of valid evidence. Non-liability is thus the natural state and a basic presumption concerning every individual, from the moment of birth until death, and any claim that avers the opposite can only be credible if it is supported by evidence. According to yet another legal maxim derived from *istiṣḥāb*, 'Certainty may not be overruled by doubt.' Applying this to the subject under review would mean that since non-liability is the state of certainty that must prevail, and the claim of liability represents the state of doubt, the former prevails over the latter, and the accused is presumed innocent until proven guilty.[40]

Article (8) of the *Mejelle* proclaims that non-liability is the basic norm. Thus when a man destroys the property of another, and then they differ on the amount thereof, credibility is given to the word of the defendant and evidence is required from the owner to prove what the defendant has not acknowledged. If the plaintiff has no evidence to support his claim, the defendant's version will be upheld. But the plaintiff can ask that the defendant takes an oath that he has told the truth.

To give another example: A claims that B is indebted to him, or that B is obligated to work for him according to a contract. A would need to prove his claim in the event of B's denial, and B's word would prevail when supported by an oath. This is because B, who denies the claim in reality, holds on to the original state of non-liability, and this is upheld unless the contrary is proven by lawful evidence.

The principle of non-liability, or presumption of innocence, is not overruled by a mere accusation, for doubt does not negate certainty. The certainty here is the prior innocence of the accused. The principle of legality also entitles the accused to defend himself and attend his own trial. This is established in a *hadīth* in which the Prophet is reported to have advised ʿAli ibn Abi Ṭalib, upon the latter's departure as judge to the Yemen:

فإذا جلس بين يديك الخصمان فلاتقضين حتى تسمع من الآخرِ كماسمعت من الأوّل.

> When the litigant presents himself before you, do not pass a judgment unless you hear the other party in the same way as you hear the first.[41]

In a similar vein, Islamic law does not permit the judge to sentence a person in his absence. The defendant must, in other words, be present in the court or be represented by an authorised person.[42] An exception is made in cases where an agreement is reached between two courts situated in two localities, one of the plaintiff and the other of the defendant, and they cooperate with one another. The Ḥanafīs reject trial *in absentia* altogether, but the Shāfiʿīs allow it in cases of *prima facie* evidence, and cases where the evidence presented by the plaintiff is conclusive and sufficient for the judge to issue a judgment.[43] There is some disagreement among the Ḥanafīs and Shāfiʿīs about whether accusation in itself can weaken the force of the original principle of non-liability: the Ḥanafīs maintain that it does, but the Shāfiʿīs hold that a mere claim or accusation does not affect the original absence of liability, or the innocence, of the accused. It is important, as one observer has rightly noted, that the presumption of innocence is strictly upheld, as the accused will otherwise be faced with the onerous, if not impossible, task of proving that he did not commit the crime.[44]

Anyone, whether the individual or the state, who accuses a person of an offence must prove it beyond reasonable doubt.[45] The burden of proof lies on the plaintiff, a principle derived from the *ḥadīth*:

البيّنة على المدّعى واليمين على من أنكر.

> The burden of proof is on him who makes the claim, whereas the oath is [incumbent] on him who denies.[46]

The plaintiff, in other words, may ask the court to put the defendant on oath if the latter denies the claim. If the claimant is required to prove his allegation, it follows that until such proof is forthcoming, the defendant is presumed to be innocent. This is also upheld in another *ḥadīth*, which provides that:

لو يعطى النـاس بدعواهـم لادّعى ناس دماء رجـال وأمـوالهـم،
ولكن اليمين على المدعى عليه.

> If men were to be granted what they claim, some will claim the lives
> and properties of others. The burden of proof is on the claimant, and an
> oath is incumbent on him who denies.[47]

According to Ibn Qayyim al-Jawziyya, if the claimant supports his claim by evidence, the court will adjudicate in his favour, otherwise the last word is that of the defendant and the court shall credit what he says, provided he takes a solemn oath to affirm that he is telling the truth.[48]

Punishment is not executed unless there is proof to establish guilt, and hearsay evidence is not admissible in the execution of penalties. Ibn Taymiyya wrote that there was at the time of the Prophet a woman in Madina who had a reputation for debauchery, and the Prophet said concerning her 'If I were to stone anyone without evidence, I would have stoned this woman.'[49] Ibn Taymiyya also quoted on the same page a statement of the caliph 'Umar b. al-Khaṭṭāb to the effect that no-one may be punished on the basis of suspicion and mistrust. Al-Qarāfi and Ibn Farḥūn have specified that proof (al-thubūt) is evidence that is sound and free of doubt and loopholes; it has met all its proper conditions and is focused on a definite result. Ibn Qayyim has observed that offenders are not punished without proof and proof comes either from the offender when he or she makes a confession, or what might amount to a confession, or else is provided independently. In both cases, the proof must be sound, free of doubt and clear of espionage.[50]

Confession in crimes, but not in civil disputes, can be withdrawn even after the sentence has been passed or during its execution. Once a confession is so withdrawn, particularly in the prescribed *ḥadd* offences, the punishment may not be carried out. For withdrawal in this manner gives rise to doubt (*shubha*), which would in turn obstruct the enforcement of punishment.[51] For a confession to be valid, the confessor must also be in full possession of his faculties. Confession must, in addition, be true in that it does not seek to conceal the truth in order merely to protect another person, or group of persons. When the cause and underlying intention of a mendacious confession is known to the judge, he is under duty to reject it.[52] A valid confession needs to be specific and categorical. If it is ambiguous to an extent that it requires interpretation, it is not admissible. Hence it is not enough if someone says merely that 'I committed adultery,' or that 'one of us committed theft.' Both statements are vague as they fail to provide relevant details and do not, therefore, amount to valid proof.[53]

Judicial decisions must be based on apparent truth, which is substantiated by valid evidence. The hidden truth, should there be any, is considered to be a matter between the individual and his Creator and it lies beyond the immediate concern of the court. In al-Shaʿrāni's phrase 'God Most High has ordered us to settle disputes among people on the basis of visible proof, and leave the rest to the Day of Judgment.'[54] This conclusion is supported by the following *ḥadīth,* in which the Prophet is reported to have said:

إنّمـا أنـا بشـر، وإنّكـم تختصـمون إلـيّ ولعلّ بعضكم أن يكون
ألحن بحجته من بعض فأقضى له على نحو ما اسمع منه، فمن
قضيتُ له من حقّ أخيه بشيئ فلايأخذ منه شيئا فأنما أقطع له
من النار.

I am but a human being. When you bring a dispute to me, some of you may be more eloquent in stating their case than others. I may consequently adjudicate on the basis of what I hear. If I adjudicate in favour of someone a thing that belongs to his brother, let him not take it. For this would be like taking a piece of fire.[55]

The Prophet has, in other words, confirmed that he adjudicated disputes on the basis only of evidence that was presented to him. Yet the *ḥadīth* is equally clear that ostentatious evidence that seeks to distort the truth gives rise to blame and punishment in the hereafter, and must be avoided.

Evidence must be allowed to be given in an atmosphere of impartiality. It is a generally agreed-upon rule of the *Sharīʿah* law of evidence that the judge must avoid inculcating witnesses, but should instead hear what they have to say.[56] But the evidence they give must inspire conviction. The judge may therefore examine and scrutinise the testimony and ensure that it is free of loopholes, that it is neither contrived nor controversial. The judge may, however, accept doubtful testimony if it can be attached to what is credible and sound. This may consist of clues, indications, etc. But if none of this is available, the judge rejects the doubtful testimony altogether.[57] The Qur'ān demands impartiality in the administration of justice. The witnesses, the judge and the enforcement authorities are accordingly required to:

كونوا قوامين بالقسط شهداء لله ولو على أنفسكم أو الوالدين والأقربين إن يكن غنيا أو فقيرا فالله أولى بهما فلا تتبعوا الهوى أن تعدلوا.

Stand firmly for justice as witnesses to God, even if it be against yourselves, your parents and your relatives, and whether it is (against) the rich or poor, for God can best protect both. Follow not the lust (of your hearts) lest it detracts you from the course of justice (4:135).

The Qur'ānic guideline with reference to sentencing is that it proscribes excess in retaliation, and prohibits punishments that are out of line with the offence itself. We note once again the following Qur'ānic directive, which is addressed to all parties in judicial disputes, including the enforcement authorities and the state:

فمن اعتدى عليكم فاعتدوا عليه بمثل مااعتدى عليكم.

Whoever is aggressive toward you, your response to them must be proportionate to the pain that was inflicted on you (2:194).

The Qur'ān further lays down the principle that no-one may be accused or punished for an offence committed by another person:

ولاتكسب كل نفس إلا عليها ولاتزروا وازرة وزر أخرى.

Everyone is accountable for his own deeds, and no soul shall bear the burden of another (6:164).[58]

This is reiterated in a *ḥadīth* to the effect that:

لا تجنى نفس على نفس.

No person may be incriminated with a crime committed by another person.[59]

A Companion by the name Abū Rimtha has reported an encounter he had with the Prophet as follows:

انطلقت مع أبى نحو النبي صلى الله عليه وسلم، ثم إنّ رسول الله صلى الله عليه وسلم قال لأبى: ابنك هذا؟ قال: إى ورب الكعبة، قال: حقّا؟ قال: أشهد به، قال: فتبسم رسول الله صلى الله عليه وسلم ضاحكا من ثبت شبهى فى أبى، ومن حلف أبى على، ثم قال: إنه لايجنى عليك ولا تجنى عليه، وقرأ رسـول الله صـلى الله عـليه وسـلم: ولاتزروا وازرة وزر أخرى.

I went together with my father to the Messenger of God, peace be on him, who asked my father 'Is this your son?' My father said, 'Yes, by the Lord of the Kaʿba.' The Prophet said 'truly—*ḥaqqan?*' The man said then 'I testify (that I told the truth).' The Prophet then smiled and laughed about my father's doubt concerning (his relation with) me and his swearing on it. Then the Prophet said: 'But he is not incriminated on your behalf nor are you incriminated on his behalf,' and then the Prophet recited the *āyah* 'and no soul shall bear the burden of another.'[60]

The Qur'ān further provides in an address to the Prophet:

إنّا أنزلنا إليك الكتاب بالحق لتحكم بين الناس بما أراك الله ولاتكن للخائنين خصيما.

We revealed to you the scripture with the truth that you may judge between people by that which God has shown to you, and be not thou a pleader for the treacherous (4:105).

This verse was revealed concerning a dispute between a Muslim and a Jew. The Muslim, Ibn Ubayraq, had stolen a coat of mail, and, having hidden it in the house of a Jew, afterwards accused the latter of the theft; he was supported in his false accusation by his tribe. The Prophet cleared the Jew of the charge but Ibn Ubayraq fled and renounced Islam. The following two verses were also revealed concerning the same case:

ومن يكسب إثما فإنما يكسبه على نفسه... ومن يكسب خطيئة أو إثما ثم يرم به بريئا فقد احتمل بهتانا وإثما مبينا.

> Whoever commits a sin only makes himself liable for it…and whoever commits a delinquency and then throws the blame thereof upon the innocent—has burdened himself with falsehood and a flagrant crime (4:111–112).[61]

This Qur'ānic principle marked a departure from ancient Arab excesses in retaliation and revenge. The Arabs sometimes doubled the penalty or claimed more than one life in retaliation. They often demanded exaggerated sums in diyyah (blood money) and held the whole tribe responsible for the crime of one of its members.[62] A well-known exception to this principle is the case of ʿāqila, which is a pre-Islamic Arabian custom that was subsequently adopted by the *Sunnah* and consensus (*ijmāʿ*), and it required the kinsmen of the offender to pay the blood money in unintentional homicide. According to al-Awzāʿī and Dāwūd al-Ẓāhirī, the offender himself does not participate with his ʿāqila in the payment of diyyah, but he does according to Abu Ḥanīfah and Mālik; and according to al-Shāfiʿī, he participates only if the ʿāqila is unable to pay the *diyya*. We learn that during the time of ʿUmar b. al-Khaṭṭāb, the ʿāqila included colleagues at work (*ahl al-dīwān*).[63] This has led Maḥmūd Shaltūt to the observation that the proper purpose of ʿāqila is cooperation and help in respect of an unintended crime. It is not meant to transfer the responsibility of the offender to another person, which is why the ʿāqila is not required to participate in the diyyah of a deliberate crime.[64]

ʿĀqila also served as a kind of social insurance so that compensation could be paid to the victim of a crime even when the offender himself could not afford to pay it. And then, of course, ʿāqila played a role in strengthening the voice of the family, clan and tribe in crime prevention as they bore responsibility for the payment of *diyya*. *ʿĀqila* evidently played a useful role in the tribal milieu of Arabia, which was probably why the practice was continued even after the advent of Islam. It is doubtful, however, that it could be meaningfully applied in modern conditions, where tribal ties no longer carry significance. Even by the time of the second caliph ʿUmar, a certain change in the locus of ʿāqila was considered. Indeed, the present day nation-state has assumed some of the roles that ʿāqila played in earlier times, and new developments such as those pertaining to life insurance, social security law and labour unions nowadays play a role similar to the ʿāqila for certain eventualities. If the social cooperation rendered by the ʿāqila is realised and substituted by these modern entities, then ʿāqila may no longer apply. In Saudi Arabia, one observer reported that 'the state assumes responsibility for the payment of blood money where the *ʿāqila*, the mutual liability group of agnatic relatives, is unable to pay it to the heirs of the victim.'[65] It thus appears that even in Saudi Arabia, the original locus of *ʿāqila*, the position has changed and the concept of state insurance has effectively assumed its role.

Muslim jurists have formulated a number of legal maxims which complement the principle of legality in the *Sharīʿah*. One of these provides that 'the conduct of reasonable men (or the dictate of reason) alone is of no consequence without the support of a legal text.' This obviously means that no conduct can be declared forbidden (*ḥarām*) on grounds of reason or on the judgement of reasonable men alone, and that a legal text is necessary to render the conduct in question an offence. No-one, therefore, should be deemed a violator because of committing an act which is not forbidden by the clear provision of the law.[66] The substance of this principle is also upheld in another legal maxim which declares that 'Permissibility is the original norm,' (*al-aṣlu fi'l-ashyā' al-ibāḥa*).[67] The majority of *ʿulamā'* have thus reached the conclusion that all things are permissible unless the law has declared otherwise. Consequently, no-one may be accused of an offence in the absence of a legal text.

A third legal maxim in this connection provides that 'No-one bears any obligation unless he is capable of understanding the law which imposes it; nor may anyone be required to act in a certain manner unless he is capable of knowing the nature of the act he is required to do or avoid doing.'[68] This principle indicates that the law, which creates an obligation or an offence, can only be addressed to a competent person who is capable of understanding it, and that it must be physically possible for him to comply with the law when he knows of it. To make the knowledge of the law possible for the citizen, the legal text must be publicised and made accessible to all. Consequently, no crime is committed until the text which creates it has been publicly announced and brought to the knowledge of the people.[69] These conclusions are supported by several passages in the Qur'ān. To quote but a few:

وما كنّا معذّبين حتى نبعث رسولا.

We do not punish until We have sent a messenger (to give warning) (17:15).

وما كان ربك مهلك القرى حتى يبعث فى أمّها رسولا يتلوا عليهم أياتنا وما كنا مهلك القرى إلا وأهلها ظالمون.

Nor was thy Lord the one to destroy a population until He had sent in its midst a messenger rehearsing to them Our signs (28:59).

رسلا مبشرين ومنذرين لئلا يكون للناس على الله حجة بعد الرسل.

Messengers who gave good news as well as warnings, so that people should have no plea against God after the (sending of) messengers.(Al-Nisā', 4:165)

People are thus accountable for their deeds on the basis of the message and scripture that is conveyed to them. The principle contained in these Qur'ānic passages is that without prior warning, scripture and guidance, there shall be no punishment. Thus according to ʿAwdah 'in the absence of a clear text which may require affirmative action or abandonment of a particular conduct, the perpetrator or abandoner incurs no responsibility and no punishment can be imposed.'[70] Anyone who looks into the *Sharīʿah*, ʿAwdah adds, will find that there is a text for every punishable offence, although the approach may differ with regard to the types of offences, as we shall presently explain.[71] Commenting on the same Qur'ānic passages, Khallāf explained, and this is the majority position, that a person who has lived in complete isolation, so that no message, law or guidance has been communicated to him, is *non-compos mentis* (*ghayr mukallaf*). Such a person could not therefore be rewarded for his good deeds or punished for his crimes. For it is a prerequisite of responsibility (*taklīf*) that the law is communicated to its proper audience.[72]

There is evidence in the Qur'ān to the effect that punishment must not be applied retroactively:

قل للذين كفروا إن ينتهوا يُغفر لهم ما قد سلف وإن يعودوا فقد مضت سنت الأوّلين.

Say to the unbelievers that if they desist (from unbelief), what they have done in the past will be forgiven (8:38).

Elsewhere in the Qur'ān, it is provided with reference to pre-Islamic marital practices that:

ولاتنكحوا ما نكح أباؤكم من النساء إلاّ ما قد سلف إنّه كان فاحشة ومقتا وساء سبيلا .

And marry not those women whom your fathers married, except for what had already happened in the past (4:22).

Abu Zahrah draws the conclusion from these verses that the Qur'ān forbids applying the penal law of Islam to offences that were committed prior to the advent of Islam. This would, in principle, establish the non-retroactivity of penalties under the *Sharī'ah*.[73] The substance of these Qur'ānic declarations is confirmed in the following *ḥadīth*. When 'Amr ibn al-'Āṣ embraced Islam, he pledged allegiance to the Prophet and asked if he would be held accountable for his previous transgressions. To this, the Prophet replied:

أما علمت يا عمرو أن الإسلام يهدم ما كان قبله؟

Did you not know, O 'Amr, that Islam obliterates that which took place before it.[74]

It is also noted that when the Prophet conquered Mecca, he did not question Abu Sufyān and his wife about their previous conduct and acts of hostility against Muslims, nor did he question the man who had killed his uncle Ḥamza, even though his death caused him deep sorrow. The only exception Abū Zahrah has noted concerning this principle is with reference to a new and more lenient law, in that the new law has a retroactive effect when it is in favour of the accused.[75]

The *Sharī'ah* does not advocate a rigid approach in its implementation of the principle of the rule of law. Broadly speaking, the *Sharī'ah* employs three different methods for implementing the principle of legality in criminal law. In the case of serious crimes, which pose a major threat to society, the *Sharī'ah* specifies both the offence and the punishment—the punishment so specified may fall under the *ḥudūd*, just retaliation *qiṣāṣ* and blood-money *diyya*. For offences which pose a relatively lesser threat to public safety, the *Sharī'ah* does not specify the penalty but defines the offence, and provides general guidelines about the punishment. These are the *ta'zīr* offences where the *Sharī'ah* specifies the conduct but empowers the judge to select the type and extent of its punishment, out of a range of approved penalties. *Ta'zīr* offences consist primarily of conduct which the *Sharī'ah* has defined as transgression (*ma'siya*). It is not for the judge to define the offence; he can only specify punishment for conduct that has already been determined as criminal by a legal text (*nass*).

While discussing the common perception that the judge has a free hand in dealing with *ta'zīr* offences, 'Abd al-Qādir 'Awdah points out that the *Sharī'ah* imposes certain restrictions on the powers of the judge. It is a mistake to say that *ta'zīr* offences are not regulated by the text or to suggest that the judge is at liberty to determine both the crime and its punishment. The judge must, first of all, determine whether the conduct is a transgression (*ma'siya*) according to clear text of the *Sharī'ah*. The offence must then be proved through lawful evidence. The judge selects only that type of punishment which the *Sharī'ah* has validated. 'Awdah goes on to illustrate this by referring to a number of *ta'zīr* offences and the textual authority on which they are based. The list includes consumption of forbidden substances, breach of trust, cheating in weights and measurements, gambling, perjury, usury, obscenity and insult, bribery, unlawful entry into private dwellings, blocking public passages, and espionage. In all of these, the Qur'ān and *Sunnah* provide the textual authority which renders the conduct a *ma'siya*. When meting out punishment for any of these offences, the judge must select an approved penalty, ranging from a mere warning to fines, flogging and imprisonment, and decide whether the sentence may be suspended or be carried out promptly. The judge, in other words, enjoys discretionary powers in regard to *ta'zīr* offences, which 'Awdah characterises as *sultah al-ikhtiyār* (power to select) as opposed to *sultah al-tahakkum*, or the power to legislate at will. In Islamic constitutional theory, neither the judge nor any other organ of government enjoys unlimited powers of this latter type.[76]

In regard to *ta'zīr* offences which violate the public interest (*al-maslahah al-'āmma*), the *Sharī'ah* does not specify the nature of the offence but provides only general guidelines on the type of conduct that is deemed to be harmful to society. The reason for this is that offences of this type are on the whole unpredictable and cannot be specified in advance. An act may be permissible and yet the circumstances in which it is committed, or some of its attributes, are such that would violate public interest. While in principle the *Sharī'ah* penalises only acts that amount to transgression, it makes an exception by authorising the judge to penalise conduct which, though not forbidden by textual authority and, therefore, not a *maʿṣiya*, is prejudicial to public interest and causes harm (*ḍarar*) to society.[77] Examples of this kind of *taʿzīr* are restrictions on the liberty of the insane for the sake of public safety and preventing him from harming the community, or the detention without proof of an accused on grounds of public interest, that is, to facilitate investigation and prevent a possible escape.[78]

In all of this, whether *taʿzīr* is in relation to a transgression (*maʿṣiya*) or harm (*ḍarar*), the punishment must be proportionate to the offence and should remain within moderate limits. Based on the authority of the *Sunnah*, the jurists have further added the proviso that *taʿzīr*, in general, must operate at a level below the severity of the prescribed penalties (*ḥudūd*).[79] *Taʿzīr* punishment may also be invoked in the case of prescribed (*ḥadd*) offences where the specified punishment cannot be enforced due to insufficiency of evidence, or owing to doubt about the fulfilment of their necessary conditions. In both cases, the judge has powers to impose, by way of *taʿzīr*, a lesser punishment as may be considered appropriate.

There is some disagreement among the leading *madhāhib* as to the quantitative limits of *taʿzīr* penalties. While some jurists, especially of the Mālikī School, have specified no limits and have referred the matter to considerations of *maṣlaḥah* and the *ijtihād* of the judge, others have held that *taʿzīr* penalties in each category must be below the level of the relevant *ḥadd* punishment. This is the view of some Ḥanbalī jurists. According to another view, which is upheld by many Ḥanafī, Shāfiʿī and Ḥanbalī scholars, *taʿzīr* must not exceed the lowest of all the *ḥadd* penalties across the board, which means that it may not exceed forty lashes of the whip in any case. Another opinion on this, which is held by some Ḥanbalī ʿulamāʾ, has it that *taʿzīr* punishment may not exceed ten lashes of the whip absolutely, and there is some authority in the *ḥadīth* in support of this. Having said this, however, *taʿzīr* punishment may also consist of a mere verbal reprimand, imprisonment, and according to some, also of banishment, depending on the nature of the offence, the conditions of the offender and considerations of public interest.[80]

Next I present an analysis of the two allied concepts *tuhma* and *ẓann*.

V. Accusation (*al-tuhmah*) and Suspicion (*al-ẓann*)

Accusation may be defined as 'An unproven attribution of crime to someone which is accompanied by a demand for judicial redress.' In this definition, accusation is an unproven claim and it is this factor that differentiates accusation from indictment and sentence, which are accompanied by proof. The demand for judicial redress in this definition also differentiates accusation from a casual attribution of criminal behaviour to someone, which is not intended to involve indictment and adjudication. Accusation is often made by the crime victim or by an interested party, but it may, in principle, be made by anyone, including members of the public and the police. It is also necessary that the subject of an accusation is a crime and a violation which renders the perpetrator liable to punishment.[81]

Accusing someone of a crime without proof necessarily partakes of suspicion (al-ẓann), which is generally not encouraged. The principle here is laid down in the Qur'ānic address to the believers to:

$$\text{يَآيها الذين آمنوا اجتنبوا كثيرا من الظن إنّ بعض الظن إثم ولاتجسسوا.}$$

Avoid indulgence in suspicion, for suspicion in some cases is wrong; and do not spy on one another (49:12).

The Prophet has reiterated the Qur'ānic directive in at least two *ḥadīths*, one of which declares that:

$$\text{حسن الظن من العبادة.}$$

Thinking well of others is a form of worship.[82]

In another *ḥadīth* the Prophet warned the believers to:

$$\text{إيّاكم والظن فإن الظن أكذب الحديث ولا تحسسوا ولا تجسسوا.}$$

Beware of suspicion, for suspicion is the worst form of lying, and do not spy.[83]

Commentators have equated suspicion here with accusation. What is prohibited, as al-Qurṭubi noted, is baseless accusation such as accusing someone of adultery and drunkenness without evidence. To say that suspicion here means accusation is also borne out by the subsequent phrase in both the Qur'ān and *ḥadīth*: 'And do not spy.' For it may occur to someone to accuse a person of some wrongdoing so as to spy on him afterwards.[84]

Syed Quṭb has drawn the conclusion, from the verse quoted above, that arrest on the basis of mere suspicion is a violation of the personal rights of the individual. No-one may be arrested for anything other than an offence which is apparent, and no-one may be chased in hidden ways or spied upon in order to be incriminated. The suspect may only be arrested and convicted for a crime that can be proved against him or her by means of lawful evidence, which must preclude espionage. In support of this conclusion, Syed Quṭb has quoted a *ḥadīth* on the authority of Mujāhid in which the Prophet is reported to have instructed the believers to:

إنا قد نهينا عن التجسس ولكن إن يظهر لنا بشيئ نأخذ منه.

Avoid spying. You may accuse people for what is apparent, but leave alone that which is not.[85]

The renowned Companion, 'Abd Allāh Ibn Mas'ūd, is also reported to have said:

ولا تجسسوا، خذوا بما ظهر لكم.

Espionage is forbidden for us. We may only incriminate people with what is apparent.[86]

Commenting on the same Qur'ānic verse (49:12), al-'Alwānī has observed that no-one may be subjected to frisking or search of his/her person or home, and there must be no surveillance, the recording of conversations over the telephone or elsewhere, or any invasion of privacy in any other manner on the basis merely of a dubious suspicion that he or she might have committed a crime. This is because 'unfounded suspicion is the worst possible kind of suspicion, and one who acts on such suspicion is a wrongdoer.'[87] This is also the conclusion that both al-Awad and al-Saleh have drawn from their combined reading of this and two other Qur'ānic verses on the privacy of the home (24:27–28). Searching and eavesdropping on persons, their personal correspondence and their properties are therefore unlawful as they partake of espionage and violate the personal right to privacy.[88]

To think well of others (*husn al-zann*), as opposed to suspicion (*sū' al-zann*), is described as an act of spiritual merit that encapsulates the spirit of fraternity among Muslims. Al-Sulamī has rightly labelled it one of the devotions of the heart (*min afᶜāl al-qalb*) that a believer does for the sake of God. What it actually means is best manifested in a *hadīth*, which provides that a true believer is the one who nurtures love for his brother and wishes for him what he would wish for himself, and dislikes for him what he would dislike for himself.[89] It is also an act of good faith to be trusting of others and give a positive interpretation to what they do, unless there is evidence for one to be suspicious of their intentions.

In one of its juristic manifestations, thinking well of others has meant that a witness is deemed to be upright and just unless he has a reputation for what may cast doubt on his character. Imam Abu Hanīfah has gone so far as to admit the testimony of a transgressor (*shahādat al-fāsiq*) on the assumption, as al-Ghazālī also agrees, that people cannot have knowledge of the hidden thoughts and intentions of others, and transgressor in question might have quietly regretted what he had done and asked God for forgiveness! Then his testimony is admissible, especially if no better-qualified witness is available.[90] Al-Ghazālī adds that confronting others with probing questions, without any credible basis of suspicion, also partakes of malice (*sū' al-zann*), which should be avoided. When someone offers his goods for sale to another, for example, and the latter has known that the seller has been a government officer who might have taken bribes, or a dishonest lender who might have cheated others or indulged in usury (*ribā'*) etc., none of this would entitle the buyer to face the seller with a question as to where and how he obtained the goods he offers for sale. Questioning of this kind is not permissible unless the buyer specifically knows that the goods offered for sale are stolen or usurped goods, for example.[91]

People who engage in trading activity in the market place should neither be questioned nor searched for the sole purpose of ascertaining the lawfulness or otherwise of the goods they possess. This is endorsed, al-Ghazālī adds, by the precedent of the Companions, who did not question trades and transactions in the market place, whether by Muslims or non-Muslims, even though they knew that some of those activities were suspicious. Only some of them are known to have asked questions in circumstances where doubt about the legality of a transaction or contract became dominant and overwhelming, and warranted questioning. Similarly, it is always possible to doubt whether meat that one buys in the butcher's shop has been properly slaughtered, or on the contrary came from a dead carcass that was not ritually slaughtered. Yet no-one should actually face the butcher with curious questions of this sort, a position which is once again supported by the precedent of the caliph ʿUmar b. al-Khaṭṭāb.[92] Al-Ghazālī has discussed these situations in the light of the renowned *ḥadīth*, which instructs the believers to: 'Abandon that which you find doubtful in favour of what you find yourself in no doubt about—*daʿ mā yurībukum ilā mā lā yurībukum*. Al-Ghazālī observes that this *ḥadīth* does have a message for the pious. If a person wishes to stay clear of doubt, he may well abandon the trade or purchase of goods of questionable origin, and no harm will have been done.

The doubt referred to in this *ḥadīth* is that which is overwhelming. For complete purity is rare to come by and what is meant here is that one should abandon things in which doubt and suspicion predominate.[93] The *ḥadīth* provides moral advice, since it speaks mainly of abandoning something which might seem doubtful to one, yet people's aptitude for and capacity to question is subjective. This is not to say that the *ḥadīth* does not relate to the subject of *ẓann*, but what it tells us concerning *ẓann* is that the *ẓann* which provides the basis of action or of questioning another person is that which is dominant and overcomes certainty about the goodness of the matter in question.

One other area where the pre-Islamic Arabs tended to indulge in unwarranted suspicion was in the treatment of women. An exaggerated sense of manliness that smacked of jealousy and unwarranted suspicion was also noted among menfolk during the Prophet's time. This subject has consequently featured in the *ḥadīth* where the Prophet warned against such behaviour, especially within the family, between man and wife, and in relation to women generally. Although bravery and manliness (*ghīra, murū'ah*) are not bad qualities in themselves, over-indulgence in them is not recommended. One of the unwarranted facets of excessive manliness has been denounced in the following *ḥadīth*:

وأمّا (الغيرة) التى يبغضها الله فالغيرة فى غير ريبة.

One of the manifestations of manliness (*ghīra*) that is disliked by God Most High is when a man indulges in it without there being any ground for suspicion.[94]

Al-Ghazālī quoted this *ḥadīth* and followed it with the comment that what is highlighted in this *ḥadīth* amounts to malice (*sū' al-ẓann*), which the Qur'ān has prohibited. The *ḥadīth* objects to the behaviour of some men who do not want their women to go out to the market, or see other men (in a permissible way), even though the Prophet had permitted women to attend the mosque for congregational prayer and to go out to the market or visit relatives.[94]

Muhammad Asad has observed that the Qur'ānic prohibition of unfounded suspicion, when read together with the relevant *ḥadīth*s on the subject of suspicion and espionage, calls for a constitutional enactment. The enactment in question should prohibit the government from indulging in activities that compromise the inviolability of the citizen's dignity and right to personal security. To subject the citizens, other than those previously convicted of felony and crime, to secret police supervision 'would be entirely out of bound in a truly Islamic state. Arrest on mere suspicion would be a breach of constitutional law.' Asad adds that imprisonment or internment without previous trial and conviction by a duly established court of law would clearly 'contravene the principle of the inviolability of the human person laid down so unequivocally in the Qur'ān and *Sunnah*.'[96]

It is further suggested that the Qur'ānic verse quoted above alludes to two types of suspicion, one of which is permissible (*al-ẓann al-mubāḥ*) and the other blameworthy and forbidden (*al-ẓann al-sū'* or *al-ẓann al-madhmūm,* and according to some, *al-ẓann al-muḥarram*). When suspicion is based on a conviction supported by clues and circumstances that may be said to be reasonable, it is permissible, or even praiseworthy, but when it lacks any such basis, it is blameworthy and forbidden. This binary division of suspicion is indicated in the verse itself, which clearly does not forbid suspicion altogether. Māwardī has observed that when suspicion is enforced by signs and manifest indications, it may provide a valid basis for action. This is when there is a distinct possibility that if steps are not taken, a crime is likely to be committed. Thus, when a trustworthy person reports that a man took a woman to a secluded place and the possibility of murder or of assault seemed prominent, in situations like this, 'it is permissible to resort to espionage, investigation and search in order to seize the opportunity of detecting acts of transgression and lawlessness before they are committed.' In the event, however, when there is no fear of criminality, or any crime in the process of being committed, or any imminent possibility of someone's modesty being violated 'it is not permissible to spy on anyone,' or to search and arrest them on that basis.[97] Thus, it is concluded that suspicion under circumstances that give rise to reasonable doubt is permissible and may form the basis of appropriate action. The grounds of suspicion may either be related to the attending circumstances, or to the character and reputation of the individual, or to both. Suspicion that is supported by these factors differs from mere doubt in that unlike doubt, suspicion is supported by the attending clues.[98] Suspicion of this kind must overwhelm the mind of the observer before he questions another person as a result of it or makes it the basis for action.

Accusation may be private (*fardī*) or public (*ʿāmm*). Private accusation is made by the victim of the crime or his representative, and it usually involves litigation between the parties involved. When, for example, the victim of theft accuses a person of having stolen his personal property, in this type of accusation the claim itself is seen a grounds for suspicion that may form the basis of arrest. Public accusation, on the other hand, is a right of society at large, which may be exercised by any one of its members. Public accusation by a fellow citizen who is not a party to the offence partakes of *hisbah*, that is, enjoining good and preventing evil, which is normally resorted to by one who is a witness to an incident. This type of accusation gives rise to the fear of abusive action whereby individuals may accuse one another on insufficient grounds, or out of malice. The fear, therefore, that the reputation of innocent individuals may be jeopardised without cause, and that such individuals are put under pressure as a result, is more prominent in this type of accusation.

There is also the additional concern that public accusations, if left unchecked, might strain the time and resources of law enforcement agencies. The public is on the one hand encouraged to be alert to criminality and evil, yet safeguards are often necessary to avoid harm to innocent individuals. Whereas the private accuser is generally required to support his accusation by some form of evidence, the public accuser is not faced with a similar requirement. For he or she is a carrier of *hisbah* and his or her position is analogous to that of a witness. A witness is normally not required to support his statement by evidence. Public accusation is, however, not treated as a testimony against the accused person. This is because the judge needs to verify the probity (*ʿadālah*) of the witness, which he is not in a position to do in a public accusation, and until this has actually taken place, the allegation is not given the same weight as that of a private accusation. Public accusation is therefore treated as a weak form of accusation, which carries a lesser weight than the testimony of witnesses.[99]

From the viewpoint of its validity or otherwise, accusation is once again divided into two types: valid accusation (*al-tuhmah al-ṣaḥīḥah*) and void accusation (*al-tuhmah al-fāsidah*).

A valid accusation is a credible accusation that is granted a hearing by a judge. Such an accusation is valid when it fulfils the following three conditions. Firstly, it must be well defined and specific, so that it is addressed to a particular person and solicits adjudication, which is not possible unless the subject matter and person or persons involved therein are clearly identified. An example of an unclear accusation would be when someone accuses another of theft in which the stolen goods are not identified, or when the accuser mentions a name and simply says 'I accuse so and so,' without mentioning what that person might have done.[100]

Secondly, a valid accusation is one which could be proven and must be free of inconsistency and contradiction. An accusation of murder, for example, where the victim's body is not found is not credible, nor is it credible when an accuser accuses two persons of individually committing the same crime, or when a man known to be poor claims that someone has stolen a huge sum of money from him.

Thirdly, the end result of an accusation must be feasible and, when proved, lead to indictment and sentencing; it is not, in other words, an exercise in futility. An example of an unfeasible accusation would be to accuse someone of stealing his own property, or of something too trivial, such as accusing someone of stealing 'a grain of wheat.'[101]

A void accusation is one that is devoid of credibility and does not warrant attention. It is an accusation which fails to fulfil one or more of the requirements of a valid accusation as discussed above.

Without wishing to enter into the minutiae, Muslim jurists have also sub-divided valid accusation into three types, namely, strong, weak, and intermediate.

A strong accusation (*al-tuhmah al-qawiyyah*) is one that is supported by overt circumstances, such as accusing someone of theft who is known to have committed similar offences in the past. A weak accusation (*al-tuhmah al-ḍaʿīfah*) is, on the other hand, that which is not supported by circumstances. An example of this would be to accuse an upright person of good reputation with theft. An intermediate accusation (*al-tuhmah al-mutawassiṭah*) is one in which neither of the two sides of a claim can be given preference over the other—such as accusing someone of theft who is obscure and about whose past conduct no information is available.[102]

VI. Arrest and Detention

In an attempt to specify the powers of the law enforcement authorities with regard to arrest and detention, Muslim jurists have discussed two sets of criteria, one of which refers to the character of the accused, and the other to the objective bases of suspicion. With reference to the former, the accused may fall under any of the following three categories:

Firstly, when the accused person is not known for criminality and corruption; there is no criminal record and the person evidently does not belong to what is phrased in Arabic as *ahl al-tuhmah*, the deviant type. Muslim jurists are in agreement that this type of accused may neither be arrested nor detained on the basis of a mere suspicion. It is added that this is precisely the type of suspicion, which the Qur'ān has proscribed and declared to be sinful. A mere suspicion in this case is not enough to warrant arrest unless it is accompanied by credible evidence. There is disagreement, however, as to whether the accuser himself may be liable to punishment, and the dominant of the two variant views on this validates a deterrent punishment for the accuser. This is necessary in order to prevent the miscreants from soiling the good name of upright and innocent individuals by launching hostile and malicious claims against them. Imam Mālik has held the view that the accuser should not be punished unless it can be proved that he had acted out of malice in order to harm the accused. The judge should not pay heed to such claims and should not even grant the claimant the opportunity to take an oath to fortify his claim. The Mālikī and the majority rulings on this issue pursue the same objective, which is to deter attack on the good name and reputation of upright individuals.[103]

Secondly, when the accused person is obscure and has no reputation either for uprightness or deviation. This type of accused may be arrested and detained according to the majority ruling for the purpose of investigation. Imam Mālik is also in agreement with the majority on this and the ruling here is founded in a *ḥadīth* in which Abū Hurayrah has reported that 'the Prophet, peace be on him, has detained a man on an accusation for a day and a night,' for the purpose apparently of investigation.[104]

أن النبي صلى الله عليه وسلم حبس رجلا فى تهمة يوما و ليلة .

Abū Dāwūd also records a different version of the same *ḥadīth* narrated by Bahz bin Ḥakīm which reads that 'the Prophet (pbuh) detained a man for an accusation and then released him.'[105] Then also Al-Tirmidhī has recorded, it seems, the same *ḥadīth* with a slight variation in the text. On this occasion, the *ḥadīth* reads 'the Prophet (pbuh) detained a man on an accusation for a portion of the day and then set him free.'

أن النبي صلى الله عليه وسلم حبس رجلا فى تهمة ساعة من نهار

ثم خلى سبيله .

There is apparently some discrepancy between these *ḥadīth* reports just reviewed with regard to the precise duration of detention period, whether it is 24 hours or a portion of time within the same day. What is clear from all these reports and constitutes a common theme between them is the validity of detention for a brief perid of an accused person for purposes of investigation. I might attempt to reconcile the ḥadīths under review by saying that detention may be within the same day or upto 24 hours.

While quoting the first of these three reports, Ibn Qayyim wrote that 'the agreed upon principles among the leading imams support this position.' For they agree, Ibn Qayyim added, that the judge is under duty to summon the defendant when there is a claim against him in order to adjudicate between them. But then if the accused has traveled a distance and it is not possible to adjudicate the case within the same day, the judge would have little choice but to detain the accused. This is valid not only in criminal litigation but also in financial disputes. Ibn Qayyim added that detention does not necessarily mean imprisonment in a confined space. It means restricting a person's freedom of movement and it may be in any place, including his own house. The judge may also assign a person to watch over the accused and follow his movements, or take a surety from him.[106]

To limit the initial period of preventive detention to 24 hours, as indicated in the *ḥadīth*, seems to be the preferred position to begin with. Some jurists have recorded the view that this may be extended to two days, and then to three days. But then there is disagreement as to the maximum duration of preventive custody. There are basically two opinions on this, one of which, held mainly by the Shāfiʿīs, has determined it to be one month. If by this time the facts are still not known, the accused should be released forthwith. The second view on this refers the matter to the discretion and *ijtihād* of the head of state and his representatives, with the recommendation that the detention should not be lengthy and be terminated whenever possible without delay.[107] Al-Māwardī explains that some jurists have stated a maximum limit of one month of detention for purposes of investigation. Others have suggested different time limits, 'but the best view is that the Imam may specify the limit as he deems fit.'[108] This latter view would bring the issue under the umbrella of *siyāsah sharʿiyyah*, a subject, which I have discussed elsewhere.[109] Suffice it here to note that siyāsah sharʿiyyah itself may be regulated by means of statutory legislation and it would in principle be valid for the Imam to impose statutory limitations on preventive detention.

Thirdly, when the accused is known for wrongdoing and the accusation against him appears consistent with his reputation and record. The majority of jurists have in this case validated preventive detention for purposes of investigation. According to one view, the accused may be detained for a longer period than one month, if the charge against him gains further ground, but he may neither be beaten nor persecuted. The preferred view is that the matter should be determined by the authorities who should mainly consider the strength or weakness of the accusation and may detain the accused for a longer period than the accused whose condition is unknown.[110] The detention here is basically aimed at facilitating investigation and it is not meant to either punish or intimidate the accused. It seems that beating this type of person is also permitted, although the ʿulamā' have recorded different views on this, as I shall later elaborate. A mere denial, even under oath, by the accused of the charges laid against him, is not enough to warrant his release, and it is essential that the truth or falsehood of the accusation is established through evidence. The ruler and judge may consequently detain him for the duration of the investigation. Those who have validated beating, and this includes Mālikī and Ḥanbalī jurists, maintain that beating should be by the whip. The length of detention is not specified according to the preferred view, although some ʿulamā' have held, as noted above, that detention for investigation may not exceed one month.[111] In response to the question as to whether the judge or the Imam or both have discretion to order detention for the purpose of investigation, the jurists have disagreed but the preferred view is that the order may be issued by either.[112]

The second of the two sets of criteria under discussion refers to the nature of the activity itself and the visible aspects of suspicious conduct that prompts the arrest and detention of a suspect. The proponents of this view proceed on the assumption that knowledge of the personal character of individuals is often not available to law enforcement authorities, and it is therefore preferable that the decision whether or not to detain a person should be based on objective and visible factors, which must contemplate the violation or suspicious conduct itself. Thus a person may not be arrested on mere suspicion, which is not substantiated by circumstantial evidence and clues (*al-adillah wa'l-qarā'in*). Suspicion alone should not be mistaken for evidence, for it is neither evidence, nor a *qarīnah*, and if an arrest were to be based on it, there must be something more than a mere doubt (*al-shak*) which turns it into a permissible suspicion (*al-ẓann al-mubāḥ*). An example of unfounded suspicion would be to arrest someone on suspicion of burglary without there being any clue to support that suspicion. This is the impermissible, or malicious, suspicion (*al-ẓann al-sū'*) which the Qur'ān has proscribed as it violates the individual's right to personal security. The Prophet has equated this kind of suspicion with the worst kind of lie (*akdhab al-ḥadīth*) as it has no basis in reality and originates in malice.[113]

In their attempt to distinguish the permissible suspicion (*al-ẓann al-mubāḥ*) from the blameworthy suspicion (*al-ẓann al-madhmūm* or *al-ẓann al-sū'*), the majority of 'ulamā' prefer to combine the two criteria (i.e. the subjective and the objective) into a single formula. It is accordingly held that suspicion is forbidden in regard to individuals who have no reputation of wrongdoing and who are, by all appearance, upright, and there is also no objective basis, nor an apparent motive or circumstance for suspicion.

As for the question whether preventive detention is permissible, it is stated that since accusation is an unproven claim, and preventive detention is a serious restraint on personal liberty, the question naturally arises whether it is at all justified to detain a person on the basis of a mere accusation. The other and equally persuasive side of this argument, as already indicated, is that it is often necessary to detain the accused for the purpose of investigation so as to prevent his possible escape. Muslim jurists have held three different views on this, one of which maintains that pre-trial detention is unlawful; the second view validates preventive detention only in crimes that invoke a prescribed (*ḥadd*), or retaliatory (*qiṣāṣ*) punishment. The third view, which is held by the majority of jurists, validates preventive detention generally.

The first view, which is held by Ibn Ḥazm al-Ẓāhirī, and also by some Shāfiʿī and Ḥanbalī *ʿulamā'*, proceeds from the original principle of non-liability (*barā'ah al-dhimmah al-aṣliyyah*) and maintains that the accused is not liable for anything prior to proof. Detaining the accused on the basis of accusation alone is tantamount to oppression and a violation of his right, which must be avoided. The proponents of this view have quoted in support the precedent of the caliph ʿUmar al-Khaṭṭāb in a case in which one ʿAbd Allāh ibn Abī ʿĀmir had his leather bag stolen while on a journey together with a group of others. One of the men in the group was suspected of the theft and was questioned for it but he denied the charge. Abu ʿĀmir later reported the case to the caliph who asked as to how many of them were travelling and the caliph was informed of this. Abu ʿĀmir then said: 'O Commander of the Faithful! I had intended to bring the accused tied up before you.' To this the caliph expressed anger and said 'You tie him up and bring him without any evidence? I shall not write nor ask anything about this.' Abu ʿĀmir then said that the caliph refused to take any action.[114] The caliph evidently disapproved of the accused being tied up in fetters, which is equivalent to detention, while there was no evidence to support the accusation.

Imam Abū Ḥanīfa's disciple, Abū Yūsuf, has also advanced a forceful argument to the effect that no one should be detained on the basis of a mere claim by another person. To quote Abū Yūsuf:

It is not permissible to imprison a person because of the accusation of another person. The Prophet, peace be on him, did not arrest people on the basis of accusation (*al-qadhaf*) only, but it is proper to bring the accuser and the defendant together. If the former produces positive evidence in support of his claim, the judgment will be issued in his favour, otherwise a surety is taken from the defendant and he is released. If the defendant subsequently clarifies something (it may be considered) otherwise he should not be pressurised. This should also apply to everyone who is detained on suspicion. The Companions of the Prophet, peace be on him, were cautious about imposing punishments (lest they harm the innocent).[115]

The basic outline of the generally approved procedure is in conformity with this view, and the procedure may be expanded as follows: when the plaintiff presents his claim against the defendant and the judge has no reason to believe that it is unfounded and controversial, it becomes the duty of the judge to summon the defendant to attend a court hearing concerning the claim.[116] If the plaintiff subsequently presents valid evidence, the court adjudicates on its basis; otherwise the court takes a guarantor (*kafīl*) from the defendant and releases him there and then. The strength of this position impresses itself when it is acknowledged that detention is a punishment and it may not be imposed in anything less than what is obligatory and proven, or there is an imminent fear of escape. No one should be detained on the basis of an unfounded accusation, and no one may be incarcerated until the facts are established.[117]

The second view on preventive detention is held by the majority of the Ḥanafīs and it validates preventive detention of the accused in the prescribed offences of *ḥudūd* and cases of retaliation (*qiṣāṣ*), but not in pecuniary claims. This view is based on the analysis that imprisonment is the most that can possibly be ordered in pecuniary claims, after the claim is proven, hence it would be excessive to impose that punishment prior to proof and on the basis only of a claim. But since the *ḥudūd* and *qiṣāṣ* offences involve punishment of greater severity than imprisonment, the latter may be imposed for the purpose of investigation.[118]

Thirdly, the majority view which validates preventive detention in all crimes, including financial crimes, is based on the analysis that setting the accused free during the investigation and trial is likely to lead to miscarriage of justice if he escapes, tries to influence the witnesses, or destroys incriminating evidence. The majority have quoted in authority for this the *ḥadīth* we have reviewed earlier in which the Prophet (pbuh) has detained an accused person for a short period and set him free afterwards.

According to yet another *ḥadīth* on the authority of a Follower (*tābiʿī*), Azhar b. ʿAbd Allāh bin Jāmiʿ al-Harazī, which is a *mursal ḥadīth*, it is reported:

A group of people brought a claim of theft against some weavers to a Companion, Nuʿmān bin Bashīr, who detained the accused persons for a few days and then released them. The plaintiffs protested to Nuʿmān that 'you released them without beating them or testing their veracity,' to which Nuʿmān replied: 'What would you have done? You might have beaten them and procured your goods, but if you punished them wrongfully, you would be liable to retaliation yourselves.' The accusers then asked: 'Is this your judgment?' Nuʿmān replied: 'This is the judgment of God and His Messenger.'[119]

حدثنا أزهر ابن عبد الله الحرازى، أنّ قوما من الكلاعيين سُرق لهـم متاعٌ، فاتهموا أناسـا مـن الحاكـة، فأتو النعمـان بن بشير صاحب النبى صلى الله عليه وسلم فحبسهم أياما ثم خلى سـبيلهم، فأتوا النعمان فقالوا: خليـت سبيلهم بـغير ضرب ولا امتحان، فقال النعمان: ماشئتم، إن شئتم أن أضربهم فإن خرج متاعكم فذاك وإلا أخذت مـن ظهـوركم مثـل مـا أخذت مـن ظهورهـم فقالوا: هذا حكمـك؟ فقال هذا حكـم الله وحكـم رسولٌ الله صلى الله عليه وسلم.

The conclusion has thus been drawn that if detention were impermissible, Nuʿmān would not have detained the accused persons nor would have he said that this was the judgment of God and His Messenger.

Quoted in support is also the Qur'ānic verse, which validates a brief detention of witnesses, in the case of a bequest, which is made during a journey but the testator has later died. The text thus provides:

تحبسـونهمـا مـن بعد الصلوة فيقسمان بالله إن ارتبتـم لانشترى به ثمنا ولو كان ذا قربى ولاتكتم الشهادة.

(If you doubt their testimony), then detain them after the prayer, and let them swear by God (saying): We will not take for it a price even if it be a relative nor will we hide the testimony...(5:106).

The text thus permits the temporary detention of witnesses that are suspected of perjury, in order to verify the truth of their testimony. The detention here is evidently precautionary, not punitive, and is intended to prevent a misappropriation of the property of a deceased person, and the text is therefore quoted to validate preventive detention for the purposes of investigation. 'Detain them after the prayer,' in the text quoted above, evidently refers to a brief detention, presumably until the next prayer time on the same day, and may well be within the perimeters of the mosques and may not even involve detention in the usual sense of the word.

As for the argument that detention violates the presumption of innocence, it is stated that this presumption remains intact, and detention prior to proof is not a punitive but a precautionary measure, which is justified to prevent an escape, especially in claims that are supported by credible clues (*al-qarā'in*).[120]

VII. The Issue of Beating the Accused

Al-Shāṭibī wrote that the *'ulamā'* disagree about the permissibility of beating the accused; those who validate preventive detention of the accused also validate beating him (or her), since both inflict punishment and partake of the attributes of one another. Imam Mālik has validated the detention of the accused, and his followers also uphold the permissibility of beating. Al-Shāṭibī, himself a Mālikī, upheld the Mālikī position when he added that 'if beating and detention were not permitted, it would be difficult to retrieve the properties of the people from thieves and usurpers.'[121] It is difficult to ascertain the majority position on this issue, since some of the references made in *fiqh* books to 'majority ruling' or 'predominant position,' turn out to be somewhat doubtful. What seems certain is that many jurists have upheld the validity of beating during detention only if the accused is a known criminal, and they are almost unanimous in saying that beating is not permissible when the accused is known to be a person of good reputation and integrity. The majority position may nevertheless be stated as follows: When the accused is known for criminality and corruption and has been arrested for serious crimes such as murder and theft, he may be beaten and detained 'until his condition becomes known.' But if the accused is not known for criminality, he may be held in preventive custody but may not be beaten.[122]

Disagreement among the *'ulamā'* prevails over the permissibility or otherwise of beating a person who is obscure, and his past record cannot be verified. A number of early jurists, including Aṣbagh, Ibn Ḥazm and al-Ghazālī, proscribe beating during investigation altogether, including that of the accused who has a criminal record.[123] Both the opponents and the proponents of beating have referred to evidence that consists of several reported *ḥadīth*s and incidents that took place during the time of the Companions. The evidence remains somewhat interpretational and inconclusive—some of which has been quoted by both sides, each drawing a totally different conclusion from it.

Al-Māwardī spoke in support of beating when he wrote that 'depending on the strength of the accusation, it is permissible for the *amīr* (governor) to give the accused a *taʿzīr*-based beating (*ḍarb al-taʿzīr*) but not a beating that is *ḥadd*-based, in order to find out the truth concerning his condition and the accusation levelled against him. If he makes a confession after having been beaten, the confession is admissible, but not if it is made during the beating.' Māwardī then adds that if the accused later confirms the confession he made under pain of punishment, his subsequent confirmation will be taken into account.[124] Māwardī has not explained how a *taʿzīr* –based beating differs from a *ḥadd*-based beating. One might speculate perhaps that he meant a lighter beating than what may be acceptable for a confirmed criminal. This is a point of ambiguity in his writing. And then he clearly states that a confession made during beating is not admissible but one that is made after it is. The logic of this position also seems to be less than sound. A contemporary writer on the subject, Fahd al-Suwaylim, has reviewed the detailed evidence and reached the conclusion, without specifying any particular type or class of accused persons, that beating is permissible provided that it is not excessive but enough to pressurise the accused whose accusation is supported by circumstantial evidence, including his past record, but adds that this does not include inhuman methods of torture such as electric shocks, nail pulling and the like.[125]

My own examination of the evidence leads me to the conclusion that passing an affirmative judgment on the permissibility of beating during interrogation can only be sustained with reference to dangerous criminals, but that taking a general position of the kind that Suwaylim has taken is ultimately self-defeating and futile. To validate beating during interrogation is untenable simply because it fails to meet the basic requirement of *Sharīʿah* that a confession must be voluntary and free of duress. The accused may not, in other words, be forced to make a confession. He is entitled to remain silent and refuse to give self-incriminating evidence.

The accused may also choose not to respond to questions. If he or she does respond and it is later determined that the answers were false, he or she may not be charged with, or punished for, giving false testimony. In the event where the accused confesses to a *ḥadd* offence, he or she may retract his or her statement and thereby nullify the confession. The accused may likewise not be made to make a confession under hypnotism, truth serum or under the influence of drugs.[126] The main argument against the exercise of coercion in order to extract a confession is presented by al-Ghazālī, and although it is said to be a minority view,[127] it stands on a stronger foundation, and draws support from several *ḥadīth*s which al-Ghazālī has quoted and which may be summarised as follows:

Firstly, the *ḥadīth* of Farewell Pilgrimage in which the Prophet declared, in an address to the believers:

فإن الله تبارك وتعالى قد حرّم دماءكم وأموالكم وأعراضكم إلا بحقها.

Everything that belongs to a Muslim, his blood, his property and his honour is forbidden to his fellow Muslim.[128]

'Everything that belongs to a Muslim,' naturally includes his personal safety from beating and persecution, unless it is in the course of justice. The substance of this *ḥadīth* is confirmed by the *ḥadīth* quoted above, of al-Nuʿman bin Bashīr, who released a group of persons who had been accused of theft for lack of evidence; had beating and torture been permissible, Nuʿmān might have beaten them in order to procure a confession. According to yet another *ḥadīth*, the Prophet has said concerning a woman who had a reputation for debauchery and corruption:

لو رجمت أحدا بغير بيّنة رجمت هذه

If I were to stone anyone without evidence,
I would have stoned this woman.[129]

It is thus concluded that the Prophet did not resort to punishment, even concerning a person who had a reputation for wrongdoing.

Ibn ʿAbbās has reported an incident in which a slave woman complained to the Caliph ʿUmar b. al-Khaṭṭāb that her master accused her of adultery and forced her to sit on fire that resulted in injury to her vagina. The caliph then asked her if the man had seen her doing what he accused her of doing, to which she replied 'No'. She was then asked if she had confessed to anything, to which she also replied in the negative. The caliph then asked the man the same questions of whether he had seen her committing adultery, and whether she had confessed to anything herself. To both of these, the man replied in the negative. The caliph then said 'By God if I had not heard the Messenger of God saying that 'the master is not retaliated for his slave nor the father for his son,' I would have retaliated in the like manner.'[130] Then the caliph flogged the man one hundred lashes and told the woman that 'you are now free from his bondage.'

The conclusion has thus been drawn that the Caliph ʿUmar was so incensed that he punished the man for the torture he had inflicted on the woman based only on suspicion and unproven accusation.

Al-Ghazālī has gone so far as to say that beating is prohibited even in accusations involving hardened criminals. A mere reputation or past record of criminality is not enough to warrant beating the accused before trial. If the accused had committed a crime in the past and was punished for it, then punishing him again on that basis is oppressive. To say that one accusation is proven by a previous incident is equally nonsensical and unjustified. The life and right to safety of every individual are sacrosanct and a departure from this position is warranted only on the basis of proof of criminality.[131]

As for the relevance of *maṣlaḥah* to the issue of pretrial beating, al-Ghazālī has observed that punishing the accused on the basis of the supposed benefit, or *maṣlaha*, of the community in the name of crime prevention is tantamount to certainty being overruled by doubt. Even if beating the accused is considered a *maṣlaha*, it falls into conflict with a greater *maṣlaha*, which is the sanctity of people's lives and properties. A *maṣlaḥah* based on doubt is thus given preference over one based on certainty. Al-Ghazālī has thus reached the conclusion that *maṣlaḥah* is not the right context by which to determine the issue. For there are opposing interests involved, one of which is that of the accuser, and society at large, on the one hand, and that of the accused person on the other. The former is in need of proof whereas the latter is not; the latter should therefore take priority, not vice versa. 'The *Sharīʿah* does not permit punishing anyone other than a criminal, and a crime needs to be proven. When there is no proof, there is no crime and therefore no punishment.'[132]

Al-Ghazālī then refers to the view that validates beating the accused person charged with theft in the hope of recovering stolen goods from him. This is unjustified, al-Ghazālī says, for two reasons, one of which is that he may very well be innocent and attacking him on the basis of doubt is unjustified. The other weakness here is that beating the accused under accusation of theft means that a property-related interest is given priority over the inviolability of the human person, which is unjustified. The principle to be upheld is once again the same: that there is to be no punishment without proof of a crime. When this is neglected, corruption sets in and our effort must be to avert corruption at its source.[133] This is also the view, as already noted, of Ibn Ḥazm al-Ẓāhirī and one of the early Mālikī jurists, Aṣbagh, who have considered beating the accused totally impermissible. The proponents of this view have added that there is no report of any incident where the Companions might have beaten or tortured the accused without proof, despite the relatively high crime rate that was experienced in that period. This is because the Companions had a sound understanding of the *Sharīʿah* guidelines, which maintain a restrictive, rather than expansive, approach concerning proof of the *ḥudūd* offences. The *Sharīʿah* outlook on this is expounded in the *ḥadīth* in which it is provided that 'anyone who commits any one of these heinous acts (i.e. the *ḥudūd* crimes), let it be concealed in God's concealment.'[134]

Al-Ghazālī also wrote that beating the accused forces him to make a confession, and a confession under duress is of no value.[135] A reference is here made to the *ḥadīth* in which the Prophet proclaimed:

تجاوز الله عن أمتى الخطاء والنسيان ومااستكرهوا عليه.

God has forgiven my community for what they do by mistake, out of forgetfulness, and under compulsion.[136]

There is general agreement on the principle that confession obtained under duress is null and void. Imam Mālik has said that 'confession to a crime obtained after a threat, a promise, imposition of restriction on one's movement, beating or imprisonment is invalid and fails to provide a basis for punishment.'[137] The Ḥanafī jurist al-Sarakhsī also wrote: 'when the judge compels a man by threatening him, or beating him, or subjecting him to restriction or imprisonment to incriminate himself in respect of a prescribed offence (*ḥadd*) or retaliation (*qiṣāṣ*), the confession is null and void.' Al-Sarakhsī then quotes the caliph ʿUmar's statement, cited above, that a man is never secure when he is in pain and frightened and incriminates himself.[138]

The proponents of pretrial beating have quoted the following evidence in support of their position:

1 Anas bin Mālik reported that a Jewish man crushed the head of a woman in between two stones and the case was brought before the Prophet, where the victim barely managed to identify her attacker. The Prophet did not release the accused until he confessed to his crime, for which he was retaliated against in a like manner.[139]

عن أنس بن مالك رضى الله عنه: أن جارية وجد رأسها قد
رضّ بين حجرين، فيسالوها من صنع هذا بك؟ فلان؟ حتى
ذكروا يهوديا. فأومأت برأسها، فأخذ اليهودي فأقرّ، فأمر به
رسول الله صى الله عليه وسلم أن يرضّ راسه بالحجارة.

The conclusion drawn from this *ḥadīth* is that the Jew did not make a confession at first and it appears that he was threatened or beaten until he made one, hence the permissibility of beating the accused during investigation. However, bearing in mind the circumstances here, it seems rather a doubtful case from which to generalize the permissibility of beating during investigation.

2 It is reported in connection with the story of Ḥāṭib Ibn Abi Baltaʿa that when the Prophet decided to conquer Mecca, Ḥāṭib wrote a letter to the Meccans about the Prophet's intention, and sent it with a woman he trusted. When the Prophet learned of this, he sent Ali ibn Abī Ṭālib, Zubayr and Miqdād to stop her and retrieve the letter. So they went riding on horses until they found the woman and asked her to hand over the letter. She said 'I have no letter with me.' But she was told: 'Either you hand over the letter or your clothes will be searched inside out.' Then she brought the letter out of the pleats of her hair.[140]

سمعت عليا عليه السلام يقول: بعثنى رسول الله صلى الله
عليه وسلم أنا والزبير والمقداد، فقال: انطلقوا حتى تأتوا روضة
خاخ فإن بها ظعينة معها كتاب فخذوه منها...فإذا نحن
بالظعينة فقلنا هلمى الكتاب، فقالت: ما عندى من الكتاب،
فقلت: لتخرجنّ الكتاب أو لنلقينّ الثياب، فأخرجته من
عقاصها.

The fact that the said Companions threatened the woman and pressurised her is taken to point to the permissibility of applying punitive tactics on an accused person for the purposes of investigation.[141]

3 Anas ibn Mālik has reported that the Prophet sent out a reconnaissance party to Badr. On their way to Badr, they met some camel

riders of the Quraysh tribe and there was among them a black slave of the clan of Bani al-Hajjāj. The Companions seized the man and questioned him about Abu Sufyān and his followers. The man said: 'I do not know about Abu Sufyān but these are Abu Jahl, Shībah, ʿUtbah and Umayyah ibn Khalaf.' They beat him until he said: 'Yes I can tell you this is Abu Sufyān.' So they let him go, but then he was asked the same question again, and again he denied knowing anything about Abu Sufyān. Upon hearing this, they beat him again. The Prophet had by then finished his prayer and when he noted what had happened, he said: 'By the One in Whose hands my life reposes: you beat him when he told you the truth and you released him when he lied to you.'[142]

والذى نفسى بيده إنكم لتضربونه إذا صدقكم وتدعونه إذا كذبكم.

In this episode, since the Companions beat the man on the basis of suspicion, it is said to be indicative of permissibility for authorities to threaten an accused person and beat him until he tells the truth. But drawing such a conclusion is unwarranted since the Prophet himself is reported to have cast doubt on what the Companions had done.

4   In connection with the incident of the slander of the Prophet's wife, ʿĀʾishah, it is reported that the Prophet summoned ʿĀʾishah's servant, Barīrah, and questioned her about the incident. ʿAlī, who was present on the occasion, struck Barīrah hard and told her to reveal the truth to the Prophet. Barīrah spoke and told them all that she knew about ʿĀʾishah, and her account was nothing but good. She then told them about the household work she had done during the day, but this did not bring any new information either.[143]

It is then concluded form this incident that ʿAlī suspected Barīrah of hiding information and struck her on that basis, which indicates the permissibility of what he did, especially in view of the fact that the Prophet did not object to his action.[144] Ibn Qayyim has observed that 'Beating is permissible for someone who is believed to know the truth but denies it, and the ʿulamāʾ are in agreement on this.'[145] With specific reference to 'the accused who is known—*idhā ʿurifa*—to be in possession of (stolen) goods but conceals them and denies it—he is beaten in order to confess, and there is no doubt in this. He is beaten in order to fulfill an obligation, which is to return the stolen property to its owner.'[146]

Having upheld the permissibility of beating notorious criminals, Ibn Qayyim adds that they should be first tested with detention, and then beaten, but only with a whip. Then he raises the question which many have raised as to whether the beating should be authorised by the governor (*amīr*) or the judge (*qāḍi*), to which the preferable answer is that the *amīr* but not the *qāḍi* should authorise it. This is because the 'only legitimate beating that a judge can order is related to the prescribed offences (*ḥudūd*) and (*ta ᶜzir*), which can, however, only be imposed after acquisition of the proof of the offence in question and knowledge of its causes.'[147] The *qāḍi*, in other words, should not be in a position to order punishment both before *and* after proof of the crime, and if a degree of arbitrariness is involved in pre-trial beating, it should not be undertaken by the *qadi*. It is also the task of the *amir* and not directly of the *qāḍi* to combat criminality and corruption, and to deal with hardened criminals. The judge's main concern is to vindicate the rights of the people through valid reasoning and proof, and the court should as far as possible be kept clear of controversial practices and duties which properly belong to the police.

Ibn Farḥūn has also referred to Ibn Qayyim on the issue of beating and has, in fact, quoted the above passage in reference only to:

One who is accused of crimes such as theft, highway robbery, murder and adultery. These may be interrogated and pressurised in proportion to the nature of the accusation and their reputation for such (crimes). They may sometimes be beaten, or detained without beating, depending on their past record and reputation. Ibn Qayyim al-Jawziyya al-Ḥanbalī has said... (here follows the passage that I quoted above).

Ibn Farḥūn closes his discussion by saying once again that 'It is permissible to beat or detain this category of accused persons when there is valid *Sharīᶜah* evidence (to warrant it).'[148]

The Mālikī jurist al-Bājī has written with reference to

The accused who is obscure and has no criminal record, the manifest *ẓāhir* ruling of the *Mudawwanah* requires that he may not be beaten but may be asked to take an oath (as to his innocence), and according to one opinion, he should be released without taking an oath. The position, therefore, is that if the accused has a corresponding reputation, he may be threatened, detained and put on oath, but if he has no such reputation, he may not be subjected to any of these, and if he is an upright person, his accuser may be punished.[149]

Ibn Farḥūn quotes al-Bājī's statement, as above, *in toto,* only to agree with it and confirm it.[150]

Al-ʿAlwāni has also discussed the views of some ʿulamā' on this issue and has, in particular, quoted Ibn ʿĀbidin's opinion, which is as follows:

'Beating one who is accused of theft is a matter of judicial policy, so opined al-Zaylaʿī. A *qāḍi* may do what is politically expedient, as policy matters are not the exclusive domain of the Imam.'

Having quoted Ibn ʿĀbidīn, al-ʿAlwānī then responded that

'there is nothing to support the opinions offered by these scholars.... Moreover none of these reasons refute or even weaken the evidence gathered by the majority of jurists that it is illegal to obtain a confession through the use (or threat) of force. Their opinions would be valid if there were contributing circumstances indicating clearly that the accused was guilty....'[151]

Clearly the ʿulamā' disagree about the legality of beating. Ibn Qayyim, al-Bājī and Ibn Farḥūn have restricted beating during interrogation to only one class of accused persons, namely notorious criminals, especially in cases of theft and highway robbery, where the veracity of a possible confession can be ascertained by the subsequent discovery or otherwise of the stolen goods that the accused might have concealed.

Moreover, having summarised the evidence in the *Sunnah* in support of beating the accused, we note that none of the four *ḥadīth*s quoted above provide conclusive evidence, as virtually every one of them is open to interpretation. Ibn Ḥazm al-Ẓāhirī has discussed most of the relevant *ḥadīth*s and explained why they are doubtful as basis for action:

With regard to the first report, he notes that it is vague and does not establish the fact of whether the Prophet threatened or punished the Jew before he made a confession; it remains, in other words, inconclusive.[152]

With reference to the second report, it is suggested that the Prophet knew for a fact that the woman was carrying the letter in question; so it was not a case of mere accusation, but one which involved acting on the basis of knowledge. This *ḥadīth* is therefore not relevant to the subject.

As for the third *ḥadīth*, the Prophet actually expressed disapproval of punishing the black man, and his remark intimates that those who punished the accused should have been more careful in the first place. It cannot, therefore, establish the permissibility of pretrial beating.

With reference to the fourth *ḥadīth* concerning Barīrah, there is once again some doubt in respect of the precise detail of what happened on the occasion. For the same *ḥadīth* has been reported in some collections with the words that 'some of the Companions rebuked her (*intaharahā*) and told her to tell the truth to the Messenger of God...' There is no mention of beating Barīrah in this version of the *ḥadīth*, and the facts of the matter remain in doubt.

To sum up, the permissibility of beating the accused during investigation requires decisive proof, which is available neither in the Qur'ān nor the *Sunnah*. What remains for us to discuss here is the case for considerations of public interest (*maṣlaḥa*), which the advocates of beating have used as the centerpiece of their juristic reasoning. Al–Shāṭibi has examined the evidence from the viewpoint of *maṣlaḥah* and I summarise his argument as follows:

With regard to beating the accused, the *ʿulamāʾ* are in disagreement. Those who have validated detention of the accused have also validated beating, for detention is a form of torture and so is beating. The advocates of this view have equated their position with that of the responsibility of the trustee in the manufacture of goods, such as a tailor who receives a piece of cloth from a client to make a dress. The trustee (*amīn*) is normally not responsible for damage to or loss of the goods in his custody unless he is shown to be negligent. But the *ʿulamāʾ* have held that the trustee in the manufacture of goods is a guarantor who is responsible for the loss of goods that are placed in his custody.

I may intervene here to explain that the analogy between beating a detainee and the responsibility of a trustee has an aspect in common, which is that both involve a measure of arbitrary judgment, as the upright and the miscreant are in both cases treated on the same footing. But then it is stated that if beating and detention of the accused were not allowed, it would be difficult to protect peoples' properties against thieves and usurpers, as producing incriminating evidence is usually difficult, especially in the case of theft. The benefit or *maṣlaḥah* that is involved in holding the trustee responsible for the loss of goods in his custody is upheld by general consensus (*ijmāʿ*), and the same logic is now extended to the case of beating the accused.

As for the objection that beating in this case might mean torturing the innocent, which amounts to prejudice (*ḍarar*), al–Shāṭibi wrote:

'To do otherwise might be even more harmful. This is notwithstanding the fact that no-one validates beating on the basis of a mere claim, but only when the latter is accompanied by supportive clues (*qarā'in*) that in the thought and judgment of the observer create a reasonable suspicion. The innocent is therefore not very likely to become a victim of prejudice; but if he does so, then that partakes of a pardonable error, somewhat similar, that is, to the error that is possible in the case of a craftsman who is held responsible for the damage and loss of the goods he has received into his custody.'

As for the objection that beating is futile if it leads to a confession that is in any case null and void, it is said 'If it leads to retrieving the stolen property, then it is beneficial.' If the accused who is beaten or threatened with beating makes a confession, which leads to the discovery of stolen goods, then the confession in question may also be validated. Beating the accused also serves as a deterrent, which dissuades people from criminality and corruption.[153]

The whole of this argument is thus premised on considerations of public interest, which also involve the possibility of mischief (*mafsadah*) arising in the process. In the event of a conflict between *maṣlaḥah* and *mafsadah*, the issue is normally determined on rational grounds, which takes into consideration the balance of evidence and the attending circumstances of each case.

I submit that the *maṣlaḥah* in question might have warranted a judgment in favour of beating the accused in earlier times when the police were on the whole poorly equipped with crime detection facilities. Although criminality remains a menace to society no less than it ever was perhaps, the police and law enforcement agencies are nevertheless better equipped now and can utilise more advanced methods, from finger-printing to laboratory analyses and data collection methods that were not possible in medieval times. This might mean that we ought to now give preference to the prevention of evil (*dar' al-mafsadah*) over the principle of securing a benefit, a position that is harmonious with the general guidance of *Sharīʿah* and the legal maxim that 'the prevention of harm takes priority over the securing of a benefit.'

Comparing the evidence for and against the permissibility of pretrial beating, it seems that the evidence against it is more persuasive, and also in harmony with the basic presumption in the *Sharīʿah* of original non-liability (*barā'a al-dhimma al-aṣliyya*) as the normal state unless proven otherwise. The case of dangerous criminals against whom society needs to be protected may be looked at individually within the context, perhaps, of *siyāsah sharʿiyyah*. As already noted, this doctrine entitles the head of state and the judge to exercise discretion in order to provide an adequate response to exceptional situations where the normal rules of law might fall short of providing one. The government may accordingly devise a special procedure for dangerous criminals and treat the issue on that basis. As for the permissibility in principle of pretrial beating, the case against it is clearly a stronger one. Since pretrial beating is aimed at extracting a self-incriminating confession from the accused, and confession under duress is invalid, it must therefore be seen as an exercise in futility and *ultra vires*.

VIII. Right to Counsel

The *Sharīʿah* recognises the right of both plaintiff and defendant to present evidence and to have access to counsel during pretrial interrogation, at the trial and, if the accused is convicted, at the execution of the sentence. The principle that applies here is that of *wakālah* (agency), and the parties are both equally entitled to appoint a representative. This is because it is possible that the party concerned is not sufficiently knowledgeable to present his or her case effectively, or that he or she is unable to attend court. There is no disagreement among the ʿulamāʾ about the validity of representation in all civil claims involving disputes over the Right of Man (*ḥaqq al-ādamī*), but the jurists have held different views on *wakāla* concerning matters that involve a violation of the Right of God (*ḥaqq Allāh*).

Representation (*wakālah*) may be in criminal or in civil disputes, and it may be with remuneration or without. If it is with remuneration, it is like *ijārah* or employment, and becomes binding on the basis of a contract between the principal (*muwakkil*) and the agent (*wakīl*). The terms of the contract, such as the agent's fees, and duration of time, are specified, and neither of the parties may withdraw unilaterally without the agreement of the other. But if *wakālah* is without remuneration, it becomes an act of charity on the part of the agent, and he is bound by it when he accepts to represent. The agent and the principal are both entitled, in this case, to terminate their agreement whenever they wish without the agreement of the other. The agent's freedom to terminate the *wakālah* is, however, restricted if his termination is harmful and leads to a loss of rights.[154]

Ibn Farḥūn has recorded a variant opinion on representation for fees in criminal disputes, as there is an element of uncertainty regarding the duration of time. *Wakālah* in criminal disputes could be lengthy and protracted unless the work involved is accurately defined. *Wakālah* is thus permissible when the agent is paid on daily or hourly basis.[155] If someone appoints a special *wakīl* by name to represent him in a particular dispute, the *wakīl* may not assign another person to act on his behalf, unless the principal had known that the *wakīl* he named might not personally attend to his case. The acting *wakīl* in this case is answerable to the principal party whose case he has undertaken, even if he has not been named in the original agreement.[156] The principal is in all cases entitled to dismiss his *wakīl* if the latter fails to fulfill his duty, or procrastinates, or is suspected of fraud or impropriety in representation.

In matters which involve admission or denial, either party to the dispute may appoint no more than one counsel or *wakīl*. A valid admission made by the *wakīl* normally binds the principal, provided that it is relevant to the case he has undertaken. In civil disputes, the admission of the *wakīl* is not valid if it deprives the principal of property or assets that he has lawfully owned.[157]

The presiding judge has some discretion in the acceptance of representation in the disputes he adjudicates. The judge may thus refuse to accept a counsel or attorney if it is known that the latter was specifically chosen in order to inflict harm on the opponent, or indeed a *wakīl* who is notorious for distortion, squabbling, and disturbance. It is for the judge to prevent this so that the court environment and the people at large are protected against distorted wrangling.[158]

There is disagreement among jurists about the permissibility of *wakālah* on the basis of win or lose assignments that partakes of the nature of *juʿalah*, or giving a prize. The *wakīl* is thus told that if he wins the case, he will be paid a fee but he will be paid nothing if he loses. Imam Mālik has considered this manner of *wakālah* to be reprehensible, but his disciples have held that the *wakīl* is entitled to *ajr al-mithl*, or the usual fee that is charged according to the market price. The reason Imam Mālik considered the *juʿalah*-based *wakālah* to be reprehensible is because uncertainty that is involved, and the possibility of it leading to conflict. According to another report from Imam Mālik, which Ibn Farḥūn has also recorded, this kind of agreement (i.e. no-win, no-fee) is permissible because of people's need for it. This latter view would appear to be in harmony with the fact that *juʿalah* is a valid contract in *Sharīʿah* and the issue that is raised here is also a typical case of *juʿalah*, and there is no compelling evidence to make an exception to that basic position of permissibility.[159]

The Ḥanafīs have expressed reservations about *wakālah* with regard to the prescribed offences of *ḥadd* that consist mainly of the Right of

God. Thus it is said that in *ḥadd* offences such as adultery and wine-drinking, the issue before the judge is usually in respect of the sufficiency or otherwise of proof, as these offences usually do not involve litigation, and judicial proceedings regarding them consist mainly of the presentation of evidence, often with no plaintiff or private litigant. Since the *ḥadd* offences of adultery and wine-drinking usually do not involve a private claim, representation in them is said to be unnecessary. If the proof consists of confession, then *wakālah* is not valid in confessions, and if it consists of testimony, once again, there is no need for *wakālah*. But if the offence in question consists mainly of a violation of the Right of Man, such as a slanderous accusation, the dominant Ḥanafī view permits representation on either side.[160] The Shāfiʿīs have generally concurred with the Ḥanafīs, and consider representation in prescribed (*ḥudūd*) offences to be invalid, except in slanderous accusation, on the analysis that the Sharīʿah advises restraint in the proof of the *ḥudūd* offences wherein representation (by the state prosecutor) usually seeks to promote and facilitate proof.[161]

It will be noted, however, that this whole argument is somewhat lop sided since representation may seek to disprove and deny the charge, just as it may also seek to secure the proof of the *ḥudūd*. This is why the Mālikīs and the Ḥanbalīs maintain the view that representation is valid in all offences, including the *ḥudūd*. The head of state may be represented by the public prosecutor in such offences, just as the defendant may also wish to be represented in court. This is the majority view, and it applies equally to offences involving just retaliation (*qiṣāṣ*) and deterrent punishment (*taʿzīr*). For they too involve violations of the Right of Man, and *wakāla* in them is valid, despite some differences of opinion that have arisen over the details. The right to be represented by a counsel is thus a general right that extends to all disputes.

A question arises concerning the consent of one's opponent in the event where only one of the two sides resorts to *wakālah*. Imam Abu Ḥanīfa has held that *wakāla* in such a case is not valid without the consent of the other litigant, who may well be unable to have a representative *wakīl* and may also be unable to defend himself well. The opponent's consent is not necessary, however, according to this view, in situations of necessity, such as traveling or illness, or when a woman does not wish to mix with men and appoints a *wakīl* to handle the case on her behalf. This is valid even without the consent of the other party. The majority, that is, the Shāfiʿīs, Mālikīs, Ḥanbalīs and the two disciples of Abū Ḥanīfa, Abū Yūsuf and al-Shaybānī have ruled, however, that *wakālah* is permissible generally with or without the consent of the opponent. They maintain that the disagreement of one litigant should not deprive the other of his or her right to representation. One of the parties may well be unable to defend himself and wish to be represented, just as it is possible that the other party is more capable of defending himself personally, and decides not to appoint a *wakīl*. Now if we make these decisions contingent on the consent of the other party, it might cause harm, and lead to delays if the consent is not granted in good time.[162]

Muslim jurists are generally in agreement that the purpose of representation, whether in civil litigation or crime, is to vindicate the truth and facilitate justice. Representation may not, in other words, seek to distort justice and advocate falsehood by recourse to deceitful and time-consuming methods. Hence, it is forbidden for a person to represent another in the event where the former knows that his principal is in the wrong.[163] Representation is valid, however, in the event where the representative only doubts the veracity of his client's claim. Textual authority for these views is found in the Qur'ānic address to the Prophet: ولا تكن للخائنين خصيما 'Be not a pleader on behalf of the treacherous' (4:105).

Some jurists have gone so far as to maintain that it is not permissible for anyone to litigate on behalf of another unless he knows the truth of the matter. If it appears to him to be a right cause, he should accept representation, but he should otherwise reject it. Representation is therefore unlawful in the event where it seeks to distort the truth in pursuit of falsehood.[164] Support for this position also comes from the *ḥadīth*, reported by ʿĀ'ishah, that the Prophet, peace be on him, said:

$$\text{أبغض الرجال إلى الله تعالى الألد الخصم.}$$

The most disliked man before God Most High is one
who stubbornly litigates in pursuit of falsehood.[165]

According to another *ḥadīth*:

$$\text{ومن خاصم فى باطل وهو يعلم لم يزل فى سخط الله عز وجل}$$
$$\text{حتى ينزع.}$$

One who litigates in pursuit of falsehood while he knows it shall remain
afflicted with the wrath of God until he disengages himself from it.[166]

Court decisions must accordingly be founded on what is known to be the truth, and everyone involved, including the judge, witnesses, and litigants are bound by this requirement.

IX. Trial and Evidence

The discussion in the following pages highlights aspects of court procedure on trial and evidence, and offers a review of the guidelines of the Qur'ān and *Sunnah* on the subjects of testimony (*shahādah*), confession (*iqrar*), evidence in general (*bayyinah*) and circumstantial evidence (*qarīnah*).

A Trial Procedure

It is the responsibility of the judge to ensure a fair trial in all the disputes he adjudicates. There is much detail in the *fiqh* literature on the subject of *adab al-qāḍi*, which is concerned with the due process of trial in the court of *Sharīʿah*, salient points of which are summarised in the following pages.

It is important that disputes are promptly received and impartially adjudicated. The judge may not, therefore, delay a case presented to him unless it is for a valid reason. He may not leave the court, or make himself inaccessible, except in times of recess and rest. Should there be a delay in court proceedings whereby the court cannot proceed with a hearing as expected, the parties may not be held in suspense and should be informed of the delay promptly.

It is not permissible for a judge to adjudicate a case in favour of his close relatives, parents or children, nor may he act as a witness in their favour, although it is said that he may issue a judgment if it is against them, but not for them. The most reliable view is that he should not adjudicate for or against his relatives at all. The judge may also not rely, in the issuance of judgment, on his personal knowledge of facts, but should only rely on facts determined by valid evidence.[167]

The judge must ensure that the disputing parties are treated equally in the court session in every respect, in words or acts or in the manner of address and seating arrangement, regardless of their wealth, social status and religion. The parties must attend the court hearing together, and neither may be granted a hearing in the absence of the other. The judge may not give priority in giving his attention to some litigants over others. The judge is also advised not to greet or welcome either of the parties in his court, and he may not engage in confidential conversation with them individually or together. Nor should he speak to one group in a language that the other does not know. If one of the parties greets the judge, he may merely return the greeting. The judge may not accept invitations or gifts from either of the litigants, or to invite them to his own private residence.[168]

The head of state and government leaders are not entitled to preferential treatment in the court of *Sharīʿah*. Early precedent confirms this: In one case it is reported that a dispute arose between the second caliph ʿUmar and his fellow companion, Ubay b. Kaʿb, and they went to Zayd b. Thābit for adjudication. When the judge passed a pillow to the caliph, the latter responded by saying that 'This is the first incident of your injustice,' and he sat in front of the judge on a par with his opponent.[169] Later the caliph ʿUmar issued instructions in a renowned letter addressed to his judges, directing them '…to let all men be equal in your presence, in your court and in your judgement so that the strong does not hope to swerve you into injustice, nor is the weak led to despair of your justice…' This letter contained further instructions to the effect that the judge may not adjudicate when he is in a state of anger, irritation, severe depression, hunger and thirst. Al-Kāsānī, who recorded this letter, also added that the judge should not overexert himself by holding exceedingly lengthy court sessions, but allow himself adequate breaks and make sure that he does not adjudicate in a state of fatigue.[170]

The court of *Sharīʿah* must maintain a level of decorum that inspires respect and confidence. Al-Kāsānī, who wrote in late 6/12th century, went on record to say that it was customary for the court to have a guard (*jalwāz*), who stood behind the judge with a whip in his hand to keep order when the court was in session. The court should have a clerk who records the proceedings, as well as helpers (*aʿwan*) who summon and bring litigants to the court. A translator should also be in attendance if needed. The judge is strongly advised to seek the counsel of those learned in *Sharīʿah* and community affairs in person or writing, and benefit from their advice. Kāsānī supports this by citing *hadīths* to the effect that the Prophet himself and the early caliphs were assiduous in consultation, and this should therefore be a feature of adjudication in *Sharīʿah* courts.[171] Prior to court hearing, it is proper for the judge to warn the litigants that the one who litigates in pursuit of falsehood and seeks to distort the truth calls upon himself the wrath of God Most High. The one who takes a false oath in order to take what belongs to his brother must prepare himself for painful punishment in the hereafter. The judge also warns the witnesses in similar terms.[172]

Imam Abu Ḥanīfa and his two disciples, Abū Yūsuf and al-Shaybānī, held the view that the judge should not give any advice to the witnesses and let them give testimony on their own initiative. Abū Yūsuf is reported to have subsequently changed his view so as to say that the judge may advise the witness, if this will help to facilitate his testimony. For it is possible that a witness may be unable, due to self-consciousness in the court environment, to express himself well. The judge could help this by addressing the witness with such expressions as 'did you testify such and such…' The judge may not, however, confound the witnesses in any way, or address them with matters that might make their task difficult. In the event of a discrepancy between the testimonies of witnesses, the judge may separate them and ask them factual questions to verify details. Should there be significant discrepancies in the testimonies of witnesses, the judge must reject them altogether.[173]

Witnesses must all be treated with dignity. This is the directive of a *ḥadīth*, which addresses everyone to 'Honour the witnesses for it is through them that God vindicates the rights (of people).'[174] Witnesses cannot, therefore, be made to wait at the office door of the judge. Similarly, priority in court hearings may be given to the party that has brought witnesses over those who have not.[175]

The judge must expedite the presentation of evidence and avoid, as far as possible, any delay in the testimony of witnesses. This is why some judges have given priority to the presentation of evidence and started the court hearing by admitting the witnesses first. When the disputing parties are present, the judge asks the plaintiff to present his claim, which should be presented in such terms that it is clearly understood by the other party and the judge himself. Should there be substantial ambiguity in the claim, the defendant may not be asked to give any response. The judge should communicate this to the plaintiff and ask him to correct his statement of claim and order both parties to leave the court. In the event that the claim is too lengthy and arduous, the judge may order the claimant to specify the gist and purpose of his claim. If the defendant has understood the nature of the claim against him, the judge may ask him for a response. Should the claim be very detailed and the defendant require a written version for him to look at, he should be provided with one.[176] Neither of the disputing parties may present evidence until the plaintiff has presented his claim, and it is clearly communicated to the parties concerned.[177]

B. A Brief Review of the Qur'ān and *Sunnah*

The Qur'ān directs witnesses not to conceal the truth and to be ready to testify to it (2:282), especially when they are invited to do so, which is why giving testimony in the cause of justice is a collective duty (*farḍ-kifā'ī*) of the community, and a particular duty of witnesses without whose testimony the truth may never be known or discovered. To conceal the truth or to conceal one's testimony (*kitmān al-shahāda*) is consequently forbidden (*ḥarām*).[178] This would explain the meaning of the *ḥadīth* in which the Prophet is reported to have said:

$$ \text{ألا أخبركم بخير الشهداء؟ الذى يأتى بشهادته أو يخبر بشهادته} $$

$$ \text{قبل أن يسئلها.} $$

Should I inform you of the best of witnesses: it is the one who comes forth to testify (even) before he is asked to do so.[179]

In another *ḥadīth*, it is reported that the Prophet laid down a basic guideline for giving testimony, saying:

$$ \text{اذا علمت مثل الشمس فاشهد والاّ فدع.} $$

When you know something, like you see the sun, then testify to it, but leave it alone otherwise.[180]

In yet a third *ḥadīth*, the Prophet is reported to have declared:

$$ \text{ومن أعان على خصومة بظلم فقد باء بغضب من الله عز وجل.} $$

The one who helps to advance what is an unjust litigation verily calls upon himself the wrath of God Most High.[181]

The Prophet has equated perjury to *shirk*, that is, associating partners with God in His divinity, in a brief statement which he is reported to have repeated three times. The Companion, Khuraym b. Fātik, reported that one day after the morning prayer, the Prophet stood and said:

'False testimony is tantamount to associating other deities with God.'

And then he immediately cited the Qur'ānic *āyah* which seems to draw the same kind of parallel as the Prophet drew between false testimony and disbelief. The *ayah* he read addressed the believers:

. . .فاجتنبوا الرجس من الأوثان واجتنبوا قول الزور حنفاء لله غير

مشركين به. . .

Shun the filth of idol worship and shun lying; turn unto God while ascribing no partners to Him (22:30–1)

Some of the restrictions on testimony have been explained in another *hadīth*, reported by ʿAbd Allāh b. ʿUmar:

إن رسول الله ردّ شهادة الخائن والخائنة وذى الغمر على أخيه

وردّ شهادة القانع لأهل البيت وأجازها لغيرهم.

The Prophet, peace be on him, rejected the testimony of the perfidious man or woman, the one who bore a grudge against his brother, and that of the servant for members of the household he served, but permitted it to others.[182]

Circumstantial evidence, clues and indications are admitted as evidence and bases of judgment, and their validity is confirmed in several places in the Qur'ān, especially with reference to the story of the Prophet Yūsuf (Joseph). A reference has thus been made to the bloodstained shirt of Yūsuf, which his brothers brought to their father, the Prophet Yaʿqūb (Jacob). Yūsuf's brothers apparently claimed that Yūsuf was attacked and killed by a wolf: 'and they brought his shirt with false bloodstains—*wa jā'u ʿala qamisihi bi-damin kadhib*' (12:18). The story has it that Yūsuf's brothers threw him into a deep well but brought his bloodstained shirt to their father and made up the rest of the story. Upon examining the shirt, Yaʿqūb noted that the shirt was otherwise intact and made the perceptive remark, 'it must have been a kind wolf to have devoured Yūsuf without even tearing his shirt.' Muslim jurists arguing for the admissibility of circumstantial evidence frequently quote this Qur'ānic episode.

Without wishing to enter details, it may briefly be stated that in another place, the Qur'ān has referred to people who are in need, but refrain from begging for help from others, by saying that they can be known by their facial appearance in the phrase *taʿrifunum bi-simāhum* (you know them by their expression) (2:273). Reports in the *hadīth* also show that the Prophet similarly issued judgment on the basis of facial appearance and indications of ethnicity and traits (*qiyāfah*) in determining claims of paternity.[183] Speaking in support of the admissibility of circumstantial evidence, Ibn Qayyim al-Jawziyya has cited numerous instances of it in the *ḥadīth*. Thus the Prophet said in one *ḥadīth*, for example that the 'signs of a hypocrite are three...,' and in another *ḥadīth*, he validated the conclusion that when a person attends the mosque regularly, he is a believer.[184] Both of these tend to confirm the point that the truth of a person's character is made known by certain signs.

C. Testimony of Witnesses

When a witness presents himself for testimony, his precise identity by reference to date and places must be recorded. The court only admits the testimony of upright (*'adl*) persons, which is why witnesses are asked to take an oath prior to giving testimony. If a witness is not an upright person, taking an oath will not qualify him to be a witness. A variant view on this is held by the Ẓāhiri School, which requires witness as to be sworn in prior to giving testimony. Ibn Ḥazm, who held this view, gave as a reason the spread of corruption among people. Ibn Qayyim has recounted the Ẓāhirī position and tends to support it, at least partially, when he writes that it is better to do so especially in the event where the judge might have doubts about the trustworthiness of a witness. Testimony may be taken in the presence of the litigating parties or in their absence, but when the party concerned attends, he is informed of the names and identities of witnesses and the contents of their testimonies. The court hears the litigant's reaction to the testimony. Should there be an objection to the reliability and just character of the witness, the court may look into the matter and may even refuse to admit him as a witness. Otherwise, the testimony is admitted and may be relied upon as a basis of judgment. The court may not entertain a litigant's request for a witness to repeat his testimony in his presence. In the event where the judge disqualifies and rejects a witness, his decision on this point may be appealed against and reversed by a higher court.[185]

The testimony of a witness is not admissible unless it is based on a personal knowledge of facts 'which is decisive and free of doubt, and not simply [based] on what he knows on the basis of probability.' This ruling is derived from the Qur'ān, where it is stated in the context of the story of Prophet Yūsuf that the eldest of the brothers told their father that 'we testify only to that which we know' (12:81 وما شهدنا إلا بما علمنا). What is based on a probability (*ẓann*) may, however, be joined with certain knowledge and given in testimony, but probability alone is not admissible as a basis of testimony.[186]

Knowledge, which is a prerequisite of testimony, may be based on one of the following grounds:

1) Reason alone, which may be based on axiomatic and self-evident truth, such as saying that three is larger than two.

2) Reason in combination with what is known through the five senses. Thus when a blind person testifies to the identify of an individual whom he recognises by his voice and speech, his testimony is accepted. The knowledge that is obtained here is based on intellectual cognition and the senses, and it is certain even if the blind witness cannot see his subject. This is also true of the testimony of a dumb person that is given by gesture, provided that all doubt is eliminated as to the reliability of his testimony. Certain smells and tastes are likewise identified by the senses, with the aid of reason.

3) Knowledge is often based on continuous testimony (i.e. *tawātur*) that establishes irrefutable certainty. This may be illustrated by saying, for example, that ʿUmar b. al-Khaṭṭāb was the second caliph of Islam who ruled following the death of his predecessor Abū Bakr. Although no one in recent times has seen the caliph ʿUmar b. al-Khaṭṭāb, or the event of his accession to the caliphate, what is said of him in this factual report is nevertheless proven by *tawātar*, which generates certain knowledge.

4) Knowledge is sometimes based on inference, such as when stolen goods are found in someone's position and the person has no alibi or explanation to establish his innocence. This is circumstantial evidence. An actual example of this is the incident in which the Companion Abū Hurayra had seen a man vomiting wine. When the caliph ʿUmar b. al-Khaṭṭāb asked him 'Did you see him drinking it?' Abū Hurayra said, 'I saw him vomiting it.' The caliph observed that naturally, he could not have vomited it without having drunk it. This is establishing a fact by way of inference and the observation of circumstance. The testimony of an expert surgeon on the cause and age of a certain injury or defect may also be cited as another example of knowledge based on inference and deduction.[187]

Notwithstanding the relatively clear and affirmative stance the Qurʾān and *Sunnah* take on the admissibility of circumstantial evidence, scholastic jurisprudence tends to restrict its scope, and tends to rely heavily on the testimony of witnesses. Documentary evidence is accepted, as explained below, on a restricted basis, and often only after its endorsement and confirmation by witnesses. Modern reform measures taken in recent times have adjusted that position in favour of the admissibility of circumstantial evidence, including documents and expert opinion. This may be seen as an inevitable outcome of the discovery and advancement of new scientific methods of establishing facts, such as photography, sound recording and the like, which have become generally accepted, and because modern statutory legislation also imposes certain limits on testimony as a means of proof.

The Ḥanbalī doctrine which has prevailed in Saudi Arabia reluctantly recognises written documents as valid testimony, but under new regulations in that country, *Sharīʿah* courts accept such documents as wills, contracts, financial documents and other registered documents without confirmation by witnesses. The testimony of a scientific expert, which may be of a circumstantial nature, is also admissible in the *Sharīʿah* courts of Saudi Arabia. It is also interesting to note that in Saudi Arabia, the 'testimony of non-Muslim against Muslims is admissible in the absence of Muslim witnesses, and in criminal cases, the testimony of a non-Muslim carries the same weight as that of a Muslim.'[188]

The judge may not adjudicate until he asks the defendant this last question: 'Is there anything else you may wish to give in evidence.' And the defendant is actually heard to say 'No'.[189] This is to all intents and purposes equivalent to what is similarly known in the English legal system as 'The last word is that of the defendant.'

When one of the litigants makes a confession before the judge at a time when no-one else is present, and later that same litigant denies what he said, the judge may not adjudicate on the basis of what he heard unless it is confirmed independently. Should there be no evidence forthcoming, the judge may refer the case to a higher court, in which case the judge himself can act as a witness. But the judge cannot be judge and witness in his own court. It is also in conformity with the objectivity of justice that the judge bases his judgment not on his personal information but on objective evidence.[190]

The judge must verify the probity of witnesses by recourse to the procedure of validation (*tazkiya*, or *taʿdīl*). The judge accordingly interviews persons who know the witnesses and confirm that they are upright and fit to perform the role. These are in effect witnesses on witnesses, known as *shuhūd al-tazkiya*, who must themselves be upright persons, yet the conditions that apply to them are not as strict as in the case of primary witnesses (*shuhūd al-taṣdīq*). Hearsay evidence, which is not acceptable from primary witnesses may, for example, be accepted from secondary witnesses, and the minimum number of two, which applies to primary witnesses, need not apply to secondary witnesses. Similarly, whereas close relatives cannot be witnesses for or against one another, they can be witnesses of *tazkiyah* in any order, provided that they are not involved in the dispute itself, or in the testimony of the primary witnesses.[191]

D. Confession (*Iqrār*)

Confession is a valid and binding means of proof, and there is no disagreement on this provided that it is free of doubt, given voluntarily, and not induced by a threat, pressure, enticement or duress.[192] Confession (*iqrār*) is defined as reporting (*ikhbār*) of a certain fact or truth or affirmation thereof by a competent person in a way that is clear of suspicion and doubt. Since a reasonable person is not normally expected to tell a lie in order to incriminate himself, when such a person does make a confession, it is admissible and constitutes a binding proof. As a means of proof in criminal disputes, confession is stronger than testimony, although less frequent of occurrence as people do not normally volunteer to confess. Notwithstanding its ranking as the strongest proof, confession is, however, confined in scope, and is basically non-transient (*hujjah qāsirah*) in that one person's confession cannot prove anything in respect of another person. Thus, when A makes a confession that he killed B and that C helped him in the act of killing, this confession is proof only against A. If C confirms A's confession, he would be guilty by his own confession, and not because of what A might have said. Confession by one person may, however, be used as evidence against another when it is supported by circumstantial evidence.[193]

Confession provides a proof in criminal charges when it offers sufficient detail. A brief confession that fails to provide such details therefore falls short of providing a proof. Thus when a person merely says that he killed another person, this kind of statement does not provide a proof by itself unless it is backed up by such detail as the mode of killing, place and time, any weapon used, and the nature of relationship, if any, between the parties or any communication that might have occurred between the killer and his victim. It is possible, for instance, that the killing in question occurred in relation to a right or fulfillment of an obligation, which may significantly affect the question of responsibility and punishment. This would explain why only a detailed confession is regarded as proof that can eliminate doubt.[194] Moreover, a mere claim by someone that he confessed under duress is not accepted in the absence of indications to support his claim. This is because duress is contrary to the norm: when people say things, they are presumed to have said them without duress, (unless there are indications such as seizure, incarceration, beating etc.,) in which case the claim may be considered reasonable and can be pursued.[195]

Confession must be made by a person who is in possession of his faculties, and this precludes children and the insane and those who are in a state of sleep or intoxication. A confession made by an intoxicated person is upheld only if it is confirmed after he regains consciousness, but then that will be regarded as a new confession. Intoxication in this context is described as a condition which eliminates the power of reason such that a person 'cannot distinguish the earth from the sky or a man from a woman,' according to Imam Abu Ḥanīfah. His disciple Abū Yūsuf has described an intoxicated person somewhat differently as one whose words do not make sense. In other words, a person is intoxicated if he does not know what he says. Abū Yūsuf's view on this is the preferred view, which is upheld by the majority of jurists.[196]

Some schools and jurists have held that in grave offences, especially what is known as *ḥudūd*, confession should be repeated and confirmed before it is admitted as a basis of judgment. Thus the Ḥanafīs, the Ḥanbalīs and the Zaydi Shīʿa have held that confession to a charge of *zinā* should be repeated four times, apparently by analogy to four witnesses, and if it is not repeated, it falls short of conclusive proof. In addition to the caution that is embedded in this ruling, it is favourable to the accused as it affords him an opportunity to retract his confession, repent and reform himself. Since the Qur'ānic text on the subject of *zinā* (al-Nūr, 24:2–6) makes a provision for repentance, it is advisable to encourage repentance, and repetition tends to favour that prospect. The Ḥanafīs have even extended this to all other offences, including the *taʿzīr* offences, and require that confession must in all criminal charges be repeated twice.[197] This is in addition to the general position that all the schools have taken to, that the accused may retract his confession in *ḥudūd* crimes.

Al-ʿAwwa, who has discussed these scholastic positions in some detail, finds this distinction between the *ḥudūd* and *taʿzīr* crimes to be less than warranted, and maintains instead that the more cautious ruling on the revocability of confession concerning the *ḥudūd* should be applied to all offences. This would appear to be sound advice, and tends to find support, as ʿAwwa has said himself, in the *Sunnah* of the Prophet. The *ḥadīth*, for example, which proclaims that punishments (*al-ḥudūd*) must be suspended on grounds of doubt, refers to all punishments, and not only to the *ḥudūd* or any particular type of punishment.[198]

Confessions made under duress are invalid. This duress might consist of imposition, or a threat of imminent imposition, of intolerable bodily pain, punishment or harm that is credible and overwhelms the victim such that it extracts self-incriminating statements from him. The confession, in other words, is made when the person making it is convinced that the pain or punishment he is threatened with will be inflicted and the threat carried out, unless he makes the confession in question. Duress that eliminates consent (*al-riḍā*) and also vitiates the will power (*al-ikhtiyār*) of its victim is duress in its full sense (*ikrāh tāmm*), and it creates a fear of death on the part of its victim. Duress that eliminates consent but does not affect the will power of its victim is incomplete or deficient duress (*ikrāh nāqis*), which normally falls short of creating a fear of death on the part of its victim. This refers to such means of duress as imprisonment and beating that does not create the fear of death. Only complete duress provides a defence in criminal cases, except in killing and grievous injury. The claim of duress, however strong, is unlikely to succeed in these cases, but it may provide a valid defence in other crimes. Incomplete duress can provide a valid defence in civil transactions and private claims. For example a contract of sale that is signed under duress of this latter kind may well be invalidated as a result.[199]

Muslims jurists have discussed a number of conditions that must be fulfilled for duress to vitiate a confession, and these are related to the severity of the threat and the state of mind that it creates on the part of its victim. It is not our purpose to go into detail here, but merely to say that confession made as a result of such duress is null and void and does not provide the basis of conviction and punishment, regardless of whether or not the pain and punishment that elicited the confession was imposed in the course of vindicating the truth or in fulfilment of a right.

Ḥasan Ibn Ziyād, a disciple of Imam Abu Ḥanīfa, is reported to have held that beating a thief in order to extract a confession from him was permissible on the analysis that theft usually occurs in circumstances of secrecy where it is difficult to provide witnesses. But he held that the beating must not 'cut the flesh, or reveal the bone.' It is reported, however, that he soon regretted and revoked his verdict, which he had given in response to a question addressed to him by a certain thief. He then followed the thief to the door of the emir and noted that the thief had confessed under beating and surrendered the stolen goods. Ibn Ziyād made the remark that he had 'Never seen injustice so closely resemble justice,' yet he upheld his revocation and maintained that confession obtained through beating was invalid.[200] Furthermore, when a self-incriminating confession is obtained as a result of 'duress by a ruler, or judge and the person under duress confesses to a crime which carries the death punishment or mutilation, such as murder and theft, and the person is executed as a result, or his hand is mutilated, the official who compelled him is liable to just retaliation (*qiṣāṣ*).'[201]

There is a consensus among jurists to the effect that a subsequent revocation of a confession, even without any claim of duress, by the person who made it in the first place is acceptable in matters pertaining to the Right of God, but not in matters pertaining to civil claims, or what is known as the Right of Man. Thus, when a person confesses to have committed adultery (*zinā*) and then retracts his confession at any stage prior to punishment or during its execution, his confession is nullified and retraction is accepted. This is because *zinā*, as well as most of the other *ḥudūd* offences, are offences pertaining to the Right of God and their punishment is suspended on grounds of doubt. Revocation of a confession in these cases represents a doubt, which consequently suspends the punishment. But in civil and financial matters, such as when a person offers a valid confession in respect of a debt he might have owed to another, his subsequent revocation is not accepted. However, if a confession turns out to have been fabricated and unreliable in the first place, it will be of no account regardless of whether it is subsequently revoked or not.[202]

When a person remains silent in response to a question and refuses to make a statement of any kind, it is preferable, according to al-Kāsāni, to take his silence as a denial rather than otherwise. The explanation offered for this is that 'a reasonable and upright person is not expected to remain silent when he is expected to tell the truth or vindicate the right of another person while he is able to speak...silence is therefore better to be taken as implied denial (*inkāran dalālatan*).'[203] In the event where the defendant speaks but says things that are non-committal, such as when he says that 'I do not confess nor do I deny' and persists in this, some jurists have taken this as a denial, whereas others have taken it to be equivalent to an admission, but the former view is again preferable, for the words so expressed actually amount to silence, and silence, as explained above, is tantamount to denial.'[204]

E. *Bayyinah, Qarīnah*, Documentation and Circumstantial Evidence

Ibn Qayyim al-Jawziyya, has refuted the somewhat parochial view of proof and evidence taken by conventional jurisprudence, which almost confines it to the testimony of witnesses. Both Ibn Taymiyya and Ibn Qayyim assert that this view is not substantiated in the Qur'ān. Ibn Qayyim has quoted Ibn Taymiyya at length and agreed with him that the Qur'ān does not confine evidence to two male witnesses, or to one man and two women, as the sole basis of judgment. Ibn Qayyim quotes the principal Qur'ānic verse on this subject (2:282) and then also quotes Ibn Taymiyya's analysis of it. The relevant Qur'ān text is as follows:

يآيها الذين أمنوا إذا تداينتـم بدين إلـى أجل مسمى فاكتبوه وليكتب بينكم كاتب بالعدل ولايأب كاتب أن يكتب كما علّمه الله فليكتب وليملل الذى عليــه الحق وليتق اللـه ربه ولاييخس منه شيئا فإن كان الذى عليه الحق سفيها أو ضعيفا أو لايسـتطيع أن يـــملّ هـو فليملل ولـيه بالعدل واسـتشهدوا شهيدين من رجالكم فإن لم يكونا رجلين فرجـل وامرأتان ممـن ترضون من الشهداء.

O you who believe! When you contract a debt for a fixed period, record it in writing. Let a scribe record it in writing between you equitably. No scribe should refuse to write as God has taught him. So let him write and let him who incurred the debt dictate, and let him observe his duty to his Lord, and diminish naught thereof. But if he who owes the debt is of low understanding, or weak, or unable to dictate himself, then let his guardian dictate it equitably. And call to witness from among your men two witnesses, but if two men are not at hand, then a man and two women, that you approve as witnesses…(2:282).

Ibn Taymiyya wrote that in this verse, God Most High enjoined the believers to protect their rights by means of written records, and the indebted person to dictate the facts of the loan transaction to a scribe. But if the indebted person cannot dictate, his guardian may do so. Then the creditor is ordered to testify and endorse the document by bringing two male witnesses, or one male and two females. Then the witnesses are ordered to be ready to give testimony when the occasion arises. The verse then continues with the instruction that if the parties are on a journey and cannot find a scribe to document their loan transaction for them, they may vouch for it by way of a pawn or mortgage. All of this, Ibn Taymiyya pointed out, is meant to 'advise, instruct and educate the believers as to the ways by which they can safeguard their rights'.

To safeguard one's right in a certain way is one thing, and the ways by which a judge adjudicates is another. This is because 'the method of adjudication (*ṭuruq al-ḥukm*) is a wider subject which can hardly be confined to two males or female witnesses.'[205] If the text had, in other words, intended to expound the means of proof in a court of justice, it would have mentioned more than just two of these, namely documentation and witnesses. The text in other words, is educational and not an exclusive legal text, since it contains guidance for people as to how they can stay clear of conflict when they conduct loans and trading transactions among themselves. But if they trust one another, or when the transaction consists of a spot trade in which the parties' liabilities are settled there and then, they may not need to record it in writing. The whole of this text, in other words, consists of education and advice, and it is not meant to provide either a definitive or a comprehensive ruling on the means of proof in courts of justice.

Evidence can be divided into two types, *bayyinah* and *shahādah*, and the way in which evidence is given may be in speech, in writing and even by gesture for a person who is unable to speak. Whereas *shahādah* refers to testimony given by a qualified witness in court, *bayyinah* is a wider concept and includes a variety of proofs and evidence that enlightens, explains and elucidates rights, including the knowledge of the *qāḍī* himself. Whereas the Shāfiʿī jurists tend to consider *bayyinah* and *shahādah* to be synonymous, Ibn Qayyim al-Jawziyya, Ibn Farḥūn and many others have considered *bayyinah* to be a larger concept. This means that *bayyinah* also includes confession, circumstantial evidence (*qarīnah*), solemn oath, denial of oath, documentary evidence, informed opinion (*raʾy al-khabīr*), *al-qiyāfah* (facial appearance) and *al-firasah* (intuitive judgment).

Ibn Qayyim has discussed some twenty six types of evidence under the general rubric of *bayyinah,* and also considers *shahādah* to be a special form of *bayyinah*. He explains that the Qur'ān uses the term *bayyinah* to mean not only *shahādah* but also argument, proof and clear evidence, and cites a number of passages (including 57; 25; 29; 35; 6:57) to this effect. The word '*bayyinah*' in the Qur'ān has nowhere been confined to witnesses, but includes evidence in general. The Qur'ān uses *bayyinah* for both material and non–material evidence, though the jurists have subsequently confined it to certain material forms such as oath-taking, documentation and *qarīnah*. Religious and rational argumentation by Prophets and Messengers is included in the meaning of *bayyināt* in the Qur'ān (cf. 57:2). In reference to judicial disputes, *bayyinah* has, however, been confined to its material forms only.[206] There are also instances where the Prophet used the term *bayyinah* to include a sign, proof, evidence and argument. One *ḥadīth*, for example, declares that 'proof (*bayyinah*) is upon the plaintiff, and the oath is upon the defendant.' Ibn Qayyim thus wrote:

> In general *bayyinah* is the name for all matters that clarify and explain a right, and whoever confines it only to the evidence of two witnesses or four witnesses or one male witness alone, clearly neglects the full significance of *bayyinah*. *Bayyinah* in the Qur'ān does not only mean two male witnesses but includes argument, proof and clear sign (of any kind) whether presented separately or all together.[207]

Signs and circumstantial evidence can often bring important facts to light and can certainly provide a stronger argument than the testimony of a single witness. Thus *bayyinah, dalālah, ḥujjah, burhān, ʿalāmah* and *amārah*, which come close to one another in meaning, all fall under *bayyinah,* just as they can be subsumed under *qarīnah*. When circumstantial evidence and a *qarīnah* is clear and indisputable, it can provide the basis of a judgment if it is coupled with an oath. This is applied, for example, where there is a dispute regarding the ownership of a tool between a tailor and a carpenter. Based on the available and undisputed *qarīnah,* the tool is given to the person whose type of work the tool would be most relevant to.

> Ibn Qayyim further elaborates on the meaning of *bayyinah*:
> The objective of the Lawgiver is that the truth should be vindicated in whatever way possible; all facts and arguments that serve that purpose should be made evident. When the real situation is ascertained and elucidated, it should be treated as an established fact, otherwise the Right of God and the right of His creatures will be rendered of no value. Manifestation of the truth does not therefore depend on any particular method. There may indeed be many standards and procedures for its ascertainment.[208]

Ibn Qayyim is thus saying that any evidence that leads to the discovery of facts is acceptable as *bayyinah,* and a court may rely on it provided that it is lawfully procured. *Shahādah*, on the other hand, consists of 'information which is true and is given in a judicial assembly by using the expression '*shahādah*' to prove a right or interest against another person.'[209] Such information must originate in certainty, not in supposition or conjecture, and when it is verified by the court through cross-examination and *tazkiya*, the court has to accept it and base its judgment on it.[210]

In the event where the claimant/plaintiff is only able to present one witness instead of two, he may do so if he can substantiate his claim by taking an oath in support of his claim. Ibn Qayyim has convincingly argued this point and wrote: 'A group of well-respected and prominent judges among the predecessors have held that the judge may issue judgement on the basis of the testimony of only one witness without it even being supported by an oath by the claimant in the event where the judge is convinced of the reliability of the testimony of that witness,'[211]

Documentation is a valid means of proof in *Sharīʿah* as we saw in the Qurʾānic text just reviewed. There is no problem concerning the admissibility of written documents and records when they are reliable, such as verified and registered documents whose safety from manipulation and forgery is guaranteed. The doubt that has arisen in the writings of many prominent jurists, including the Imams Abu Ḥanīfa, Mālik, Shāfiʿī and Aḥmad ibn Ḥanbal, is precisely because of the possibility of the distortion and forgery of written documents. This may be explained by reference to the prevailing conditions of the time in which these Imams expounded their doctrines, namely the inefficient means of transport and communication, as well as low levels of literacy, which were major factors in the cautious attitude they took towards the admissibility of hand-written documents. For such documents were often presented before the court when the person who wrote them was out of reach, and no registered or verified endorsement of them was available to establish their authenticity.

Hand-written papers that were presented in the courts took any of the following three forms, as Imam Aḥmad b. Ḥanbal has expounded.[212] Firstly, when the document is endorsed and confirmed in court by the party who wrote it, or when the judge is convinced of its authenticity; in this case the judge admits it as a means of proof and adjudicates on its basis. Secondly, when the judge is not so convinced, and confirmation by the party who wrote it is also lacking; in this case the judge does not admit it as evidence unless necessary confirmation either by the writer or witnesses is forthcoming. Thirdly, when the document in question

is in the custody of the judge, such as in court records, the judge admits
it if he is convinced of its veracity, failing which he may refuse to admit
it as evidence. Thus when the judge is convinced of the authenticity
of a written statement of a person, such as a witness, which may have
been preserved under seal, the judge admits it without question. The
judge may admit papers and written documents that he remembers as
having been filed in his court previously, but he must in all cases refuse
to admit documents when he is not convinced of their reliability.[213]

Another element of doubt about hand-written documents arose
in conjunction with the written but unregistered wills of individuals.
Claims and counter-claims were often presented regarding the veracity
of wills that were supposedly written and left behind by the deceased.
The basic position on this was that the document by itself did not
provide a proof unless it was verified and proven to be genuine. As for
verified documents, whether verified by the testimony of witnesses or
by the personal recognition of the judge, or any supportive but conclusive indications that they are genuine, the written words are in every
respect equivalent to spoken words and there is no difference in their
strength as a means of proof before the court.[214]

Salim al-ʿAwwa has referred to Ibn Taymiyya's analysis and drawn
the conclusion that in respect of proving or disproving of criminal
offences, the *Sharīʿah* does not impose any restrictions on the means of
proof and evidence. The judge is granted the discretion to adjudicate
on the basis of any evidence he finds convincing, whether it is through
witnesses, documentary or circumstantial evidence, or indeed all evidence, regardless of whether or not a reference has been made to it in
the Qur'ān and *Sunnah* or the writings of Muslim jurists.[215]

Al-ʿAwwa continues what is in effect a logical follow-up to Ibn
Taymiyya's conclusion, on which he and his disciple Ibn Qayyim had
based their ruling of the *āyat al-mudāyanah*. Thus it is noted that the
Qur'ān refers to two male witnesses, or one male and two female, only
on two occasions, one of which is in the *āyat al-mudāyanah* as already
discussed. The other reference to witnesses in the Qur'ān occurs in
sura al-Ṭalāq, and in the context of divorce, which is as follows:

فإذا بلغـن أجلهـن فـأمسكوهن بمعروف أو فارقـوهـن بمعروف
وأشهدوا ذوى عدل منكم وأقيموا الشهادة لله .

And when they (divorced women) complete their waiting period,
either retain them with kindness or release them in a decent manner,

and bring two just witnesses from among you, and give testimony for
the sake of God (65:2).

It thus appears that the two references to testimony in the Qur'ān occur
in the context of loans and contracts, one of which facilitates the proof
of credit-based transactions, and the other a disputed divorce. Both
fall under the broad category of civil claims, or civil litigations, and
have nothing to do with criminal offences. Although the testimony of
witnesses is also accepted as a means of proof in criminal offences, the
means of proof in this context are not confined, in the affirmative sense
of proving a criminal claim, or in the negative sense of disproving it,
to any particular method. For there is a difference between what may
be described as a lawful disposition (*al-taṣarruf al-qānūnī*) such as a loan
contract, and a factual incident (*al-wāqiʿah al-mādiyyah*), especially in
the form of a criminal offence. The former is a lawful transaction that
is openly concluded, and its material elements are voluntarily expressed
and recorded, and witnesses are called to attend their proper conclusion; whereas the latter is a crime that is normally committed in secrecy,
and no criminal is expected to call witnesses to observe the crime he
commits. On the contrary, the perpetrator of a crime takes precautions
so that no-one can see the crime he commits. It is therefore only fair
and reasonable to expand upon the means of proof in the context of
crime, especially when it enables the accused to disprove the charges
he faces. This is because of the sensitivity of the issue, which is to avoid
the possibility of punishing an innocent person. For this is deemed,
according to the teaching of the *Sunnah*, to amount to a greater miscarriage of justice compared to the possibility of a guilty person escaping
punishment. None of this is, however, meant to lower the standard of
scrutiny in the proof of criminal offences, and the overall reliability of
evidence that is presented in court.

What needs to be stressed is that the means of proof in a criminal
trial should not be confined to any particular method. The accused
should in particular be able to rebut the charges against him by all
means at his disposal. Only in respect of certain offences, the charge
of adultery (*zinā*), for example, where the Qur'ān stipulates four eye
witnesses, the judge may not adjudicate on the basis of anything less
than the stipulated method. It is reasonable to conclude from this that
in criminal investigation and trial, a fairly open approach should be
taken towards the means of proof and the evidence that is presented
by the accused to prove himself innocent. This is because non-liability or innocence is a basic presumption of *Sharīʿah* and no unnec-

essary structure can be recommended to erode the substance of that presumption.

We turn now to evidence that is presented against the accused by the police and prosecutor. Although the means of proof here are not confined to any particular method, a more restrictive approach to evidence and a higher standard of caution in its admissibility are recommended. Basic authority for this approach is furnished in the directive of the *ḥadīth*, which requires that punishments are suspended in all cases of doubt. A more restrictive approach is also in order in the context of lawful dispositions, or *taṣarrufāt qānuniyya*, such as marriage and divorce, and transactions that have a bearing on the rights and properties of others. This is because the law makes documentation and testimony a requirement of a valid conclusion thereof. Since they are normally not concluded in secrecy, it is relatively easy to have them testified and documented.[216]

There is a certain perception in the writings of some commentators that the *Sharīʿah* law of evidence is 'rigid and does not permit the judge to evaluate and exercise discretion, by way of comparison and preference, in relation to some types of evidence over others.' Unwarranted conclusions have often been drawn that criminal adjudication and trial procedures in Islamic law stipulate specific methods of proof which tie the hands of the judge, such that he cannot adjudicate on any other basis, even if the evidence in question falls short of establishing the facts. ʿAwwa argues that this is unfounded and a closer examination of the *Sharīʿah* rules of evidence and trial shows that the judge is not constrained by such rigidities. The judge is not bound to admit evidence, whether consisting of testimony of witnesses or any other type of evidence, which he finds less than convincing, even if the evidence in question conforms to all the prerequisites of admissibility. What is more, the judge is not permitted to issue judgement on the basis of such evidence if the truth is made clear to him by other means. Thus in a charge of *zinā* when four witnesses have testified that a certain woman has committed it, and the judge then discovers that the woman in question is a virgin, he must reject the witnesses, acquit the woman, and punish the witnesses on charges of slander (*qadhf*). The judge in all cases 'evaluates the grounds of the claim that is brought before him in the light of its circumstances and does not adjudicate unless he is certain that the claim is supported by incontrovertible evidence.'[217]

In Malaysia, legislation has been introduced, under the various State Enactments, to regulate the admissibility of the Islamic law of evidence in the Shariah courts. The Shariah Evidence Ordinance of Sarawak

1991 and the Shariah Court Evidence (Federal Territories) Act, 1997 are among the more comprehensive on the subject. Both laws have drawn a distinction between *bayyinah* and *shahāda*. *Bayyinah* is thus held to be a wider concept than *shahādah,* and the lines of distinction between them come close to Ibn Qayyim al-Jawziyya's aforementioned differentiation.

The Sarawak Shariah Evidence Ordinance 1991, in Section (3), defines *bayyinah* as evidence or proof which proves a right or interest, and includes *qarīna*. *Qarīna* is, in turn, defined as 'a fact which is connected with another fact in any of the ways which are stated in *ḥukum Syara'*, or which are set out in this Ordinance.'

Shahādah is a special type of *bayyinah* and it is defined in the Sarawak Ordinance 1991 as follows:

Shahādah means the evidence which has the quality of truth given in a court by using the expression *ashhadu* to prove a right or interest of a person against another person, and if it is accepted, it binds the judge.

Under Sarawak Ordinance (Sec. 830), *shahādah* is signified by the usage of expression 'I bear witness—*ashhadu*.' *Shahādah* is also intended to prove a right or interest that may consist of the Right of God, or the Right of Man, or a combination of both. Muslims are competent under the Sarawak Ordinance (S. 83) to give both *shahādah* and *bayyinah,* whereas non–Muslims are entitled to give *bayyinah*. The *bayyinah* of an expert who is not a Muslim against a Muslim may be accepted in *Sharīᶜah* courts. A witness who gives *shahādah* must be competent, upright (ᶜ*adl*) and impartial, and not involved in good or in bad relations with a party in the case. Yet these restrictions do not apply to the one who gives *bayyina*. Section (85) of the Sarawak Ordinance entitles wife and husband as well as father and child to give *shahādah* or *bayyinah* against one another, but they can only give *bayyinah* for one another. A witness who is not upright may not give *shahādah* but may give *bayyinah* (83–3).[218]

Articles (119) to (129) of the Syariah Court Evidence (Federal Territories) Act 1997 also makes similar provisions on the requirements, such as upright character, and other qualifications of witnesses who give *shahādah* or *bayyinah*. It also provides for the cross-examination or *tazkiyah* of witnesses by the *Sharīᶜah*. This may consist of open or secret examination, and the taking of an oath. Section (119) provides that:

After the witness has given his evidence, the judge shall question him, to ensure the credibility of the witness.

Explanation: If it is said that a witness is not telling the truth or if any witness is just but has made a number of mistakes in the evidence or the witness has forgotten facts or it is said that the witness is just but he denies the claim, the Shariah Judge cannot give judgement, unless he decides whether the witness is just or not by open examination in the court or by secret examination.

The distinction that the Malaysian law draws, implies that *shahādah* requires the fulfillment of stricter conditions, whereas *bayyinah* can be given by a person who may not qualify as a *shāhid*. Unlike *shahādah*, which binds the judge, *bayyinah* does not bind the judge and it is left to the judge to accept or to reject it.

Concluding Remarks

In conclusion, it may be said that criminal judicial procedure in the *Sharīʿah* remains largely open to the prospect of refinement and growth within the general framework of *siyāsah sharʿiyyah*. The textual guidelines of the Qurʾān and *Sunnah* on criminal procedure examined in this essay generally point to the same direction, namely that Islamic law supports any procedure that advances the cause of justice and fair treatment and does not, in so doing, violate considerations of public interest, or *maṣlaḥah*. *Siyāsah sharʿiyyah* is itself predicated on *maṣlaḥah* and it is, as such, changeable since it must respond to the exigencies of time and circumstance and cannot, as it were, be predicted and legislated in advance. Even if the broad outlines of *siyāsah sharʿiyyah* on criminal procedure were to be codified, the head of state and judge would still be left with a measure of discretionary power which they could utilise in response to exceptional and emergency situations adequately dealt with under the normal rules of *Sharīʿah*.

There is a daunting gap between the theory and practice of *Sharīʿah* in the area of criminal procedure. Even a cursory glance at the juridical guidelines of *Sharīʿah* and the prevailing practices of government in present-day Muslim countries is enough to determine the nature of the challenge. Al-ʿAlwānī observes that 'it is indeed shameful for us today to see that certain Muslim majority states are not at all concerned with human dignity and rights and that they willfully ignore the guarantees designed to protect those rights... Their tyranny serves only to distort the truth of Islam and the ways in which it upholds justice'.[219] Some of these governments have indeed become immersed in mistrust, suspicion and espionage against their own people to an alarming extent. The sensitivities voiced by the normative guidelines of Islam and the juristic heritage of its leading ʿulamāʾ is a far cry from actual practice in many quarters of the Muslim world today. Rulers and governments in many Muslim countries pay only lip service to constitution and the rule of law. Conformity to the rule of law and the idea of service to the general public has yet to become a visible reality. It is not surprising, therefore, to see that resistance and insurgency, in Muslim societies, against oppressive government practices, have done so usually from an Islamic platform. Without wishing to condone violence in any form, the fact remains that resistance movements are often driven to despair, extremism and violence by the barbarism of these rulers, and the absence of reciprocity and dialogue. If the world community views Muslims as trigger-happy and violent, this is due, in no small measure, to the mistrust, conspiracy and suspicion that oppressive Muslim governments have practised against their own citizens.

As an appendix to this chapter, I enclose the text of a 1979 International Conference resolution of concern to human rights and Islamic criminal justice.

Appendix

RESOLUTION

Whereas the First International Conference on the Protection of Human Rights in the Islamic Criminal Justice System has been held in Siracusa, Italy, at the International Institute of Higher Studies in Criminal Sciences, 28–31 May 1979:

Whereas it has been established to the satisfaction of all participants from both Islamic and non-Islamic nations that the letter and spirit of Islamic law on the subject of the protection of the rights of the criminally accused are in complete harmony with the fundamental principles of human rights under international law as well as in complete harmony with the respect accorded to the equality and dignity of all persons under the constitutions and laws of Muslim and non-Muslim nations of the world:

Whereas the basic human rights embodied in the principles of Islamic law include the following rights of the criminally accused, *inter alia*:

1) The right of freedom from arbitrary arrest, detention, torture, or physical annihilation;
2) the right to be presumed innocent until proven guilty by a fair and impartial tribunal in accordance with the Rule of Law;
3) the application of the principle of legality which calls for the right of the accused to be tried for crimes specified in the Qur'an or other crimes whose clear and well-established meaning and contents are determined by Shari'ah law or by a criminal code in conformity therewith;
4) the right to appear before an appropriate tribunal previously established by law;
5) the right to a public trial;
6) the right not to be compelled to testify against oneself;
7) the right to present evidence and to call witnesses in one's defence;
8) the right to counsel of one's own choosing;
9) the right to a decision on the merits based upon legally admissible evidence;
10) the right to have the decision in the case rendered in public;
11) the right to benefit from the spirit of mercy and goals of rehabilitation and resocialization in the consideration of the penalty to be imposed; and
12) the right of appeal.

Whereas the aforementioned rights of due process of law contained in Islamic law are in complete harmony with the prescriptions of the International Covenant on Civil and Political Rights which has been signed or ratified by many nations including a significant number of Muslims and Islamic nations and which reflects generally accepted principles of international law contained in the Universal Declaration of Human Rights of 1948 and the U.N. Declaration on the Standard Minimum Rules for the Treatment of Offenders;

Now therefore the participants of the Conference, in their individual capacities, desirous of upholding the aforementioned principles and the values they embody and desirous of ensuring that the practices and procedures of Islamic and Muslim nations conform thereto, solemnly declare that:

Any departure from the aforementioned principles would constitute a serious and grave violation of Shari'ah law, international human rights law and the generally accepted principles of international law reflected in the constitutions and laws of most nations of the world.

A thorough re-examination of the working of criminal law—whatever its nature and source—now in force in various parts of the contemporary Muslim world, in the light of the Criminal Justice Resolution of 1979 reproduced above, must be undertaken as a matter of urgency.

NOTES

1. Cf. Herbert Parker, *The Limits of the Criminal Sanction*, 140 ff.

2. Cf. Mutawalli, *Mabādi Niẓām al-Ḥukm*, 4th ed., 148; ʿAbd Allāh, *Naẓariyyah al-Dawla*, 300; al-Saleh, 'The Right of The Individual to Personal Security.' in Bassiouni, *Islamic Criminal Justice*, 56.

3. Badawi, *Daʿāʾim*, 91; Fuʾād Aḥmad, *Uṣūl Niẓām al-Ḥukm*, 263; al-ʿĪlī, *Hurriyyāt*, 363.

4. Ghazawī, *al-Ḥurriyyah*, 25.

5. Cf. Cherif Bassiouni, *The Islamic Criminal Justice*, 19.

6. Muslim, *Mukhtaṣar Ṣaḥīḥ Muslim*, 473, *ḥadīth* no. 1775.

7. Abū Dāwūd, *Sunan Abi Dāwūd*, ed., al-Bughā, 704, *ḥadīth* 4893.

8. Bukhārī, *Ṣaḥīḥ al-Bukhārī* (Khan's trans.) K. al-Hudud, VIII, 510, *ḥadīth* 776; Abū Yūsuf, *al-Kharāj*, p. 163.

9. Tirmidhi, *Sunan al-Tirmidhi*, III, 255, K. al-Birr, *ḥadīth* 84.

10. *Ibid.*, Kitāb al-diyyāt, IV, 16, *ḥadīth* no. 1395.

11. Bukhārī, *Ṣaḥīḥ al-Bukhārī*, I, 110, *ḥadīth* no. 48.

12. Abu ʿUbayd, *al-Amwāl*, 42.

13. Al-Ṣanʿānī, *Subul al-Salam*, III, 192; al-Zuhaylī, *al-Fiqh al-Islāmī*, VII, 230.

14. Bukhārī, *Ṣaḥīḥ al-Bukhārī*, (Khan's trans.), VIII, 512, *ḥadīth* 778.

15. Tabrizi, *Mishkāt*, vol. III, *ḥadīth* 4957.

16. Khallāf, *Siyāsa Sharʿīya*, 31.

17. Abū Dāwūd, *Sunan, Kitab al-diyyāt, bab. al-qiṣāṣ min al-nafs, ḥadīth* 4537; Abu Zahrah, *Tanẓīm*, 230.

18. Id., *Kitab al-diyyāt, bab al-qawad min al-ḍarba, ḥadīth* 4536.

19. Ibn Saʿd, *Ṭabaqāt*, III, 293; Fuʾād Aḥmad, *Uṣūl*, 266; Osman, *Huqūq al-Insān*, 79.

20. Cf. al-Shāṭibi, *Muwāfaqāt*, II, 3–5 and *passim*; Kamali, *Islamic Jurisprudence*, 271 ff.

21. Tabrizi, *Mishkāt*, III, 1061, *ḥadīth* 3570; al-ʿĪlī, *Hurriyyāt*, 369; Bassiouni, *Islamic Criminal Justice*, 56.

22. Abū Yūsuf, *al-Kharāj*, 190.

23. Al-Tabrizi, *Mishkāt*, III, 1061, *ḥadīth* 3570; Abū Yūsuf, *al-Kharāj*, 164.

24. Abū Yūsuf, *al-Kharāj*, 175; see also Ibn Farḥūn, *Tabṣira*, II, 158.

25. Abū Yūsuf, *al-Kharāj*, 190–191.

26. Māwardī, *Aḥkām*, 220.

27. Abū Yūsuf, *al-Kharāj*, 51–63; al-ʿĪlī, *Hurriyyāt*, 369; see also al-Saleh, 'The Right of the Accused to Personal Security,' in Bassiouni, *Islamic Criminal Justice*, 85.

28. Abū Yūsuf, *al-Kharāj*, 162; al-ʿIlī, *Ḥurriyyāt*, 370; Shishani, *Ḥuqūq al-Insān*, 577.

29. Cf. Mahmassanī, *Arkān*, 107–108; Māwardī, *Aḥkām*, 86.

30. Al-Nabhān, *Niẓām al-Ḥukm fi'l-Islām*, 167.

31. Cf. Enayat, *Modern Islamic Political Thought*, 128.

32. Cf. Abu Zahrah, *Tanẓīm*, 34–35; Mutawalli, *Mabādi*, 387; Ghazawi, *al-Ḥurriyyāt*, 26. For a discussion of citizenship from the Islamic perspective, the reader is referred to my book, *Freedom of Movement, Citizenship and Accountability of Government: An Islamic Perspective* (forthcoming).

33. Muslim, *Ṣaḥīḥ: K. al-Imārah, B. Wujub tāʿat al-umarā' fi ghayr ma ʿṣiya wa taḥrīmuhā fi'l ma ʿṣiya, hadīth no.* 39. This *hadīth* is reported unanimously (*muttafaq ʿalayh*).

34. Abū Dāwūd, *Sunan* Abū Dāwūd, *hadīth* 2625.

35. Mawdudi, *Human Rights in Islam*, 33.

36. ʿAwdah, *al-Tashri ʿ al-Jinā'i*, I, 56.

37. *Id.*, I, 562.

38. Mahmaṣṣāni, *Arkān*, 94.

39. Abū Yūsuf, *Kitāb al-Kharāj*, 152.

40. Cf. Zuḥaylī, *Ḥaqq al-Ḥurriyya fi'l-ʿĀlam*, 96–97; Kamali, *Principles of Islamic Jurisprudence* (chapter on *Istiṣḥāb*), 384–397.

41. Abū Dāwūd, *Sunan*, vol. 3, *hadīth* no. 3582; Māwardī, *Aḥkām*, 67; Mahmaṣṣānī, *Arkān*, 107. See for details Kasani, *Bada'i'*, VIII, 3819.

42. Al-Shaʿrānī, *al-Mīzān*, II, 165; see also al-Awad, 'The Rights of the Accused,' in Bassiouni, *Islamic Criminal Justice*, 94.

43. Kasani, *Bada'i'*, VIII, 4918.

44. Cf. Saleh, 'The Right of the Individual to Personal Security,' in Bassiouni, *Islamic Criminal Justice*, 66.

45. Maḥmaṣṣāni, *Arkān Ḥuqūq al-Insān fi'l-Islam*, 106.

46. Bayhaqi, *Sunan: K. al-Daʿwa wa'l bayyināt, B. al-bayyinah ʿala al-mudd'ai wa'l yamin ʿala muda'a ʿalayh*.

47. Muslim, *Mukhtaṣar Ṣaḥīḥ Muslim*, p. 280; *hadīth* 1053; Ibn Qayyim, *al-Turuq al-Ḥukmiyya*, 94.

48. Ibn Qayyim, *al-Turuq*, 28.

49. Ibn Taymiyya, *al-Siyāsa*, 153.

50. Al-Qarafi, *al-Furuq*, IV, 54; Ibn Farḥūn, *Tabṣirah*, I, 131; Ibn Qayyim, *I'lām*, II, 87.

51. Al-Shaʿrāni, *Kitāb al-Mīzān*, II, 137; el-Awa, *Punishment in Islamic Law*, 128.

52. Ibn Qayyim, *al-Ṭuruq al-Ḥukmiyya*, p. 5; Saḥnūn, *Mudawwana*, VI, 293; Fahd al-Suwaylim, *al-Muttaham*, 184.

53. Al-Sharbini, *Mughni al-Muḥtāj*, IV, 150; Fahd al-Suwaylim, *al-Muttaham*, 187–188.

54. Al-Shaʿrāni, *Kitāb al-Mīzān*, II, 166.

55. Abū Dāwūd, *Sunan Abū Dāwūd* (Hasan's tran.), III, 1016, *ḥadīth* no. 3583.

56. Al-Shaʿrāni, *al-Mīzān*, II, 169.

57. Māwardī, *Aḥkām*, 71.

58. Shaltut, *al-Islam*, 327; see also al-Shaʿrāni, *Kitāb al-Mīzān*, II, 125.

59. Al-Shawkānī, *Nayl al-Awṭār*, VII, 94 (Cairo: 1347).

60. Abū Dāwūd, *Mukhtaṣar Sunan Abi Dāwūd*, ed. Al-Bughā, 643, *ḥadīth* 4495.

61. Cf. al-Bahi, *al-Dīn wa'l-Dawlah*, 394.

62. Shaltūt, *al-Islām*, 327.

63. Ibn Ḥazm, *Muḥallā* (Cairo: 1347), II, 55; Mahmassani, *al-Awzāʿi*, 138.

64. Shaltūt, *al-Islam*, 327.

65. Layish, 'Saudi Arabian Legal Reform,' 283.

66. ʿAwdah, *al-Tashri al-Jinā'i al-Islami*, I, 115. The Arabic version of the maxim reads: *lā ḥukm li-afʿal al-ʿuqalā' qabl wurūd al-naṣṣ*.

67. Al-Ghazālī, *al-Mustaṣfa*, I, 63; al-Āmidī, *al-Ihkām fi Uṣūl al-Aḥkām*, I, 130.

68. Khallāf, *ʿIlm Uṣūl al-Fiqh*, 173.

69. Cf. ʿAwdah, *Tashri* ʿ, 117.

70. 'Awdah, *al-Tashri* ʿ, I, 115.

71. Ibid., I, 133.

72. Khallāf, *'Ilm Uṣūl al-Fiqh*, p. 98.

73. Abu Zahrah, *al-Jarīma wa'l-'Uqūba*, p. 185.

74. Muslim, *Ṣaḥīḥ*: K. al-Īmān, B. al-Islām yahdim ma qablah wa kadha al-hijrat wa'l-ḥajj, *ḥadīth* no. 192; Abu Zahrah, *al-Jarīmah wa'l-'Uqūba*, 343.

75. Abu Zahrah, *al-Jarīmah*, 323; al-Saleh, 'The Right of the Individual to Personal Security,' in Bassiouni, *Islamic Criminal Justice*, 63.

76. Ibid., 138–149; see also al-Saleh, 'The Right of the Individual to Personal security,' in Bassiouni, *Islamic Criminal Justice*, 60.

77. Abu Zahrah, *al-Jarīma*, 209.

78. Al-Māwardī explains that some jurists, like ʿAbd Allāh al-Zubayri al-Shāfiʿī, have stated a maximum limit of one month of detention for the purposes of investigation. Others have suggested different time limits, but the best view is that the Imam may specify the limit as he deems fit: *Kitāb al-Aḥkām al-Sulṭāniyya*, 192; 'Awdah, *al-Tashri al-Jinā'i*, I, 150.

79. Abu Zahrah, *al-Jarīma*, 208; 'Awdah, *al-Tashrī*ʿ, 308.

80. See details Ibn Qayyim, *al-Ṭuruq*, 124; see also al-Māwardī, *al-Aḥkām*, 205.

81. Cf. Ibn Qayyim, *al-Ṭuruq al-Ḥukmiyya*, 93–94. Fahd al-Suwaylin, *al-Muttaham*, 23.

82. Abū Dāwūd, *Mukhtaṣar Sunan Abī Dāwūd*, ed. al-Bughā, 717, *hadīth* 4993.

83. Bukhārī, *Ṣaḥīḥ al-Bukhārī* (Khan's trans.), VIII, 58, *hadīth* 90; Muslim, *Sahih Muslim, kitab al-birr wa'l-Ṣilla, bab al-nahy 'an al-tajassus.*

84. Cf. al-Qurṭubi, *al-Jāmiʿ li-Aḥkām al-*Qur'ān, XVI, 331.

85. Syed Quṭb, *Fi Ẓilāl al-Qur'ān*, VI, 3346.

86. Ibid., VI, 3343; al-Shaʿrāni, *Kitāb al-Mīzān*, p. 166.

87. Al-'Alwāni, 'The Rights of the Accused in Isam,' *AJISS*, 11 (1994), 363.

88. Al-Awad, 'The Right of the Accused Under Islamic Criminal Procedure,' in Bassiouni, *Islamic Criminal Justice*, p. 104; al-Saleh, *loc cit*, 68.

89. Sulami, *Qawā ʿid al-Aḥkām* (Rayyan edn.), 160–161.

90. Ghazālī, *Iḥyāʾ*, II, 124–25.

91. Ghazālī, *Iḥyāʾ*, II, 120–21.

92. *Id.*, II, 121.

93. Ghazālī, *Iḥyāʾ*, I, 123.

94. Ghazālī, *Iḥyā*, II, 47. Abū Dāwūd, *Mukhtaṣar Sunan*, ed., al-Bughā, 368, *hadīth* 2659.

95. *Id.*, II, 48.

96. Asad, *Principles of State and Government*, 85–86.

97. Māwardī, *Aḥkām*, 252.

98. Cf. al-Qurṭubi, *Aḥkām al-Qur'ān*, XVI, 331–332; al-Dusuqi, *Ḥāshiya al-Dusuqi*, IV, 144; al-Jundi, *Damānāt*, 185–186.

99. Al-Kāsāni, *Badā'iʿ al-Ṣanā'iʿ*, VI, 277; al-Sharbini, *Mughni al-Muḥtāj*, IV, 437.

100. Al-Dusuqi, *Ḥashiyah al-Dusūqi*, 144; al-Sharbini, *Mughni al-Muḥtāj*, IV, 464.

101. Ibn Abidin, *Ḥāshiya*, V, 544; al-Qarafi, *al-Furūq*, IV, 72; Ibn Farḥūn, *Tabṣirat al-Ḥukkām*, I, 148; Ibn Juzay, *Qawānīn*, p. 304.

102. Ibn Farḥūn, *Tabṣirat*, II, 145; al-Māwardī, *al-Aḥkām*, 219.

103. Ibn Farḥūn, *Tabṣirat*, II, 156; Ibn Taymiyya, *Majmuʿ Fatāwā*, XXX-IV, 236; Ibn Qayyim al-Jawziyya, *al-Ṭuruq*, p. 101; al-Jundī, *Damānāt*, 182.

104. Abū Dāwūd, *Sunan Abū Dāwūd*, Kitāb al-Aqḍiyah, Bāb fī al-Habs, *hadīth* no. 1381.

105. *Ibid., hadīth* no. 3630.

106. Ibn Qayyim al-Jawziyya, *al-Ṭuruq al-Ḥukmiyyah*, , 101.

107. Al-Māwardī, *al-Aḥkām al-Sulṭāniyyah*, 152; Ibn Qayyim, *al-Ṭuruq*, 103; Ibn ʿĀbidīn, *Ḥāshiyah*, IV, 188; al-Bajī, *al-Muntaqā*, VII, 166.

108. Al-Māwardī, *al-Aḥkām*, 220.

109. Kamali, 'Siyāsah Sharʿiyyah or the Policies of Islamic Government,' *AJISS*, 6 (1989), 59-81.

110. Ibn Farḥūn, *Tabṣirat*, II, 158; al-Bajī, *al-Muntaqā*, VII, 166; al-Zaylaʿī, *Baḥr al-Rāʾiq*, V, 46.

111. Ibn Qayyim, *al-Ṭuruq*, 104-105; al-ʿĪlī, *Ḥurriyyāt*, 369.

112. Al-Māwardī, *al-Aḥkām* (Matbacah al-Sacadah edn.), 220; Ibn Qayyim, *al-Ṭuruq*, 104; Ibn ʿĀbidīn, *Ḥāshiyah*, IV, 15.

113. Al-Qurṭubī, *al-Jāmiʿ li-Aḥkām al-Qurʾān*, VII, 6152; al-Jundī, *Ḍamānāt*, 182-186.

114. Al-Ṣanʿānī, *al-Muṣannaf*, I, 217; Ibn Ḥazm, *Muḥallā*, II, 16.

115. Abū Yūsuf, *al-Kharāj*, II, 190-191.

116. Ibn Qayyim al-Jawziyya, *al-Ṭuruq al-Ḥukmiyyah*, 102; Shishānī, *Ḥuqūq al-Insān*, 376.

117. Cf. Shishānī, *Ḥuqūq al-Insān*, 377.

118. Al-Zaylaʿī, *Baḥr al-Rāʾiq*, V, 6; Suwaylim, *al-Muttaham*, 92

119. *Id., K. al-Ḥudūd*, b. Fiʾl-Imtiḥān biʾl-Ḥarb, *ḥadīth* 4382.

120. Al-Māwardī, *al-Aḥkām*, 220; Ibn Farhun, *Tabsirah*, II, 329.

121. Al-Shāṭibi, *Iʿtiṣām*, II, 120.

122. Cf. Shishāni, *Ḥuqūq al-Insān*, 376.

123. Ibn Taymiyya, *Majmu ʿ Fatāwā*, XXXIV, 238; see also al-Māwardī, *Aḥkām*, 220; Ibn Qayyim, *al-Ṭuruq al-Ḥukmiyya*, p. 105; Ibn Farḥūn, *Tabṣira*, II, 154 & 158.

124. Māwardī, *Aḥkām*, 220.

125. Fahd al-Suwaylim, *al-Muttaham*, 116–117.

126. Al-ʾAlwani, 'The Rights of the Accused,' (part two), *AJISS* 11, (1994), 507.

127. Suwalim, *al-Muttaham*, 101–102.

128. Bukhārī, *Ṣaḥīḥ al-Bukhārī*, (Khan's trans.), VIII, 511, *ḥadīth* 776.

129. Ibid., VIII, 559, *ḥadīth* 839; Ibn Taymiyya, *al-Siyāsa*, 153.

130. Al-Ḥākim, *al-Mustadrak*, II, 216; al-Bayhaqi, *al-Sunan*, VIII, 36.

131. Ghazālī, *Shifāʾ al-Ghalīl*, 111.

132. Al-Ghazālī, *Shifāʾ al-Ghalīl*, 110; see also idem., *al-Mustaṣfā*, I, 297. Ibn Ḥazm, *Muḥallā*, VIII, 141; al-Bājī, *Muntaqā*, VII, 166; Ibn Farḥūn, *Tabṣira*, II, 158.

133. Id., 110.

134. Ghazālī, *Shifāʾ al-Ghalīl*, p. 111. *Ḥadīth* also recorded in the *Muwaṭṭā* of Imam Malik, *ḥadīth* no. 12 in *Kitab al-Ḥudūd*.

135. Al-Ghazālī, *Shifāʾ al-Ghalīl*, 110.

136. Al-Ḥākim, *Mustadrak*, II, 198. Bukhārī, has recorded the same *ḥadīth* with slight variation in wording. See *Ṣaḥīḥ al-Bukhārī* (Khan's tran.), VIII, 527, *ḥadīth* 805.

137. Saḥnūn, *al-Mudawwanat al-Kubrā*, VI, 293.

138. Al-Sarakhsi, *Mabsūṭ*, XXIV, 70.

139. Muslim, *Mukhtaṣar Ṣaḥīḥ*, p. 272, *ḥadīth* 1028.

140. Abū Dāwūd, *Sunan Abi Dāwūd*, ed. al-Bughā, p. 366, *ḥadīth* 2650.

141. Ibn Qayyim, *al-Ṭuruq al-Ḥukmiyya*, 9; Ibn Farhūn, *Tabṣira*, II, 139.

142. Abū Dāwūd, *Mukhtaṣar Sunan Abi Dāwūd*, ed. al-Bughā, 372, *ḥadīth* 2681.

143. Al-Bukhārī, *Ṣaḥīḥ*, VI, 12; Muslim, *Ṣaḥīḥ*, IV, 2133.

144. Ibn Farhūn, *Tabṣira*, II, 137; al-Tarablisi, *Muʿīn al-Ḥukkām*, p. 171.

145. Ibn Qayyim, *al-Ṭuruq al-Ḥukmiyya*, p.106; al-Shāṭibi, *Iʿtiṣām*, II, 120.

146. Ibn., p. 108.

147. Ibn Qayyim al-Jawziyya, *al-Ṭuruq al-Ḥukmiyya*, 104.

148. Ibn Farhūn, *Tabṣira*, II, 157–158.

149. Al-Bājī, *al-Muntaqā*, VII, 166.

150. Ibn Farhūn, *Tabṣira*, II, 162.

151. Al-'Alwani, 'The Right of the Accused in Islam,' (Part Two), *AJISS* 11 (1994), 512—quoting Ibn ʿĀbidin, *Ḥāshiya*, III, 259.

152. Ibn Ḥazm, *Muḥallā*, VIII, 132; See also Suwaylim, *al-Muttaham*, 116.

153. Al-Shāṭibi, *al-Iʿtiṣām*, II, 120.

154. Ibn Farhūn, *Tabṣira*, 5, 184.

155. *Id.*, I, 185.

156. *Id.*

157. *Id.*, I, 179.

158. *Id.*, I, 180.

159. *Id.*, I, 184.

160. Al-Kāsani, *Badā'i 'al-Ṣanā'i ʿ*, VI, 21.

161. Al-Shirāzi, *Muhadhdhab*, I, 349; al-Sharbīni, *Mughni al-Muḥtāj*, II, 221; Awad, 'Rights of the Individual Under Islamic Procedure,' in Bassiouni, *Islamic Criminal Justice*, 97.

162. Al-Kāsani, *Bādā'i ʿ*, VI, 22; Ibn Qudāmah, *al-Mughni*, V, 89–90; al-Shirāzi, *Muhadhdhab*, I, 355.

163. Al-Mardāwi, *al-Inṣāf*, V, 394; al-Buhūti, *Kashshāf al-Qannā ʿ*, III, 483.

164. Ibn Farhūn, *Tabṣira*, I, 185.

165. Tirmidhi, *Sunan al-Tirmidhi*, *ḥadīth* 2976.

166. Abū Dāwūd, *Sunan*, III, 305; al-Bayhaqi, *al-Sunan al-Kubrā*, VI, 82.

167. Māwardī, *Aḥkām*, p. 75; Ibn Farhūn, *Tabṣira*, I, 47; 'Afifi, *al-Ḥuqūq al-Maʿnawiyya*, p. 65.

168. Ibn Farhūn, *Tabṣira*, I, 47–52; ʿAfifi, *Ḥuqūq*, p. 62.

169. Kāsani, *Bādā'i ʿ*, IX, 4096.

170. Māwardī, *Aḥkām* (Maṭba ʿa al-Saʿāda edn.), 59; Kāsani, *Bādā'i ʿ* (Ali Yūsuf Publishing), IX, 4093 & 4102.

171. Kāsāni, *Badā'i ᶜ*, IX, 4099–4102.

172. *Id.*, IX, 4096.

173. *Id.*

174. *Id.*IX, 4102.

175. *Id.* IX, 4102.

176. Ibn Farḥūn, *Tabṣira*, I, 55.

177. Ibn Qayyim al-Jawziyya, *al-Ṭuruq*, (Adāb edn.) p. 24.

178. 'Awdah, *al-Tashri' al-Jina'i*, I, 60.

179. Abū Dāwūd, *Mukhtaṣar Sunan Abi Dāwūd*, ed. Al-Bughā, 512, *ḥadīth* 3596.

180. Zuhaylī, *al-Fiqh al-Islāmī*, VI, 559 quotes the *ḥadīth* on the authority of Ibn ᶜAbbās. The context in which the *ḥadīth* occurs is the requirement of eye-witnessing, immediately following the theme of whether or not a blind person can be a witness. See also ᶜAfifi, *al-Ḥuqūq*, p. 71; Bahnasi, *Naẓariyya al-Ithbāt*, 14.

181. Abū Dāwūd, *Mukhtaṣar Sunan*, ed. Al-Bughā, 512, *ḥadīth* 3598.

182. *Id.* 513, *ḥadīth* 3600.

183. Ibn Farḥūn, *Tabṣira*, 241–243.

184. Ibn Qayyim al-Jawziyya, *al-Ṭuruq al-Ḥukmiyya*, (Adab edn.), p. 97.

185. Ibn Farḥūn, *Tabṣira*, I, 56–59; Ibn Qayyim al-Jawziyya, *al-Ṭuruq*, 125.

186. *Id.*, I, 243.

187. *Id.*, I, 244; Ibn Qayyim al-Jawziyya, *al-Ṭuruq*, p. 187.

188. Cf. Layish, 'Saudi Arabian Legal Reform,' 283.

189. Ibn Farḥūn, *Tabṣira*, I, 97.

190. *Id.*, See also for details Ibn Qayyim al-Jawziyya, *al-Ṭuruq*, 174 ff.

191. Kāsāni, Badā'i ᶜ (Ali Yūsuf Publishing) IX, 4096–4099.

192. Ibn Qayyim al-Jawziyya, *al-Ṭuruq al-Ḥukmiyya*, 174.

193. ᶜAwdah, *al-Tashri ᶜ al-Jinā'i*, I, 303–304.

194. ᶜAwdah, *al-Tashri ᶜ al-Jinā'i*, I, 303–304.

195. Ibn Qudāmah, *Mughnī*, V, 273; ᶜAwdah, *al-Tashri ᶜ*, I, 313.

196. ᶜAwdah, *al-Tashri ᶜ al-Jinā'i*, I, 306.

197. Kāsāni, *Badā'i ᶜ*, VII, 50.

198. ᶜAwwa, *al-Fiqh al-Islāmī*, 182; *idem. Fi Uṣūl al-Niẓām al-Jinā'i*, 309.

199. *Id.*, 307.

200. Sarakhsī, *al-Mabsūṭ*, IX, 180.

201. ᶜAwdah, *al-Tashri ᶜ al-Jinā'ī*, 314.

202. *Id.*

203. Kāsāni, *Badā'i ᶜ al-Sanā'i ᶜ*, vol. VIII, 3925.

204. *Id.*

205. Ibn Qayyim al-Jawziyya, *al-Ṭuruq al-Ḥukmiyya*, 70–71.

206. Ibn Qayyim al-Jawziyya, *al-Ṭuruq al-Ḥukmiyya*, 24; ʿAfifi, *al-Ḥuqūq al-Maʿnawiyya*, 71.

207. Ibn Qayyim, *al-Ṭuruq al-Ḥukmiyya*, 16f.

208. Ibn Qayyim, *Iʿlām al-Muwaqqiʾin*.

209. Muḥammad Salām Madkūr, *al-Qaḍaʾ fiʾl-Islām*, Cairo: Dār al-Nahḍ ah, 1964, 84.

210. Bahnasī, *Naẓariyyat al-Ithbāt*, 14.

211. *Id.*, 75ff.

212. As quoted by Ibn Qayyim al-Jawziyya, *al-Ṭuruq*, 84.

213. *Id.*, 185–86.

214. *Id.*, 185–86.

215. Al-ʿAwwa, *al-Fiqh al-Islāmī fī Ṭarīq al-Tajdīd*, 179.

216. *Id.*, 180–181.

217. *Id.*, 179–180.

218. Cf. Ahmad Ibrahim, *The Administration of Islamic Law in Malaysia*, 699f.

219. ʿAlwāni, 'The Right of the Accused' *AJISS* 11 (1994), 518.

CHAPTER THREE

The Right to Privacy
(*Ḥaqq al-khuṣūṣiyya*)

I. Introductory Remarks

The notion of privacy and all it includes varies in different societies and cultural settings. What people expect to be included in this right or deem to fall outside its ambit is often changeable, even within one society in historical terms, or in relationship to a particular turn of events. This might explain the absence of a comprehensive definition of privacy, or of a consensus among scholars of comparative law about the essential elements of the right to privacy. Judges have often shown a reluctance to draw clear lines of division between the private life of the individual and what might be said to be the domain of public life, or vice versa.[1] Justice Louise D. Brandies of the United States is said to have coined a simple definition over 100 years ago. No judge has actually given a complete definition since then. Brandies wrote simply that 'privacy is the right to be left alone.'[2] According to another commentator, an 'infringement of privacy may be described as interference with another person's seclusion of himself, his family or his property from the public.' An infringement of privacy can occur in various forms, including unreasonable intrusion upon a person, appropriation of their name or likeness, unreasonable publicity, and publicity that places another person in a false light.[3]

According to an alternative definition, the right to personal privacy is the 'immunity of the person, [and their right] to safeguard and protect what is private and confidential against detection, surveillance and the interference of others, including his friends and relatives and the state, without his consent, and his entitlement to defend [his privacy] against intrusion.'[4]

It is evident in this definition that the right to privacy is meaningful when one lives in society and enjoys a wide level of interaction with others. It would hold little meaning, in other words, for the one who lives in isolation from others. The right to privacy also takes for granted the personal freedom of the individual to reveal confidential information about himself to anyone he wishes by a grant of permission, conversation and correspondence, or through direct contact, within the limits of decency and public morality. Physical exposure of what is private (ʿawra) in the Islamic context may not be publicly exercised, nor is a worshipper totally free to violate the rules of ʿawrah on religious occasions and during worship, even behind closed doors. But most of the limitations that one must observe in public are omitted when one is behind closed doors and within the privacy of one's home. A person's home is the most immediate manifestation in law of his right to privacy against the outside world, and is protected by the Sharīʿah provision of istiʾdhān, that is, the requirement of asking an owner's permission to enter his house. This is a right that puts others under an obligation not to pry or intrude on the privacy of the individual, and places relatively fewer constraints on the bearer of this right himself and the manner in which he wishes to exercise it.

The right to privacy refers not only to the sanctity of an individual's home but to all other aspects of privacy, such as that of personal correspondence, the confidentiality of one's private activities, personal conversations and financial affairs. It is basically a generic right, which includes everything that is regarded as personal and private, and which an individual dislikes to share with others. It has certain manifestations which are fairly obvious, such as the prohibition of entering the private home without the permission of its residents, but some of its aspects are less tangible and relate to individual states of mind and attitudes. That which is considered to be secret and confidential (al-sirr) can thus be a matter of the state of mind of a person, and may include all that he or she thinks should be concealed from others. It may consist of matters pertaining to a real person or may concern a corporate personality, and the subject-matter may also pertain to either private or public affairs, professional matters, and matters of concern to family and social relations.[5] The directives of the Qur'ān and Sunnah on privacy are general in that they do not specify the scope of what may or may not be included. The demands, for example, in the Qur'ān and Sunnah, to avoid ill-founded suspicion concerning others, and to avoid enquiring into private and confidential affairs of others, tend to lay down the basis of a right, but do not specify the scope of that right.

Given the nomadic lifestyle of the Arabs at the advent of Islam, their desert-like environment and the relative absence of physical barriers that could separate the private home from the outside world, it is notable that the Arabs have shown a high level of sensitivity towards the privacy of the home. The concern to protect the private life of the individual both within and outside the family unit is clearly conveyed in the Qur'ān and also in the normative teachings and *Sunnah* of the Prophet. The emphasis that is thus laid on the privacy of the home, and on the immunity of the individual against prying and espionage, were also complementary and supportive of other interests, such as those relating to the preservation of the family unit and the protection of private ownership.

For a totally different set of reasons, the sensitivities of the Arabs' nomadic lifestyle, and their rigorous protection of the right to privacy, relate well to the concerns of modern society. This is despite the fact that modernity has brought with it housing facilities that give little cause for concern for privacy, even in contemporary Arabia itself, unlike the borderless environment of the desert. Yet it is ironical that the physical boundaries and structures of the modern era have long been penetrated by some of the latest instruments of modernity. The computerisation of data, electronic devices, a globalisation of the means of communication, and aggressive detection and policing strategies present the modern man with a concern for his privacy no less perhaps than the nomadic Arab of pre-modern times. The complexities generated by these new developments naturally require specific responses in order that the integrity and meaning of an individual's right to privacy be preserved.

The comparison between nomadic and modern urban lifestyles serves to show how different lifestyles can each present a threat to the right to privacy that is different only in form. The basic concern about the integrity of this right, which emanates from the intrusive and inquisitive attitudes of others, has remained a constant preoccupation of modern society almost everywhere. Indeed, the basic data of the Qur'ān and *Sunnah* on the protection of the right to privacy remains relevant to the conditions of contemporary society, despite the long interval of time and the vast changes of circumstance. The evidence in the Qur'ān and *Sunnah*, which we will presently discuss, tends to be thematic, and addresses only certain aspects of the right to privacy, such as the privacy of the home, the need to ask for permission prior to entering a private dwelling, the prohibition of espionage (*al-tajassus*) and what might be seen as preliminaries to espionage, namely suspicion (*al-ẓann*) and exposing the hidden weaknesses of others. I shall review these and respond to the question of how the law regulates instances of conflict between the proper exercise of this right and considerations of public interest. What are the circumstances, in other words, where other considerations might take priority over the right to privacy?

The discussion that follows begins with the privacy of the home, where relevant passages in the Qur'ān and *Sunnah* on the subject of *isti'dhān* are discussed. This is followed, in the next section, by similar coverage of espionage, and then two related themes, namely suspicion (*al-ẓann*) and looking into someone's personal correspondence, are addressed in the succeeding two sections. Section six addresses a theme that takes some prominence in the *Sharīʿah*, namely the concealment of the private affairs of others (*satr al-ʿawrāt*). The next section addresses the confidentiality of personal conversation, and is followed, in section eight, by a discussion of the deceased person's right to privacy. The last section discusses restrictions on the right to privacy in such areas as the testimony of witnesses, the solicitation of a legal opinion and *fatwā*, the role of personal consent in the disclosure of confidential information, and considerations of public interest (*maṣlaḥa*).

II. The Privacy of the Home (*Ḥurmat al–Maskan*)

This is in many ways the centrepiece of the right to privacy in *Sharīʿah*. One might note at the outset that a private home or dwelling (*maskan, manzil, bayt*) is more of a concept than a physical structure of any particular kind. For a private dwelling can mean a conventional home or apartment that has well-defined boundaries and walls, or other structures that might have been erected in a place that is not owned by its occupier; it can also include a flimsy structure that may fail to provide a physical barrier against intruders. Yet in all its various manifestations, the private dwelling is, according to the Qur'ānic view, a place where one resides and where others are not allowed to enter without one's permission. The individual's home is his private preserve, his castle so to speak, and an exclusive place where he feels safe from the intrusion of others. This is maintained in the Qur'ānic passages which outline the importance of seeking permission (*isti'dhān*), and its protection against the intruding eyes of outsiders. As such, the Qur'ān tends to define the home (*bayt*) by a description of some of its attributes.

A home is thus signified as a place of rest, where an individual seeks peace, and has the exclusive prerogative to grant or to refuse permission for others to enter it.

The privacy of the home is the subject of several passages in the Qur'ān, but the passage reviewed below focuses on *isti'dhān* (asking for permission), which signifies the starting point of the Qur'ānic exposition on the right to privacy. The text enjoins the believers:

يا أيها الذين آمنوا لا تدخلوا بيوتا غير بيوتكم حتى تستأنسوا وتسلّموا على أهلها ذلكم خير لكم لعلكم تذكرون. فإن لم تجدوا فيها أحدا فلا تدخلوها حتى يؤذن لكم، وإن قيل لكم ارجعوا فارجعوا هو أزكى لكم والله بما تعملون عليم. ليس عليكم جناح أن تدخلوا بيوتا غير مسكونة فيها متاع لكم والله يعلم ماتبدون وماتكتمون.

Do not enter houses (*buyutan*) other than your own (*buyutikum*), until you have asked permission and saluted their inmates. This is better for you, so that you may be mindful. But if you find no-one therein, do not enter them until permission is given to you. If you are asked to go back, then go back, for this is certainly purer for yourselves, and God knows all that you do. It is no sin for you to enter uninhabited houses which might serve a good purpose for you; and God knows what you do openly and what you conceal (24:27–29).[6]

Reports indicate that this verse was revealed following a complaint to the Prophet by 'a woman from the Anṣār' in Madina, who lived in an apparently crowded household together with her father and other relatives. She complained that she did not enjoy privacy because members of the household, especially the men, moved about and at times entered upon her when she wanted privacy. One might also note in this connection that the pre-Islamic Arabs were not particularly observant of the rules and etiquettes of privacy, and that partly because of the hot climate, they often took off their clothes in the company of their spouses. In the pre-Islamic period, people used to freely visit the houses of others without obtaining prior permission, and this became a source of inconvenience for their residents. The Qur'ān thus laid down new rules, the most important among which was the requirement to obtain permission.[7] People can disallow entry for a variety of reasons. They may refuse to see someone because of the inconvenience it might cause, or because they do not wish to expose their private lives. A refusal could also be due to psychological problems, such as anger, or a recent quarrel within the family, preparation for other expected visitors, or because people might not be well. Permission for entry is therefore necessary to avoid sudden inconvenience to the host. Having stated this, Syed Quṭb recommends that permission to enter a house nowadays should be sought by telephone. For it is socially undesirable for visitors and guests to arrive unannounced and expect hospitality and welcome without prior appointment.[8]

The procedure of entering other people's homes expounded in this verse focuses on two points, one of which is to ask for permission, and the other is to greet the inmates. The word '*tasta'nisū*' (lit. familiarise yourselves) in this text is taken to be, for all intents and purposes, equivalent to '*tasta'dhinū*' (ask for permission), since the two often coincide,[9] although one might add that '*tasta'nisu*' is more specific about identifying oneself by name, and introducing oneself and then asking for permission. The main purpose is, of course, to avoid intrusion and startling others in the privacy of their homes. The occupant must be approached with courtesy and tact, and even then the latter has the undiminished prerogative to refuse permission and tell the visitor to simply turn back without giving any reason or explanation. To seek permission and to greet the inmates are two aspects of the proper manner of honouring a person's right to privacy, and achieving excellence of conduct in this situation.

The text under review begins with a prohibition on entering dwellings that are inhabited by other people, and this is followed by the provision of asking for permission. The subsequent portion of the text reinforces the need for *isti'dhān* by stating that when an inmate refuses to grant permission, the visitor must not persist and must leave. There is further elaboration of this portion of the verse in a *ḥadīth*, quoted below, which states that if the inhabitants do not respond after three attempts at *isti'dhān*, the visitor must leave, although some commentators have noted from the general reading of the text that it is preferable to leave at once after a refusal, rather than repeat one's attempt at *isti'dhān*, or even wait outside the door in question.[10] Imam Mālik has observed that the *Sunnah* concerning *isti'dhān* is three attempts, and no more, unless the person knows that he has not been heard by the inmates, in which case a further attempt may be made in order to make oneself heard.[11] Al-Kāsānī has added that the three attempts to obtain permission must be separate if they are to fulfill the requirement. If someone repeats the request for *isti'dhān* three times one after another, this counts as one attempt only and fails to fulfill the possibility of triple *isti'dhān*.[12] The succeeding portion of the verse relaxes the requirement of *isti'dhān* in the case of uninhabited dwellings when entering them might serve a useful purpose. Commentators have elaborated that 'uninhabited dwellings' here applies also to public places, shops, government offices, guesthouses and hotels, which are normally open to visitors, and permission to enter them, is not a requirement for those who go there for a lawful purposes. But even so, visiting particular quarters within public places, such as hotel rooms occupied by guests, or private office quarters within government buildings and so forth, are not exempt from the requirement of *isti'dhān*.[13]

The Shāfiʿī jurist al-Sulami (d. 660/262) has discussed the relevance of general custom (*ʿurf*) in this context, arguing that *ʿurf* should be the basic indicator by which to differentiate public and private places, and thereby judge the need to obtain permission to enter the latter. There is customarily no need, Sulami writes, to obtain permission to enter public baths, government offices and courthouses once they open their doors to the public. But this does not eliminate the need for obtaining permission to enter certain parts of such premises, which may be private, and general custom determines them as such. Permission is either based on *ʿurf*, as shown in these examples, or it is based on the word of the inhabitants; where the former is not known or is doubtful, the latter needs to be solicited and obtained. Entering public schools may not require permission, but entering a church may well do since 'the worshippers or inmates of a church may dislike a Muslim to enter.' Custom sometimes also facilitates permission to enter private dwellings by stipulating a certain method or procedure for it. Permission to enter is in principle only granted by an adult, but custom seems to approve a child reporting the permission of the owner (his or her father perhaps) to the visitor who knocks at the outside door.[14] Entering compounds with several apartments does not customarily require advance permission, but if some of the inhabitants object to someone's entry, it is not permitted.[15] These were some of the examples that al-Sulamī gave from his own time. They may be liable to change because of changes in custom, but the basic rule he advocated on the normative role of custom in determining the applicability of *isti'dhān* remains valid.

Some juristic disagreement has arisen as to whether or not the verse under review was mainly educational, and conveyed moral advice rather than an obligation. Many have understood it to be educational, but the preferred view (*al-ra'y al-rājih*) on this is that the verse conveys an obligation. This is due to the imperative form of the Arabic, *li-yasta'dhinakum*, and also the fact that the *Sunnah* of the Prophet on this supports the idea of obligation.

The definitive language of the Qur'ānic text and the fact that it is conveyed in general terms (ʿāmm) also means that it is applicable to everyone, including one's relatives, men, women and even children, government authorities and the police without any exception. This is also true of the prohibition at the beginning of the text, which is conveyed in general terms without exceptions. Al-Alūsi has thus observed that 'Seeking permission before entering a private home is obligatory (*wājib*) on all of God's creatures.'[16] The right to the privacy of one's home is thus established by a clear text, and so any exception to or qualification of the terms of this text must be founded on evidence that is equally clear and decisive. This text is also clear on the point that only the inhabitant of a dwelling is entitled to grant permission to enter, provided that the person concerned is in full possession of his faculties. Children and servants are not normally entitled to grant such a permission, but as already noted, the rules of custom also play a role in who may or may not be entitled to grant permission to enter.[17]

It is also noted in the relevant commentaries that the requirement of *isti'dhān* represents a Qur'ānic reform, since Arab traditions had hitherto not taken a clear stand on this before. People often entered other people's dwellings without asking for permission or greeting the inhabitants. They simply declared themselves by such utterances as 'It is me' (*anā, anā*) or '*laqad dakhaltu*' (I've come, or I've entered), and they did so regardless of the inconvenience they might cause to the inhabitants. Thus according to one *ḥadīth*, Jābir b. ʿAbd Allāh narrated that 'I went to the Prophet's house concerning the debt he owed my father. I knocked at the door and the Prophet, peace be on him, asked 'Who is it?' and I said 'I,—*anā*.' The Prophet repeated '*anā anā*' as if he disliked hearing it.'[18]

عن جابر أنه ذهب إلى النبى صلى الله عليه وسلم فى دين أبيه فدققت الباب، فقـال: من هذا؟ قلت: أنا. قال: أنا، أنا كأنه كرهه .

The matter of access to the Prophet is the subject of a Qur'ānic verse, where the following instruction is given:

يآيهــا الذيــن آمنوا لاتدخلوا بيوت النـبي إلا أن يؤذن لكـم إلى طعام غيــر ناظريــن إناه ولكــن إذا دعيتــم فادخلوا فإذا طعمتــم فانتشروا ولامســـتأنسين لحديــث إن ذلكــم كان يؤذى النـبي فيستحى منكم.

O believers, do not enter the Prophet's houses unless you are admitted for a meal and (not so early as) to wait for its preparation. But if you are invited, enter, and when your meal is ended, then disperse. Do not linger for conversation. Such (behaviour) causes annoyance to the Prophet (33:53).

Clearly the Prophet's friends treated him with familiarity, dropped in without notice, waited for a meal to be served, and stayed after the meal to engage in conversation with one another. Yet this behaviour was unseemly, especially when the Prophet became head of state. He needed a measure of seclusion from the people to ensure privacy for himself and his family.

This interpretation is supported by the next section of the same verse, though the subject is different: 'And when you ask the women (i.e. the Prophet's wives) anything, ask them from behind a curtain. That is purer for your hearts and their hearts,' (33:53).

وإذا سألتموهن متاعا فسألوهن من وراء حجاب.

The issue of privacy of the Prophet and his household is also the subject of another Qur'ānic verse where it is provided that:

إن الذين ينادونك من وراء الحجرات أكثرهم لايعقلون.

Those who call you from the back of the apartments—
most of them do not understand. (49:4).

The Arabs used to walk to the back of the Prophet's house, where the private apartments of his wives were situated, and shout 'Muḥammad' to summon him. The Prophet disliked this behaviour, which was rightly attributed to their ignorance. The correct advice was thus given as follows:

ولو أنهم صبروا حتى تخرج إليهم لكان خيرا لهم.

'If they would wait until you come out to them, this would be better for them,' (49:5).

In conformity with the style of Qur'ānic legislation, the injunction on *isti'dhān* is set out in the language of exhortation and persuasion, reminding its audience of the greater purity and refinement of character solicited by this legislation. The language of persuasion was deemed appropriate since the new rulings sought to reform the unruly practices of the Arabs, which had persisted among the nascent community of believers. The legal terms of the text thus made a moral appeal, so as to make *isti'dhān* a feature of the day-to-day life of the Muslim community. The Prophet reinforced and elaborated on Qur'ānic guidelines in his *Sunnah*, and reports indicate that Qur'ānic reforms were on the whole well received and adhered to by the Companions, some of whom observed the requirement of *isti'dhān* almost to the letter, although it is also noted that triple *isti'dhān* was not commonly practised, a point we will return to later. Although repetition for a third time was generally understood to be the last repetition, Imam Mālik has rightly held that triple *isti'dhān* may be exceeded if one is sure that the inmate has not actually heard the visitor's request for permission.[19]

The initial phrase at the beginning of the verse quoted above proscribes entering 'houses other than your own,' which might raise a question about the significance of ownership in this context, and whether one is allowed to enter one's own house without any restrictions. Is the owner, in other words, allowed to enter his own house whenever he wishes? In answer to this, it is stated that the emphasis is on occupancy, not ownership, hence the fuller reading of the text might be rendered as '...Do not enter houses other than your own, which you occupy.' The owner, or property manager, is in exactly the same position, therefore, as anyone else, and must obtain permission before entering a place he owns (or manages) but which is occupied by others.[20]

Commenting on the Arabic word '*maskan*' (home), al-Isfahāni wrote that it signifies a place where one finds security from fear, a place where one feels at ease, with a sense of peace, privacy and assurance about one's person, property and honour.[21] Similar Arabic words, such as '*al-bayt*' and '*al-manzil*' and '*al-dār*' convey the same meaning, and they all signify a place in which one actually lives, regardless of whether or not it is suitable for living, and whether the occupancy is temporary or long-term. The physical structure of the house and the materials from which it is made are irrelevant; whether weak or strong, a cave or tent, a mobile home or a caravan, every home enjoys the same protection, regardless of its location, monetary value and other attributes. 'House' in this sense also includes all its attachments, such as the roof, doors, windows, basement, garden etc., provided that they all belong to the same unit. Proof of ownership or possession is also not a requirement. Even a squatter home to which its legal owner has turned a blind eye will most likely be protected for the purposes of the exercise of the right to privacy.[22] In the event where a place which has no separate compartments is shared by several inhabitants, they all enjoy equal right of entry without seeking the permission of the others, such as in the common rooms of dormitories, shops, and hospitals. The position would, however, be different if the dwelling in question has separate compartments, in which case residents would need to seek permission of their respective inmates prior to entry.[23]

It is reported that the Prophet limited the number of requests for entry to three at any given time. The *hadīth* in question thus provides that:

$$\text{الإستئذان ثلاث، فإن أذن لك وإلا فارجع.}$$

Asking for permission is (allowed up to) three times;
if it is not granted to you, you must return.[24]

It is further stated that there should be a slight pause in between the three attempts, so as to prepare inmates and give them time to receive a visitor. The first time is for alerting, the second for allowing time for the inmate to change into suitable attire, and the third is to obtain a reply about whether or not to enter. This is what the Companions Abu Hurayra and a leading Successor, Qatāda b. Diʿāma, are reported to have said.[25]

Despite the affirmation in one *hadīth* that إنما جعل الإذن لأجل البصر: 'The purpose of *istiʾdhān* is to validate viewing,'[26] a blind person is not exempted from the requirement of *istiʾdhān*. This is because the Qurʾānic injunction on *istiʾdhān* is unqualified and general (ʿāmm), and also because hearing in this case is taken as a substitute for viewing. Hence a person who can hear, even if unable to see, falls under the same ruling.[27] On a broader note, it is suggested that personal privacy and the sanctity of the home can be violated in many different ways, including by hearing, touching and smelling that which is private, and the failure of one or more of these faculties does not suspend the requirement of *istiʾdhān*.

As for the question of whether repeating a request to enter three times is a requirement in every case, the *'ulamā'* have responded that it is not a requirement, and should the permission be granted upon the first request, there is no need for a repetition. Repetition is not a part of the original injunction; it is a supplementary addition by the *Sunnah*, which emphasises the basic right to privacy, and lays down a limit as to when to stop repeating one's request for permission to enter. It is further stated that repetition beyond this limit may annoy the inmate, and compromise the integrity of his right to privacy.[28] There is, however, a variant view, attributed to Qatāda b. Diʿāma, to the effect that triple *isti'dhān* is the correct interpretation of the Qur'ānic term '*tasta'nisū*' (familiarise yourselves), and it is therefore a requirement in every case.[29] This is, however, a weak opinion, and the majority position is that repetition should be resorted to only when appropriate, but it is not a requirement as such, is preferable. Finally, notwithstanding the sequence of the Qur'ānic text, it has been deemed to be preferable to greet the inmates first and then ask for permission to enter.[30]

The authority quoted for this interpretation is the *ḥadīth* which requires that 'greeting precedes speech,'[31]

السلام قبل الكلام.

and more specifically the *ḥadīth* on the authority of ʿAbd Allāh b. ʿUmar which provides that:

عن أبى هريرة فيمن يستأذن قبل أن يسلم، قال لايؤذن حتى يسلم.

'If someone asks for permission before greeting,
answer him not until he greets.'[32]

According to yet another *ḥadīth*, Kalda Ibn al-Ḥanbal reported that he conveyed some foodstuffs that Safwān b. Umayya had sent for the Prophet. Kalda then said:

عن كلدة بن حنبل أنّ صفوان بن أمية بعثه إلى رسول لله صلى الله عليه وسلم بلبن وجداية وضعا بيس، والنبى صلى الله عليه وسلم بأعلى مكة فدخلت ولم أسلم فقال ارجع فقل السلام عليكم.

> I entered on the Messenger of God, peace be on him, when he was in Makka, without greeting him or asking for permission to enter, and he told me to return and say *as-salāmu ʿalaykum*, then enter.[33]

Al-Jundi has recorded the view that the proper procedure as to which should come first, greeting, or *istiʾdhān*, depends on the circumstances. If a visitor actually sees the inmate first, then greeting should precede *istiʾdhān*, but when this is not the case, greeting may follow *istiʾdhān*.[34] It is then stated that the first position, which is to start with the greeting is, perhaps, in greater harmony with contemporary custom: when someone knocks at the door, or rings the bell, the inmate or his employee usually comes out; normally, one would greet him first and then seek his permission to enter after the greeting.

But if one disregards the correct etiquette of visiting and neither greets the inhabitants nor asks for permission, one has already committed a violation of the law. This is the purport of the following *ḥadīth* reported by ʿUbāda b. al-Ṣāmit:

عن عبادة بن الصامت رضي الله عنه أن رسول الله سئل عن الإستئذان في البيوت فقال: من خلت عينه قبل أن يستأذن ويسلم فلا إذن له، وقد عصى ربه.

> The Prophet, peace be on him, said: 'One who has viewed (the inside) before asking for permission (and before greeting), there can be no permission for him.'[35]

The *ḥadīth* thus makes it clear that when a person asks for permission but takes the liberty to look inside before it is given, then waiting for permission after that is a futile exercise and permission in this case is of no value. This is because the basic requirement of *istiʾdhān* is to validate viewing what is inside, and if one views first, permission becomes redundant.

Hudhayl b. Sharaḥbīl has narrated a similar *ḥadīth* wherein he said that 'A man came and stood at the door of the Prophet's house—according to one report, it was Saʾd b. Abi Waqāṣ—asking for permission, but was actually facing what was within. The Prophet then told him. 'From you (to expect) this! Asking for permission is to validate viewing.'[36]

فقال النبى صلى الله عليه وسلم: هكذا... أو هكذا. فإنما الإستئذان من النظر.

This confirms the previous *hadīth* that the one who asks for permission must not look into a private space until permission is given.

Isti'dhān is of two types, general and specific. The general *isti'dhān* (*al-isti'dhān al-ʿāmm*) applies to the public at large, whereas special *isti'dhān* (*al-isti'dhān al-khāṣṣ*) applies to relatives and residents of the same household. The distinction here originates in another Qur'ānic verse which provides further instructions on the etiquettes of privacy:

يآيها الذين آمنوا ليستئذنكم الذين ملكت أيمانكم والذين لم يبلغوا الحلم منكم ثلاث مرات من قبل صلوة الفجر وحين تضعون ثيابكم من الظهيرة ومن بعد صلوة العشاء ثلاث عورات لكم ليس عليكم ولاعليهم جناح بعدهن طوافون عليكم بعضكم على بعض.

O you who believe! Let those whom your right hands possess and those of you who have not attained puberty ask permission of you three times: before the morning prayer, and when you take off your clothes at noon time (when resting) and after the prayer at night. These are the three times of privacy for you. There is no sin for you, nor for them to visit each other, outside these times… (24:58).

Two notable features of this verse are the extension of the rules of privacy to members of one's family and household, and the assigning certain times of the day as times of privacy and rest wherein others, including relatives, servants and children, are advised not to disturb one. Commentators have explained that the three periods specified in the verse, namely early morning, midday, and late evening, were customary times of rest for the Arabs, when they did not welcome visits, and yet they would still have untimely visitors. The text is worded such that *isti'dhān* is made a requirement only at the three times specified, but not during the longer intervals in between. It would therefore not be correct to say that *isti'dhān* within the family is a requirement that extends from early morning to late evening. This is confirmed in the last sentence of the verse, which removes the requirement of asking for permission 'outside these times.' The distinction between this verse and the one discussed earlier is that one is specific while the other is general. The earlier text laid down the general rules of *isti'dhān* that addressed everyone, whereas the second verse is concerned with what is termed as special permission, in that *isti'dhān* is required during these specified times and within the physical context of the family unit.

The word *ẓahīra* (noon time), according to Muhammad Asad, occurs only once in the Qur'ān, and may have, in this verse, been metonymically used to imply daytime as opposed to the time after the nightfall prayer and before the prayer of daybreak. This is why it is rendered as 'middle of the day.' Moreover, the number 'three' used twice in the verse is not enumerative or exclusive, but places emphasis on the recurrent occasions on which even the most familiar members of a household must respect each others' privacy.[37] According to another Qur'ānic verse:

وإذا بلغ الأطفال منكم الحلم فليستئذنوا كما استئذن الذين من قبلهم كذلك يبين الله لكم آيته.

And when the children among you attain puberty, they too should ask for permission, even as those mentioned before them ask permission. God thus makes His commandments plain to you. (24:60).

According to a *ḥadīth* narrated by ʿIkrima, some persons from Iraq asked the renowned Companion ʿAbd Allāh b. ʿAbbās a question concerning the Qur'ānic passages cited above. The Iraqis said that 'None of us have practised what this verse requires.' They quoted the text, and Ibn ʿAbbās responded to their question as follows: 'God Most High loves *al-satr* (privacy) and out of His grace and mercy revealed this text at a time when people hardly lived in proper houses. Under those circumstances, people's privacy was not assured, even in their households, as they could easily be disturbed by a servant or a child or by members of the family, which is why the text here stipulates that permission should be obtained so as to protect personal privacy.' Then the situation changed, and God enabled people to live in better houses, and so almost no-one has since needed to observe the directive of this verse.[38]

عن عكرمة أن نفرا من أهل العراق قالوا: يا ابن عباس، كيف ترى فى هذه الأية التى أمرنا فيها بما أمرنا ولايعمل بها أحد قول الله عز وجل: يآيها الذين أمنوا ليستأذنكم والذين لم يبلغوا الحلم منكم ثلاث مرات من قبل صلاة الفجر وحين تضعون ثيابكم من الظهيرة ومن بعد صلاة العشاء وثلاث عورات لكم ليس عليكم ولاعليهم جناح بعدهن طوافون عليكم. قال ابن عباس: إنّ الله حليم رحيم بالمؤمنين يحب الستر، وكان الناس ليس لبيوتهم ستور ولا حجاب، فربما دخل الخادم أو الولد أو يتيمة الرجل والرجل الى أهله، فأمرهم الله بالإستئذان فى تلك العورات، فجاءهم الله بالستور والخير فلم أر أحدا يعمل بذلك بعد .

The following *ḥadīth* is an explanation of the Qur'ānic verse on the subject of *isti'dhān*:

عن عطاء بن يسار أن رسول الله صلى الله عليه وسلم سأله رجل فقال: يا رسول الله أأستأذن على أمى؟ فقال: نعم، قال الرجل: أنى معها فى البيت، قال رسول الله صلى الله عليه وسلم: استأذن عليها، قال الرجل: إنى خادمها، فقال رسول الله صلى الله عليه وسلم: استأذن عليها، أتحب أن تراها عريانه؟ قال: لا، قال: فاستأذن عليها .

'Atā' bin Yasār reported that a man asked the Messenger of God: 'O Messenger of God, do I (need to) ask my mother for permission?' To this the Prophet replied 'Yes'. Then the man said: 'I live with her in the house'. To this the Messenger of God responded 'Ask her permission when you enter'. The man further added 'I serve her'. Then the Messenger of God said 'Seek her permission. Do you wish to see her naked'? The man said 'No'. To this, the reply came 'Then ask her for permission'.[39]

The requirement of *isti'dhān* among relatives is a part of the general ruling of the Qur'ān on *isti'dhān*, and is not confined to a particular time. Yet *isti'dhān* among close relatives (*maḥārim*) refers not only to one's mother or sister but also to father and brother, regardless of senility or advanced age. Entering upon them must therefore be preceded by *isti'dhān*.[40]

The rules of *Sharīʿah* concerning the privacy of the home may be extended by analogy to private cars, boats and caravans. To extend the concept of *bayt* to a private boat finds support in the Qur'ānic usage of *bayt* in reference to a ship. A supplication of the Prophet Noah which the Qur'ān recounts thus reads:

رب اغفر لى ولوالدىِ ولمن دخل بيتي مؤمنا.

O My Lord! Grant forgiveness to me, my parents, and those
who entered my house (baytī) in safety. (17:28).

The word *bayt* here refers to the ship (Noah's Ark) that carried Noah and his followers.[41]

It may be said in this connection that a caravan is a closer parallel to the home and should therefore qualify for the same protection as a home. A car that is put away in a garage is clearly under custody (*ḥirz*) and a protected property that falls under the same rules that apply to theft. A car that is parked in a public place or when driven on the road may not fulfil some of the requirements of custody (*ḥirz*) which relate to theft, but is protected by the rules of privacy nevertheless, and no-one is entitled, therefore, to look into the parts that are not exposed to the naked eye. Yet violating the rules of privacy here may present a somewhat mitigated case when compared to violating the sanctity of the private home. Custody (*ḥirz*) is also of two types, one of which refers to houses and residential units in the protective custody of their occupants. The other type of *ḥirz* is when a guardsman is assigned to guard a house, ship, car or any other object. Thus when a car is parked in a guarded place, or when a residential unit is guarded, the rules of privacy and theft apply to them even when they are not occupied.[42] Boats, private vehicles, and caravans are thus protected by the requirements of permission and greeting prior to entry. These are thus not only protected by the general rules of *Sharīʿah* relating to private property, but also by the rules concerning the privacy of the home.

The legal maxim of *fiqh* stating that 'It is not permissible for anyone to interfere in the property of another person without the latter's permission,'[43] clearly protects the right of ownership. The one who violates the private property of another may be guilty of theft or other property offences, and the specific rules of *Sharīʿah* will apply to the case. But even if one does not commit a property offence, such as burglary or theft, and merely invades the space of a home's owner or occupant by a surreptitious and unsolicited search for information, one will have violated the owner's right to privacy. The circumstances of each case may provide relevant evidence to substantiate the nature of the charge. There may be private places in a car, boat or caravan where confidential papers are kept, and the owner may be a celebrity or one who is privy to important confidential information. These, and other such factors as the manner of entry into such vehicles, and a possible search for information could help to specify the nature of the offence. This also applies to passengers on a bus, aircraft, train or boat who are not allowed to search for papers or other items in the various sections of the vehicle.[44]

The more formalised procedure mentioned in the *ḥadīth* of asking for permission three times, and then the requirement that one must discontinue asking and leave, had, by the time of the second caliph ʿUmar, become a practice that was almost forgotten. This is indicated in the *ḥadīth* referred to earlier, of Abu Mūsā al-Ashʿari, which Abū Dāwūd has recorded in two or three slightly different versions, as given below: one from al-Ashʿari himself, the other from Abu Saʿīd al-Khudri, and the third an extended version of al-Ashʿari's. All three concur on the facts of the incident but differ somewhat in respect of detail. Yet all the three show that the Caliph ʿUmar appeared surprised to hear that triple *istiʾdhān* was what the Prophet had stipulated. I summarise al-Ashʿarī's report first.

عن أبى بردة عن أبى موسى أنّه أتى عمر فاستأذن ثلاثا... فلم يؤذن له، فرجع، فبعث إليه عمر: ماردك؟ قال: قال رسول الله صلى الله عليه وسلم: يستأذن أحدكم ثلاثا، فإن أذن له وإلا فليرجع. قال: ائتنى ببينة على هذا، فذهب ثم رجع، فقال: هذا أبيّ، فقال أبى: ياعمر لاتكن عذابا على أصحاب رسول الله صلى الله عليه وسلم، فقال عمر: لأكون عذابا على أصحاب رسول الله صلى الله عليه وسلم.

Abu Mūsā al-Ashʿarī reported that he went to see the caliph ʿUmar, knocked at the door of his house and asked for permission three times, but no permission was given for him to enter, so he left. Later, the caliph sent for him and asked him the reason why he turned back, to which al-Ashʿari replied that he did what was required of him in the *ḥadīth* and he cited the *ḥadīth*, that 'If any of you asks for permission thrice and it is not given, he must return.' The caliph then asked al-Ashʿarī if he could find a witness to confirm the *ḥadīth*. Al-Ashʿarī went and brought Ubayy b. Kaʿb as his witness. Ibn Kaʿb confirmed the *ḥadīth*, and told ʿUmar 'not to penalise the Companions of the Messenger of God (by asking them to bring witnesses).' ʿUmar then said: 'I am not penalising the Companions of the Messenger of God.'[45]

Abu Saʿīd al-Khudrī's version confirms this but adds the point: 'I was sitting with a number of the Anṣār, when Abū Mūsā turned up obviously upset. We asked him the reason why, and he said that ʿUmar ordered me to go and see him. I went and asked for permission three times...'[46]

عـن أبى سعيد الخدرى، قال: كنت جالسا فى مجلس مـن مجـلس الأنصار، فجاء أبو موسى فزعا، فقلنـا له: ما أفزعك؟ قال: أمرني عمر أن آتيـه، فأتيته فاستأذنت ثلاثا فلم يؤذن لـى، فرجعت، فقال: مامنعك أن تأتينى؟ قلت: قد جئت فاستأذنت ثلاثا فلم يؤذن لـى، وقد قال رسول الله صـلى الله عليه وسلم: إذا استأذن أحدكم ثلاثا فلم يؤذن له فليرجع، ...

One additional section to al-Ashʿarī's version that appears in some reports has it that ʿUmar added in his response to al-Ashʿarī that 'I do not accuse you of anything, but the *ḥadīth* of the Messenger of God is forceful/harsh—*shadīd*.'

فقـال عمر لأبى موسى: إنى لم أتهمـك ولكـن الحديـث عن رسول الله صلى الله عليه وسلم شديد.

According to yet another report, ʿUmar said 'I do not accuse you of anything, but I fear that people tend to spread through concerning the *ḥadīth* of the Messenger of God.'[47]

فقال عمر لأبى موسى: أما إنى لم أتهمـك ولكـن خشيـت أن
يتقول الناس على رسول الله صلى الله عليه وسلم.

It thus appears that ʿUmar thought of the *ḥadīth* as severe in its requirement presumably both of triple *istiʾdhān* and turning back when no response is given. This episode confirms that triple *istiʾdhān* was not a familiar practice of the Companions in Madina. It may thus be concluded that the *Sunnah* concurs with the Qurʾān regarding the basic requirement of *istiʾdhān*, and a certain repetition that would naturally occur when no response is heard, but the repetition aspect of it may be considered to be circumstantial and relevant perhaps to housing arrangements, and to customary practices in Arabia. These have little relevance to modern housing conditions, which have changed dramitcally over time, and custom too has undergone parallel changes. What is important is the principle of *istiʾdhān* itself and the protection that it offers to the right to privacy. The manner in which that principle is upheld and applied may vary, and there can be no objection to this. If a sound device, a doorbell or telephone, is used to obtain permission without one going through the prescribed procedure, this should also be acceptable. What is important is to maintain the principle itself.

One might add here that Abu Mūsā al-Ashʿari had perhaps taken the instruction of the *ḥadīth* he cited a little too literally. The *ḥadīth* naturally stipulated triple *istiʾdhān* only when the first and second attempts failed to bring a response. If the first attempt brought a response, repetition would not be necessary. And then the question of one's distance from the entrance, and the audibility of the request for permission etc., are also relevant. If the living quarters in the house are close, and three requests for permission are not answered, further repetition may be pointless and intrusive. But this may not be the case when the living quarters are far from the entrance, or when other circumstantial factors make for a delayed response.

The issue of housing structure and design is today even more relevant to the proper observance of *istiʾdhān*. The more secure and secluded house of today does not necessarily provide its inhabitants with greater protection, or more privacy, from the prying eyes and ears of intruders. Modern detection devices and instruments of intrusion become more and more sophisticated while houses became more exclusive. The issue is therefore not so much the physical attributes of a dwelling but of the observance of the principle of its inmates right to privacy, and how effectively the principle of *istiʾdhān* can therefore be observed, regardless of the physical attributes of a place.

The requirement of *isti'dhān* is omitted in the following four situations:

(1) Emergencies such as fire, flood and situations that present an immediate danger to life. This is a corollary of the general rule of *Sharīʿah* (also a legal maxim) that 'Necessity makes the unlawful lawful.'

(2) Criminality and sin that is openly committed, and can be seen without recourse to detection and espionage. A crime is evident if it is detectable directly by the senses. Examples of this include the sighting of a thief who carries the goods he has stolen, or a smell or sound which indicate that a crime is being committed.[48]

(3) The arrest of criminals. Government authorities may order entry into a house without permission in order to arrest a criminal hiding there. This may only be done under an order from the competent authorities.[49]

(4) Lastly, the requirement of *isti'dhān* is omitted when someone is invited and then accompanied by the messenger who conveys the invitation, as provided in the following *ḥadīth*:

إذا دُعي أحدكم إلى طعام فجاء مع الرسول، فإن ذلك له إذن .

> When any of you is invited for a meal and comes together with
> the messenger, this becomes a substitute for permission.[50]

This may be extended by analogy to other means by which a message or an invitation is communicated, such as a telephone call, a written invitation or other modes of communication which do not involve a protracted delay in delivery. For the preceding *ḥadīth* points to promptness in communication. With reference to social custom, one might also add that *isti'dhān* is not a requirement when one goes to an 'open house', such as during the *ʿId al-Fiṭr*, or the days immediately following it, in Malaysia, when people specify a particular day, or a part thereof, for receiving visitors and guests. This may be said, in some cases at least, to be equivalent to the prior communication that is envisaged in the *ḥadīth*.

III. Espionage (*al-Tajassus*)

Al-Ghazālī has described espionage as to 'search for signs in order to know what is otherwise not known and not permitted by the *Sharīʿah*.'

Signs can be either clear and visible without detection, in which case there is no question of espionage, or they can be hidden, and not known without a search. To search for such signs with a purpose to discover what is hidden is espionage.[51]

Al-Ghazālī's definition is comprehensive in that it has no specific context and it can include espionage both by Muslims against Muslims and non-Muslims as well as espionage by enemy powers. Some other definitions of the term by early Muslim jurists tend to associate espionage with warfare and hostile activities by enemy forces. Al-Dughmi has discussed these and has himself defined espionage as consisting of 'search and surveillance for hidden information and enemy secrets by means of detection devices in order to discover and utilise the information sought after in preparation for a particular purpose.'[52] Al-Jundi has almost paraphrased al-Ghazālī's definition by saying that 'espionage consists of a search for information in order to discover and expose about people what they consider to be private and confidential, either by viewing or listening, while they are unaware, or searching through their notes and documents without their permission.'[53]

Al-Dughmi's definition is contextual in that espionage is signified as a state-based activity, and a spy (*al-jāsūs*) is one 'who collects information for his homeland and government.' From the viewpoint of his own government, he is a loyal soldier and patriot who serves his people, whereas he is a dangerous enemy when looked at from the other side. From an Islamic viewpoint, a spy who works for the Muslims and gathers information on the enemy is a 'struggler in the way of God... and loyal to God, His Messenger and the believers.' But when a Muslim spies for enemy forces, he is a traitor and even more dangerous than enemy spies.[54] From the Islamic point of view, a spy (*jāsūs*) is defined as 'a person, Muslim or non-Muslim, who pries secretly into the privacies of Muslims and reports on them to the enemy, be it on military or non-military matters, during peace time or war.'[55] Thus there is a clear attempt to convey the impression that espionage as a term does not apply to a person who spies for Muslims against an enemy. A spy (*jāsūs*) is also a person who operates for the enemy and collects information on Muslims.

It is perhaps not necessary to confine the scope of espionage to any particular context, since it may either be related to warfare, as was the case in much of the early history of Islam, or to the political, economics of today, and scientific matters. The means and methods of espionage have also dramatically changed over the course of time, often because of the spread of mass media and communication.[56] It is no exaggeration to say that about ninety percent of information on enemy powers is nowadays gathered from press and media coverage, radio, television and the internet, and only about ten percent of espionage activity is carried out by professional spies. The conventional aspect of direct viewing and hearing often associated with espionage in the sense of violating the privacy of a home has also changed in that more effective methods, such as hidden cameras, bugging devices etc., are being used. Ships and sub-marines in the high seas and spy planes in the air make extensive use of unconventional methods, all of which, nevertheless, fall under the broad concept of espionage.

Espionage is forbidden by the text of the Qur'ān, as in the following:

يَآيهـا الذيـن آمنوا اجتنبوا كثيرا مـن الظـن إن بعـض الظـن إثـم ولاتجسـسوا ولايغتـب بعضكـم بعضـا أيحـب أحدكـم أن يأكـل لحم أخيه ميتا فكرهتموه.

O you who believe, avoid indulgence in suspicion, for surely much of suspicion partakes of sin; and do not spy (*lā tajassasū*) or let some of you backbite against others. Would any one of you like to eat the flesh of his dead brother? Surely you would abhor it. (49:12).

This is the most direct Qur'ānic injunction on espionage, and the reference to eating the flesh of 'your dead brother' leaves no doubt that espionage is not contextualised in the Qur'ān in the same way that it has been in some juristic writings of later origin. Espionage is, in other words, not confined to warring enemies, since it can equally occur between brethren in faith. There are other Qur'ānic passages that relate to relations with enemies forces, but they are in the nature of manifest (*ẓāhir*) statements of a lesser degree of clarity than the one just quoted, which is a clear text (*naṣṣ*) on the subject. Two Qur'ānic verses that are quoted in support of espionage against the enemy are concerned with warfare:

يَآيها الذين آمنوا خذوا حذركم فانفروا ثباتا أو انفروا جميعا.

O you who believe! Take precautions and either go forth in parties or go forth together.... (4:71)

To take precautions in warfare includes having knowledge about enemy forces, their tactics and strategies, and these cannot be known without recourse to espionage. The other passage quoted in support of such espionage also addresses the Muslims to:

وأعدوا لهم مااستطعتم من قوة ومن رباط الخيل ترهبون به عدو الله وعدوكم.

Make ready for them all that you can of (armed) forces and of tethered horses, so that you may apprehend the enemy of God and your enemy…(8:6).

'All that you can prepare' includes military preparation, technological and scientific know-how and knowledge of the size, location and other details of the enemy power and its state of preparation. Thus the verse is also seen to validate espionage against an enemy.

The standard Qur'ānic declaration on *tajassus*, quoted earlier, carries its best-known meaning, which is to pry into the affairs of others and seeking information about them that they would dislike to be known by or exposed to others. This kind of spying is carried out without the knowledge of its victims and it may be by way of listening to their private conversations, watching over their activities, or opening their letters. The essence of espionage, according to al-Qurṭubi, is 'to search for what is hidden to you.'[57] The phrase '*lā tajassasū*' in the verse under discussion proscribes exploring and exposing the hidden failings and weaknesses of others, and things they do in the privacy of their homes.[58] The purpose of *tajassus* in this verse is detection and the uncovering of the privacy of others (*tatabbuʿ al-ʿawrāt*) by unlawful means. The victim may be an individual, group of individuals, or the whole community or state, Muslims and non-Muslims alike.[59]

Within the given framework of its discourse, the main Qur'ānic injunction, quoted earlier, is seen as an unqualified and general (*ʿāmm*) prohibition on espionage addressed to everyone, including government agencies and the police, and it applies to all varieties of espionage, including espionage by governments against individuals or vice versa, opening letters, eavesdropping and so forth. Some *ʿulamā'* have identified espionage as one of the grave sins (*al-kabā'ir*) and evaluated it as *ḥarām*, not only among Muslims themselves but also in relation to non-Muslim citizens.[60] It is a flagrant violation of the right to privacy, and a transgression against the *Sharīʿah*. People are entitled to keep their failings and weaknesses hidden and to conceal what they see as confidential to themselves, and neither the state nor society has a right to supervise the private lives of individuals. 'It is a right of every Muslim to keep their private lives to themselves,' wrote al-Jundi, 'and his right also to conceal, when he falls into a sin or violation, and society has no right to supervise his private life.'[61]

Espionage and exposing the hidden weaknesses of upright individuals is forbidden, regardless of the motive. This is understood from the explicit text of the Qur'ān and *hadīth*, and their unqualified prohibition of espionage. The qualified Qur'ānic prohibition on suspicion or *zann*, on the other hand, is such that it leaves room for evaluation and the prospect of classifying some varieties of *zann* as well-founded or even praiseworthy. But the fact that the Qur'ān and *Sunnah* both speak of espionage alongside backbiting (*ghība*) and suspicion (*zann*) indicates that the prohibition of espionage is all-embracing, and equally applies to those who might be engaged in a good cause, such as the *muhtasib*, that is, the market inspector and officer in charge of *hisba*, who is not permitted to use espionage as a means of promoting *hisba* (i.e. enjoining good and preventing evil). As a government officer, the *muhtasib* must act on the basis of what he knows by direct observation without recourse to espionage, eavesdropping or other methods of a search for evidence. The basic guidelines that govern the activity of the *muhtasib* are that he must not amount to inflicting harm on anyone; that his judgement is based on knowledge and not mere doubt. The evil that the *muhtasib* pursues must be evident (*zāhir*) rather than known only to a person's confidantes or close relatives, and concealed from the public gaze. Should there be a need for search and detection, it is no longer the concern of *hisba*. An evil is self-evident when it is obvious enough to leave no room for recourse to interpretation and *ijtihād*. If *hisba* is carried out in situations of necessity, it is important for the *muhtasib* to know that necessity is also measured according to circumstance.[62]

Another restraint on *hisba* is that it applies to evil conduct and crime as it occurs, so that the *muhtasib* is in a position to prevent it, or to bring about a change to an on-going situation. He may intervene when he sees wine-drinking, or to prevent rape or *zinā* when they are seen to be taking place or are imminent. In the event where a crime has already been committed, and the *muhtasib* or a member of the public then learns of its occurrence, this is no longer the concern of *hisba* but of the due processes of law and justice. To give another example, when someone attacks another and causes an injury, once the attack has already occurred, it is a crime that may be prosecuted and not a matter of concern to *hisba* as such. But if the *muhtasib* actually observes it while it is occuring, he is entitled to take suitable action to prevent it. *Hisba* in respect of crimes that are imminent but have not yet occurred is limited to verbal advice and admonition only, which may not turn into punitive action or verbal abuse.[63]

The caliph ʿUmar b. al-Khaṭṭāb clarified the position when he said that the government acts on what is evident; the one who exhibits good character should not be suspected of anything but good, and only God knows the inner secrets of people.[64] The prohibition of espionage also includes eavesdropping and listening to other people's confidential communication. Al-Ghazālī held it to be impermissible for one to listen, behind closed doors, to the sound of (string) musical instruments, or try to detect the smell of alcohol. It is also unlawful for anyone to search and frisk the clothes another person is wearing in order to detect what is hidden underneath, or to enter the house of another person to know what is inside. Similarly, neighbours may not be asked to report on one another. Only when there is enough ground for suspicion, such as a report by 'upright persons who offer [the information], without being asked, that so and so is busy drinking inside,' and signs of criminality or imminent evil are noted, the lawful authorities may 'enter the house without asking for permission,' in order to take preventive or investigative action.[65] Some ʿulamā of the Mālikī school have considered eavesdropping to be a form of espionage,[66] and it is the subject of the following *hadīth* which is as follows:

مـن استمع إلى حـديـث قوم وهـم له كارهون صـب فى أذنيـه الآنك يوم القيامة.

The one who listens to other people's confidential speech, which they do not wish to be heard by others, will have scorching lead poured into his ears on the Day of Judgment.[67]

Listening to other people in a way that they would dislike may be directly, by way of eavesdropping, or through the planting of bugging, or by using a disinterested intermediary (*al-fuḍūli*), all of which fall under the general and prohibitive terms of this *hadīth*. This also applies to children, servants and neighbours who may be used as informants and spies by others. All of this is impermissible regardless of the purpose of the espionage, and none of it can be justified in the name of the promotion of good and the prevention of evil, or *hisba*, which may not rely on surreptitious methods or espionage. One exception noted in this connection is in the context of a prospective marriage. A person who intends to marry a woman may enquire into the character of his prospective wife by talking to neighbours and children. This may be said to fall under the rules of necessity (*ḍarūra*), which should be delimited by the extent of the need.[68]

Reports indicate that peeping through door cracks and eavesdropping from behind closed doors were a cause for concern during the Prophet's time, and provoked a rigorous response from him—as in the following *ḥadīth* reported by Anas b. Mālik:

أن رجلا اطّلع من بعض حجر النبى صلى الله عليه وسلم فقام إليه النبى صلى الله عليه وسلم بمشقص أو بمشاقص فكأنى أنظر إليه يختل الرجل ليطعنه .

A man peeped into a room of the Prophet, peace be on him. The Prophet stood up, holding an arrowhead. It is as if I am just looking at him, trying to stab the man.[69]

Another *ḥadīth* on the same subject is even more specific:

من اطّلع فى بيت قوم بغير إذنهم ففقئوا عينه فلا دية ولا قصاص .

For the one who pries into other people's homes without their permission, it is permissible for them to gouge out his eye, and if they do so, they are not liable to pay compensation (*diyya*) or accept retaliation (*qiṣāṣ*).[70]

Abū Dāwūd has recorded a slightly different version of the first of these two *ḥadīths* as follows:

عن أنس بن مالك أن رجلا اطّلع من بعض حجر تالنبى صلى الله علبه وسلم فقام إليه رسول الله صلى الله عليه وسلم بمشقص أو مشاقص، قال: فكأنى أنظر إلى رسول الله صلى الله عليه وسلم يختلُه ليطعنه .

A man spied on some of the rooms of the Prophet's household and the Prophet picked up a sharp instrument and tried to pierce his eye with it.[71]

The wording of this *ḥadīth* suggests that the Prophet wanted to attack the eye of the intruder without warning him. Although the attempt was unsuccessful and the man disappeared, the *ḥadīth* implies that the Prophet had actually meant to do it. Muslim jurists have consequently concluded that the victim of a similar attempt is entitled to act similarly in order to defend his right to privacy, and if he strikes the intruder with a sharp instrument, a stick or stone which injures or kills him, there is no liability for *qiṣāṣ* or compensation. It also appears that no prior warning is necessary.[72] This is the majority opinion held by the Shāfiʿīs, the Ḥanbalīs, some Ḥanafīs and the Shīʿa Imamiyya, all of whom agree on the right of the victim to gouge out the eye of the culprit. It is further added that what is proposed in the *ḥadīth* is the only effective means by which to deter intrusion, and that other measures would not amount to an effective defence against an assailant. This is partially due to the surreptitious nature of the offence, and the difficulty of providing evidence to prove it.[73]

Some jurists have added, however, that a warning should be given first and if the intruder still persists, then action may be taken according to the terms of the *ḥadīth*. Al-Jundi considers this view to be preferable.[74] Most of the Ḥanafīs and Mālikīs have, however, taken a different view of the *ḥadīth* in question by arguing that its wording is symbolic, and intended to point to the enormity of the conduct in question, and is not to be taken literally. The Prophet himself, it is said, pressed an item through the door crack in order to repel the man, and to show his anger, but it is not certain whether he intended to actually injure the prying eye. The proponents of this view, mainly the Ḥanafīs, further add that the ruling of this *ḥadīth* has been abrogated by the Qurʾānic verse to the effect that:

$$\text{وإن عاقبتم فعاقبوا بمثل ماعوقبتم به .}$$

If you punish, then your punishment should be equivalent to the pain
inflicted on you. (16:126)

The victim of such an intrusion is nevertheless entitled to act to defend his right to privacy, and if he strikes the culprit or throws something at him, which injures him, there is no liability for compensation, even if the culprit is really injured.[75] The position here is analogous to the right of self-defence. One is accordingly entitled to use force against an assailant (*al-ṣā'il*) on one's person or property. If the attack can be repelled by the use of force that falls short of injury and a lethal strike, this is preferred, but even if it leads to injury, there is no liability for it. The purpose here is to repel an intruder, as it is a case of self-defence, but not to take revenge or punish, for these are matters for the due procesess of law, which are not included in the right to self-defence.[76] The immediate nature of this right to self-defence is indicated in the *ḥadīth* where it reads that 'there is no blame on you if you did so,' that is, if you actually gauged out an intruder's eye. But there will be liability for compensation if the gouging of an eye is after the event and premeditated. To this it is added that if someone deliberately looks at another person's private parts, the latter is not permitted to gouge out the former's eye; and looking at the inside of a person's house may also be said to be analogous to this, and so this too does not warrant the said response.[77] The judge is authorised to punish intrusions of this kind by a suitable deterrent punishment, but not to order the gouging out of the eye of the intruder.

Two other questions may briefly be discussed here, one of which is whether or not eavesdropping or listening behind the door of someone's house entitles the house owner to an attack that could destroy the hearing ability of the intruder. The answer to this question is in the negative, simply because of the absence of textual authority to validate it, whereas in the case of intrusive viewing, the gouging of the eye is mentioned in the text, but no analogy between the two is warranted. The intrusive listener would instead be liable to a deterrent (*ta'zīr*) punishment for spying.

A second question that arises here is hypothetical. What if a third person holds down the unauthorised viewer so that the resident of the house may gouge out his eye? Would this be lawful? The answer here, too, is in the negative in that the house resident is not entitled to do so, and if he actually does gouge out the eye of the intruder, he is liable to payment of compensation (*diyya*) for the eye, and whoever held down the intruder is liable to a deterrent *ta'zīr* punishment.[78] To this analysis Abū Zahrah has added that the permission to gouge out the eye is meant to emphasise the sanctity of a private residence, but is not a punishment. The offence does not carry a pre-determined penalty, but the judge is entitled to determine its punishment under the principal of *ta'zīr*.[79]

Espionage is permitted in situations of necessity, and in order to arrest a criminal when there is a basis on which to establish a valid suspicion. Thus when an upright person whose word can be trusted reports that a murder is about to be committed, and that he saw the potential victim being taken by the suspect to a certain place, or that a woman is being abducted and raped, then it is permissible for a law enforcement officer to resort to espionage. This is especially warranted in situations where a loss of life, or an attack on the honour and dignity of others is at stake, and it is feared that evidence to bring the criminal to justice would otherwise be lost.[80] Since Islamic governments are under an obligation to establish security, and to ensure that lives and properties are protected, they may resort to espionage in situations where grave crimes are being committed or when the criminal has fled the scene. But even so, recourse to crime-detection espionage should be based on circumstantial evidence, such as credible clues (*al-qara'in*) and reports by reliable individuals.

'Espionage without a valid cause is forbidden (*haram*).' This is the conclusion drawn by al-ʿAqqād in his study of the precedent of the second caliph ʿUmar b. al-Khaṭṭāb.[81] 'No one has the right,' wrote the author of *Nihāyat al-Muḥtāj*, 'to resort to espionage, or a search and surveillance of people's homes, on the basis merely of doubt. But if there is well-founded suspicion about the perpetration of a crime, such as the presence of an apparent clue, or a report by an upright person, then recourse to spying is permissible, and it even becomes obligatory if it is feared that a crime such as murder and rape will not be otherwise detectable. But espionage is not permitted outside these situations.'[82]

The normal rule is that when a crime that has already been committed can be proven by other evidence, recourse to espionage is not permitted. But this stipulation is ignored when a crime is suspected to be about to occur. Al-Māwardī envisaged the same scenario when he wrote that espionage and intruding into the privacy of others, when founded on mere doubt, was not permissible unless it be a matter of saving a life or preventing an imminent attack on the lives and properties of others.[83] From his enquiry into the relevant evidence on the issue, Rākān al-Dughmi reached a similar conclusion when he wrote that espionage is generally *haram*, and recourse to it should be confined to situations of necessity. The test here is that without recourse to espionage, the criminal is not likely to be tracked down, and there is a real fear of someone being killed, or a rape or *zina* committed. Anything less than these situations will not justify recourse to espionage.[84]

One should also note that the government has no authority to spy on people, in the name of public security, or to make espionage a means of gathering information for the promotion of particular viewpoints and policies. This is the sort of unjustifiable espionage that the Prophet denounced in his saying:

إن الأمير اذا ابتغى الريبة فى الناس أفسدهم.

When the ruler chases the private lives of the people on the basis of doubt, he will not fail to spread corruption among them.[85]

It is also reported that someone told the renowned Companion ʿAbd Allāh Ibn Masʿūd, while pointing at a wine-drinker, that 'This is so and so, and wine is dripping down his beard,' to which he replied 'Espionage is forbidden to us. But if something becomes evident to us, we may act on it.'[86]

هذا فلان تقطر لحيته خمرا، فقال: إنا قد نهينا عن التجسس ولكن إن يظهر لنا بشيئ نأخذ به.

Military engagement with enemy powers is a recurrent theme in the literature on the subject, and in this scenario, the Prophet himself is known to have authorised espionage. Muslim rulers have all, to varying degrees, resorted to it in order to gather information on the military capability and tactics of the enemy. Among the Companions who were assigned such tasks by the Prophet himself, certain individuals such as Hudhayfa b. al-Yamānī, Qays b. Saʿd, Naʿim b. Masʿūd etc., are well-known. They conducted secret service activities against enemy forces, and also in respect of internal security matters. They were on the whole considered heroes who served their homeland and religion by risking their lives, and therefore earned spiritual rewards.[87] The first caliph Abū Bakr is also known to have sent out spies when the tribes rebelled and refused to pay the *zakah* tax in connection with the ensuing wars of apostasy. The renowned army commander during the time of the first caliph, Khālid b. al-Walīd, 'had numerous spies whom he sent out and received information from every day.'[88] Abu ʿUbayda b. al-Jarrāḥ, the army commander who led the battle against the Romans during the time of the caliph ʿUmar, regularly received information from spies on the deployment of enemy forces.[89] The *Sharīʿah* thus permits spying on an enemy, and it is even considered a duty in times of war.

The notion that espionage was a necessary part of preparation for war thus became well-entrenched, but a certain unwarranted extension of state espionage activities within home territory also became noticeable. During the Abbasid era, the postal services incorporated espionage in their normal duties. 'The Ṣāḥib al-Barīd (Post Master) carried out surveillance duties on government officers and also assigned espionage duties to his officials against enemy powers.'[90] The Abbasid Caliph al-Manṣūr (754-775) is said—in an interview—to have singled out four state officials who were like four pillars to the throne, on whose services he greatly relied. These were the Chief judge, the Chief of police, the Tax collector, and 'after hesitating and biting his fingers thrice, he sighed and said... The Ṣāḥib al-Barīd.'[91] It thus appears that Muslim rulers resorted to espionage in matters of state security and warfare, crime prevention and internal security, as well as 'informing themselves on the conditions of their subjects.'[92] All of this seems to have been justified in the name of necessity and public interest (ḍarūra, maṣlaḥa). The principle of prohibition nevertheless remains, and commentators who write on espionage have on the whole declared it to be prohibited by the clear authority of the texts. Thus espionage is clearly a case of conflicting interests, and limiting its practice to the extent of necessity and serving the public interest has remained a perennial challenge for ruling authorities.

In this context, the night patrol of Madina by the caliph ʿUmar b. al-Khaṭṭāb also merits attention. On one of three reported occasions, the caliph was accompanied by his colleague, ʿAbd al-Raḥmān Ibn ʿAwf, for the purpose of informing himself of the conditions of the people. ʿAbd al-Raḥmān recounted the story as follows: as the two of them were walking in Madina one night, they saw lamp-light coming from a house in the distance; they approached the house and found that its front door was closed but they could hear the noise of people within. 'ʿUmar took me by the hand,' and asked whose house it was. ʿUmar then said that it belonged to Rabīʿa b. Umayya b. Khalaf and that the people inside seemed to be drunk. ʿUmar then asked ʿAbd al-Raḥmān's view as to what they should do. ʿAbd al-Raḥmān replied that the Qurʾān had forbidden espionage and he quoted the verse concerning it. The caliph turned around and they left the scene.

Al-Ghazālī, who quoted this report, drew the conclusion that this is clear evidence for 'the obligatoriness of concealment (al-satr) and for an abandonment of searching for what is hidden (tark al-tatabbuʿ).'[93] Ghazālī went on to quote a *ḥadīth* in support of this view, in which the Prophet had addressed Muʿāwiya by saying, 'If you try to expose the hidden failings of people, you will surely spread corruption among them.'[94] Al-Ghazālī added that espionage is not permissible concerning someone who is behind closed doors, nor is anyone entitled to enter such places without obtaining permission first.

The second report on the night patrol of the caliph ʿUmar has it that one night, while on an inspection tour of the town, the caliph heard the voice of a man singing in a house. The caliph entered to find a woman next to the man and some wine that he was drinking. The caliph warned the person by calling him 'O enemy of God,' and rebuked him for his sinful indulgence. The man replied 'And you, O Commander of the Faithful! Do not be so hasty (in your rebuke). If I have disobeyed God in one instance, you have done so on three counts.' The man then quoted three brief passages from the Qurʾān, one on the prohibition of espionage, the other on the prohibition of entering houses from the rear, instead of the normal [front] entrance, and then the prohibition on entry without permission, and told the caliph that he had violated all three injunctions. The caliph asked if the man had anything good to say about himself, and the man replied 'Yes' and said that if the caliph granted him pardon, he would never repeat what he had done. Then the caliph pardoned him and went out and left the house.[95]

And lastly, it is reported that on another one of his night tours of Madina, the caliph ʿUmar saw a man and a woman engaged in illicit intercourse. The caliph reported this to his fellow Companions the following day and asked them for their response to an incident of adultery that the caliph himself had seen—could he enforce a *ḥadd* punishment on that basis? The Companions replied that 'You are the Imam,' but ʿAlī b. Abī Ṭālib had a different view and said that the *ḥadd* punishment could not be applied on that basis. The Qurʾānic mandate on that matter was that four eyewitnesses must testify, and the caliph too had to comply with that requirement. There was some hesitation, as Ghazālī has noted, over the question of whether the Imam could in such a case act on the basis of his personal knowledge, but as it turned out, the caliph accepted ʿAlī's advice and took no action concerning the case. 'This is clarion evidence,' Ghazālī added 'that the *Sharīʿah* demands a concealment of sins. *Zinā* is a grave sin and yet the judge may not punish anyone for it on the basis of his personal observation.'[96] As for the question of the likely consequence of that sin in the Hereafter, Ghazālī quotes a *ḥadīth* on the matter and draws the conclusion that 'God Most High wishes that the sin in question be concealed in this life. He is far too Noble and Merciful to disclose it in the Hereafter. But if He exposed it in this world, He is too Noble to disclose it again in the Hereafter.'[97]

The accuracy of these reports and any of the conclusions drawn from them have, however, been questioned. I have quoted al-Ghazālī's version of the reports mainly because I thought he drew the right conclusions from them, notwithstanding a certain vagueness in the factual details of his version of the reports. Al-Jundi has, in this connection, raised some doubts, for example, concerning the details in which these night patrols were reported, and regards them to have been tainted by isrā'īliyāt (accretions of Jewish origin).[98] The man in the second of the three reports is said to be Abu Mahjan al-Thaqafi, a wine drinker whom the caliph had flogged more than once. When the caliph took him by surprise that night, he is said to have addressed the caliph by telling him that he had committed espionage and then cited three Qur'ānic passages on the subject. It is unlikely that a person in a drunken state would be able to recite the Qur'ān under the circumstances in which the incident took place. Jundi strongly refutes the suggestion that the caliph ʿUmar committed espionage ʿin view of his reputation for piety and exquisite knowledge of the Qur'ān. Similar weaknesses have also been noted in the other two reports, which need not perhaps be detailed here, but which led al-Jundi to the conclusion that what the caliph ʿUmar did on his night patrols were instances of siyasa sharʿiyya (Sharīʿah-based policy), and also of ḥisba, that were designed to uproot corruption. But even then, when it became clear to ʿUmar that he might have violated the sanctity of the private home, he desisted and proceeded no further.[99]

To substantiate this viewpoint, Jundi refers to the views of ʿAbbās Maḥmūd al-ʿAqqād and ʿAbd al-Fattāḥ al-Sayfi on ʿUmar's night tours of Madina, both of whom have held that the caliph was sensitive, and repentant about having violated people's privacy in those incidents, all of which indicate that he was acting in good faith, whereas espionage often originates in suspicion.[100] Without wishing to go into detail, Jundi also recounts other instances of night tours in which the caliph ʿUmar, usually accompanied by another Companion, rushed to the help of poor families with children, and took measures to improve their conditions. There are a number of such reports which clearly suggest that ʿUmar busied himself in the service of the people, and was their benefactor rather a spy against them.

Some elements of espionage might have been present in these three incidents. But since the caliph himself took corrective action on those occasions, this alters the picture, and absolves the caliph of the charge. Many have drawn the conclusion that the caliph's night tours were attempted in a totally different spirit from spying, so much so that he did not even believe that he was indulging in espionage, and whenever he was alerted, he showed remorse and left the scene. What needs to be added here is that since the caliph himself regretted his surprise visits and took no further action on what he had seen on those occasions, his precedent should not be taken as evidence to validate surprise nocturnal visits or espionage activities by state authorities. This would be a misinterpretation of the caliph's precedent.

IV. Private Correspondence

Opening other people's personal letters and confidential correspondence falls under the Qur'ānic prohibition of espionage. The subject has also been specifically addressed in a *hadīth* in which the Prophet is reported to have said:

من نظر فى كتاب أخيه بغير إذنه فكأنما ينظر فى النار.

> The one who looks at the letter of his brother without his permission truly looks into the fire of hell.[101]

Unauthorised peeping into other people's letters and personal correspondence is tantamount to espionage, especially when one is deliberately searching for information on another person. But if it is a casual look due to curiosity more than anything else, it is still sinful even if it does not amount to espionage as such. Letters and messages sent by post, email, and fax are regarded as deposits (*wadīʿa*) on behalf of their senders and the persons to whom they are addressed. A deposit is like a trust (*amāna*) in the hands of its carrier and the postal service. The sender/depositor is entitled to his rights of privacy and ownership, and these must be respected by post office employees and others. The recipient also cannot divulge confidential information that the sender has addressed only to him. This applies to all correspondence, packets and parcels, whether registered with the postal service or not. In addition, the post office is bound by contractual obligation to safeguard the confidentiality of their customers' correspondence and communication, whether by telephone or other means. Violations of contract and *amāna* that are prejudicial to the customer amount to a punishable offence. In the case where a third party is harmed by a breach of trust and the disclosure of confidential information, the harm thus inflicted may provide a case for financial compensation, penal sanction, or both,

on the authority of the *ḥadīth*–cum legal maxim that 'Harm may neither be inflicted nor reciprocated.' لاضرر ولا ضرار.[102] What this *ḥadīth*
means is that inflicting harm is unacceptable in the first place, but when
a harm has been inflicted, the perpetrator is liable to compensate for it.
The culprit himself and the post office would be liable in this context
for payment of compensation. Another *ḥadīth* quoted in this connection provides that:

كل المسلم على المسلم حرام دمه و ماله وعرضه.

'All that belongs to a Muslim is unlawful to his fellow Muslim: his
blood, his property and his honour.'[103]

Official correspondence, letters and communication belonging to the
government are also protected by the *Sharī'ah* ruling on the prohibition
of espionage. This is because the Qur'ānic address to the believers to
refrain from espionage applies to all instances of it, whether by individuals or government, the government against the individual or vice versa.
Confidential information contained in official records is thus protected
and it is not permissible for members of the public to look into them
or to reveal them. The office holders themselves are under contractual
obligation to safeguard what is placed in their care and custody, and to
protect the confidentiality of the information entrusted to them.[104]

The sanctity of personal correspondence applies equally to non-
Muslims. This is the purpose of the *ḥadīth* al-Bukhārī has recorded
concerning a letter that a Jew had sent to a certain destination. The
ḥadīth, which is narrated by Abu Hurayra, is somewhat inconclusive in
the context, but what it does provide is that the Prophet had mentioned
to his Companions a letter that a Jew had addressed to a friend and had
enclosed a large sum of money with it, thought to be one thousand
dinars. The money was enclosed in a separate wooden container.[105]

عـن أبى هريرة رضى الله عنـه عن رسول الله صلى الله عليـه
وسلـم: أنـه ذكره رجـلا من بنـى اسرائيل أخـذ حشبة فنقرهـا
فادخـل فيها ألف دينار وصحيفة منه إلى أصحابه، وقال عمر بن
أبى سلمة عـن أبيه عـن أبى هريرة: قال النبى صلى الله عليـه
وسلم نجر خشبة فجعل المال فى جوفها وكتب إليه صـحيفة
من فلان إلى فلان.

The facts of this *ḥadīth* tend to confirm that valuables enclosed with personal correspondence are protected, and unless there is reason to believe that an offence is being committed, no-one is entitled to ask questions about them. This is inferred from the fact that the Prophet himself asked no questions about it, even though he had known about the sum that was enclosed with the letter.

Penal sanctions or damages that are imposed under the principle of *taʿzīr* (deterrence) allow the judge a certain degree of flexibility in determining the type and quantity of punishment in the light of attendant circumstances. In cases of necessity, or imminent danger, or when the community interest is at stake, jurists have held that personal letters and messages, whether belonging to the individual or to the state, may be opened. This judgement could be based on the report of a trustworthy individual, or a reasonable suspicion, and the rule of law here is in conformity with the maxim that 'Harm must be eliminated,' but only to the extent that is necessary. Another legal maxim that applies here is that 'Necessity must be measured by its true proportion.'

In his comment on the *ḥadīth* that 'The one who looks into the letter of his brother truly looks into the fire of hell,' al-Baghawi has noted that it is concerned with letters and correspondence that involve confidential information between the sender and addressee and where a breach of privacy would be prejudicial and offensive. But the *ḥadīth* does not include written material and information that is not confidential, such as academic texts and information meant for everyone. Opening letters and correspondence of this type is not forbidden because of the principle that knowledge should be disseminated and its benefit made available to everyone. It is said, on the other hand, that the language of the *ḥadīth* is general, and does not make any explicit exception in favour of textbooks or knowledge-based information. According to this view, all correspondence and indeed everything sent by post is included, and if there is knowledge and benefit in it, its owner has the greatest entitlement to it.[106] This is in my opinion a preferable conclusion. For there is no compelling reason to specify the general terms of the *ḥadīth* on the grounds of a rather weak argument advanced in favour of the dissemination of knowledge. It is also difficult, once one makes such an exception, to draw a line between knowledge-based information and that which is personal. Moreover, the contents of a parcel or envelope can only be known once it is opened, an act that violates the right to privacy. There may be exceptional situations where such a violation does not necessarily occur. Yet it seems preferable to stay clear of doubtful reasoning and follow the unqualified terms of the *ḥadīth* as they are. The norm of the *Sharīʿah* in regard to opening personal letters is that it is prohibited, and a cautious approach to the interpretation of that *hadīth* would be more harmonious with that norm.

An exception may once again be made on the grounds of necessity (*darūrā*). A letter or parcel that is manifestly suspect and is itself an instrument of espionage, violence or commotion may be opened, if necessary by the order of the government, and may involve coercion in order to defend people against imminent harm. The principle here is elucidated in an incident which occurred during the lifetime of the Prophet. It is reported that when the Prophet was planning to conquer Mecca, Ḥāṭib bin Abi Baltaʿa wrote in secrecy to the people of Mecca to inform them of the Prophet's imminent plan. A woman was given the task of delivering the letter by Abu Baltaʿa. The matter came to the Prophet's knowledge and he immediately sent two of his Companions, ʿAlī b. Abī Ṭālib and Zubayr b. al-ʿAwām to intercept the woman. They did so and when she was asked for the letter, she denied that she was carrying it. She was then told to bring out the letter or face being searched and stripped of her garments. Having been threatened in such terms, the woman brought out the letter, which she was hiding in her hair locks.[107] Al-Baghawī has quoted this as evidence in the *Sunnah* to validate looking into the private correspondence of another in emergency situations and in order to prevent an imminent harm.[108] Al-Dughmī has also commented that it is permissible to open private letters when evidence and circumstance suggest this to be the only way by which to protect the community against imminent harm.[109] Ibn Farḥūn has considered it to be a matter that falls within the ambit of a *Sharīʿah*-oriented policy, or *siyāsah sharʿiyyah*, especially with regard to the use of force, which should normally be unnecessary and should be preceded by no more than a threat (*al-tahdīd wa'l-irʿāb*). Questions as to whether one may or may not resort to a threat, and how it should be conducted, should, in other words, be determined within the framework of *siyāsah sharʿiyyah*.[110]

It may be added here that in the interests of providing clarity and guidance, the terms of *siyāsah sharʿiyyah*, or *Sharīʿah*-based policy, should be determined by the legislative assembly and parliament as they currently exist in Muslim communities. Since the *Sharīʿah* itself does not represent the applied law of the land in many Muslim countries, it would be unrealistic to expect that the post office and its employees would have enough knowledge of *siyāsah sharʿiyyah* to determine the finer aspects of their procedures. It is therefore all the more advisable to have clear legislative guidelines to determine these procedures.

V. Suspicion (*al-Ẓann*)

It is not an exaggeration to say that nearly all violations of the right to privacy are predicated on suspicion. Often, authorities or an individual suspect something on the part of others and tend to vindicate or eliminate this suspicion by recourse to espionage or other violations of privacy. Suspicion may thus be said to be at the root of attempts to violate the right to privacy.

As already noted, the Qur'ān has not just proscribed espionage but also suspicion, and declared it to be mostly sinful. The *Sunnah* is equally emphatic on the subject of unfounded suspicion, which is seen to be the starting point of defamation and espionage. The Prophet has thus warned the people to:

إياكم الظن فإن الظن أكذب الحديث ولاتجسسوا ولاتعيروا.

> Beware of suspicion, for suspicion may be totally untrue and may amount to the worst form of lying; and do not spy on one another and do not expose each other's hidden failings.[111]

In a comment on this *ḥadīth*, al-Ghazālī wrote that ill-founded suspicion (*sū' al-ẓann*) is tantamount to inner *ghība* (*al-ghība bi'l-qalb*), which is the origin of the outer or manifest *ghība* that is articulated in words. Espionage also originates in *sū' al-ẓann*. Just as manifest *ghība* is prohibited, the *ghība* of the heart is also forbidden. What this means, al-Ghazālī adds, is that one should not act on an ill-founded suspicion so long as one can find an interpretation that exonerates a person. One is advised to remind oneself that what one suspects may be due to a mistake or forgetfulness on the part of another, if there is room for such an interpretation. This kind of *ẓann* is often founded on positive thinking and intuition (*tafarrus*) that is often stimulated by a sign which propels thought in that direction. *Tafarrus* tends to suppress negative suspicions in favour of positive interpretations. All of this applies, once again, in the absence of certainty, and in instances where people's speech and conduct are open to interpretation. As for that which is discovered with certainty and definitive observation, one need not make it the subject of speculation and *ẓann* at all.[112]

Suspicion with malice has been declared *ḥarām* in another *ḥadīth*, alongside harming the blood or honour of a Muslim. The *ḥadīth* thus provides that:

إن الله حرّم من المسلم دمه وعرضه وأن يظن سوء الظن.

God has forbidden (aggression on) the life and personal honour of a
Muslim, and making him the target of an ill-founded suspicion.[113]

Commenting on this *ḥadīth*, al-Jundi noted that the reference is to
suspicion that is based on mere doubt without any clues or indications,
and pursuing it further means attaching a value to it, which the *ḥadīth*
has clearly advised against.[114]

Suspicion that originates in malice and has no evidential basis is not
worth pursuing, is best abandoned altogether. This is preferable, ranks
as an act of worship, and is the subject of another *ḥadīth* which simply
states that: حسن الظن من العبادة 'Benevolent thoughts—*ḥusn al-ẓann*—partake of sincere worship.'[115]

From the viewpoint of reality and substance, Muslim jurists have
also drawn a distinction between two types of suspicion. One of these
is a strong and well-founded suspicion (*al-ẓann al-mu'akkad*), which has
an evidential basis and may even justify a decision or *ḥukm* to be based
on it. The other variety is termed weak or unfounded suspicion (*al-
ẓann al-ḍaʿīf*), which is no more than a hunch or a doubt (*al-shakk*); it
has no evidential basis and no decision may be based on it. The former
is sometimes referred to as *tafarrus* (intuition), as mentioned above,
which is insightful and clear of malice, whereas the latter is founded on
malice and is basically forbidden.[116]

From the viewpoint of its attributes, suspicion or *ẓann* is once again
divided into two types, namely praiseworthy suspicion (*al-ẓann al-
maḥmūd*), which is based on good faith and aims to prevent evil, and
reprehensible suspicion (*al-ẓann al-madhmūm*), which is the opposite of
the former and is sinful. This is the sort of *ẓann* which is mentioned in
the Qur'ān in reference to the hypocrites, that:

وظننتم ظن السوء وكنتم قوما بورا.

You conceived an evil thought and you are a people lost in
wickedness. (48:12).

This is also the kind of suspicion that the Prophet described as the
worst kind of lying. It is a lie because it does not correspond with
reality, has no basis in truth, and can be more misleading and decep-
tive than a simple lie. Reprehensible suspicion concerning a person
who is evidently upright is forbidden, but it is permissible concerning

people of ill repute who are known for criminality or corruption. Suspicion in this case is not, in other words, entirely discouraged. In evaluating a *ẓann*, whether praiseworthy or reprehensible, jurists refer to the personal character and record of the person in question, as well as to the nature of the activity or conduct that has given rise to suspicion.

If these two criteria, namely the personal record and the suspected act of a person reinforce one another, the resultant suspicion is praiseworthy. In the event, however, where the personal character and reputation of an individual are not known, reference is generally made to clues and objective indications concerning the activity that has given rise to suspicion. Suspicion can be considered by judicial authorities only if supported by evidence, and only then can a warrant of arrest or preventive detention be issued.[117]

In a chapter entitled '*Ḥuqūq al-Muslim*,' that is, the right of Muslims over one another, al-Ghazālī's recounts six rights a Muslim has on other Muslims, one of which is the avoidance of suspicion concerning a fellow Muslim. This is a right of every Muslim over others in so far as it helps all of them to stay clear of rumour and backbiting. The six rights in question are stipulated in a renowned *ḥadīth* which need not be detailed here. As far as the avoidance of suspicion is concerned, this is the subject of another *ḥadīth* narrated by Anas b. Mālik, which is as follows:

> The Messenger of God, peace be on him, spoke with one of his wives at a time when a man passed by. The Prophet called the man and told him, 'O so and so, this is my wife Safiya.' The man said: 'I was not suspecting you of anything.' Then the Prophet said that Satan penetrates the thoughts of people like the blood in their veins.[118]

According to another report, the Prophet added these words to the *ḥadīth*:

$$ \text{إن الشيطان يجري مجرى الدم.} $$

The devil (and his evil thought) infiltrates a man like the flow of blood in his veins.[119]

The Prophet obviously tried to prevent suspicion concerning himself, despite his eminent reputation for piety and trustworthiness. What transpires in this *ḥadīth* was subsequently taken up by the caliph ʿUmar

b. al-Khaṭṭāb, who is quoted to have said 'The one who puts himself in a suspicious situation should not blame others who might accordingly suspect him.' ʿUmar is also reported to have raised the whip over a person who was speaking to a woman on the street, until the man told him that he was speaking to his wife, to which the caliph responded that people had not seen them as such, and that he should not arouse people's suspicion.[120]

VI. Concealing the Privacy of Others (*Satr al-ʿAwrāt*)

This is one of the major themes of the *Sunnah*, and the instruction that the Prophet gave on this subject is forceful in that it is not confined to moral guidance alone but involves legal rulings. Jurists have understood much of the *Sunnah* on the subject to be of legal import, and have based some of their conclusions on it. Our review of the leading *ḥadīths* here begins with those that underscore the virtue of hiding other people's weaknesses:

من سترمسلما ستر الله فى الدنيا والآخرة.

He who conceals the privacy of a Muslim, God will conceal his hidden failings both in this world and the Hereafter.[121]

Another version of the same *ḥadīth* has it that

لايستر عبد عبدا فى الدنيا إلا ستره الله يوم القيامة.

'The one who conceals the hidden failings of others does not fail to enjoy God's forbearance over his failings on the Day of Judgment.'[122]

It is further provided in another *ḥadīth*:

لاتؤذوا المسلمين ولاتعيروا ولاتتبعوا عوراتهم فإن من يتبع عورة
أخيه المسلم يتبع الله عورته.

Do not annoy your fellow Muslims; do not impute evil to them, and do not expose their nakedness. For behold, anyone who exposes the nakedness of his Muslim brother, God will expose his own nakedness.[123]

The concealment of that which is private is reported, in yet another widely-quoted *ḥadīth*, as an integral part of fraternity between Muslims:

المسلم أخو المسلم لايظلمه ولايسلمه، من كان فى حاجة أخيه فإن الله فى حاجته، ومن فرّج عن مسلم كربة فرّج الله عنه بها كربة من كرب يوم القيامة ومن ستر مسلما ستره الله يوم القيامة .

Muslims are brethren of one another. A Muslim does not inflict injustice on his brother, nor does he abandon him or refuse to help him when he suffers from injustice. The one who helps his brother in need, God helps him at his own moment of need, and the one who relieves a Muslim of hardship, God relieves him of hardship on the Day of Resurrection. And the one who safeguards the privacy of a Muslim, God will conceal his failing on the Day of Resurrection.[124]

Al-Ghazālī has observed that the urge to violate the privacy of another person emanates from malice and inner resentment on the part of those who are inclined to store-up their malice and wait for an opportunity. And then when they find a convenient moment, they raise the curtain of disgrace and thus sever the bond of fraternity. When this becomes the case and malice becomes pervasive and uncontrolled, isolation from one's brothers is preferable. One should not, therefore, expect an observance of the ties of fraternity from individuals who are filled with rancour and malice, and who are ready to attack and expose the faults of others at any opportunity.[125]

The Prophet has clearly declared that exposing the hidden failings of fellow Muslims is the antithesis of the fraternity and affection that Islam consistently emphasizes. The same attitude seems to have been encouraged with regard to non-Muslims, as we read in another *ḥadīth*:

إنك إن اتبعت عورات الناس أفسدتهم أو كدت أن تفسدهم .

If you try to expose the nakedness of people (ʿawrāt al-nās), you are bound to spread corruption among them.[126]

The general language of this *ḥadīth*, and the reference therein to people at large, confirms that it is addressed to Muslims and non-Muslims alike.

A benevolent attitude is nurtured by being reserved with others regarding their private affairs. The right of neighbours tends to feature prominently in this connection. This is also understandable by virtue of the fact that knowledge of the private affairs of others assumes a degree of familiarity with them, and this is usually the case among neighbours. One of the rights of a neighbour that is emphasised is that one should avoid asking them questions that seek to uncover what they wish to keep to themselves. One should also turn a blind eye to those private matters of one's neighbours that one happens to observe, and also avoid listening to rumours about them.[127] The Prophet has been quoted to have said, concerning one's neighbours, that 'A man is not a (true) believer until his neighbour is safe from his prejudice.'[128].

Neighbourhood (*al-jiwār*) is a wide concept in the *Sharīʿah*, and includes not only the person(s) next door, but also those with whom one sits, which could include a colleague at work, or a classmate, and also a companion on a journey. Being good to one's neighbours and to one's guests are important aspects of the Islamic ethos, and the *Sunnah* is emphatic on this point, as shown in the following *ḥadīth*:

من كان يؤمن بالله واليوم الآخر فليكرم ضيفه، ومن كان يؤمن بالله واليوم الآخر فلا يؤذ جـاره، ومـن كان يؤمـن بالله واليوم الآخر فليقل خيرا أو ليصمت.

He who believes in God and the Last Day, let him honour his guest; he who believes in God and the Last Day, let him avoid annoying his neighbour; and one who believes in God and the Last Day, let him say that which is good, or remain silent.[129]

In another *ḥadīth*, a parallel is drawn between dishonouring a Muslim and indulging in usury (*ribā*). The honour of a Muslim is necessarily compromised by anyone revealing that which he dislikes to be revealed. The *ḥadīth* thus provides that:

إن من أربى الربا الاستطالة فى عرض المسلم بغير حق.

To indulge in excess regarding the honour of a Muslim without a just cause is equivalent to the worst form of *ribā*.[130]

One of the instances of 'annoying one's neighbours' is to open a window or an aperture that overlooks their home in a way that exposes them to onlookers. This is prohibited by the renowned *ḥadīth* that 'Harm may neither be inflicted nor reciprocated—*lā ḍarara wa lā ḍirār*.' The one who opens such a window of the like is therefore required to close it or to remove it altogether. The precedent for this is the *ḥadīth* of Samura b. Jundub who had a palm tree with its branches stretching far into the house of his Anṣari neighbour. Each time Samura and his son entered the neighbour's house in order to reach his tree, it caused annoyance to the neighbour. The Anṣari complained to the Prophet. So the Prophet asked Samura if he would sell his tree to the neighbour, which Samura declined to do. He was then asked if he would like to move it away from where it was, to which Samura also replied in the negative. The Prophet then ordered the Anṣari to 'Go and chop down the tree,' and told Samura that he was bent on inflicting harm on his neighbour.[131]

It is also reported that the Caliph ʿUmar b. al-Khaṭṭāb wrote a letter to the governor of Egypt, ʿAmr b. al-ʿĀṣ, in which he briefly said: 'It has been brought to my attention that Khārija bin Ḥudhāfa has constructed a window that overlooks his neighbour and violats their privacy. Upon receiving my letter, you may proceed to demolish it, God willing, and peace be upon you.'[132] In a similar report, it is noted that one Ibn Lahia wrote a letter to the caliph ʿUmar concerning 'A man who had opened a window overlooking his neighbour.' The caliph responded that a bed should be placed below the window and a man should stand on it. If he could thus see the contents of the neighbour's house, it should be closed down; otherwise it should not be obstructed. This has led Abu Yaʿlā al-Farrā to the conclusion that building a high rise overlooking other houses is not necessarily objectionable. The objection arises when a new structure exposes a neighbour to unsolicited viewing.[133] The *Mejelle* ruling on this is more specific when it provides that 'Overlooking women's quarters in a house, such as the courtyard, kitchen, and water-well areas, is counted as an exorbitant harm (*ḍarar fāḥish*), which must be eliminated.'[134] This ruling clearly lends support to a distinction between two types of windows, one of which is for viewing and which is low enough to violate the privacy of someone else's home, and the other, which is higher and primarily built for access to light. Another point to be noted here is that the exposure of those quarters that are frequented by women is the material factor. When such exposure occurs, it is immaterial whether it is during summer time or winter, daytime or night. What is not prohibited is being able to view places that are not frequented by women in the adjoining household, such as a guestroom, garden and the like. But it is noted, once again, that this aspect of the matter should be determined by reference to the prevailing custom of the locality.[135]

According to the clear instructions of *Sunnah* on the subject of covering the private parts (*'awrah*) of one's body, men and women are both asked not to expose their bodies in public. Thus it is reported that on one occasion the Prophet saw a man bathing naked outdoors, and soon after the Prophet addressed the people in the mosque to tell them that:'God Most High is modest and guarded and He loves modesty and *satr*. When any one of you take a bath, let him cover his body.'[136]

إن الله عـز وجـل حـي سـتير يحـب الحياء والسـتر فإذا اغتسـل أحدكم فليستتر.

It is almost certain that Arabian women during the time of the Prophet did not practise veiling and were not confined to staying in their homes. The Prophet had not ordered veiling and had allowed women to go out to the mosque for ritual prayer. Then the verse of veiling was revealed in Madina, which ordered the wives of the Prophet and other women 'to lower their garments close around them (when they go abroad). That will be better so that they may be recognised and not annoyed,' (33:59).

يآيها النبي قل لأزواجك وبناتك ونسـاء المؤمنين يدنيـن عليهـن من جلابيبهن ذلك أدنى أن يعرفن فلا يؤذين.

The Prophet's widow ʿĀʾisha is reported to have said that when this verse was revealed, the Madinan women of the Anṣār (helpers) began to cover themselves and many also confined themselves to their houses. Concerning the Anṣār women of Madina, Umm Salama is reported to have said that when this verse was revealed, 'the women of the Anṣār would go out of their homes while wearing a head cover made of black cloth.'[137]

لما نزلت سورة النورعمدن إلى حجور أو حجوز، شكّ أبو كامل، فشققنهن خمرا.

In another Qur'ānic verse revealed in Madina on the subject of veiling (*satr*), women were directed to 'draw their veils over their bosoms,' (24;31)

وليضربن بخمرهن على جيوبهن.

'Ā'isha is reported to have said concerning this verse that many women, especially those of the Emigrants (*muhājirāt*), used to wear garments with a slit in the area of the neck, which exposed a part of their chests. When this verse was revealed, they began to 'wear covers which would hide their heads, necks and chests.'[138] As time passed by, the rules of *satr* and veiling were made more and more restrictive until 'Āisha is reported to have said in a *mursal* (discontinued) *ḥadīth* that on one occasion 'when Asmā', the daughter of Abu Bakar, came, she was wearing a light garment; the Prophet disapproved and told her: 'O Asmā', when a girl reaches womanhood, it is not proper for her to reveal [anything of herself] except her face and hands.'[139]

إن أسماء بنت أبى بكر دخلت على رسول الله صلى الله عليه وسلم وعليها ثياب رقاق، فأعرض عنها رسول الله صلى الله عليه وسلم وقال: يا أسماء إن المرأة إذا بلغت المحيض لا تصلح أن يرى منها إلا هذا وهذا وأشار إلى وجهه وكفيه.

According to the instruction of another *ḥadīth*, it is provided that

ولا ينظر الرجل إلى عرية الرجل، ولا المرأة إلى عرية المرأة، ولا يغض الرجل إلى الرجل فى ثوب واحد ولاتفضى المرأة إلى المرأة فى ثوب.

A man may not look at the private parts of another man, nor a woman at the private parts of another woman; a man may not share the same cover with another man (in bed), nor may a woman sleep under the same cover with another woman.[140]

In another report, a phrase is added at the very end of this *ḥadīth* which reads: إلا ولدا أو والدا except for one's father and child.'[141]

'*Awrah* is divided into strict (*mughallaẓa*) and light (*mukhaffafa*). The strict '*awrah* for a man consists of penis, testacles and rectum, the rest is light ʿawrah. Strict ʿawrah for a woman is said to be her entire body except for the face, hands, feet and her chest.

All this is firstly concerned with the ritual prayer (ṣalāh), during which the ʿawrah must be covered, but the jurists of the various schools of law have extended these rules to all other times. Muslims are thus instructed not to look at the ʿawrah of another person, or even their own, unless it is for a valid reason such as medical treatment. The ʿawrah of a woman is between the navel and the knee when she is at home by herself or in the company of her close relatives (maḥārim) or other Muslim women. But when she is in the company of strangers of the opposite sex, or even non-Muslim women, her ʿawrah extends to all of her body except her face and hands.

The Mālikīs have relaxed some of these rules by saying that the strict ʿawrah for a man is confined to his private parts and for a woman it is all of her body except the hands and feet, head and chest and the corresponding area to the chest at the back.

The Shāfiʿīs have held that the thigh above the knee section of the male body is not really ʿawrah, based on a ḥadīth in which one of the companions, Anas b. Mālik, reported that 'On the day of (battle of) Khaybar the Prophet's lower garment slipped off his thighs such that I could see the whiter section of his thigh.'[142] The Ḥanbalī school has also held as a result of this ḥadīth that a man's navel and knee are not included in his ʿawrah.[143]

Many commentators have discussed the subject of ʿawrah and found weaknesses in the authenticity of some of these rulings, especially in view of the various customary practices that have influenced them in different times and places. Muhammad Shaḥrūr has discussed some of these and quoted in detail the divergent ruling that nearly all the schools have for female slaves. It seems that the schools of law have persuaded themselves to apply different rulings to slave women and free women. Slave women are on the whole treated, as far as ʿawrah is concerned, on the same footing as a man, and their ʿawrah is a lesser issue than that of free women. This is tantamount to double standards of which Shaḥrūr is critical.[144] For women are women and a ʿawrah of a free woman and the slave woman need not be different. Others have highlighted the role of custom, and it appears that some of the details of the scholastic rulings do not have clear support in the sources.

Old Persian and Greek customary practices have influenced the practices of veiling and segregation in Muslim societies. Heavy veiling and strict segregation of the genders, as has been widely practised among

Muslim communities in later periods, do not relate well to the general pattern that can be discerned in Arab society during the time of the Prophet. Women at that time evidently did not practise veiling, and the ruling that treats the entire body of a woman as ʿawrah, with some minor exceptions, might seem somewhat exaggerated. The conclusion that can be drawn here is that the Qurʾān and *Sunnah* direct Muslims to guard their modesty and avoid shameful and indecent exposure. Shaḥrūr has discussed the source evidence for this in detail, and I do not propose to elaborate further on it. It seems in order, however, to say that the sources of *Sharīʿah* lay down a basic principle that needs to be upheld.[145] The manner in which that principle has been observed has clearly varied over time, and has taken different dimensions among different Muslim communities. General custom (ʿurf) that is in keeping with the spirit of the principle of decency may therefore be said to be a correct indicator of what may or may not be included in the light ʿawrah, and what may or may not be included in the notion of personal privacy.

On the subject of guarding private and confidential information, the *Sunnah* provides a basic guideline, which is that when a person of integrity falls into error and commits a sin which he feels guilty about, and does not declare it to anyone, others should not pursue it either—as per the instruction in the following *ḥadīth*:

من أتى شيئا من هذه القاذورات فليستر بستر الله تعالى فان من يبد لنا صفحته نقم حد الله عليه.

Anyone who commits these filthy acts (probably the *ḥudūd* offences), let it be concealed with God's forbearance unless it becomes evident to us, and when this is the case we shall apply God's punishment to him.[146]

To speak out concerning a transgression committed in privacy by someone who has kept quiet about it is a transgression in itself, and the *ḥadīth* clearly discourages this. Al-Ghazālī has raised, in this connection, the question of whether one should reveal an (unreported) offence, such as adultery or theft, if one is put under pressure to own up to it. Al-Ghazālī argues that if one is asked a question by the Sultan, for example, concerning one's property, which it is feared the Sultan might usurp, or when the Sultan asks concerning something one might have committed but which is only known to God Most High—it is better for 'one to deny it and say 'I have not committed either adultery or theft', even at the expense of telling a lie.' One should also refuse to give in to pressure concerning the privacy of one's brother and refuse to answer questions about it.[147]

According to a *ḥadīth* recorded in the *Sunan* of Abū Dāwūd, one Mawlā told ʿUqbah Ibn ʿĀmir that 'We have neighbours who indulge in wine-drinking.' To this ʿUqbah replied 'Conceal it,' but Mawlā showed reluctance and said 'I feel like going to bring the police on to them.' Then ʿUqbah said: 'Woe to you, give them a chance. For I heard the Messenger of God saying:

من ستر عورة مؤمن فكأنما أحيا موؤودة عن قبرها.

The one who sees the private failing of another and hides it, it is as if he resuscitates a child that was buried alive in its grave.[148]

The Prophet has encouraged everyone to make an effort to conceal the private affairs and hidden weaknesses of others, and declared this an act of spiritual merit:

ومن ستر على مسلم ستر الله عليه فى الدنيا والآخرة، والله فى عون العبد ما كان العبد فى عون أخيه.

The one who conceals (the privacy of) a Muslim, God will conceal his privacy in this world and the hereafter. God helps His servant when the latter is helpful to his brother.[149]

The Qur'ānic verse on the prohibition of espionage that was quoted earlier (49:2) draws a parallel between three things that are often inter-related: unfounded suspicion, backbiting, and espionage, and it seems that the latter two of this trio originate in the first. Whereas the reference to suspicion (*al-ẓann*) in this verse is somewhat flexible, inso-much as it says that 'Suspicion in most cases is sinful,' it is categorically prohibitive on backbiting and espionage. The reason for this is that suspicion supported by clues is not forbidden, as we elaborated earlier, but the Qur'ān is absolutely prohibitive of back-biting and espionage. Exposing the hidden weaknesses of others '*kashf al-ʿawrāt*' and '*tatabbuʿ al-ʿawrāt*,' which is often the end-result of back-biting and espionage, is also addressed in a number of *ḥadīths*. Thus, it is provided in one that:

يامعشـر من آمن بلسـانه ولم يدخل الإيمـان قلبه، لاتغتابوا المسلمين ولاتتبعوا عوراتهم فإن من اتبع عوراتهم يتبع الله عوراته، ومن يتبع الله عورته يفضحه فى بيته .

To the one who has professed the faith by his tongue and has not internalised it into his heart: do not backbite against the Muslims or expose their hidden weaknesses, for the one who does that, God will expose his weakness, and when God exposes someone's hidden weakness, he will be humiliated (and his nakedness will even be exposed) within his own house.[150]

The *ḥadīth* here advises against superficial conformity to the guidance of the faith. The one who professes the faith but does so superficially as to have no inhibitions about exposing other people's weaknesses is not entitled to God's protection. The attitude of dignified silence concerning other people's failings is also advised concerning one's own occasional failure in that one should not declare it, but try instead to suppress it. But the one who announces misdeeds, whether his own or those of others, is known as *mujāhir bi'l-maʿāṣi*, that is, one who boastfully broadcasts his sinful conduct, and it is basically to such persons that the above *ḥadīth* applies.

Some ʿulamāʾ have elaborated on the criteria of distinction between the two types of people, namely those who make their evil conduct overt (*mujāhir*), and those who try to conceal it (*mustatir*), and they argue that a concealer of sin (*mustatir*) is someone who commits a sin in the privacy of his home, or a place not frequented by others, and does not make it known himself either. But he who commits a sin in a place that is not hidden from others, such as his neighbours, even if in his own house, is a *mujāhir*, and does not enjoy the protection granted to a *mustatir*. The distinction between the two, also helps us to ascertain the limits of privacy, and the protection the law extends to it. That distinction—between the broadcaster of evil and the concealer of it—does not, however, apply to someone who confesses to his evil by telling the truth, and wishes to repent and reform himself, for he is not a *mujāhir*. On a similar note, a defiant wrongdoer who conceals his evil conduct in order to escape detection is also not a *mustatir*.

More generally, it has been observed that people are of two types, the first of whom are those who are mindful of their behaviour and public image, and are not known for corruption or sin. When they slip into committing a sin which they do not declare, others should not expose them either, nor should they talk about the sin, as this would partake of backbiting. It is with regard to these people that the Qur'ān advises the public to exercise restraint:

إن الذين يحبون أن تشيع الفاحشة فى الذين آمنوا لهم عذاب أليم فى الدنيا و الآخرة.

Those who love to spread evil concerning the believers will suffer a painful chastisement in this world and the Hereafter.(24:19)

'Concerning the believers,' in this verse means believers who are people of integrity and qualify as *mustatir*. As for the second type, those who have a reputation for corruption, and declare their own misdeeds openly, they have little regard for what others say about them. These are the *mujāhir* who are unashamed of their conduct, and encourage others to follow their way. They are not entitled to protection, and there is no *ghība* (backbiting) concerning them.[151]

The wealth gained by someone who enriches himself by divulging information concerning the private life of others, is unlawful, and that person is the subject of the following *hadīth*:

من أكل برجل مسلم أكلة فإن الله يطعمه مثلها من جهنم، ومن كسى ثوبا برجل مسلم فإن الله يكسوه مثله من جهنم.

The one who gains his feed at the expense of another Muslim (by revealing information that dishonours him behind his back), God will visit the equivalent in Hellfire upon him. The one who clothes himself at the expense of another, God will engulf him in the fire of Hell in a like manner...[152]

And lastly, the rules of concealment (*satr*) are to be abandoned in the following four situations:

1. When exposure serves to prevent a grave offence, such as murder, adultery or theft, in which case concealment is tantamount to condoning it and exposure is permissible on the basis of necessity (*ḍarūra*). Necessity must, on the other hand, be measured accurately.[153]

2. When exposure is conducive to public security, fighting manifest corruption, and ensuring the safety of people's lives and properties.

3. Exposure is permissible concerning a *mujāhir*, that is, a person who declares his misdemeanor himself and has no remorse over or inhibition about it. It is unwarranted to conceal the misdemeanor of he who does not care to conceal it himself.

4. When exposure secures a manifest benefit, or *maṣlaḥa*, for the community.[154]

VII. Confidential Conversation (*Kitmān al-Sirr*)

The Qur'ān and *Sunnah* inculcate the ethics of trustworthiness (*amāna*) most comprehensively, and discourage the betrayal of trust (*khiyāna*) so strongly that *amāna* becomes a central feature of the ethos Islam. When someone speaks to another in confidence, it becomes an *amānah* of the latter to keep the conversation to himself, and not to reveal it to others. The Qur'ān thus directs the believers as follows:

يَآيها الذين آمنوا لاتخونوا الله والرسـول وتخونوا أمانتكـم وأنتـم تعلمون .

O believers, do not be unfaithful to God and the Messenger, or be unfaithful to your trusts while you know it (and know the nature of what is involved). (8:27)

The term *amānāt* (trusts), which occurs in this verse in its plural form, without any qualification, includes all varieties of trust, including confidential conversation that take place in an atmosphere of trust between people.[155] To underscore the broad scope of *amānāt*, the Qur'ān not only reminds people about matters that are seen and heard but also warns against suspicion that originates in the minds and hearts of people. In observing one's *amāna*, one needs to be vigilant, lest one acts out of suspicion. Al-Ghazālī commented on this verse by saying that when one speaks in confidence to one's friends and relatives, the secrecy of the conversation that transpires is a trust, and it is forbidden to divulge it to others, and doing so would be disloyal. This trust is not confined to the spoken word, but extends to that which is seen even if not spoken about, and also things that are neither seen nor heard, but which occur in the mind. This message can be read in the following Qur'ānic verse:

إن السمع والبصر والفؤاد كل أولئك كان عنه مسؤولا.

Truly the ear, the eye and the heart are all answerable (to their Creator). (17:36)

Everyone who possesses these faculties is therefore enjoined to use them responsibly, since each has a role to play in the trust that the Qur'ān seeks to uphold. It is a form of *khiyāna* (betrayal of trust), therefore, to reveal a secret that is entrusted to one.[156] If someone solicits information about it, the request should be denied, even at the expense of telling the truth. For telling the truth is not an absolute obligation at all times. Just as a man is permitted to conceal his own defects, it is permissible for him to do the same regarding others. Since another person, his friend or brother, has entrusted him with confidential information, they become like one soul in two bodies, which is the essence of fraternity. The trust here should also be observed in action so that a person does not behave in such a way as to go against the nature of that trust.[157]

The evidence of the *Sunnah* is emphatic on the question of honouring a trust, to the point that disregarding it is equated with a flaw in the integrity of one's faith. Thus it is tersely declared in a *ḥadīth* that: لا إيمان لمن لا أمانة له. 'The one who has no *amāna* has no faith.'[158] The substance of this *ḥadīth* amounts to a prohibition of exposure or betrayal of what has been said to one in confidence, especially if this betrayel is likely to be harmful to one's friend and confidant.[159] The confidential nature of speech is sometimes indicated in the manner in which it is conveyed, or the context and circumstances of its address. This is the purport of another *ḥadīth* wherein the Prophet is reported to have said:

إذا حدّث الرجل بالحديث ثم التفت فهى أمانة.

When a man speaks (to another) and having finished his speech looks around (lest anyone else might have heard it), it becomes confidential.[160]

When he quotes this, al-Ghazālī adds that the *ḥadīth* clarifies what amounts to a betrayal of *amāna*, which is to divulge something that has been said to one in confidence. He then recounts an incident in which the Umayyad caliph Muʿawiya spoke in confidence to Walīd ibn ʿUtbah, apparently concerning Walīd's father. Walīd then told his father, who was a Companion, that the Commander of the Faithful had confided in him something that he thought he should not conceal from his father. ʿUtbah's response to this was that Walīd shculd not divulge it. For as long as he kept a confidential maːter to himself, he would be safe, but if he declared it, it would be held against him. Walīd then said that the matter was of concern to the relationship between son and father, to which ʿUtbah once again responded by saying that he would prefer to know that his son would not degrade his tongue by divulging a confidential conversation. To do so is *ḥarām*, especially when it is harmful to others, and it is blameworthy even when it is not harmful.[161]

It is also known that the Prophet himself spoke in confidence with his Companions. According to a report that al-Bukhārī has recorded on the authority of Anas b. Mālik, on one occasion 'A man was talking to the Prophet in confidence in the mosque. The Prophet continued talking to him in that way until some of the Companions fell asleep, and afterwards the Prophet got up and offered the prayer with them.'[162]

It is forbidden to disclose confidential information that occurs in consultation or in a meeting, whether of two or more persons, which is held in an atmosphere of trust. Thus according to another *ḥadīth*:

إنمـا يتجالس المتجالسان بـالأمانـة، فلا يحـل لأحـد أن يغشـى على صاحبه مايكره.

The participants of a council are bearers of a trust (*amāna*), and it is not permissible for any one of them to reveal what the others would dːslike to be exposed.[163]

The same message is conveyed, slightly differently, in another *ḥadīth* as follows:

لايجوز لأحـد أن يدخل على المتناجين فى حال تناجيهما.

It is not permissible for anyone to enter a meeting wherein peoplː are engaged in consultation.[164]

According to the instruction of yet another *ḥadīth*:

لايجلس بين الرجلين إلا بإذنهما.

When two persons are sitting together, a newcomer is not allowed to sit between them without their permission.[165]

While the stranger is here required to be sensitive to any confidential conversation that may be taking place between two persons, the reverse of this is also true in that in a company of three, two persons should not engage in confidential conversation in a way that isolates the third. This is the subject of another *ḥadīth* which provides that: 'Two of the three may not engage in confidential talk without the third, as this is likely to cause him distress.'[166]

لايتناجى اثنان دون الثالث، فإن ذلك يحزنه.

A slightly longer version of this *ḥadīth* merely adds the phrase 'until they join the crowd,' in which case the restriction will cease as of that moment.

What this implies is that confidentiality can place a wedge between people if it is not handled with sensitivity to others, and it seems that confidentiality in the context of meetings and social encounters should not, as far as possible, be used in a way that is abrasive or hurtful to others. Abū Dāwūd has also recorded what seems to be a follow-up to the *ḥadīth* just quoted. Here it is provided that the Companion ʿAbd Allāh b. ʿUmar asked the Prophet a question: 'What if there are four (people)?' and the Prophet said that two of them engaging in confidential conversation would not cause any harm.[167]

عن أبن عمر، قال: قال رسول الله صلى الله عليه وسلم مثله،

قال أبو صالح: فقلت لابن عمر: فأربعة؟ قال: لايضرك.

The concept of *amāna*, in the sense of confidentiality and trust is extended, according to another *ḥadīth*, to all consultative councils except for those that promote criminality and sin. To quote the *ḥadīth*:

المجالس بالأمانة إلا ثلاث مجالس: سفك دم حرام، أو فرج

حرام أو اقتطاع مال بغير حق.

All (private) meetings are deemed to be confidential, except for three: those that discuss unlawful bloodshed, adultery, and misappropriation of the property of others.[168]

Al-Ghazālī has drawn the conclusion that the bearer of confidential information about someone's shortcomings should refrain from speaking about the weaknesses of his friend and associate, both in his presence and his absence. If occasions when other people speak about his friend arise, he should not participate, and should also remain silent when questioned about his friend. He should neither confirm nor deny other people's statements regarding the weaknesses of his friend, even if they were made after a split or termination of friendship with that person. One should also avoid revealing information about the friends and family of a former friend, or quoting what other people have said about him.

Friends are, on the other hand, allowed to say good things about one another. This is because silence is advised only with regard to confidential matters and matters which a friend would dislike to be disclosed to others. But there are also occasions when one should not remain silent, and where silence is not justified. Speaking out on such occasions may even partake of enjoining what is good (*amr bi'l-maʿrūf*). On such occasions, one must be honest without malice. To speak badly of others in a way they would dislike also partakes of backbiting (*ghība*), which is forbidden in its own right.[169]

The question then arises as to who actually qualifies for this kind of protective attitude, so that others will protect them and not reveal their hidden weaknesses. In answer to this, al-Ghazālī writes that one should try to ignore the occasional failure or sin, or some bad aspect of character, that one might know about another person. For people often make a mistake, then regret and rectify it, and one or even a few weaknesses of character of this kind should not be given too much weight. For one should not expect others to be more perfect than oneself might be, nor should one think that people can be free of defects. For 'there is no one on the face of the earth who do not combine both good and bad qualities.' When the good qualities predominate, the person is termed a 'noble believer—*al-muʾmin*' who is entitled to fraternity and protection.[170] In the more legalistic language of al-Shāfiʿī, which al-Ghazālī also quotes, a just (*ʿadl*) person is he whose good deeds are greater than his violations (*maʿāṣi*). For there is no Muslim who obeys God all the time or disobeys Him all the time. The person who obeys God most of the time is *ʿadl* in respect both of matters pertaining to the Right of God and those pertaining to the Right of Man. Everyone is under a duty to observe silence concerning the failings of an upright person, both in words and thoughts. For thinking ill of such a person is likely to partake of suspicion (*sūʾ al-ẓann*). The avoidance of suspicion often means giving his words and deeds a good interpretation if at all possible.[171]

Consultation (*shūrā*) is a general Qur'ānic dispensation that applies to community affairs as well as to personal relations between individuals (cf. 3:159). The one who gives or receives counsel is bound to be entrusted with confidential information of one kind or another, which becomes an *amāna* for him. This is the subject of a *ḥadīth* which simply states that المستشار مؤتمن. 'The one whose counsel is solicited is the bearer of *amāna*.'[172] The ruling of this *ḥadīth* may be extended by analogy to consultant physicians, family doctors and lawyers, who are usually entrusted with confidential information by their clients. They are under duty therefore not to divulge such information. It is reassuring to note that what is recommended here is harmonious with the professional ethics that prevail in these areas. Customary practice is in this case harmonious with the normative guidance of the *Sharīʿah*.

That revealing the personal secrets entrusted to one is proscribed by the *Sharīʿah* also leads to the conclusion that a threat to reveal these secrets is not permissible either. All threats are thus proscribed, regardless of whether or not the threat occurs in the context of personal relations, of official duty, or between individuals and governments and so on. For such a threat might well amount to blackmail, and its harm might be no less than actually revealing the secret in the first place. The threat of revealing, or betraying, an *amāna* is therefore not permissible, and falls under the same prohibition that applies to the breach of that *amāna* in the first place.[173]

Al-Bukhārī has recorded a long *ḥadīth*, on the authority of ʿĀ'isha, wherein she said that she and the other wives of the Prophet were once sitting when the Prophet's daughter, Fāṭima, walked in. The Prophet welcomed her and she sat on his right side. The Prophet then confided something to Fāṭima which made her weep, and when he noticed her sorrow, he confided something else to her which pleased her a great deal. Later when ʿĀ'isha asked Fāṭima what had transpired between her and the Prophet and urged her to tell her, Fāṭima replied: 'I would not disclose the secrets of the Messenger of God.' When the Prophet died, ʿĀ'isha asked Fāṭima the same question again, and this time Fāṭima said that now she would reveal what had taken place between her and the Prophet on that occasion: What made her sad, Fāṭima said, was that the Prophet had told her that 'Gabriel used to review the Qur'ān with me once every year, but this year he reviewed it with me twice, and therefore I think that my time of death approaches.' Fāṭima wept on hearing this, but then she became very happy when the Prophet told her: 'Will you not be pleased, O Fāṭima, that you will be the chief of all the believing women among my followers.'[174]

It would appear from this *ḥadīth* that certain secrets can be revealed after the death of the person concerned, especially when they contain a message that is not harmful, or even be beneficial, or brings closeness between people. Fāṭima had evidently guarded the Prophet's secret because she did not want to cause grief to the rest of the Prophet's family with the sad news, and also because the latter statement might have offended ʿĀ'isha since in some ways ʿĀ'isha was as close to the Prophet as herself. But these concerns no longer presented themselves in the same way after the Prophet had passed away.

Silence is the recommended advice of Islam in the event where no benefit is likely to be realised by speech. It is consequently regarded as a sign of piety and virtue to say something only when a benefit is likely to be achieved by it. Thus according to the express terms of another *ḥadīth*:

من كان يؤمن بالله واليوم الآخر فليقل خيرا أو ليصمت.

The one who has faith in God and believes in the Last Day, let him say something good, or remain silent.[175]

In yet another *ḥadīth* of a similar type, the Prophet underscored this point when he said:

كفى بالمرء إثما أن يحدث بكل ما سمع.

It is enough of a sinful conduct for anyone to repeat everything that he hears.[176]

To observe the privacy of the confidential conversation that takes place between friends and relatives can thus be said to be an integral part of the Islamic ethos. It is also a significant feature of the Arab image of an honorable person, which has found expression in the Arabic proverb that ' The chest of the noble is like a graveyard of secrets.' (*ṣudūr al-aḥrāri qubūr al-asrār*).[177]

Two people married to each other cannot reveal confidential information tabout their spouses to other parties within or outside the family. For matrimony creates a sacred bond between two persons which must be honoured and protected. Anything known by the spouses concerning one another is a trust in their keeping, and should be guarded. Revealing confidential information is a breach of this trust and amounts to disrespect to the nobility of marriage. This is upheld in the *ḥadīth*, narrated by Abu Saʿīd al-Khudri, wherein the Prophet is reported to have said:

من أعظم الأمانة عند الله يوم القيامة الرجل يفضى إلى امرأته وتفضى إليه ثم ينشر سرها.

The most perfidious of people before God on the Day of Resurrection is a man who confides in his wife and she confides in him and then he divulges her secrets (to others).[178]

This *ḥadīth* prohibits the revelation of marital secrets by either of the spouses, particularly in reference to conjugal relations. This is a given, and neither spouse needs to articulate to the other that their conjugal relations are strictly confidential.[179] They are covenanted to one another, and responsible for honouring their covenant, in the way the Qurʾān addresses the believers: 'and honour your promise, for you are held responsible on account of your promise,' (17:34).

وأوفوا بالعهد إن العهد كان مسئولا

Any futile or careless speech that compromises the trust and nobility of the marriage contract is either forbidden (*ḥarām*) or reprehensible (*makruh*), depending on the nature and severity of the words or conduct in question. The basic guidelines here are provided in two other *ḥadīths* as follow:

لا يدخل الجنة قتّات.

The one who carries words among people in order to spread corruption shall not enter Paradise.[180]

And then the *ḥadīth* already quoted that:

من كان يؤمن بالله واليوم الآخر فليقل خيرا أو ليصمت.

The one who believes in God and the Last Day, let him say what is good or remain silent.[181]

More specifically, it is reported in a long *ḥadīth* that Abū Dāwūd has recorded that the Prophet entered upon a group of his Companions and asked if there was anyone among them who spent the night behind closed doors with his wife, in privacy and confidence, and then the next day recounted what had transpired between them. There was no response. Then the Prophet addressed a group of women with the same question, and they responded 'But by God, they speak about such things, men and women both do.' The Prophet then said that those who divulge their marital secrets are 'like two devils that meet one another in the market-place and they mate with one another while the people are watching them.'[182]

إن مثل من فعل ذلك مثل شيطان وشيطانة لقى أحدهما صاحبه بالسّكّة فقضى حاجته فيها والناس ينظرون إليها.

Shawkānī, who recorded this *ḥadīth*, then drew the conclusion that 'this *ḥadīth*, together with the one narrated by Abū Saʿīd al-Khudrī, indicates that divulging marital secrets, by either spouse, concerning their sexual relations, is prohibited.' For both these *ḥadīths* are emphatic on the enormity of the conduct they refer to. But if either of the spouses speaks only about the occurrence of sexual intercourse without further elaboration, they will have committed what is *makruh*. This is designed to protect the sanctity of marital life against corrupt and indulgent elaboration that is demeaning, and contrary to *murū'a* (manliness, chivalry) and magnanimity. If these is a useful purpose in divulging marital secrets, such as when mentioned to a medical doctor or judge, there should be no objection, since this will most likely be covered by the rule of necessity (*ḍarūra*). Yet what is divulged in this situation should be the bare minimum needed.

VIII. The Privacy of the Deceased Person

The general guideline of *Sharīʿah* concerning deceased persons is that their failings should not be disclosed, and nor should they be made the victims of backbiting or derision. For the personal dignity of the dead is sacrosanct under the *Sharīʿah*, and must at all times be protected against abuse. Thus a *ḥadīth* asks the believers to:

أذكروا محاسن موتاكم وكفوا عن مساويهم.

Mention your deceased persons for their virtues, and restrain yourselves from discussing their failings.[183]

This is endorsed in another *ḥadīth* which provides that:

إذا مات أحدكم فدعوه لاتقعوا فيه.

When any of your fellow humans die, leave them alone and refrain from discussing their weaknesses.[184]

When a deceased person is insulted or slanderously accused, his relatives may demand that the offender is punished for it, or demand financial compensation if they have suffered injury or loss as a result.[185]

As for the grounds on which the *Sharīʿah* permits the disclosure of information about individuals (as in the case of testimony, or *fatwā* etc., discussed below), the rules that apply to the living also apply, as far as possible, to the dead. Thus where a testimony or an issuance of *fatwā* or the public interest require a disclosure of confidential information about deceased persons, it is permissible to obtain it, although the general guidance of *ḥadīth* advises a degree of restraint even greater than that which applies to the living.

One aspect of the privacy of the deceased that Muslim jurists have discussed at length is the ritual of bathing them (*ghusl*), which naturally involves some exposure of their bodies. Bathing the dead prior to burial is obligatory (*wājib*), or, according to some Mālikī jurists, (*mandūb*) or recommended, according to a *ḥadīth* wherein the Prophet said that a Muslim has six rights over other Muslims, one of which is that he is bathed after he dies.[186] The question then arises as to what parts of the body are considered private (i.e. ʿawra), and may not be exposed, and the answer is the same whether the person is alive or dead. The rules of ʿawrah differ only by reference to gender, but they do not differ by reference to life or death. In the case of males, ʿawrah consists of the abdominal section of the body below the navel down to the knee, which may not be exposed, especially during prayer. This is clear in the *ḥadīth* in which the Prophet is reported to have said: 'Do not reveal your thigh or look at the thigh of either the living or the dead.'[187]

لا تكشف فخذك ولاتنظر إلى فخذ حي ولا ميت.

A stranger of the opposite sex is not permitted to bathe a deceased person. Moreover, bathing a deceased person of either sex must be carried out so that the private parts are not revealed. It is recommended that a cover be placed on the private parts when the deceased is washed. It is also recommended that the person who bathes the deceased does not touch the private parts directly, as touching is equivalent to viewing, and both violate the deceased's right to privacy. The hand of the person who washes should also be covered when washing the deceased. In the absence of water, recourse may be had to dry ablution, or *tayammum*. The corpse of a martyr (*shahīd*) who has fallen in *jihād* is not washed. Otherwise the requirements of washing and of *satr* (covering the private parts) apply equally to all, including discerning children, and they are observed as a mark of respect for the privacy and dignity of the deceased.

It is preferable that a male person's body is washed by a male and that of a female by a female. A man may therefore not wash a woman except in cases of necessity where a member of the same sex is not available, and vice versa. Preference in this case is given to the spouse or relative of the deceased person over other people of the opposite gender.

The marital tie subsists for a time after the death of the spouse, and it terminates upon expiry of the waiting period (*ʿidda*), which, in the case of death, is one hundred and thirty days. The spouse of a deceased person thus continues to remain a spouse until the expiry of *ʿidda*. Thus it is reported that two prominent Companions, namely Abū Bakr and Abu Mūsā al-Ashʿarī, had willed that their respective spouses should bathe them when they died and their wishes were carried out. When the Prophet, peace be on him, died, it is reported that ʿAlī b. Abī Ṭālib bathed him, and his widow ʿĀ'isha said later that she had not known at the time that a wife could undertake the bathing of her deceased husband's body and that she would have done it herself if she had known about it at the time.[188]

One might note, however, that in al-Kāsānī's rendering of the ruling of the Ḥanafī school of *fiqh*, unlike the wife who is entitled to bathe her deceased husband, the husband does not have the same right to bathe the body of his deceased wife. Two reasons are given, one of which is that *ʿidda* is observed only by the wife, not by the husband, which means that marriage subsists after the death of a spouse only from the wife's perspective, not that of the husband. The second and controversial point is that the husband's relation to his wife resembles ownership (*milk al-nikāḥ*) which terminates when the subject of this 'ownership' is no longer alive. One cannot, in other words, have a right concerning a 'property' that is no longer in existence. Kāsānī thus wrote that 'It is not permissible for him to bathe her—*lā yaḥillu lahu ghuslihā.*'[189] With due respect to al-Kāsānī's erudition in *fiqh*, he applies flawed logic here, which violates the essence of the 'compassion and friendship,' by which the Qur'ān characterises marriage (30:21). It is also irregular to postulate two different capacities for marriage, whereas in practice the contract of marriage and the experience of marital life do not bear out this dualistic approach.

When a married woman dies, say during a journey, and there are women with her as well as her husband, the women should bathe her and not her husband—'according to us—*indanā,*' say al-Kāsānī who represents the Ḥanafī school. But he adds that the Shāfiʿīs entitle the husband to bathe his deceased wife. The Shāfiʿīs have, much to their credit, ignored the Ḥanafī viewpoint on this matter altogether, and have referred instead to a *ḥadīth* in which the Prophet is reported to have said to his wife ʿĀ'isha, who transmitted the *ḥadīth,* that: 'Should you happen to die (before me), I will bathe you, put a shroud on you, and pray on you.'[190] The Shāfiʿīs have also relied on the report that when Fāṭima, the wife of ʿAlī (and the Prophet's daughter) died, ʿAlī bathed her. These two *ḥadīths* establish the validity of the Shāfiʿī ruling, which is also based on the premise that 'The marriage subsists putatively on the grounds of the needs of the deceased wife in the same way as it would subsist when the husband dies.'

The Ḥanafīs have interpreted the *ḥadīth* of ʿĀ'isha with the reading that when the Prophet told her 'I will bathe you—*ghasaltuki,*' he meant that he 'would provide the means for bathing her.' A similar and even weaker explanation is given to ʿAlī's *ḥadīth,* which another Companion, ʿAbd Allāh b. Masʿūd, apparently refuted and discussed with ʿAlī until ʿAlī said to Ibn Masʿud 'Did you not know that the Prophet told me that Fāṭima is my wife in this world and in the next.'[191] This case, in other words, was a special case, according to this reading, which need not be generalised, and the husband is therefore not entitled to the right that ʿAlī enjoyed.

The rules of privacy also extend to shrouding the deceased. The shroud should be clean, preferably three pieces of white cloth that cover the entire body in a dignified manner. The use of perfume is recommended because it honours the deceased person. The Prophet's widow, ʿĀ'isha reported that

كفن رسول الله صلى الله عليه وسلم فى ثلاثة أثاب .

The Prophet's body was shrouded in three pieces of white cloth.[192]

In another *ḥadīth* also reported by ʿĀ'isha, the Prophet's body was washed with his shirt still on, and ʿAlī and Usāma b. Zayd, who washed him, rubbed the Prophet's body by moving their hands over his shirt.[193] When the coffin is carried, the procession walks behind the deceased person and not in front, although some say the opposite. This is also to show respect for the deceased person. It is reprehensible (*makruh*) to speak loudly at the funeral procession, or to load the coffin on a beast; rather, it should be carried on human shoulders, unless circumstances dictate otherwise.[194] As a mark of respect for the deceased, the Prophet has also instructed his followers by saying: 'When you see a funeral, you should stand up until it passes by or is laid down.'[195]

إذا رأيتم الجنازة فقوموا لها حتى تخلفكم أو توضع.

It is reported that the Prophet himself stood when the funeral of a Jew passed by. His Companions mentioned to him that the deceased person was a Jew, but the Prophet repeated the same instruction that 'When you see a funeral, you should stand up.'[196]

كنـا مـع النبى صلى الله عليه وسلم إذ مرت جنازة، فقام لهـا،
فلما ذهبنا لنحمل، اذا هى جنازة يهودي، فقلنا يا رسول الله،
إنما هي جنازة يهودي، فقال: إن الموت فزع، فإذا رأيتم جنازة
فقوموا.

IX. Restrictions on the Right to Privacy

This section addresses the grounds and circumstances in which the *Sharīʿah* permits the exposure of confidential information about individuals, and these include testimony, *fatwā*, public interest, the consent of the party concerned and *ḥisba*. We have already discussed how *ḥisba* restrains the right to privacy in the context of crime prevention, and need not address that point again. We turn now to the subject of testimony.

1) Testimony (*Shahāda*)

Testimony by its very definition involves the disclosure of information, before a judge, that would otherwise be unknown to him. Testimony

may thus be said to involve a certain innate violation of privacy. The
Qur'ān demands that the witness must reveal the truth, and also makes
it a general duty that those who know the truth come forward and
give testimony in the cause of justice. Thus it is enjoined in the Qur'ān
that:

ولاتكتموا الشهادة ومن يكتمها فإنه آثم قلبه.

And do not conceal testimony, for whoever conceals it, his heart is
tainted with sin. (2:283).

According to the recognised rules of evidence in the *Sharīʿah*, a testimony in the cause of justice may be given without solicitation only
in matters pertaining to violations of the Right of God, but even so,
it is not always recommended for witnesses to volunteer a testimony
unless it is requested by the party concerned or by a court of justice.
Yet if one knows that a divorced couple still live in sinful cohabitation
with one another, or when one knows of a 'marriage' between close
relatives, or when a certain individual is noted for misappropriating the
assets of a charitable endowment (*waqf*), and since all of these involve
violations of the Right of God, these may be reported and testified to
without prior solicitation, or court summons. For it is provided in a
ḥadīth that:

خير الشهداء من أدى شهادته قبل أن يسألها.

The best of witnesses are those who give testimony without having
been asked for it.[197]

However, if testimony is concerned with what is known as the Right
of Man, especially when the right-bearer himself is alive and present, it
may not be given unless it is solicited. Thus when a debtor defaults in
repaying his creditor, or when a man fails to support his wife, or fails
to pay her dower, no-one should volunteer to be a witness unless this
is requested by the right-bearer or a court. The authority for this ruling
is also given in a *ḥadīth* wherein the Prophet spoke disapprovingly of
certain people, and this included 'A person who gives testimony without having been asked for it.'[198]

ويشهد الشاهد ولايستشهد.

It is a collective duty (*farḍ kifā'ī*) of witnesses to give testimony in the cause of justice in the event when there are many persons who can serve as witnesses, but it becomes a personal duty (*farḍ ʿayn*) of a witness if he or she is the only person who can do so.

This is the majority ruling, but the Mālikīs and Ḥanbalīs have held that giving testimony is always a personal duty in matters pertaining to the Right of Man. The authority for this is provided in the following verse:

ولايأبى الشهداء إذا ما دعوا.

The witnesses should not refuse when they are called on (to give evidence). (2:282).

The text here refers to testimony when a witness is called upon to give it. Witnesses may not, therefore, volunteer to reveal confidential information concerning others, whether alive or dead, in private claims, and should also give testimony only when asked to do so. This is also the general advice concerning testimony in prescribed crimes (*ḥudūd*) such as adultery and theft. Since the *ḥudūd* are generally classified under the Right of God, or community rights, the witness is basically at liberty to offer testimony or not. If it is given voluntarily, there is no objection to it, but there is considerable evidence in the sources which encourages silence concerning the perpetrators of these crimes, especially at the pre-arrest and pre-trial stages. There are several reports of persons who approached the Prophet and confessed the offence of adultery they had committed, but the Prophet encouraged them to revoke their confession and repent in silence.[199] This is because the *ḥudūd* are the Rights of God, and God's attributes include generosity and forgiveness. There is no great fear, it is said, attached to the loss of God's rights, but that fear is very real concerning the Right of Men in their private claims and disputes. The witness is therefore advised to conceal the failings of the perpetrator of *ḥudūd*, but to be ready to give testimony when called upon in private disputes among individuals. It should be added that concealment (*al-satr*) is recommended in the *ḥudūd* except in cases of fear of a possible miscarriage of justice, and fear that an innocent person may be convicted if testimony is not volunteered, or when the perpetrator is known to be unrepentant and a dangerous criminal. It is also recommended not to volunteer testimony for the crime of theft if the perpetrator has already returned the stolen goods to their owner.[200]

It thus appears that revealing the misdeeds of others in a testimony that might violate their privacy does not always go against the right to privacy as such. It may on the contrary become a collective or a personal duty of the witness to disclose information, and in certain circumstances, it may only be recommendable or even optional for him or her to do so. The only reservation to be noted here is that secret information on others in private disputes may not be revealed by a witness unless his or her testimony is solicited.

The *Sharīʿah* also permits the cross-examination and impugnment (*al-jarḥ*) of witnesses before courts of justice, and also in the case of the transmitters of *ḥadīth*, by those who are qualified to attempt such impugnment. Cross-examination and impugnment may involve the disclosure of personal and private information about individuals, and probe into their personal lives, whether they are dead or alive. The rules of *al-jarḥ* actually require, both in the cases of witnesses and transmitters of *ḥadīth*, that a vague and imprecise reference to the faulty or unjust character of a witness is unacceptable. It is thus not enough merely to say that so and so is a transgressor, but one has to specify how, and this may inevitably entail the disclosure of secret information about individuals, which may amount to backbiting, and yet is permissible by general consensus. An exemption here is granted on condition, however, that disclosure, or an impugnment of testimony, is attempted not due to hostility or a personal vendetta of any kind, but for the sake of a worthy cause. Another requirement is that the disclosure of defects and impugnment (*al-jarḥ*) are limited only to what is necessary and no more, and must not engage in insult or name-calling that may not be relevant to the discovery of truth.[201]

2) Legal Opinion and *Fatwā*

Both Al-Ghazālī and al-Nawawi have held backbiting (*ghība*) to be permissible concerning a person who is alive or dead if it serves a valid legal purpose that cannot be otherwise realised, and this includes the solicitation of *fatwā*, as explained below.[202]

Revealing a secret (*ifshāʾ al-sirr*), or the exposure of the private affairs of another person, often involve backbiting (*ghība*), and someone who asks a jurisconsult (*mufti*) or an attorney for a legal opinion may find that this requires a probing into the privacy of the person concerned. The question then arises of whether the *mufti* may or may not ask for such information, and whether the client may disclose it. In answer to this, Al-Ghazālī has suggested that it is preferable to avoid probing into the privacy of others if a legal opinion can be given without it. Suppose that a client approaches a *mufti* concerning a grievance against a relative, say his father or wife; it is safer for the client to ask general questions rather than give specific details. The one who solicits a *fatwā* on an issue of concern may ask a general question, for example, by asking about the position of a person who has a grievance against a close relative, the father, for instance, or asking about the predicament of a person who might have committed *zinā* with a close relative. This is a preferable way of approaching the issue (known as *al-taʿrīḍ*), instead of revealing what might have actually occurred. This approach of abstracting, so to speak, is likely to give a degree of objectivity to the issue without involving unnecessary probing into the privacy of individuals. But then it is also permissible to specify the subject-matter further, since this may well be deemed necessary in the context. Quoted in authority for this is the *ḥadīth* concerning Hind, the wife of Abu Sufyān, who complained to the Prophet that 'Her husband was a tight-fisted man and did not give enough provisions to her and her child,' to which the Prophet responded by saying 'Take what is sufficient for you and your child in a decent manner.'[203] As it appears, there was a certain amount of backbiting (*ghība*) in what Hind said to the Prophet, yet the Prophet listened and gave a verdict. In serious crimes, such as the offence of *zinā*, it is advisable not to accuse a person directly, for it can very well make the accuser liable to the punishment of slander-ous accusation (*qadhf*) if he fails to prove the charge through admissible evidence. But as already noted, it remains permissible to communicate with a lawyer and *mufti* in confidence and accuse another, or even backbite if necessary, for a valid purpose. Yet one must also try to exer-cise restraint in disclosure of secret information on others.[204]

3) Privacy and the Public Interest (*Maṣlaḥa ʿĀmma*)

There may be occasions when the public interest requires a disclo-sure of confidential information about individuals and organisations. A medical doctor, for example, is normally required by his profes-sional code not to reveal confidential information about his patients. In the event, however, when guarding professional secrets endangers public health, such as in the case of a contagious disease, the secrecy requirement may be overlooked and a necessary exposure made in order to enable early action to control the spread of the disease. Based on this argument, the Saudi-based Fiqh Academy, in its eighth session in Brunei (1993/1414), passed a resolution that makes it obligatory to reveal confidential information if concealing it is likely to be more harmful than revealing it. The Academy resolution was guided by two legal maxims of *fiqh*, one of which permits one to pursue of the lesser of two evils, and the other that a specific harm may be accepted in order to prevent a general one.[205] This in turn justifies a government decision to make it obligatory for medical doctors to reveal and report any contagious diseases carried by their patients. But no such requirement is valid concerning non-contagious diseases, simply because there would be no case to make for the protection of the public interest. But even when a disclosure of confidential information is required when the public interest is at stake, such a disclosure should be limited to what is deemed necessary and no more. This is the purport of another legal maxim of *fiqh* which states that 'Necessity is measured according to its true proportions.'

A similar issue of public interest may arise with regard to people who advocate theological innovation and heresy (*arbāb al-bidaʿ*), i.e., as to whether or not they should be exposed in order to protect the public against their harm. Al-Ghazālī has answered this question in the affirmative and urged that their heresy and transgression should be criticised and exposed so that the community can protect itself and take measures against their misguidance. It is necessary, however, that the publicity (*tashhīr*) that is given to the propagators of *bidʿah* is confined to the facts, and does not extend to accusations or insults.[206]

4) Authorisation and Consent

A question arises as to whether the consent one person grants to another that the latter might reveal personal secrets about himself or herself authorises the recipient of that confidential information to actually reveal or publicise it. An example of this is when someone writes another person's biography and obtains permission from his subject to disclose confidential information about him. The answer to this is generally in the affirmative, except for cases where the exposure itself amounts to transgression and harm (*ḍarar*) that violates the limits of propriety and decorum. If the writer of a personal biography reveals harmful information concerning his subject, he remains answerable and may be penalised for it, notwithstanding the personal consent of his subject. The writer and holder of secret information must therefore use his own good judgement about whether disclosing it is likely to be of benefit or not.

When a person makes a statement in which he or she reveals confidential information about himself or herself, it is treated as a confession (*iqrār*), which may be used as a basis for prosecution and conviction, should there be grounds for such a course of action. Once a person has revealed secrets about himself, they are no longer considered secrets and are therefore not protected by the safeguards that protect the right to privacy.

Broadly speaking, a person may reveal confidential matters concerning himself if there is a benefit to be obtained by this. Thus if a person speaks about the secrets of his or her scientific success, or his success in business or the arts, and this may provide a good example and advice, this is praiseworthy, but not if it becomes a source of mischief or misguidance—such as a criminal who reveals his secret methods and discusses tactics that could prove to be provocative and harmful. A person once involved in the state intelligence services is also advised not to reveal his experiences since such a revelation might prove prejudicial to the public. The basic guidance of the *Sharīʿah* on this and similar matters is provided in the *ḥadīth* which declares it as a 'Sign of piety for a Muslim to say something good or else to remain silent.'[207]

من حسن إسلام المرء أن يقل خيرا أو ليصمت.

Silence and restraint thus become the basic advice of the *Sharīʿah* in regard to revealing confidential information concerning others, and disclosure is advised only when it is deemed to be necessary and beneficial. The personal consent of an individual also provides limited relief from the general advice of restraint on the disclosure of confidential information on others.

X An Overview of Modern Law

With reference to the laws of both Britain and Malaysia (and other Commonwealth jurisdictions), the basic question often raised is about the recognition of privacy as a basic right. This is because the law in both countries remains ambivalent, notwithstanding the fact that privacy is valued in the mores and customs of both. No-one would doubt that 'a man's home is his castle', and in his private life, a person ought to feel safe from unwarranted intrusion by outsiders, including the police.

The Federal constitution of Malaysia is silent on the subject of privacy. The question thus arises of whether 'invasion of privacy' is a violation of personal liberty and could therefore be read within the meaning of Article 5(1) of the Constitution. This Article provides that 'No person shall be deprived of his personal liberty, save in accordance with law.' In *pp. v. Haji Kassim*,[208] a question that came under scrutiny in both the High Court and the Federal Court was whether an incriminating statement made confidentially by an accused person to a medical officer or psychiatrist was admissible against him. The High Court had overruled the objection that arose under section (26) of the Evidence Act 1950 and held it admissible. But the Court's judgement in doing so was informed by American textbooks, probably because of a lack of precedent in Malaysia and other Commonwealth jurisdictions. As one commentator noted, 'This gives the impression that privacy is somehow a right that is alien to Malaysia or other Commonwealth Jurisdictions.'[209]

The Malaysian courts have also admitted tape-recorded evidence, the interception of communication and phone-tapping—even though they violate a person's privacy—if they are found to be relevant and authentic. Court precedent in numerous cases points to the conclusion that the judicial discretion to exclude is rarely invoked by Malaysian judges. The court is usually not too concerned with the method of procurement of evidence. The Evidence Act 1950 seems to condone this, as it emphasises the inclusion of relevant evidence and the result seems to be that the court admits all that is relevant, but not prejudicial, and rejects all that is not relevant (cf. section 138). Since there are no local cases that deal directly with the right to privacy, the focus of the debate tends to be on ill-gotten evidence, and the discussion on whether an exclusionary rule concerning ill-gotten evidence should be adopted has never ceased. The problem in Malaysia remains a conspicuous lack of statutory recognition of privacy as a fundamental right.

There is no right to privacy as such in the laws of England and Wales either. There is also no recorded case in Scotland to establish that the right is recognised by law. However, civil law in Scotland rests on the notion of generalised rights more than in England, and this makes it possible for the courts to make an extreme invasion of privacy liable to a remedy or sanctions.[210]

English law is well-developed, on the other hand, on trespasses against personal property, which often subsumes the invasion of privacy. Even in cases where there is no actual entry to private property, the law of nuisance secures privacy to some extent. An unreasonable amount of persistent telephone calls could qualify as nuisance. There is no English precedent, however, to recognize an unqualified right of personal privacy. According to Salmond:

> English lawyers have been skeptical about the effectiveness of general declarations for the protection of rights. So English law does not recognise any general right to privacy... Common law gives no remedy to one who complains that his neighbours have spied from their windows into his premises, or have cut off an attractive view from his house by erecting a fence. No recognised tort has been committed. Nor does there seem to be any remedy for interception of telephonic or other conversations...[211]

In *Malone V. Commission of Police of the Metropolis* (No. 2),[212] the House of Lords held that although there is a right to privacy, the fact remains that there exists no prohibition in statute that renders the act of phone-tapping unlawful. Consequent to this case, the Interception of Communications Act 1985 was enacted, and it provided in section (1) that: 'it shall be a criminal offence to intentionally intercept a transmission made by post or by a public telecommunication system otherwise than under the provision of the statue.' There is nevertheless no requirement for the judicial authorisation or supervision of such an interception.[213]

In comparison, it may be noted that a judicial warrant is necessary before interception is attempted in Canada, Australia and the United States.

Article (12) of the Universal Declaration of Human Rights 1948 has recognised privacy as a basic right:

> No one shall be subjected to arbitrary interference with his privacy, family, home or correspondence, nor to attack upon his honour or reputation. Everyone has the right of the protection of the laws against such interference or attack.

The International Covenant on Civil and Political Rights 1976 specifically recommended that each member state 'should adopt such legislative measures as may be necessary to give effect to the right of persons not to be subjected to arbitrary or unlawful interference with their privacy, home or correspondence.'

The *Sharīʿah* recognises a general right to the privacy of the home, just as it also imposes a general prohibition on espionage against personal privacy and in the context of court proceedings. Incriminating evidence must be secured lawfully in order to be admissible. If the evidence in question is the result of espionage and obtained, for example, through piercing apertures through a door or by eavesdropping and phone-tapping, it cannot be used for incriminating purposes.[214] This is because the *Sharīʿah* prohibits the search of private homes, and invasions of privacy for the purposes of verifying the occurrence of a crime—unless there is independent evidence that a crime has been committed.[215]

The *Sharīʿah* also recognises the right to privacy for women within their home compounds, with a sufficiency of light and air. According to the *Mejelle*, new structures, such as doors and windows that expose places frequented by women, like the kitchen and courtyard of a house, to unsolicited viewing, is considered as excessive harm (*ḍarar fāḥish*) and a court order may be obtained for their removal. The person may consequently be compelled to 'put a stop to that *ḍarar*, by building a wall, or a wooden partition, in such a way that the women are no longer seen....'[216]

In a similar vein, when someone climbs a fruit tree in his own garden and can see his neighbour's place and the women of that house, that person must give advance notice when he intends to climb the tree. 'If he has not given notice, the judge could prevent him from going up into that tree without notice.'[217]

Fault-finding, and intrusion upon the private lives of individuals by journalists does not exonerate them from liability. Unfair and inaccurate publications that violate the principles of Islam equally fall under Qurʾānic prohibitions. 'The proprietor, the editor, the printer, the publisher, the original contributor or composer of a scandalous article or column are liable to [persecution for] defamation, notwithstanding exceptions provided in the *Sharīʿah*.'[218] The Protection that the Qurʾān has granted is not limited to the physical aspects of a person's privacy but also to their dignity and honour. The Qurʾān thus provides: 'Woe to every slanderous defamer,' and 'O you who believe, avoid suspicion as much as you can... and do not defame one another behind your backs.'[219]

Concluding Remarks

The *Sharīʿah* may be said to be protective of the right to privacy of all individuals, regardless of the particularities of race, religion or gender.

The honour and dignity of the human person is the subject of an unqualified declaration in the Qur'ān that God has 'bestowed dignity on the children of Adam,' and made the *homo sapiens* superior to the rest of His creation (17:70). Qur'ān commentators have generally concluded that this declaration makes dignity an inherent attribute and the right of all human beings.[220] The right to privacy, such as the privacy of one's home, safety from espionage, and the right to confidentiality, are among the important manifestations of human dignity. The Qur'ānic requirement that one can enter private homes only with the permission of its inhabitants, as well as the prohibition on espionage, are both unqualified in respect of gender or religion.

The private home should be safe from unsolicited viewing, intrusion and espionage, regardless of the race, gender or religion of inhabitants. The religious factor is not taken into account in respect of espionage, but only in the context of hostility and warfare. The position here is based mainly on the practical *Sunnah* of the Prophet and the precedents of his Companions but its basis in the Qur'ān may be a matter of interpretation. There is no authority in the sources, however, to validate internal government-led espionage against citizens themselves, whether Muslims or non-Muslims, except perhaps in the context of crime detection and situations of necessity. But since these two exceptions can be a given wider interpretation in relation to context and circumstances, it would be advisable to make espionage in particular cases subject to a judicial order. This will ensure objectivity and correctness, and also facilitate the admissibility of any evidence obtained there through in a court of law.

The *Sharīʿah* evidence on the right to privacy also provides a blueprint that can be utilised, and if necessary, adjusted and developed in regard to certain aspects of privacy that may not have been regulated in the source evidence. It may even be justified to say that the Qur'ān and *Sunnah* should generally be seen not as detailed legislative codes, but as sources of general guidance. There is, for instance, considerable emphasis on the privacy of the home and the etiquette of obtaining permission to enter a private home. Yet for obvious reasons, the source evidence does not specifically address aspects of the right to privacy that may now call for protective legislation because of the use of new detection devices, the computerisation of data and the internet, for these compile and store a wide range of confidential information on individuals. As it is, much of the source evidence of the *Sharīʿah* on privacy provides moral advice that should be seen as a basic framework and a set of guidelines for legislation. Legislation is needed to specify, for instance, the legal command from what may be said only to be moral advice. There is also the circumstantial factor of the drastic change in living conditions for contemporary Muslims compared to what earlier Muslims experienced at the time of the revelation of the Qur'ān and *Sunnah*. Since the *aḥkām* of the *Sharīʿah* are only enforceable in the presence of their effective causes and rationale (*ʿilal*), in the event where the basic cause of a particular ruling no longer exists, the ruling itself is also liable to change. Some of the rulings that were fit, for example, for the hot and arid conditions of Mecca and Medina may fall into this category. The determination of whether or not this is in fact the case, and whether or not the effective cause (*ʿilla*) of a *ḥukm* has collapsed, is a juridical decision that needs to be taken by means of legislative and policy measures by lawful authorities. Moral advice may also be elevated to a legal ruling, and this too requires legislative action.

To conclude, Islamic law exhibits a high level of sensitivity towards violations of the right to privacy, and the guidance it provides goes a long way to protect this right. The fact that the Qur'ān and *Sunnah* contain moral advice and religious guidance side by side with legal injunctions makes respect for the privacy of others an integral part of the social and cultural ethos of the Muslim community, and this can, in turn, be expected to play a supportive role in legislation.

NOTES

1.   Cf. Ḥusnī al-Jundī, *Ḍamānāt Ḥurmat al-Ḥayāt al-Khāṣṣah fi'l-Islām*, 36.

2.   S.D. Warren and L.D. Brandies 'The Right to Privacy' 4 *Harvard Law Review* (1890), 193.

3.   *Winfield and Jolowics on Tort*: London: edr. W.V.H. Rogers, Sweet & Maxwell, 1979, 525. See also Niazi *Islamic Law of Tort*, 90.

4.   Al-Jundī, *Ḍamānāt Ḥurmat al-Ḥayāt*, 46.

5.   Cf. Sarip Adul, *Kitmān al-Sirr wa Ifshā'uh*, 201.

6.   Cf. al-Alūsī, *Rūḥ al-Maʿānī*, XVIII, 133, wrote that 'when you greet the inmate and ask for permission to enter, you have fulfilled the requirement of this *āyah*.'

7.   Cf. Jundī, *Ḍamānāt Ḥurmat al-Ḥayāt al-Khāṣṣa,* 59, 71: Dughmī, *Ḥimāyat al-Ḥayāt al-Khāṣṣa*, 16; Niazi, *Islamic Law of Tort,* 79.

8.   Sayyid Qutb, *Fi Ẓilāl al-Qur'ān*, vol. 18, 88–89.

9.   Al-Jundī, *Ḍamānāt*, 56; Dughmi, *Ḥimāyat*, 21.

10.   Al-Shawkānī, *Fath al-Qadīr*, IV, 20; al-Dughmi, *Ḥimāyat*, 24.

11.   Al-Dughmi, *Ḥimāyat*, 25.

12.   Kāsānī, *Badā'iʿ al-Ṣānā'iʿ*, VI, 2112.

13.   See for details al-Dughmi, *Ḥimāyat al-Ḥayāt al-Khāṣṣa fi'l-Sharīʿa*, 129–131; see also Muhammad Asad, *The Message of the Qur'ān*, 538.

14.   Sulami, *Qawāʿid al-Aḥkām* (Rayyan edn.), 285.

15.   *Id.*, 288.

16.   Al-Alūsi, *Rūḥ al-Maʿāni*, XVIII, 216; al-Dughmi, *al-Tajassus wa aḥkāmuhu*, 147; *Idem, Ḥimāyat*, 27.

17.   Sulami, *Qawāʿid*, 285; Jundī, *Ḍamānāt*, 108; 'Iwad Muhammad, *Dirasat*, 116.

18.   Cf. Abū Dāwūd, *Mukhtaṣar Sunan Abi Dāwūd*, K. Al-Adab, b. *al-rajul yasta'dhinu bi'l-daqq*, *ḥadīth* 5187.

19.   There are reports which indicate that some Companions might have understood their duty of complying with the text in a rather formalistic sense. On one occasion Abū Mūsā al-Ashʿarī came to the house of ʿUmar b. al-Khaṭṭāb and knocked three times at the door but heard no reply and started to return, apparently prematurely, as ʿUmar had not heard him and then caught up with al-Ashʿari to tell him so. Cf. *Muslim, Mukhtaṣar Ṣaḥīḥ Muslim*, 374, *ḥadīth* no. 1421. See also Jundī, *Ḍamānāt*, 90.

20.   Cf. al-Jundī, *Ḍamānāt*, 62.

21.   Cf. al-Isfahāni, *al-Mufradāt*, 236.

22.   Cf. al-Khaṭīb, *Mughni al-Muḥtāj*, IV, 198; Jundī, *Ḍamānāt*, 65.

23.   Cf. al-Jundī, *Ḍamānāt*, 64; 'Iwad Muhammad, *Dirāsāt*, 113.

24. Muslim, *Mukhtaṣar Ṣaḥīḥ Muslim*, 374, *ḥadīth* no. 1421; Abū Dāwūd, *Mukhtaṣar Sunan*, *ḥadīth* 5180.

25. Al-Ṣābuni, *Mukhtaṣar Tafsir Ibn Kathir*, III, 282; al-Jundī, *Ḍamānāt*, 87.

26. Muslim, *Mukhtaṣar Ṣaḥīḥ Muslim*, 375, *ḥadīth* no. 1424.

27. Cf. al-Jundī, *Ḍamānāt*, 75.

28. Al-Alūsī, *Rūḥ al-Maʿāni*, XVIII, 135; al-Jundī, *Ḍamānāt*, 87.

29. Cf. Ibn Kathīr, *Tafsīr Ibn Kathīr*, III, 282.

30. Cf. Ibn Qayyim, *Zād al-Maʿād*, II, 430.

31. Tabrizī, *Mishkāt*, vol. III, *ḥadīth* 4653.

32. Ghazālī, *Iḥyā' ʿUlūm al-Dīn*, II, 200.

33. Abū Dāwūd, *Mukhtaṣar, K. Al-Adab, b. Kayf al-isti'dhān*, *ḥadīth* 5176; Ghazālī, *Iḥyā'*, II, 200.

34. Al-Jundī, *Ḍamānāt*, 93.

35. Abū Dāwūd, *Mukhtaṣar Sunan, Kitāb al-Adab, Bab fi'l-Isti'dhān*, *ḥadīth* 5173.

36. Abū Dāwūd, *Mukhtaṣar Sunan, Kitāb al-Adab, b. fi'l-Isti'dhān*, *ḥadīth* 5174.

37. Asad, *The Message of the Qur'ān*, 546.

38. Abū Dāwūd, *Mukhtaṣar Sunan Abi Dāwūd, K.al-Adabi, b. al-Isti'dhān fi'l-'Awrāt*, *ḥadīth* 5192.

39. Al-Bukhārī, *al-Adab al-Mufrad*, 311; Imam Mālik, *al-Muwaṭṭā'*, 683.

40. Jundī, *Ḍamānāt*, 71.

41. Dughmi, *Ḥimāyat*, 124.

42. Cf. Id., 126.

43. The Arabic version of this maxim is: lā yajūz li-aḥad an yataṣarrafa fi-milk al-ghayr bi-lā idhnihi, al-Dughmi, *Ḥimāyat al-Ḥayāt*, 123.

44. Cf. Al-Dughmi, *Ḥimāyat al-Ḥayāt al-Khaṣṣa*, 123-127.

45. Abū Dāwūd, *Mukhtaṣar Sunan Abī Dāwūd, K. al-Adab, b. Kam Marra yusallim al-rajulu fi'l-isti'dhān*, *ḥadīth* 5181.

46. *Id.*, *ḥadīth* 5180.

47. *Id.*, *ḥadīth* 5183–84.

48. Al-Māwardī, *Aḥkām*, 252.

49. Al-Qurshi, *Aḥkām al-Ḥisbah*, 96.

50. Abū Dāwūd, *Mukhtaṣar Sunan Abi Dāwūd, K.al-Adab, b. fi'l-rajul yudʿā*, *ḥadīth* 5190. Another version of this *ḥadīth*, also recorded in Abū Dāwūd, simply has it that 'A man's messenger to another is equivalent to permission.'

51. Cf. Ghazālī, *Iḥya' Ulūm al-Dīn*, II. 321: 'al-tajassus ṭalab al-amārat al-muʿarifa...[fīmā] la-rukhṣata fīhi aṣlan.'

52. Dughmi, *al-Tajassus wa Aḥkāmuh*, 29.

53. Junidi, *Ḍamānāt*, 170.

54. Dughmi, *al-Tajassus*, 29-31.

55. *Id.*, 31.

56. Cf., *Id.*, 30.

57. Al-Qurṭubi, *Tafsīr al-Qurṭubi*, XVI, 333.

58. Cf. Jundī, *Ḍamānāt*, 169.

59. Dughmi, *al-Tajassus*, 26.

60. Cf. al-Dughmi, *al-Tajassus*, 140; *Idem, Himāyat al-Hayāt al-Khaṣṣa*, 36.

61. Jundī, *Ḍamānāt*, 170.

62. Ghazālī, *Iḥyā' ʿUlūm al-Dīn*, II, 321; 'Awdah, *al-Tashri ʿ al-Jinā'i*, I, 502; Dughmi, *Himāyat*, 129.

63. Ghazālī, *Iḥyā'*, II, 321.

64. ʿAwdah, *al-Tashri ʿ al-Jinā'i*, I, 503; Dughmi, *al-Tajassus*, 149.

65. Ghazālī, *Iḥyā'*, II, 324.

66. ʿAwdah, *al-Tashri ʿ*, I, 504.

67. Al-Bukhārī, *Adab al-Mufrad*, 397, *ḥadīth* 1159; Ghazālī, *Iḥyā' ʿUlūm al-Dīn*, II, 199; al-Mundhiri, *al-Targhīb*, III, 693.

68. Al-Sanʿāni, *Subul al-Salām*, vol. IV, 199; al-Dughmi, *Himāyat al-Hayāt al-Khaṣṣa*, 69.

69. Al-Bukhārī, *Ṣaḥīḥ al-Bukhārī* (Muhsin Khan's trans.,) VIII, 171, *ḥadīth* 259.

70. Abū Dāwūd, *Mukhtaṣar Sunan, K. al-Adab, b. al-Isti'dhān*, *ḥadīth* 5172.

71. Abū Dāwūd, *Mukhtaṣar Sunan, K. al-Adab, b. al-Isti'dhān*, *ḥadīth* 5171.

72. Al-Jundī, *Ḍamānāt*, 127; al-Dughmi, *al-Tajassus*, 145.

73. Ibn ʿAbidin, *Ḥāshiya*, V, 485; Shirazi, *al-Muhadhdhab*, II, 225; al-Jundī, *Ḍamānāt*, 140.

74. Al-Jundī, *Ḍamānāt*, 143.

75. Cf. al-Dughmi, *Himāyat al-Hayāt*, 39; al-Jundī, *Ḍamānāt*, 146.

76. Jundī, *Ḍamānāt*, 154.

77. *Al-Fatwa al-Hindiyya*, VI, 89; al-Dughmi, *al-Tajassus*, 144 ff; al-Jundī, *Ḍamānāt*, 145.

78. Ibn Ḥazm, *Muḥallā*, X, 427; Jundī, *Ḍamānāt*, 149-50.

79. Abu Zahrah, *al-Jarīma wa'l-'Uqūba fi'l-Fiqh al-Islāmī: al-'Uquba*, 460.

80. Al-Māwardī, *al-Aḥkām*, 253; al-Farrā, *al-Aḥkām*, 280; Dughmi, *al-Tajassus*, 127.

81. Al-ʿAqqād, *ʿAbqariyyat ʿUmar*, 97.

82. Al-Ramli, *Nihāyat al-Muhtāj*, VIII, 45; Dughmi, *Aḥkām*, 129.

83. Al-Māwardī, *Aḥkām*, 253.

84. Al-Dughmi, *al-Tajassus*, 130.

85. Abū Dāwūd, *Mukhtaṣar Sunan Abi Dāwūd, K. al-Adab. b. al-Nahy ʿan al-Tajassus*, *ḥadīth* 4889.

86. *Id., K. al-Adab. b. al-Nahy ʿan al-Tajassus*, *ḥadīth* 4890.

87. Dughmi, *al-Tajassus*, 136.

88. *Id.*, 80.

89. *Id.*, 81.

90. *Id.*, 36.

91. *Id.*, 37, quoting *Tārikh al-Ṭabari*, IX, 299.

92. *Id.*, 127.

93. Ghazālī, *Iḥyā'*, II, 198 and 320.

94. *Ḥadīth* reported by Abū Dāwūd (already quoted).

95. Ghazālī, *Iḥyā'*, II, 199.

96. *Id.*, II, 198.

97. *Id.*, the *ḥadīth* is also quoted by Tirmidhī and Ibn Mājah.

98. Jundī, *Ḍamānāt*, pp. 204-205.

99. *Id.*, p. 199.

100. Jundī, *Ḍamānāt*, pp. 197-200.

101. Al-Suyūṭi, *Jāmiᶜ al-Ṣaghīr*, I. 165; al-Baghawi, *Sharḥ al-Sunna*, II, 74; Ibn Maflaḥ, *al-Ādāb al-Sharᶜiyya*, II, 166.

102. Ibn Māja, *Sunan, ḥadīth* 2340.

103. Abū Dāwūd, *Sunan, K. al-Adab, b. fi'l-Ghība, ḥadīth* 4882.

104. Cf., al-Dughmi, *Ḥimāyat*, 117-118.

105. Bukhārī, *Ṣaḥīḥ al-Bukhārī* (Muhsin Khan's trans.) VIII, 184, *ḥadīth* 277.

106. Al-Baghawi, *Sharḥ al-Sunna*, II, 74; See also al-Dughmi, *Ḥimāyat al-Ḥayāt al-Khaṣṣa*, 118.

107. Bukhārī, *Ṣaḥīḥ al-Bukhārī, Kitāb al-Ghazawāt, Bab al-Fatḥ: man naẓara fi kitab man yahdhur ᶜala al-muslim*.

108. Al-Baghawi, *Sharḥ al-Sunna*, vol. II, 74.

109. Al-Dughmi, *Ḥimāyat al-Ḥayāt al-Khaṣṣa*, 121.

110. Ibn Farḥūn, *Tabṣirat al-Ḥukkām*, II, 139.

111. Muslim, *Ṣaḥīḥ Muslim, Kitāb al-birr wa'l-ṣilla, bāb taḥrīm al-ẓann wa al-tajassus wa al-tanafus*.

112. Ghazālī, *Iḥyā'*, II, 175.

113. Ghazālī, *Iḥyā'*, II, 175; Ibn Maflaḥ, *al-Ādāb al-Sharᶜiyya*, I, 45.

114. Al-Jundī, *Ḍamānāt*, 172.

115. Abū Dāwūd, *Sunan Abū Dāwūd, Kitāb al-Adab, Bab fi ḥusn al-ẓann*.

116. Al-Jundī, *Ḍamānāt*, 180.

117. Al-Qurṭubi, *Tafsīr al-Qurṭubi*, VII, 6152; al-Khuli, *Adab al-Nabawi*, 136; al-Jundī, *Ḍamānāt*, 180;Niazi, *Islamic Law of Tort*, 86.

118. Ghazālī, *Iḥyā'*, II, 200.

119. *Id.*, Tabrizi, Mishkāt, vol. I, *ḥadīth* 68.

120. Ghazālī, *Iḥyā'*, II, 200.

121. Abū Dāwūd, *Mukhtaṣar Sunan, K. al-Adab b. al-Mu'ākhāt*.

122. Muslim, *Mukhtaṣar Ṣaḥīḥ Muslim*, p. 473 *ḥadīth* no. 1777.

123. Al-Tirmidhi, *Sunan*, III, 255, *Kitāb al-Birr*, *ḥadīth* no. 85.

124. Abū Dāwūd, *Mukhtaṣar Sunan Abi Dāwūd, K. al-Adab, b. al-Mu'ākhāt*, *ḥadīth* 4893.

125. Ghazālī, *Iḥyā'*, II, 175-76.

126. Abū Dāwūd, *Mukhtaṣar Sunan Abi Dāwūd, K. al-Adab, b. al-Nahy ʿan al-Tajassus*.

127. Ghazālī, *Iḥyā'*, II, 213.

128. *Id.*, II, 212.

129. Abū Dāwūd, *Mukhtaṣar Sunan, K. al-Adab, fi ḥaqq al-Jiwār*, *ḥadīth* 5154.

130. Abū Dāwūd, *Mukhtaṣar Sunan, K. al-Adab, b. fi'l-Ghība*, *ḥadīth* 4876.

131. Abū Dāwūd, *Mukhtaṣar Sunan Abi Dāwūd, Kitāb al-Aqḍiya, b. Abwab min al-Qaḍā*, *ḥadīth* 3636.

132. Ṣanʿāni, *Subul al-Salām*, I, 264; Jundī, *Ḍamānāt*, 159.

133. Al-Farrā', *al-Aḥkām al-Sulṭāniyya*, 303; see also Jundī, *Ḍamānāt*, 160.

134. Mejelle (Art 1202).

135. Cf., Ibn ʿĀbidin, *Ḥāshiya*, IV, 401.

136. Abū Dāwūd, *Sunan, K. al-Ḥammām, b. al-Nahy ʿan al-Taʿarri*, *ḥadīth* 4012.

137. *Id., K. al-Libās, b. fi libās al-Nisā'*, *ḥadīth* 4100.

138. *Id.*, *ḥadīth* 4102.

139. *Id.*, *ḥadīth* 4104.

140. *Id., K. al-Ḥammām, b. ma ja' fi'l-Taʿarri*, *ḥadīth* 4018.

141. *Id.*, *ḥadīth* 4019

142. Shawkāni, *Nayl al-Awṭār*, II, 64; Shahrūr, *Naḥw Uṣūl Jadīdah*, 357.

143. Cf., Zuḥaylī, *al-Fiqh al-Islāmī*, I, 583-584..

144. Shahrūr, *Naḥw Uṣūl Jadīda*, 357-358.

145. *Id.*, 357-365.

146. Imam Mālik, *al-Muwaṭṭā, K. al-ḥudūd*, *ḥadīth* No. 12; Ghazālī, *Iḥyā'*, III, 135.

147. Ghazālī, *Iḥyā'*, III, 135.

148. Abū Dāwūd, *Sunan, Kitāb al-Adab, Bab fi satr ʿala'l-Muslim*, *ḥadīth* 4891-4892; Ghazālī, *Iḥyā'*, II, 176.

149. Abū Dāwūd, *Mukhtaṣar Sunan Abi Dāwūd, K. al-Adab, b. fi'l-ma'unat li'l-Muslim*, *ḥadīth* 4946.

150. Abū Dāwūd, *Mukhtaṣar Sunan Abi Dāwūd, K. al-Adab, b. fi'l-Ghība;* *ḥadīth* 4880; Ghazālī, Iḥyā' 'Ulūm al-Dīn, II, 198.

151. Ghazālī, *Iḥyā'*, II, 199; al-Jundī, *Ḍamānāt*, p. 188 ff.

152. Abū Dāwūd, *Mukhtaṣar Sunan, K. al-Adab, b. fi'l-Ghība*, *ḥadīth* 4881.

153. Cf. Dughmi, *Ḥimāyat*, 65.

154. Cf. al-Jundī, *Ḍamānāt*, 191-192.

155. Al-Dughmi, *Himāyat Hayāt al-Khāṣṣa*, 57.

156. Al-Ghazālī, *Iḥyā' ʿUlūm al-Dīn*, III, 128.

157. *Id.*, II, 176.

158. Al-Haythami, *Majmaʿ al-Zawā'id*, vol. I, 196; Ibn Ḥanbal, *Musnad*, III, 135.

159. Al-Dughmi, *Himāyat Hayāt al-Khāṣṣa*, 59.

160. Abū Dāwūd, *Mukhtasar Sunan Abi Dāwūd, K. al-Adab, b. fi Naql al-Hadīth*, *hadīth* 4868; Ghazālī, *Iḥyā'*, II, 176.

161. Ghazālī, *Iḥyā'*, III, 129.

162. Bukhārī, *Ṣaḥīḥ al-Bukhārī* (Muhsin Khan's trans.) VIII, *hadīth* 307.

163. Abū Dāwūd, *ʿAwm al-Maʿbūd*, vol. XIII, 217; Ghazālī, *Iḥyā'*, II, 176.

164. Al-Ṣanʿānī, *Subul al-Salām*, vol. IV, 119; al-Dughmi, *Himāyat*, 70.

165. Abū Dāwūd, *Mukhtasar Sunan Abi Dāwūd, K. al-Adab, b. fi'l-Rajul Yajlis*, *hadīth* 4844.

166. Abū Dāwūd, *Mukhtasar Sunan Abi Dāwūd, K. al-Adab b. fi'l-Tanāji*, *hadīth* 4851.

167. Id., *hadīth* 4852.

168. Abū Dāwūd, *Mukhtasar Sunan Abi Dāwūd, K. al-Adab, b. fi Naql al-Hadīth*, *hadīth* 4869; Ghazālī, *Iḥyā'*, II, 176.

169. Al-Ghazālī, *Iḥyā' ʿUlūm al-Dīn*, vol. II, 174; see also al-Dughmī, *Himāyat*, 58.

170. Ghazālī, *Iḥyā'*, II, 174.

171. *Id.*, II, 175.

172. Abū Dāwūd, *Mukhtasar Sunan Abi Dāwūd, K. al-Adab, b. fi'l-mashwara*, *hadīth* 5128.

173. Cf. al-Dughmi, *Himāyat*, 60.

174. Bukhārī, *Ṣaḥīḥ al-Bukhārī*, (Muhsin Khan's trans.), VIII, 201, *hadīth* 301.

175. Bukhārī, *Ṣaḥīḥ al-Bukhārī, K. al-Adab, b. Man Kana Yu'min bi-Allāh*.

176. Abū Dāwūd, *Mukhtasar Sunan Abi Dāwūd, K. al-Adab, b. al-Tashdīd fi'l-Kidhb*, *hadīth* 4992.

177. Cf., Ghazālī, *Iḥyā'*, II, 176.

178. Abū Dāwūd, *Mukhtasar Sunan Abi Dāwūd, K. al-Adab, b. fi'l-Naql al-Hadīth* 4870.

179. Cf., Dughmi, *Himāyat*, 53.

180. Abū Dāwūd, *Mukhtasar Sunan Abi Dāwūd, K. al-Adab b. fi'l-Naql al-Hadīth* 4871.

181. Bukhārī, *Ṣaḥīḥ al-Bukhārī, K. al-Adab, b. Man kana yu'minu bi-Allāh*.

182. Shawkāni, *Nayl al-Awṭār*, VI, 224-225; see also Dughmi, *Himāyat Hayāt*, 54-55.

183. Abū Dāwūd, *Mukhtaṣar Sunan Abi Dāwūd, K. al-Adab fi'l-Nahy ʿan Sabb al-Mawtā, ḥadīth* 4900.

184. *Id., ḥadīth* 4899.

185. Ibn Qudāma, *al-Mughni*, vol. X, 221.

186. Kāsānī, *Badā'iʿ*, II, 75; '*Ghusl,*' *EI²*, vol. II, 1104.

187. Abū Dāwūd, *Sunan Abi Dāwūd, K. al-Ḥammām, b. al-Nahy ʿan al-Taʿarri, ḥadīth* 4015; Kāsānī, *Badā'iʿ*, II, 752.

188. Kāsānī, *Badā'iʿ*, II, 762.

189. *Id.*, 762.

190. *Id.*, II, 764.

191. *Id.*, II, 765.

192. Abū Dāwūd, *Sunan Abi Dāwūd, K. al-Janā'iz, b. fi'l-Kafan, ḥadīth* 3151

193. *Id., K. al-Janā'iz, b. fi'l-Satr al-Mayyit ʿInda Ghuslih, ḥadīth* 3141.

194. *Id.*, II, 775.

195. *Id., K. al-Janā'iz, b. al-Qiyām fi'l-Janāza, ḥadīth* 3172.

196. *Id., ḥadīth* 3174.

197. Ibn Māja, *Sunan Ibn Maja, K. al-Aḥkām, b. al-Rajul ʿind al-Shahadati la-yaʿlam Ṣaḥibuhu, ḥadīth* 2364.

198. *Id., K. al-Aḥkām, b. Karāhiyyat al-Shahāda li-man lam yustashhad.*

199. See for detail Adul, *Kitmān al-Sirr*, 118–119.

200. Saraksi, *al-Mabsūṭ*, vol. IX, 146; Adul, *Kitmān al-Sirr*, 119.

201. Al-Sakhawī, *al-Iʿlan bi'l-Tawbikh*, p. 69; Sharif ʿAdul, *Kitmān al-Sirr*, pp. 139–140.

202. Ghazālī, *Iḥyā' ʿUlūm al-Dīn*, vol.III, p.302; al-Nawawī, *Riyāḍ al-Ṣāliḥīn*, p.441.

203. Bukhārī, *Ṣaḥīḥ al-Bukhārī, K. al-Nafaqāt, b. Idhā lam yanfīq al-Rajulu fa li'l-Mar'ati an Ta'khudh.*

204. Adul, *Kitmān al-Sirr*, 142.

205. Cf., Adul, *Kitmān al-Sirr*, 143.

206. Ghazālī, *Iḥyā'*, vol. III, 302.

207. Bukhārī, *Ṣaḥīḥ al-Bukhārī, K. al-Adab, b. man kāna yu'minu bi-Allāh wa'l-yawm al-(r)khir;* see also Adul, *Kitmān al-Sirr*, 149.

208. (1970) 2 *MLJ* 115.

209. Fahda Nur Ahmad Kamar 'Exigencies and Right to Privacy,' (2001) *I.L.M.* 33.

210. B.A. Hepple and M.H. Mathews, *Tort: Cases & Materials*. London: Bullerworths, 1974, 570.

211. Salmond, *Torts*. 34.

212. (1979) 2 All ER G20.

213. Sharpe, *Judicial Discretion*, 174.

214. Cf. Niazi, *Islamic Law of Tort*, 85.

215. *Id.*, 87.

216. The *Mejelle*, (Art. 1202).

217. The *Mejelle*, (Art. 1205).

218. Islahi, *Tadabbur Qur'ān*, vol. VI, p. 510 as quoted in Niazi, *Islamic Law of Tort*, 88.

219. Cf. Asad, *Principles of State and Government*, 84.

220. For details see Kamali, *The Dignity of Man: An Islamic Perspective*.

CHAPTER FOUR

The Right of Ownership
(*Ḥaqq al-milkiyyah*)

I. Introductory Remarks

Ownership is both a freedom (*ḥurriyyah*) and a right (*ḥaqq*), but ownership as a freedom precedes ownership in the sense of a right. What this means is that everyone is at liberty to acquire ownership, say of a plot of land, but then when a person does acquire it, whether through purchase, gift, or inheritance, his ownership is no longer a possibility he is free to pursue, but an established right that is exclusive to him. Having said this, it is still not incorrect to refer to both these aspects of ownership as rights, for the liberty to acquire ownership is also a right, a type of right which is known in Arabic as *al-ḥaqq al-mubāḥ*, or a permissive right, which is different from a personal right (*al-ḥaqq al-shakhṣī*). A personal right is stronger than a permissive right in that it is exclusive and can be the subject of sale and inheritance, whereas a permissive right, although protected by law, is not an exclusive right, and can neither be sold nor inherited. This may also be said to be one of the main differences between a freedom and a right generally in that the former is a permissive right and everyone is entitled to utilise it and benefit by it, but no-one is entitled to lay an exclusive claim to it. In this way, freedom to own property resembles other civil liberties such as freedom of speech and freedom of movement, yet these can also be referred to as rights, in the sense of permissive rights. They may all be said to be liberties, which are however, like ownership, i.e., all capable of being converted into rights. To write a book is an exercise of one's freedom of expression, but then once it is written the author owns it and also has an exclusive right (copyright) over it. Similarly to travel to a certain destination is an exercise of one's freedom of movement, but when one acquires a visa and buys a plane ticket to go there, that freedom has been exercised as a right.

To be able to own property is one of the basic individual liberties recognised in both the *Sharīʿah* and in the constitutions of most Muslim countries. The *Sharīʿah* also protects the ownership of property, both movable and real, by individuals, groups, and the community as a whole, provided that it is acquired through lawful means. Private ownership is recognised, and all individuals, men and women alike, are entitled to keep what they earn or inherit. The individual also enjoys the freedom to deal with his property as he or she pleases, and to dispose of it through such means as sale, gift, bequest and other modes of lawful transaction. One of the ways that the *Sharīʿah* protects private ownership is by providing penal sanctions for those who violate the sanctity of this right. The Qurʾān forbids the taking of the property of others without their consent and prescribes severe punishments for highway robbery and theft. The courts are also empowered to deter and punish other property offences under the discretionary penalties of *taʿzīr*.

Like all other rights, the right of ownership is subject to qualifications and conditions not only in the form of taxes, charitable donations, and limitations imposed through the laws of inheritance and bequest, but also, the owner may not exercise his right in violation of the rights of others, or in such a way that may be harmful to others. Private ownership is similarly subject to considerations of public interest (*maṣlaḥah*). The government may thus expropriate private property in order to build a road, a mosque, fire station or hospital, but the owner must in all cases be paid a fair price.

The *Sharīʿah* also entitles joint-owners and neighbours to a right of pre-emption (*shufʿah*), which entitles them to a priority right to buy the remainder of a jointly-owned property, or an adjoining property, in the event where such a property is offered for sale. And then there are rules in the *Sharīʿah* that proscribe profiteering and monopolistic activities that are deemed to be detrimental to the community, and the owners therefore do not enjoy the freedom to practise them.

II. Affirmative Evidence

The *Sharīʿah* takes an encouraging stance on affluence and wealth as it encourages the acquisition of wealth through lawful means on the one hand, and imposes no quantitative limits on it on the other. Also indicative of the same affirmative outlook is the fact that the Qur'ān has in numerous places referred to property and wealth as *faḍl Allāh*, that is, the bounty and favour of God, and has encouraged the believers to exert themselves of earning it (cf. 62:10; 24:22; 9:75). The text also refers to wealth as *khayr* (blessing, benefit) in reference, for example, to assets that a deceased person leaves behind for his family (cf. 2: 180). A perusal of such references in the Qur'ān lends support to the view that exerting oneself in the quest for lawful earning in order to support oneself and one's family ranks as a form of service and *ʿibādah*. The Prophet, peace be on him, has in fact considered having wealth to be preferable to poverty, and went on record to advise, for instance, one of his prominent Companions, Saʿd Ibn Abī Waqāṣ—when he was ill and the Prophet visited him in Mecca during his Farewell Pilgrimage—that he should leave enough for his heirs so that they were not left in financial hardship. Abu Waqāṣ was feeling uneasy about the fact that he had remained in Mecca after the Prophet's migration to Madina. In reply to Abu Waqāṣ's question as to whether he should bequeath all of his property in charity, the Prophet is reported to have said,

أفأتصــدق بثلثــى مالى؟ قال: لا، قلت أفأتصــدق بشطره، قال: لا، الثلث والثلث كثير، إنك ان تذر ورثتك خير من أن تذرهم عالة يتكففون الناس.

No, one third, and one third is more than enough. For it is better that you leave your heirs in easy conditions rather than penniless, for that might prompt them to beg others for help...[1]

There are also reports to the effect that the Prophet prayed for some of his Companions, including Anas b. Mālik, in such terms as اللهم أكثر ماله وولده. 'O My Lord, increase his wealth and his offspring.' The Prophet also did so for himself, as in the following supplication:

اللهم إنى أسألك الهدى والتقى والعفاف والغنى.

O My Lord, grant me guidance (*hudā*), piety (*taqwā*), purity (*ʿiffah*) and affluence.[2]

Some of the leading companions, such as ʿUthmān b. ʿAffān, ʿAbd al-Raḥmān b. ʿAwf and Zubayr b. al-ʿAwām, were considerably wealthy, but this was never held against them. Reports also indicate that they spent their wealth generously on meritorious causes. Wealth is of course not a goal in itself, but a means of fulfilling needs and securing benefits. Anyone who utilises wealth for these purposes, wealth in their hands is a source of benefit for themselves and the community, just as it becomes a source of corruption and evil when it is spent in pursuit of corrupt and selfish ends.

Another feature of the teaching of Islam on ownership and wealth is that it discourages extravagance and waste. The Qur'ān calls reckless spenders as the 'brothers of the devil' who are ungrateful for the bounty of God (17:27). Then again, the Qur'ān demonstrates a love of beauty, and relates this at times to the reasonable use and manifestation of wealth in the life-style of those who have it, provided that this does not amount to extravagance, for 'God does not love the wasteful spenders (*muṣrifīn*)' (7:31).

إنه لا يحب المسرفين.

The moral tone of this teaching has been taken a step further in another place, where the Qur'ān validates interdiction (*al-ḥajr*) and judicial restraint in the case of weak-minded individuals (*safahā'*) that are incapable of the prudent management of their assets. The text thus provides:

ولا تؤتوا السفهاء أموالكم التى جعل الله قياما وارزقوهم فيها واكسوهم وقولوا قولا معروفا.

> And do not give your property, which God has made a means of support for you, to the weak of understanding (*al-sufahā'*), but give them maintenance and clothing out of it. (4:5).

Furthermore, the Qur'ān speaks very strongly against the evils of materialistic indulgence, and the oppressive and indolent use of property, which is referred to as lawlessness, sin (*ithm wa baghy*) and indecencies (*al-fawāḥish*) that must be strictly avoided, not just outwardly but also in the spirit of sincerity and truth (7:33). Wealth is a means of great benefit and beauty and can be used in pious pursuits, and yet the Qur'ān speaks of wealth as a testing ground by which 'We shall test you to find out who conducted himself best,' (18:7, see also 3:186). We also find in the Qur'ān a firm denunciation of hoarders and accumulators of wealth who refuse to spend it in a worthy cause, for they deprive both themselves and society of the lawful enjoyment of the bounty of God:

$$\text{والذيــن يكنزون الذهـــب والفضة ولاينفقونهـــا فى ســبيل الله فبشرهم بعذاب أليم.}$$

Those who hoard gold and silver and refuse to spend them in the way of God, warn them of a painful punishment. (9:24).

The Qur'ānic guidelines in regard to property are supportive of moderation and the avoidance of extremes. This is the clear message of the two verses that follow:

$$\text{ولاتجعل يدك مغلولة إلى عنقك ولاتبسطها كل البسط فتقعد ملوما محسورا.}$$

And do not tie your hand to your neck, nor stretch it forth to its utmost reach, so that you are then left with destitution and regret (17:29).

And then the Qur'ān speaks approvingly of

$$\text{والذين إذا أنفقوا لم يسرفوا ولم يقتروا وكان بين ذلك قواما.}$$

Those who spend, but they are neither extravagant nor mean, but remain moderate (between these extremes), (25:67).

The distinction between niggardliness (*al-shuḥḥ*) and moderation must to a large extent depend on individual circumstances, but a rough guide has been suggested by the caliph ʿUmar b. al-Khaṭṭāb, who said that 'Whoever pays the *zakāh* (legal alms), honours his guest (with hospitality), and gives in order to alleviate misfortune is free of niggardliness.'[3] Extravagance and niggardliness are both indicative of ingratitude and run contrary to the advice of moderation that is the consistent theme of a great deal of teaching of Islam.

The general evidence of the Qur'ān and *Sunnah* is not only supportive of private ownership but also provides guidelines on the proper acquisition, utilisation, expenditure, and transfer of private wealth. There is clear recognition in the *Sharīʿah* of two principal methods of the acquisition of wealth, one of which is without personal effort and includes gift, bequest and inheritance, and the other is through personal effort and labour. The Qur'ān provides affirmative evidence on both, and protects private property on the one hand, and offers prohibitive injunctions concerning theft, usurpation, fraud, hoarding, gambling and usury on the other. Thus it is provided:

يَآيُّها الذين آمنوا لاتأكلوا أموالكم بينكم بالباطل إلا أن تكون تجارة عن تراض منكم.

> O you who believe! Do not devour your wealth among yourselves wrongfully unless it is through trading by mutual consent (4:29).

The possessive pronoun in *amwālakum* (your property) in this verse clearly validates private ownership, and is further endorsed by the immediate occurrence of *baynakum* (among yourselves). The remaining portion of the text, which forbids the wrongful appropriation of the property of others, also endorses its earlier portion since it protects private property against wrongful appropriation without the consent of its owner. 'Wrongful appropriation of the property of others (*akl al-māl bi'l-bāṭil*)' is a broad Qur'ānic concept that comprises within its scope not just theft, robbery and fraud, which are usually committed by persons other than the owner himself, but also hoarding, gambling and usury in which the owner may be acting himself—but since they do not fall within the scope of trading by mutual consent, they are all forbidden. Gift, sale, inheritance and all other lawful means of the acquisition of property fall, on the other hand, under trading and transaction by mutual consent. Another instance of the wrongful appropriation of property specified in the Qur'ān is bribery, which distorts the course of justice and leads to the sinful enrichment of some people at the expense of others (2:188). It is therefore not the element of consent on its own, but this when it is combined with an exchange of values through fair-trading, that distinguishes a lawful transfer of ownership from a wrongful appropriation of the property of others. For consent may be present in bribery, but is lacking in a fair exchange of values.[4] The fact that the *Sharīʿah* forbids violations of private property under the pain of punishment in itself guarantees protection of the right of ownership.

The owner of property may be totally helpless in defending his/her right, such as in the case of orphans, where the Qur'ān declares, in a particularly emphatic tone:

والذيـن يأكلون أموال اليتامـى ظلمـا إنمـا يأكلون فـى بطونهـم نارا.

Those who wrongfully devour the property of orphans are swallowing fire into their bodies, and subject themselves to the punishment of Hell (4:10).

In numerous other places, the text validates private ownership and recognises the exclusive right of the owner. The text thus provides, in reference to the capital assets of owners, which might have been given on loan:

فلكم روؤس أموالكم لاتظلمون ولاتظلمون.

Your capital assets belong to you. You shall neither be unjust nor be the victims of injustice (2:279).

The Qur'ān also confirms private ownership in reference to livestock:

أولم يروا أنا خلقنا لهم مما عملت أيدينا أنعاماً فهم لها مالكون.

Did they not see that We created for them, by Our hands, livestock of which they are the owners. (36:71).

This verse contains an interesting combination of two things, namely God's creative action, and man's ownership of its outcome. Although God Most High is the Creator, men are still referred to as owners (*mālikūn*).

The Qur'ān also directs the owners of property to be prudent and not to jeopardise the safety of their assets: ولاتؤتوا السفهاء أموالكم.'And do not give your properties (*amwālakum*)... to the weak of understanding (4:5).' And then again:

والذين فى أموالهم حق للسائل والمحروم.

And those in whose properties there is an appointed right for the poor and the indigent (70:24, see also 51:19).

The opening words in this verse clearly acknowledge the owners' proprietary right over their assets, and only within that framework does it speak of a portion that is to be given to the poor.

The *Sunnah* reiterates these Qur'ānic guidelines and further emphasises the sanctity of private property, both as a principle in its own right and as a manifestation of fraternity between Muslims. To quote but a few *hadīths* on the subject:

إن دماءكم وأموالكم عليكم حرام الى أن تلقوا ربكم.

Your lives and your properties are forbidden to one another until you meet your Lord.[5]

لايحل مال امرء مسلم إلا بطيب عن نفسه.

It is unlawful to take the property of a Muslim without his consent.[6]

كل المسلم على المسلم حرام دمه وماله وعرضه.

All that belongs to a Muslim is forbidden to his fellow Muslim, his life, his property and his honour.[7]

كل أحد أحق بماله من والده وولده والناس أجمعين.

Every person is entitled to his own property more than his father, his son, and the whole of mankind.[8]

In another *hadīth*, recorded in *Ṣaḥīḥ Muslim,* a dispute is reported to have arisen in which a woman, Arwah bint Uways, told the Umayyad ruler, Marwān b. al-Ḥakam, that one Saʿīd b. Zayd had usurped some of her land. Saʿīd was summoned and in defending his case he said: 'How could I take her land after hearing what I heard from the Prophet, peace be on him?' Marwān asked: 'What did you hear?' and Saʿīd replied: The Prophet, peace be on him, said 'Whoever takes (even) one span of land unjustly from another, it will become a yoke over his neck to the extent of seven earths.' Marwān responded by saying 'I shall not ask you to bring evidence after this.'[9]

إن أَروى بنت أويس ادّعت على سعيد بن زيد أنه أخذ شيئا
من أرضه فخاصمه إلى مروان بن الحكم، فقال سعيد: أنا
كنت آخذ من أرضها شيئا بعد الذى سمعت من رسول الله
صلى الله عليه وسلم، قال: وماسمعتَ من رسول الله صلى
الله عليه وسلم؟ قال: سمعت رسول الله صلى الله عليه وسلم
يــقول „ مــن أخــذ شــبرا من الأرض ظلمــا طوّقه إلــى سبع
أرضين،، فقال له مروان: لأأسألك بيّنة بعد هذا.

Based on this evidence, Muslim jurists have formulated the following legal maxims, which appear in the Ottoman *Mejelle*. 'It is unlawful for anyone to take the property of another without a lawful cause' (Art. 97) and 'No-one may interfere in the property of another person without his permission' (Art. 96).

The protection of private property also represents one of the five essential values that constitute the overriding objectives (*maqāṣid*) of the *Sharīʿah*. The owner is entitled to defend his property against any violation or encroachment. Indeed, there is a promise of spiritual reward for one who does so, as mentioned in the following *ḥadīth*:

من قتل دون ماله فهو شهيد.

'He who dies in defence of his property is a martyr (*shahīd*).'[10]

The *Sharīʿah* also extends the right of self-defence, *mutatis mutandis,* to the protection of one's property. The jurists of the leading schools of law have thus drawn the conclusion that an attack on one's property entitles the victim to repel aggression by the least violent means that can repel it, but if he believes that it cannot be repelled in any other way than killing the assailant, then it is permissible for him to kill him in self-defence, in which case he will have acted within his rights.[11] This right is even recognised in respect of defending the property of others. Wāfi has quoted the Ḥanafi jurist Ibn al-Humām in this context, who wrote that: 'In the event where robbers take the property of others and the latter cry for help, and it is then given, and the robbers are confronted; it is lawful to fight and if necessary kill the robbers to retrieve the property from them.'[12] Ibn al-Humām's writing on this is representative of the positions of both the Ḥanafi and Shāfiʿī, schools.

It is thus stated that Islamic law recognises the right of all individuals to defend the private property of others in the same way as their own property, provided that the following conditions are met: First, that there is a hostile attack which requires immediate action, and which leaves no room for other alternative courses of action. Second, that the defendant uses no more force than he believes is necessary in order to repel the aggression.[13]

Private property has been subjected to the obligations of *zakāh* (legal alms), obligatory maintenance for close relatives (*al-nafaqāt al-wājiba*), inheritance, bequest, and other such requirements, which are designed to realise the benefit (*maṣlaḥah*) of the community. These provisions generally follow the basic objective of equitable distribution of property within the family and society, just as they serve the purpose of preventing a concentration of wealth in the hands of the rich alone (cf., 57:7).

Obligatory maintenance is a right of one's close relatives, such as one's spouse and young children in all cases, and also one's parents and adult offspring when they are in need. Jurists have held different opinions about the entitlement to maintenance of collaterals, including one's siblings, uncles and aunts. The Ḥanafīs tend to include the widest range, whereas the Ḥanbalīs apply entitlement to inheritance as a criterion. Poor relatives in this category would thus be entitled to support according to their entitlement to inheritance from each other. The Shāfiʿīs entitle only the ascendants and descendants to maintenance (*nafaqah*), whereas the Mālikīs have confined it to one's parents and children.[14]

Zakāh is an obligation on everyone who owns property above the quorum (*niṣāb*), for one year, and is not in such debt that a substantial part of his or her assets are absorbed by it. *Zakāh* is taken from productive assets roughly at the rate of two and a half per cent, and the state is authorised to enforce this payment and even penalise those who refuse to pay. *Zakāh* on livestock of all types, gold, silver, currencies and merchandise is generally two and a half per cent, but tends to be higher on agricultural produce and mineral resources according to the detailed conditions expounded in *fiqh* texts. The Qur'ān has objectively proclaimed *zakāh* as the right of the poor to a part of the property of the rich (51:4). This manner of reference to *zakāh* also features in the Prophet's instruction to Mu'ādh b. Jabal, who was told, upon his departure to become the judge and governor of the Yemen, to '...take it from the wealthy and give it to the poor among them' (*khudhhā min aghniyā'ihim wa ruddihā ʿalā fuqarā'ihim*). It is concluded that reference to 'the wealthy' in this text subsumes minors and the insane, so that *zakāh* is taken out of their property regardless of their incapacity to have a legally-valid intention (*niyyah*).

A divergent opinion is held by the renowned Companion, ʿAbd Allāh b. Masʿūd, to the effect that *zakāh* is an act of ʿibādah, and like all other ʿibādāt depends upon intention or *niyyah*. Since minors and the insane are incapable of *niyyah*, the levying of *zakāh* on their assets should be postponed until they gain this capacity. Yet the majority opinion has followed the general language of the text to the effect that *zakāh* is imposed on all property regardless of the personal ability or disability of its owners. This ruling proceeds on the analysis that *zakāh* combines worship (ʿibādah) and *muʾūnah* (social obligation), and that the objective of a fair distribution of wealth will suffer if *zakāh* is made dependant in all cases on *niyyah*.[15]

The *Sharīʿah* also validates interdiction (*al-ḥajr*), which limits the legal capacity of the owner because of his/her inability to manage property. Thus the prodigal and idiot may be placed under a court interdiction until such a time that the court is satisfied that he or she is capable of prudent management. The authority for this is provided in the Qurʾānic verse quoted earlier:

ولاتؤتوا السفهاء أموالكم التى جعل الله لكم قياما وارزقوهم

واكسوهم.

And do not give your property, which God has made a means of support for you, to the weak of understanding (*al-sufahāʾ*), but maintain them out of it and clothe them (4:5).

This text emphasises the community's interest in the prudent management of property. For the property that is alluded to here belongs to the weak of understanding (*sufahāʾ*), yet God has referred to it as 'your property' to confirm that it should be utilised in a manner that is harmonious with the public interest.[16] Furthermore, it is provided in a *ḥadīth* that 'People are partners in three things: water, grass and fire.'[17] An alternative version of the same *ḥadīth* adds *al-milḥ* (salt). Wāfi's interpretation of this *ḥadīth* maintains that 'fire' in this context means fuel, and includes trees, wood, forests and fuel of all kinds. Salt in this *ḥadīth* refers to the salt that is obtained easily without processing and expenditure of the kind involved in the desalination of salty water.[18] The term grass in this *ḥadīth* includes grazing land and fodder obtained from such lands that are not owned by anyone.

Imam Mālik has included mineral water in this list of shared resources, by analogy to the above-mentioned *ḥadīth* for it is found in the depths of the earth, whether solid or liquid, and it is a property of the *bayt al-māl* or 'public wealth' that is administered by the state. This wealth belongs to the community even if it is actually found in private property owned by one or more individuals. The reason for this is that the owner of the land owns the surface, and that part which he can utilise and customarily own for agriculture and building, and it is not customary for owners to use that part which is normally out of reach. For minerals buried deep down are not 'owned' by anyone and may be owned and utilised by the community as a whole. Wāfi, who quoted Imam Mālik's view, then commented that 'Imam Mālik's view on this matter is exemplary and shows greatest harmony with the spirit of the *Sharīʿah* of Islam.'[19] There is no question of course, about the public ownership of mineral wealth, which is found in unowned property, and which is easy to exploit. In that respect, the majority of jurists, including Imam Shāfiʿī, agree with Imam Mālik and this kind of resource to be the community's property, and the Imam or ruler has no authority to assign it by *iqṭāʿ* (or apportionment of land as a payment) to anyone or make it the property of anyone in particular.[20] It thus appears that private ownership, although clearly recognised in Islam, is subject to certain restrictions that are designed to protect the public interest and ensure the equitable distribution of wealth in society.

III. The Vicegerency of Man

While the *Sharīʿah* recognises the freedom of the individual to own property and takes measures to safeguard the rights of the owner, the basic theory of ownership in Islam is that the true owner of all property is God Most High, and man, in his capacity as the vicegerent of God, is a mere custodian or trustee. This is the substance of the *Sharīʿah* doctrine of the vicegerency of man on the earth (*istikhlāf fi'l-arḍ*), to which references are made in a number of places in the Qur'ān as follows:

وإذ قال ربك للملآ ئكة إنى جاعل فى الأرض خليفة قالوا
أتجعل فيها من يفسد فيها ويسفك الدماء ونحن نسبح
بحمدك ونقدس لك قال إنى أعلم مالاتعلمون .

And when thy Lord said to the angels: Lo! I am about to place a vicegerent on the earth, they said: Wilt Thou place therein one who will do harm therein and will shed blood, while we, we hymn Thy praise and sanctify Thee? He said: Surely I know that which you do not know (2:30).

وللّه ملك السموات والأرض ومابينهما .

And to God belongs the ownership/kingdom of the heavens and the earth and all that is in between (5:17 and 42:49).

آمنوا بالله ورسوله وأنفقوا مماجعلكم مستخلفين فيه .

Believe in God and His Messenger and spend of that whereof He has made you trustees (57:7).

قل لمن ما فى السموات والأرض قل لله كتب على نفسه الرحمة .

Say, to whom belongs all that is in the heavens and the earth? Say: to God. He has prescribed mercy upon Himself... (6:12)

وآتوهم من مال الله الذى أتاكم .

And to give them (the poor) of God's property that is given to you (24:33).

Commenting on these passages, Syed Quṭb wrote that human beings are trustees and custodians of the wealth that circulates among them. Trusteeship (*istikhlāf*) does not imply absolute ownership; it only implies contingent ownership, which is valid if the conditions of the trust are fulfilled. The trusteeship lapses when its conditions are not observed, when ownership returns to its original owner.[21] The conditions of valid *istikhlāf* are competence and good management. Whenever these qualities are lacking, *istikhlāf* returns to the guardian of the property or to society. Furthermore, the concept of trusteeship applies both to the individual and to society. Thus the Islamic state bears the same responsibility as the individual, each in their respective capacities, as trustees and vicegerents of God.[22] Al-Khafīf and Zuḥaylī both confirm the substance of this analysis, and observe that vicegerency in this context conveys the social responsibility (*waẓīfah ijtimā ʿiyyah*) of the owner, which is manifested in two ways: firstly that the owner ceases to be so when his exercise of ownership inflicts exorbitant harm (*ḍarar fāḥish*) on another; and secondly that the owner's property right is subjected to the benefit of other individuals, such as his neighbours and strangers, who must be given right of passage, right of flow and other ancillary rights.[23]

Vicegerency or *khilāfah* also entails a commitment to virtuous objectives such as charitable spending in the way of God, in addition to *zakāh*, by helping the needy within and outside one's family; the avoidance of waste and extravagance, or hoarding and profiteering. Another manifestation of *khilāfah* in this context is that the Imam or ruler is authorised to intervene in the event of manifest violations of these social responsibilities in the exercise of the owner's property rights.[24]

Islam's concept of ownership thus looks in two directions, one of which is to establish and protect private ownership, and the other to ensure that ownership entails social responsibility that is predicated on fraternity and cooperation within the community. The recognition in the *Sharīʿah* of public ownership side by side with private ownership clearly manifests this dual emphasis in the Islamic concept of ownership. The legal regime devised by the *Sharīʿah* seeks to balance these two interests against one another.

Some observers have, however, expressed reservations about the nature of *istikhlāf*, and whether it should actually mean the attribution of real ownership to God and not to human owners. It is thus stated that the Qurʾānic passages on the absolute sovereignty and ownership of God should not be read so as to affect the nature of financial transactions and the ownership of property by individuals. To say that God Most High is the real and absolute owner of all things is a symbolic expression of man's submission to Him, and an affirmation of God's supremacy in a way that is similar perhaps to the authority of a state over its territory, neither of which is meant to affect the ownership of individuals over parts of that whole property. One commentator thus wrote that 'The attribution of ownership to God in the Qurʾān conveys a devotional meaning only (*ma ʿnā ta ʿabbudi maḥḍ*), which has no bearing on transactions (*mu ʿāmalat*).'[25] The Qurʾān also affirms, in numerous places, that God Almighty is the Creator of the heavens and the earth (cf., 6:14). Proclamations of this kind mean that human beings are bound by the commands of God Most High in the exercise of their right of ownership. 'People are entitled to own the bounties of the earth, and ownership is a God-ordained right. Property is also not a goal in itself but a means of obtaining benefit and utilising it for the fulfilment of needs.'[26]

Report has it that two prominent Companions, Abū Dharr al-Ghifārī and Muʿāwiya b. Abī Sufyān disagreed on this question in the presence of the caliph ʿUthmān Abū Dharr. He heard Muʿāwiya saying that 'all property belongs to God.' Abū Dharr told Muʿāwiya not to repeat this and asked him a question: 'What makes you call property that belongs to Muslims the property of God?' Muʿāwiya's response was: 'May God bless you O Aba Dharr! Are we not God's servants and is He not the owner of all property?' But Muʿāwiya failed to convince Abū Dharr, and he reiterated his view that Muslims are the owners of their properties. Abū Dharr thus refuted Muʿāwiya's covert view that the government could impose restrictions on private property. And as time passed by, Abū Dharr's views prevailed, since they were also in conformity with the caliph ʿUmar b. al-Khaṭṭāb's position on the matter.[27]

Those who quote Qur'ānic evidence on God's kingdom and His absolute ownership of all things tend to overlook the fact that the Qur'ān also contains ample evidence on the normative validity of private ownership, and that God Most High has subjugated, to man's benefit and service, everything in His creation. Similarly, some of the Qur'ānic passages quoted in support of the vicegerency of man can also be quoted in support of the view that God Most High has appointed man His representative, and delegated effective authority to him to manage his own worldly affairs. Thus it declares:

$$\text{وأنفقوا مما جعلكم مستخلفين فيه.}$$

And spend of that over which We have appointed you as successors. (57:2)

Elsewhere, the Qur'ān speaks of God's purpose in assigning the earth to the custody of mankind, not only as trustees but also as heirs and right-bearers therein (cf. 44:29; 7:125; 33:27).

Thus the notion that the vicegerency of man on the earth implies a negation of private ownership is unwarranted since it could be taken to imply that the community as a whole had the right to overrule private ownership, which would be manifestly erroneous. The absolute sovereignty of God is an article of the Muslim faith on which there is no disagreement, just as there is no doubt that the Qur'ān is affirmative on the trusteeship and vicegerency of man in the earth. Man is therefore both an owner of property and also the bearer of a trust, and there is no inherent conflict between the two. Moreover, the *Sharīʿah* has taken detailed measures to protect private property against any kind of violation. It may therefore be concluded that the vicegerency of man on the earth is not in conflict with his right of ownership, nor is the latter in any conflict with the absolute sovereignty of God.

The Cairo-based Academy of Islamic Research (*Majmaʿ al-Buḥūth al-Islāmiyya*), in its first session in 1964, deliberated on the subject of ownership, and held that the *Sharīʿah* has unequivocally upheld and recognised private ownership as a basic right, and has taken detailed measures to protect it. Yet the government and the *ūlu al-amr* have been authorised to impose restrictions on the exercise of this right and on people's freedom to own property, though this is limitied to the extent that will prevent manifest abuse, and facilitate a realisation of wider interests. The state is also authorised to levy taxes on private property on the grounds of public interest, just as it may also confiscate and appropriate property that is acquired through oppressive or unlawful means. It is thus stated that the actual amount of property a person acquires is a matter of personal choice and belongs to the sphere of *mubāḥ*, and that the government may make *mubāḥ* the subject of an obligatory or a prohibitive ruling in order to realise a *maṣlaḥah* or to repel prejudice and *ḍarar*. When the government issues an ordinance to that effect, it must be obeyed.[28] Any other intervention by the government in the private property of individuals, which they have lawfully owned must be minimal, and if deemed necessary or dictated by *maṣlaḥah*, it should be involve the payment of fair compensation to the owner.[29]

Our general understanding of *istikhlāf* and its bearing on ownership must therefore be that ownership in Islam is not an absolute right in that private ownership has been subjected to the benefits both of its owner and the community at large. The *Sharīʿah* does not, therefore, permit private ownership to become a means of harm or corruption. For God Most High commands justice and the doing of good (*ʿadl wa iḥsān*). The human owner who acts in his capacity as the vicegerent and representative of God may not, therefore, use his right contrary to that trust of vicegerency and the relevant injunctions of the *Sharīʿah*.[30] The *Sharīʿah* provides a body of rules and guidelines on the acquisition of property, on its utilisation, expenditure and transfer, and also subjects it to the rights of the poor and the benefit of the community at large. The implementation of this is a faithful discharge of the trust of vicegerency both on the part of the private owner and of the community of believers.

IV. Definition and Types of Ownership

The majority of jurists (*jumhūr*), including Imam al-Shāfiʿī, define property (*māl*), which is the subject-matter of ownership, as anything that has a saleable value, and destroying which could entail compensation, even if a small amount, yet not so small that people would not consider it to be of any value, such as a grain of wheat or a handful of grass. The Ḥanafis have, on the other hand, defined property as anything that people naturally like to own and which can be stored for future use. The Ḥanafi definition of *māl* thus precludes usufruct, such as rent, which is not yet collected, and anticipated profit (*manfaʿa*) as well as certain varieties of abstract rights (*al-ḥuqūq*) as elaborated below, since they cannot be stored for future use. The majority definition includes usufruct (*manfaʿa*) and intangible assets in the definition of *māl*, and also considers these to be inheritable.[31]

Al-Qarafi defined ownership (*al-milk*) as 'A ruling of Sharīʿah (*ḥukm sharʿī*), or a juridical attribute (*waṣf sharʿī*), which is specified in a real object (*ʿayn*) or usufruct (*manfaʿa*), and enables a person to control, dispose, or exchange it in any manner he wishes provided that there is no legal impediment against it.'[32] Ownership is a *ḥukm sharʿī* in the sense that it materialises on the basis of certain grounds or causes that the Sharīʿah has determined. To say that ownership may be exchanged for value, differentiates it from permissibilities or *mubāḥāt*, such as the use of public amenities, which are not exchangeable for value. To say that ownership materialises in a real object or usufruct signifies an exchangeable value in ownership. This specification also precludes certain rights (*ḥuqūq*) that may not be exchangeable for value. The right to the custody of a child (*ḥaḍāna*) or that of guardianship (*wilāya*) are neither attached to objects nor consist of usufruct, and do not constitute the proper subject of ownership.

Yet to confine the definition of ownership to objects and usufruct and preclude rights from its scope has also provoked criticism. In addition, al-Qarafi's definition contains a weakness in that it tends to equate ownership with a Sharīʿah ruling (*ḥukm*), which cannot be the subject of a bargain or exchange per se. Muṣṭafā al-Zarqā's definition is more concise. Ownership is thus defined as 'An exclusive assignment (*ikhtiṣāṣ ḥājiz*) under the Sharīʿah which enables only the owner to control or dispose of it, unless there is a legal impediment (such as minority, insanity etc.) against it.'[33] Exclusive control or assignment in this definition means that no-one other than the owner is entitled to interfere, or exercise control over it. The fact that this definition does not confine ownership to objects or usufruct means that rights are also included, and we shall elaborate on this later.

According to an alternative definition, ownership is a 'Legal relationship (*ittiṣāl sharʿī*) between a person and an object (*shay'*), which entitles the former to an exclusive right of disposition and control over the latter.'[34]

ʿAlī al-Khafīf defined ownership as an interest that is granted under the *Sharīʿah* (*maṣlaḥah mustaḥiqqa sharʿan*),[35] whereas according to Muḥammad Yūsuf Mūsā, ownership signifies effective control (*ḥayāzat al-shay'*), which enables a person to exclusive utilisation and disposition of a thing (*al-shay'*) in the absence of any legal impediments.[36] Al-Khafīf's definition is generally worded and obviously includes both tangible objects and intangible assets, such as a copyright or other intellectual property. Muḥammad Yūsuf Mūsā's definition refers to tangible objects, as this is understood from the occurrence of the word (*al-shay'*) in the definition. It thus appears that Muṣṭafā al-Zarqā's definition avoids many pitfalls and tends to be comprehensive.

Ownership is divided into two categories, namely complete ownership (*al-milk al-tāmm*) and deficient ownership (*al-milk al-nāqiṣ*). The second classification of ownership that we will reviewed here is its division into private ownership (*al-milk al-fardī*) and communal or collective ownership (*al-milk al-jamāʿī*) as summarised below.

1) Complete and Deficient Ownership

Complete ownership is that which comprises ownership both of an object and its usufruct, whereas deficient ownership falls upon one of these but not both. Complete ownership is exclusive and permanent and enables the owner, with full capacity, to deal with his property as he pleases. Complete ownership is typically acquired through contract, gift, and inheritance, as well as through acquiring possession and control of permissible things (*istīlā' al-mubāḥ*) such as the collection of wood in the wild or hunting. Complete ownership is the most common variety of ownership in the *Sharīʿah*. Deficient ownership is less common by comparison and, as noted above, may include the object but not its usufruct, or vice versa. An example of deficient ownership that consists of the usufruct but not the corpus is when a person makes a bequest in favour of another person for the use of his house during the lifetime of the legatee, or for a term of say five years. The house (i.e. the object) thus remains the property of the testator, and his legal heirs will own only the corpus of the house, but inherit all of it after expiry of the stated terms of the bequest. The owners (legal heirs) would consequently have no control over the property, which they must vacate and make available to the beneficiary of the bequest. It would appear that ownership of the object (*ᶜayn*) is permanent and always leads to complete ownership, whereas ownership of the usufruct (*manfaᶜa*) is, according to the Ḥanafis at least, always temporary, since usufruct cannot be inherited according to them.[37]

The second type of deficient ownership is that which includes only the corpus. This is also illustrated by the previous example of bequest, in which the testator remains the owner of the usufruct but bequeaths the corpus of his property alone to the legatee. The latter, as a result, only owns the corpus. This may also occur in a charitable endowment (*waqf*) in which the dedicator (*wāqif*) retains ownership of his property (*ᶜayn*) but transfers ownership of its usufruct (*manfaᶜa*) to the beneficiary. And then there are a variety of nominate contracts which only involve a transfer of usufruct. For example in a lease (*ijāra*) contract, such as that of a rented property, the tenant owns only the usufruct, and a contract of lending (*iᶜārah*, or *ᶜāriya*) entails the transfer only of the usufruct to the borrower.

Deficient ownership that pertains only to usufruct may consist of a personal right (*ḥaqq shakhṣī*) for the beneficiary in the sense that it follows the owner rather than the property, or it may consist of a right *in rem* (*ḥaqq ᶜaynī*), which is always attached to the property, not to the owner. An example of the former is when a person bequeathes only the usufruct, say for ten years, of his orchard to another person, and an example of the latter is ownership of the right of way (*ḥaqq al-irtifāq*) or a right of flow (*ḥaqq al-majrā*), that is always attached to a property independently of the owner. This latter type of deficient ownership can only occur with regard to real property.[38]

The following three conditions must be satisfied for private ownership to materialise:

a)   The object is not a communal property that is meant to benefit the community as a whole, such as mosques, bridges and roads.

b)   It is permissible (*ḥalāl*) for the object to be owned and is as such considered a valuable asset (*māl*) from the viewpoint of the *Sharīᶜah*. This precludes forbidden objects such as dead carcasses and swine. Property that is dedicated in *waqf* is also not fit for private ownership.

c)   Ownership is realised through lawful means, precluding theft, robbery, bribery and usurpation. Ownership cannot be lawfully established if the asset in question is acquired by unlawful means.

Complete ownership of real and corporeal assets is permanent and does not weaken or terminate with the passage of time. It can be terminated by way of sale, transfer and other recognised methods of disposition under the *Sharīʿah*. This also means that one cannot buy nor sell a property for a limited period of time, nor can one terminate one's ownership of such assets by way of absolvement (*ibrāʾ*), abandonment, or simple renunciation.[39]

Deficient ownership involves the ownership of usufruct only; it can, on the other hand, be made contingent and limited to time and place and other suitable conditions. For example, the lease and hire of a car, or a bequest of the yield of agricultural land, or the temporary loan (*iʿāra*) of a horse, may all be made conditional.

Unlike complete ownership, which is normally inheritable, deficient ownership cannot be inherited, according to the Hanifis at least, and tends to expire with the death of the owner. The only recognised exceptions to this are the ancillary rights, or easements, which actually follow the property and can be inherited. The majority of jurists, including the Shāfiʿīs, Mālikīs and Ḥanbalīs, have held, however, that usufructory rights are inheritable. In the event, for example, where the tenant dies before the expiry of the contract of tenancy, his legal heirs inherit the remaining portion of the tenancy contract. This is also the case with regard to temporary loan (*iʿāra*) and also the employment contract (*ijāra*), all of which are inheritable according to the majority of Muslim jurists.

Since ownership of usufruct or *manfa ʿa* normally involves control and possession of the corporeal object (*ʿayn*), such as the rented place in the case of tenancy, or the borrowed object in the case of temporary loan, the deficient owner, or the one who is entitled to the usufruct, is responsible for the safe-keeping of the capital asset, and may be held liable for compensation in the event of transgressions or negligence relating to it, subject to some disagreement regarding detail among the leading *madhahib*.[40]

2) Ownership of Rights (*Milkiyyat al-Ḥuqūq*)

The ownership of rights is an extension of the discourse on complete and deficient ownership in the sense that some rights can be owned fully whereas certain other rights cannot be so owned.

In response to the question of whether rights can be included in the definition of *māl*, it is necessary to describe, however briefly, the main varieties of rights, as there are rights that qualify as *māl,* just as there are others which do not. When a right qualifies as *māl*, it is also likely to be a valid subject of ownership and proprietary dispositions.

Rights that are counted as *māl*, according to the majority, include a credit loan (*dayn*) and certain ancillary rights, or easements (*ḥuqūq al-irtifāq*) that are attached to real property. There is general agreement, on the other hand, that certain rights, such as the right to custody of a child, visitation rights and the right of paternity, do not qualify as *māl*, nor do they carry a financial value of their own. A more accurate exposition of their basic positions necessitates a brief discussion of the classification of rights as follows:

a) Rights that are attached to *māl* and consist of usufruct (*manfaʿa*), or the use of corporeal objects, also qualify as *māl*. Included in this category are the right of abode in a rented property, the right of transport, whether consisting of the use of animals or machines, and easements, which are attached to real property. Rights of this kind consist of the ownership of usufruct, even if someone else owns the capital asset. These are considered valuable property (*māl*) by those who include usufruct in the definition of *māl*.

b) Rights that basically consist of liberties and are in the nature of *ibāḥāt* (permissible rights), such as the right to use public roads and recreation grounds, the right to buy property and the right to conclude contracts. These are usually attached to real property or *māl*, and yet they are not considered *māl* because they cannot be possessed or exclusively controlled by any one person, nor can they be exchanged for value.

c) Rights that depend on the will of another person even if they are attached to *māl*, do not qualify as *māl*, simply because of the uncertainty and doubt in their realisation. An example of this would be the right to the unpaid price of a gold object, which only the Mālikīs recognise as *māl* but the majority do not. The reason for this is that the remittance of the outstanding sum depends on the will of the buyer, and until it is actually remitted, it is not counted as *māl*. One might add the proviso here that when timely payment is guaranteed by a guarantor or by negotiable instruments and collaterals, the assets in question may be considered *māl*.

d) Rights that attach to a legal personality (*dhimma*) such as a credit loan (*dayn*) of money or fungible goods, and the wife's right to maintenance from her husband, or indeed payment for work that is completed: whereas some jurists recognise these as *māl* and valid subjects of ownership, the Ḥanafis only regard them as putative rights (*māl ḥukmī*), which can be owned but only by way of deficient, as opposed to complete, ownership. Since there is uncertainty in possessing and utilising these rights, and they consist mainly of usufruct, they can be owned only by way of deficient ownership.

e)   Rights that attach to persons such as the right of guardianship of one person over another, the right to custody, and the right to just retaliation (*qiṣāṣ*), are normally not considered *māl* because they cannot be sold, nor have they a financial value, except for the right of *qiṣāṣ*, which has a monetary value attached to it in the event that it is converted to *diyya* (blood money). These rights are inheritable nevertheless, even if they are not considered *māl*, but they cannot be transferred by way of sale or exchange.[41]

It thus appears that some rights do carry a monetary value and are considered *māl*, just as they can be owned and transferred by way of sale, exchange and inheritance. There are rights, on the other hand, that are not considered *māl* and may or may not be the proper subject of ownership. ʿAlī al-Khafīf has equated rights (*ḥuqūq*) with benefits (*maṣāliḥ*), both of which are in the nature of usufruct (*manāfiʿ*) that is sometimes attached to real property and corporeal assets and at other times to persons. These various types of rights also vary in respect of their underlying causes and origins. Some of them originate in the rule of law, whereas others come into being as a result of personal commitments and contracts.[42] They cannot all be categorised as *māl*, nor can they all be owned in the normal sense of complete ownership, although most of them can be owned by way of deficient ownership (*milkiyyah nāqiṣah*).

3) Private and Public Ownership
(al-Milkiyyah al-Fardiyya wa'l-Jamāʿiyya)

The Qurʾānic verse which proclaims هو الذى خلق لكم ما فى الأرض جميعا. 'It is He Who created for you all that is on the earth' (2:29) has, according to the commentator, laid down the basis of the principle of original permissibility, or *ibāḥa*, in Islamic law. This is confirmed in another passage where the Qurʾān declares even more vividly:

وسخر لكم ما فى السموات وما فى الأرض جميعا منه .

We have subjugated to you all that is in the heavens and the earth. (45:13).

Thus it is observed that all things were originally permissible (*mubāḥ*) to all people, and this was the natural state of things until the emergence of private ownership, which also preceded other varieties of ownership. This is confirmed by the historical knowledge that the individual precedes society, and that social order and organisation mark a later stage in the unfolding of human history on this planet. Life in society brought with it the growth of agriculture and construction, including the collective utilisation of water, forests and pasture, which led in turn to the emergence of collective ownership.[43]

Different types of ownership, especially of land, were known to pre-Islamic Arabs, who mainly practised three types of land ownership: land that was owned by individuals, by the community, or by tribal chiefs. All three types of ownership were thus known to the Arabs at the time of the advent of Islam. Some wealthy Meccans possessed land in fertile towns not only in Mecca but also in Ṭā'if and Syria. Pastures used for grazing livestock were treated as community land. Land that the tribal chief reserved for his own cattle or for any other purpose was in the tribal sense a royal possession. Pre-Islamic Arab literature frequently alludes to such lands. When the Prophet migrated to Madina, he not only confirmed the private ownership of land by Muslims and non-Muslims, but also set a precedent by allocating land to individuals for the purposes of housing and farming, often on the basis of need, or as an appreciation of meritorious service. Later, the caliph ʿUmar b. al-Khaṭṭāb took over state property, which in pre-Islamic days was owned by the emperor of Persia or his family. The land in the sub-jugated territories consisted of two broad categories: (1) treaty land conquered without war, and (2) land conquered by force. The first category was governed by the terms of treaty, while the second cat-egory was treated as state-owned. It included land under cultivation, and arable, waste or barren land.[44]

Private ownership, whether of individual-owned, or jointly-owned property, is clearly recognised as the prototype and principal variety of ownership in *Sharīʿah*. This is also the main theme of much of the evidence of the Qur'ān and *Sunnah* on the subject. Private ownership is distinguished from collective or communal ownership in that under the former, only one or more specified individuals have exclusive rights to the object or property in question. Both the owner and the property are clearly identified and exclusive.[45] While private ownership is the default, the *Sharī'ah* also recognises collective ownership and gives it an almost equally prominent profile insofar as when there is a conflict between the two, restrictions are imposed on private ownership so as to accommodate, or give way to, communal interests. This is in fact the main feature of the restrictions on private ownership that are elaborated below.

A salient feature of public and collective ownership in the *Sharī'ah* is that it belongs to the community as a whole, which means that no single individual, or group of individuals, can be the exclusive beneficiary thereof. Abu Zahrah and al-Khafīf thus described 'public property (*al-milkiyyah al-'āmmah*)' as property that belongs to the community or a section thereof, from which all members of that community are entitled to benefit. No–one may, however, utilise it so as to deprive others, nor may private individuals own it.[46] Thus it is noted that roads, bridges, rivers, mountains and charitable endowments (*awqāf khayriyya*) belong to the community as a whole, in which everyone has a share, and the right to utilize them for their own benefit. Instances of the recognition of collective ownership in the Qur'ān refer to the mosque, which is referred to as the property of God, and also the spoils of war prior to distribution, since they belong to the community as a whole. This is also true of the assets of *bayt al-māl* and unowned barren land. The state is a trustee and manager of these assets and has no absolute authority to assign or transfer them to private individuals, unless this is in pursuit of a manifest public interest, in which case the state may transfer them to individuals for the purposes of utilisation and development.

As for barren land not owned by anyone and located outside residential areas, there is authority in the *Sunnah* that validates some private ownership over it even without the state's intervention. Thus it is proclaimed in a *ḥadīth* that:

من أحيا أرضا ميتة فهي له .

Anyone who reclaims barren land may own it.[47]

This is the majority position, although the Imams Abū Ḥanīfah and Mālik have held that the intending reclaimer must obtain the government's permission first, so as to avoid conflicts with other people. There are also reports that the Prophet himself and then the Pious Caliphs after him assigned land and mineral resources to individuals for development, utilisation and management.[48] Mineral resources of the type that are easy to exploit, such as salt or spring water, are also communal property and are treated like public pastures (*ḥimā*), and the Prophet declared that they belong only to God and His Messenger, that is, to the community of believers.[49]

Ḥimā is defined as the consecration of land and preventing private ownership and development (*iḥyā'*) thereof, in an attempt to reserve it for pasture and the grazing of livestock.[50] The Prophet thus assigned the land of al-Baqīʿ in Madina as *ḥimā* for the horses of the Anṣār and Muhājirīn. The fact that the *ḥadīth* of *ḥimā*, which declares that 'There is no *ḥimā* but for God and His Messenger' (*la ḥimā illā li-Allāh wa li-rasūlih*), is worded so as to make it the sole prerogative of 'God and His Messenger' has led some to the conclusion that no-one else is allowed to practise *ḥimā*. Having said this, al-Māwardī concludes that the Prophet did not say this for himself but for the benefit of the community, and it was this understanding which prompted the caliphs Abū Bakr and ʿUmar to assign land for similar purposes, as the Prophet had done himself.[51]

Collective ownership can be over three types of properties as follows. Firstly properties, as already noted, that are for the benefit of the community as a whole, such as public schools, roads, rivers and hospitals, as well as properties that are dedicated in charitable endowment. These cannot be converted into the private property of anyone. When we read in the Qur'ān the proclamation that 'The mosques belong to God' (*innal-masājida li-Allāh*, 72:18), it means that they belong to the community where they worship and remember God.

Secondly, properties that are easily exploited in that the labour that is expended for their utilisation is not proportionate with their value, and this includes barren land, forests and easily-exploitable mineral resources. They belong to the community and may not be privately-owned, although the state may assign them, partially or wholly, to individuals for a certain period to facilitate their exploitation and development.[52]

Thirdly, properties that are owned and controlled by the state, such as agricultural and arable land in conquered territories. Such properties, known as *kharāj* lands, were accordingly left in the hands of their occupants on condition that ownership remained with the state. The state had the authority, however, to assign these properties to individuals for development. The transfer in this case was only of usufruct, whereas ownership of the property itself remained with the state, which represented the community. The revenue realised from it, that is, the *kharāj* tax, was payable to the treasury (*bayt al-māl*). *Kharāj* is exempted, however, according to Imam Abū Ḥanīfah, in the event of crop failure due to natural calamities and disease.

A certain change occurred in the status of conquered lands during the reign of ʿUmar b. al-Khaṭṭāb, especially with regard to the agricultural lands of Iraq, where the caliph left the land with their owners and imposed the *kharāj* tax over it. Although land in the conquered territories was state-owned in principle, it nevertheless remained under the effective control of their owners in that that they mortgaged, sold, gifted and eventually passed it on as an inheritence. Hence the conclusion that ownership belonged to the original owners and the state only received the *kharāj* revenues. It is then stated that this was in conformity with the *Sunnah* of the Prophet.[53] When the Prophet conquered the lands of Khaybar, he left them in the hands of their Jewish owners and occupants on condition that they paid one half of their yield to the Muslim community. Ownership of this one-half thus belonged to the community as a whole.[54]

Based on this precedent, the juristic ruling that the ownership of conquered lands belongs to the state has been disputed, and the position is, as stated above, that ownership remained with their owners as in the case of the lands of Khaybar during the Prophet's time, and the land of Iraq during the time of caliph ʿUmar. Owners were required to give half of the yield to the state, but their ownership remained intact. Abū Yūsuf has stated that the available precedent actually lends support to both positions, either that the state distribute the land among Muslim soldiers and impose a tax of one-tenth on it, or else that it leave the land with its original owners and impose the *kharāj* land-tax on it[55] It thus appears that the government has the discretion to make appropriate decisions in order to promote the ideals of justice and the public interest (*maṣlaḥa*).

V. The Acquisition and Means of Ownership (*Kasb al-Milkiyyah*)

Ownership is over property (*māl*) and *māl* is either owned by a human being or not owned. Property that is owned by a person is *māl mamlūk* (owned property), and that which is unowned is *māl mubāḥ* (permissible property). The ownership of owned property is protected, and the *Sharīʿah* provides measures to ensure an owner's exclusive right over his property. The ownership of unowned, or permissible, property is acquired through domination (*istīlā'*), which is demonstrated by possession/occupation (*al-ḥayāza*) and any activity that is indicative of a person's intention to own.

As a means of acquiring ownership, *istīlā'* is only validated in the *Sharīʿah* in respect of property that no-one has ever owned. As soon as a person exercises *istīlā'* over unowned property, he or she becomes the owner thereof, and ownership is henceforth not transferred to another person except by lawful means, such as sale, inheritance etc. As already noted, *istīlā'* consists of activity that aims towards ownership, and the *Sharīʿah* recognises *istīlā'* in the forms of work (*ʿamal*), land reclaimation (*iḥyā'al-mawāt*), hunting (*al-ṣayd*) and the extraction of mineral resources (*istikhrāj al-maʿādin*). The acquisition of property through these methods involves activity and work. As for property that is already owned (i.e. *amwāl mamlūka*) the law speaks only of valid methods of transfer such as sale, gift and inheritance. Whereas some writers include contract among the means of acquiring ownership, others include contract under the methods of the transfer of ownership. Leaving out the detail, we can usefully specify the main categories of ways to acquire ownership below. There are seven methods:

1. Work (*al-ʿAmal*)

Earning through the effort and labour of one's hand, or manual effort combined with skill and intellectual exertion, are not only valid means of the acquisition of property in Islam but are highly recommended. All the other methods of the acquisition of wealth that are discussed below are recognised in the *Sharīʿah,* but beneficial work is superior in that it is undertaken with sincerity and devotion to a worthy cause, and is often equated with worship (*ʿibāda*) that earns the pleasure of God. Work may be the principal means of ownership in respect of both movable objects and land. A person who makes or manufactures valuable goods, or one who reclaims barren land are both examples of this. Work in this sense is the most pervasive method of the acquisition of ownership since there is some work involved in most of the varieties of the acquisition of ownership discussed here. Work as a means of ownership normally refers to lawful work that is free of legal impediments.

Much of the affirmative content of the Qur'ān and *Sunnah* on *ʿamal* is discussed in a separate volume of the present work, bearing the title *Right to Education, Work and Welfare in Islam*, which addresses work as a basic right as well as an obligation on the individual. The source evidence is instructive on the right of workers to fair pay and other benefits, just as it is assertive on the care and attention that the worker must pay to the quality and calibre of his work. Work that qualifies the worker to the pleasure of God and spiritual rewards must necessarily be of a high calibre. It was in this spirit that the Prophet spoke of work when he said in a renowned *ḥadīth*:

ما أكل أحد طعاما قطّ خيرا من أن يأكل من عمل يده وإن نبى الله داود عليه السلام كان يأكل من عمل يده.

No-one has ever eaten food purer than that which is eaten through the labour of one's hands; the Prophet (*cum-king*) David, peace be on him, used to earn his living through the labour of his hands.[56]

The Prophet also said in another *ḥadīth* that إن الله يحب المؤمن المحترف 'God Most High loves His servant who occupies himself in sustained work.'[57]

2. The Reclamation of Barren Land (*Iḥyā' al-Mawāt*)

Barren land here refers to land outside residential areas and cities that has no owner. This is also known as *arḍ mubāḥ*, or permissible land, which naturally precludes appropriated land (*arḍ mamlūka*), even if it is barren. Land that is owned and left unattended and becomes barren is still owned property and therefore not a subject of concern in this context. However, if the owner of barren land is unknown, it returns to the public treasury (*bayt al-māl*) and is treated, to all intents and purposes, as land that is not the property of anyone. Land in the vicinity of towns and villages does not fall into the category of permissible (*mawāt*) land, as it is considered to be land that serves the nearest adjacent town in various forms, including pastures, recreation grounds, cemeteries, public passages, and wood land etc. Muslim jurists have also precluded land that contains mineral wealth, such as salt, oil and gas, from *mawāt* lands. Whereas the government is entitled to assign the *mawāt* land, by way of *iqṭāʿ*, to a particular person or group of persons for the purposes of utilisation and development, land that is adjacent to towns and villages belong to those living in them and may not be assigned by way of *iqṭāʿ* to outsiders. What exactly amounts to development or reclaimation is to be understood by reference to prevailing custom in particular places and locations. Individuals may reclaim *mawāt* or barren land in the outlying areas, and anyone who reclaims and develops such land may become its owner.

The basic authority for the occupation and assignment of *mawāt* land is found in the *ḥadīth* quoted earlier, which entitles everyone, including the government, to reclaim and develop that land. The assignment is, however, limited to a period of three years during which time it must be developed, failing which it may be given to someone else. To develop and utilise the land for beneficial purposes is the basic rationale of the ruling of the *ḥadīth* on this subject. Development means making the land fertile for agriculture, or making it available for housing or any other beneficial purpose. If someone reserves barren land by placing stones or markers around it (*taḥjīr*) but does not develop it, he does not become the owner as a result of the *taḥjīr* in itself. *Taḥjīr* in this case merely gives him priority over others for three years, following which he retains no priority at all. Even during the three years, if someone else actually takes over and builds or develops the land, he becomes the owner, although this is said to be reprehensible.

To reclaim barren land, the individual, according to the majority of scholars, does not need prior authorisation from the government, but the Ḥanafis maintain that he must obtain prior authorisation so as to prevent conflict among people. According to some jurists, if the government had not known about it until after the reclamation, the reclaimer becomes its owner even without prior authorisation. According to yet another view, permission is not required for taking over land that is difficult to develop, and it is unlikely that any conflict may arise over it. The two disciples of Imam Abū Ḥanīfa, Abū Yūsuf and al-Shaybani, have concurred with the majority opinion that the *ḥadīth* itself provides the necessary authority and further authorisation from the government is not required.[58]

3. Hunting (*al-Ṣayd*)

Hunting is perhaps the oldest method of acquisition that is known to mankind. The *Sharīʿah* recognises hunting as a method of the acquisition of property that may include fish, animals, birds and valuables found in seas and rivers, such as pearls, treasure troves, gold particles etc. The Qurʾān provides the authority for hunting when it proclaims in an address to the believers that:

أحلّ لكم صيد البحر وطعامه متاعا لكم وللسيارة وحرّم عليكم صيد البر ما دمتم حرما واتقوا الله الذى إليه تحشرون .

Hunting and the eating of fish is made lawful for you, a provision for you and for seafarers; but to hunt on land is forbidden to you so long as you are on the pilgrimage (of *ḥajj*). Be mindful of your duty to God, unto Whom you will be gathered (5:96).

The latter portion of this passage refers to the period of sanctity (*iḥrām*) during the *ḥajj* season, when hunting is not permitted. But hunting is otherwise permitted. Once the game is caught, it becomes the property of the owner and can only be owned by another person by means of the lawful transfer of ownership. If a hunter catches an animal or bird which then escapes, it is no longer his property unless he immediately tries to recapture it. If wild animals are tamed and they habitually come to the place that belongs to the tamer, and then they cease to come, they are no longer owned by anyone and may be owned by whoever hunts and captures them.[59]

4. Mines and Treasure Troves

These may consist of solid or of liquid assets, and the land in which they are found is either owned or permissible land. Mineral resources that are found in private property belong to owner of the land, since the resources found therein are considered to be a part of that property according to the majority of scholars from the leading *madhāhib*, excluding Imam Aḥmad b. Ḥanbal. Imam Ibn Ḥanbal is in agreement with the majority but makes an exception in regard to flowing springs and liquids deep in the earth, which resemble water and become, therefore, the shared property of the community. This is apparently an extension of the meaning of the *ḥadīth* cited above, wherein water, fire and grass are said to belong to the community as a whole.

If the land in which mineral resources are found is permissible or unowned barren land, then the assets that are found therein are also permissible (*mubāḥ*), and belong to the community as a whole, regardless of the liquidity or solidity of the items found, and there is no disagreement on this.

According to the Mālikī opinion, which al-Khafīf has identified as preferable, mineral wealth belongs to the community as a whole, regardless of whether it is found in privately-owned property or in permissible (*mubāḥ*) land. Even the head of state is not entitled to make a grant (*iqṭāʿ*) of it to anyone in a proprietary capacity on a permanent basis, but he may do so on a temporary basis, which may extend to the lifetime of the assignee, for the purposes of utilisation and development. The assignee does not become the owner and may not transfer the assets by way of inheritance.[60]

According to a third opinion on this subject, gold and silver are exceptional and all mineral resources containing gold and silver are the property of the community, and the Imam has the authority to utilise and deal with it as he deems consonant with the public interest (*maṣlaḥa*).[61]

Al-Shishāni, who has discussed these views, concludes with a reflection on the types of mineral found, and the time and place of their finding. If the mineral wealth happens to be an essential commodity, such as petrol or gas, it should be considered community property like water and grass that belong to the people, regardless of the type of land or property in which they are found. But if the mineral wealth in question is not an essential commodity, and people's livelihood does not depend on it, it is like a treasure trove that has no owner. One fifth of it is payable to the public treasury, and the rest to the owner of the land in which it is found. If the wealth found consists of a treasure trove that is likely to have had an owner, as may be indicated by signs or writing, it is once again not permissible (*mubāḥ*) property but belongs to the Muslim community as a whole.[62]

As for a treasure trove (*luqṭa*) consisting of money or valuables found on the earth's surface or below, and has no identifiable owner, efforts should be made to find the owner, and if a Muslim establishes a claim over it, it shall be given to him, otherwise it will be treated as *luqṭa*. If a non-Muslim citizen establishes his claim to it, the government takes one-fifth and gives the rest to the non-Muslim claimant.

If the treasure is found in land owned by a person, it shall belong to the owner of the land and not the finder, and if the finder happens to be the owner of the land, the find will belong to him solely. If the land or place where the treasure is found is not owned by anyone, such as mountains or forests, it is to be given to the finder himself. If no-one claims ownership of the treasure, in the event where the treasure bears any Islamic mark or sign, it shall be deemed *luqṭa*, and if there is no hope of finding the owner, the treasure may be utilised for the needs of the poor, including the finder, if he is a needy person. In the event that the treasure bears signs of non-Islamic origin, the state may take one-fifth and give the rest to the original owner of the land to whom it had been granted by the state, or to his heirs, if alive. If the treasure cannot be traced to a previous or original owner, it shall belong to the public treasury. Abū Yūsuf has held, however, that the treasure in such a case will belong to the finder and not the owner of the land. If the treasure bears no signs or marks at all, it shall be deemed to be of Islamic origin. No *khums* (one fifth share) will be chargeable on it by the state because *khums* is chargeable on property which belongs to the category of booty (*ghanīma*). The property of a Muslim is not booty and no *khums* is imposed on it.[63]

5. Land Grant (*Iqṭā ʿ*) by the Government

Iqṭāʿ or the grant of land by the government in power consists of assignment to an individual. It is not valid in regard to land that has an owner nor is it valid over that which the government has no legitimate title.[64] When its valid perimeters are observed, *iqṭāʿ* is a recognised ground of ownership under the *Sharīʿah*. The purpose of such land-grants is, usually, a realisation of benefit for the people through the development and utilisation of resources. Once it is developed, tax, whether consisting of tithes or *kharāj*, may be levied on the land in question. Should an *iqṭāʿ* fail to realise its valid purpose, it may be revised, and the land assigned to others who may be able to develop it. This was the type of *iqṭāʿ* that was validated by the Prophet himself. Then, during the time of the Pious Caliph, *iqṭāʿ* was also practised as a way of rewarding individuals for outstanding service. The basic authority for *iqṭāʿ* is found in the *Sunnah* of the Prophet, who is reported to have given land grants to some of his Companions, including Bilāl b. al-Ḥārith, Zubayr b. al-ʿAwām. ʿUmar b. al-Khaṭṭāb, ʿAbd al-Raḥmān b. ʿAwf and others. When the Prophet established a state in Madina, there were three types of land in the city: privately-owned, unowned barren land, and grazing land for animals. The Prophet then announced, as in the *ḥadīth* already quoted, that anyone who reclaimed barren land could become its owner. Some individuals came forward and were consequently given grants of land for development, and the land so assigned became known as *iqṭāʿ*.[65] A similar situation arose after the Muslim conquest of the Persian and Roman empires, where the state had areas of land on its hands, without owners either due to the owner's demise, or his dislocation or escape. It was consequently deemed necessary to assign land to people who could utilise it.

According to reports, the first caliph Abū Bakr authorised a land-grant to Zubayr, and then Abū Bakr's successor, ʿUmar b. al-Khaṭṭāb, assigned some land on a similar basis to ʿAlī b. Abī Ṭālib and others. The caliph ʿUmar practiced *iqṭāʿ* on a wider scale in the newly conquered territories.[66] Some of the land grants made by the Pious Caliphs are known to have been to people who had rendered services to Islam and rendered distinguished service to the community, though this was practised on a fairly limited scale. In principle, the Imam may not use *iqṭāʿ* as means of showing personal favour to anyone, or for reasons other than the benefit and *maṣlaḥah* of the community, and making the land available for productive purposes.[67]

There is general agreement on the validity of the *iqṭāʿ* of barren lands, which the Imam may assign to individuals, but there is disagreement about whether *iqṭāʿ* can apply to the assets of the *bayt al-māl*. The majority of jurist approve of *iqṭāʿ* in both these capacities, but the Mālikī school and al-Shaybāni, a disciple of Abū Ḥanīfa, have held that if *maṣlaḥah* is the basic justification for *iqṭāʿ*, then *maṣlaḥah* requires that the assets of *bayt al-māl* are not alienated from anyone, and that it is not permissible for the Imam to give away anything by way of *iqṭāʿ* from the *bayt al-māl*. The Shafi'is have held that *iqṭāʿ* from the assets of the *bayt al-māl* is valid only in respect of profit but not of capital assets. The beneficiary of *iqṭāʿ* can thus own the yield but not the capital assets of *iqṭāʿ*.[68]

From the viewpoint of its purpose and objective, *iqṭāʿ* is divided into three types, namely proprietary (*iqṭāʿ tamlīk*), developmental (*iqṭāʿ istighlāl*), and usufructory (*iqṭāʿ irfāq*). These divisions are self-explanatory in that the first establishes ownership(s) whereas the second is meant to develop and utilise the land, and the third is meant to facilitate the use of public property for the convenience of certain individuals or groups of individuals, such as hawkers and petty traders, using public property, or when public property is used for access to a private property.

The main restrictions that apply to *iqṭāʿ* may be summarised as follows:

1) *Iqṭāʿ* is a prerogative of the Imam. No-one else is authorised to interfere with public property by way of *iqṭāʿ*.

2) The Imam does not assign to anyone more land than he can reclaim and develop.

3) When the assignee of an *iqṭāʿ* property fails to develop the land, the Imam must take it away and ensure that the public interest is duly protected.

4) The assignee of an *iqṭāʿ* property must not use it in such a way that inflicts harm on others.

5) Proprietary *iqṭāʿ* does not apply to public facilities such as parks, grazing lands and easily-exploited mineral resources.

Iqṭāʿ is often time-bound and must therefore comply with stipulations as to the time and manner of its use, which the Imam may impose on the grounds of public interest.[69]

A certain variation of *iqṭāʿ* has been applied by the government of Saudi Arabia in regard to the grant of petroleum concessions to American companies. The companies were evidently interested in accepting the concessions in order to make a profit. Layish, who has looked into this, has found that a combination of *Sharīʿah* principles pertaining to mineral resources, such as *iqṭāʿ*, *ijāra* (lease) and *iḥyā' al-mawāt* (the reclamation of waste land) have been relied upon in various parts of the concession agreements. This is in order to obtain the necessary legal devices that could respond to some of the new developments pertaining to the grant of concessions to foreign companies.[70] It is further noted that concession agreements provide that disputes between the parties be settled by arbitration. The Saudi authorities have 'recently decided' that the arbitration agreements 'shall not be contrary to Islamic law' and that the proceedings shall take place in Saudi Arabia in order for the award to be enforceable.[71] Layish has not explained the details any further, but the idea of deriving a combined formula from the joining-up of different contract types would fall under the notion of *talfīq* (patching-up) which is a well-recognised formula in conventional Islamic jurisprudence. One would have thought that the element of novelty here was that *iqṭāʿ* was being used for commercial purposes, and hence the need for recourse to *talfīq*. Be that as it may, Layish has further reported that the government of Saudi Arabia has also used the principle of *iḥyā' al-mawāt* as a legal basis for the gratuitous bestowal of land to entrepreneurs for the purposes of industry or workers' housing.[72]

6. Inheritance and Bequest

Inheritance is the natural corollary of private ownership in the *Sharīʿah*, and it is recognised as a legitimate means for the acquisition and transfer of ownership. The right of a number of close relatives to inherit a specified share in the property of their deceased relative is established in the clear text of the Qur'ān (cf., 4: 11–13). The legal heir becomes owner of his or her share of the estate upon the death of his or her relative, and there is no need for consent or acceptance by either of the parties. There is, however, a certain order of priorities, which the jurists have explained. The first charge on the estate is on account of funeral expenses, then any unpaid debt the deceased person might have owed, and then bequest and inheritance.

Muslim jurists have differed in regard to the precise moment when ownership is transferred to the legal heirs. The Ḥanafis have held that the transfer takes place only after the payment of outstanding debts, and the heirs are not therefore entitled to the exercise of proprietary rights independently, although they may take charge of the estate and clear the debts and any bequests that the testator might have made.[73] The owner is also entitled to bequeath up to one-third of his estate to anyone who is not a legal heir, and even to a legal heir provided that the rest of the legal heirs are in agreement.

7. Legal Alms (*zakāh*) and Charities

Since the Qur'ān has declared *zakāh* to be the right of the poor to a share of the wealth of the wealthy (51: 24–25), what its recipient consequently acquires is owned by him. *Zakāh* is one of the five pillars of Islam and very much a part of the social fabric of the society it envisages. As a manifestation of fraternity (*ukhuwwah*) among Muslims, *zakāh* is designed to protect the poor and facilitate the redistribution of wealth in the community. The Qur'ān has earmarked the revenues of *zakāh* to eight classes of people, foremost among whom are the poor and the indigent, but the beneficiaries of *zakāh* also include officials who collect and administer the *zakāh*, insolvent debtors, and others (cf., 9:60). Also included in these categories is the release of slaves in that the *zakāh* revenue may be spent for that purpose, just as the list includes the giving of help to the wayfarer (*ibn as-sabīl*). Some of the eight classes of *zakāh* recipients may no longer exist in a given situation, or may be difficult to find, in which case the state would be within its rights to entitle those who resemble the designated categories, so that the funds of *zakāh* are expended in the ways that the text has specified.[74] Prisoners who serve their sentences and need help to begin normal life in the community may be one such group. The government is also entitled to re-assign the entitlement from one category to another. Insolvent debtors, for example, may be entitled to a larger portion of the *zakāh* revenues.

VI. Restrictions on Ownership

To state the general principle at the outset, the *Sharīʿah* imposes no maximum limits on private ownership, and this means that a person may own any amount of property, whether movable or real, provided that it is acquired through lawful means.[75] The main restrictions that the *Sharīʿah* imposes on ownership are aimed at preventing harm to others, the protection of the public interest, the concern to utilise barren land, the right of pre-emption, and inheritance. These are elaborated in the following pages, but one might note at the outset that the lines of division between some of these, such as the prevention of harm, and the protection of the public interest, are not always clear-cut since they tend to converge and overlap at times. These may be outlined as follows.

1. The Prevention of Harm (*Dafʿ al-Ḍarar*)

The owner is entitled to the enjoyment of his property without restriction, provided that this does not lead to inflicting harm on others. In the event where a manifest harm is inflicted on the community or another individual through the exercise of proprietary rights, then the authorities must evaluate whether that harm is greater than the benefit that the owner seeks to realise by the use of his right. If the harm is negligible and does not warrant imposing restrictions on the exercise of the basic right of ownership, then it must be tolerated. But if the harm to others is greater by comparison, the owner's right of use may be limited to the extent needed to eliminate the harm, or, whenever possible, to reduce it to a tolerable level.[76]

The questions of whether the owner's exercise of his right is harmful, and whether that harm is excessive (*fāhish*), are often determined by reference to the prevailing custom and expert opinion. It is reported in a *hadīth* that during the Prophet's time, one Samura bin Jundub had a palm tree, and its branches extended into a garden that belonged to a man from the Anṣār, who lived with his wife. Each time Samura tried to reach the branches, it made the owner uncomfortable. So the man asked Samura if he would like to sell his tree, to which Samura gave a negative response. Samura was subsequently asked to remove the tree and cut it off, but he still refused. The man then complained to the Prophet and the Prophet asked Samura once again to consider selling his tree, but he refused again. Samura also turned down the next suggestion that he should make a gift of it to the plaintiff. The Prophet then told Samura 'You are inflicting harm.' and said to the plaintiff to 'Go and cut down the palm tree.'[77]

A similar incident is reported in which, during the rule of the caliph ʿUmar b. al-Khaṭṭāb, one al-Ḍaḥḥāk Ibn Khalifa extended a water stream within his property, which had to go through the land of Muḥammad bin Maslama. When Ḍaḥḥāk asked for Maslama's permission, he refused, but Ḍaḥḥāk went on to say that it would be equally beneficial for both of them, and that Maslama was welcome to use all the water he needed for his land first. But Maslama still refused to give permission. Ḍaḥḥāk then informed the caliph ʿUmar, who also tried to persuade Maslama to agree to the proposed extension of the water stream, which would be of benefit to both. Once again, Maslama is said to have declined the suggestion without having any reasonable excuse. So the caliph compelled Maslama and issued an order that authorised Ḍaḥḥāk to extend the canal.[78] Based on this precedent, Islamic law recognises the right of flow (*ḥaqq al-majrā*) for the owner of property, to allow him to receive water that has to flow through his neighbour's property. The neighbour may not obstruct it, and if he does, he can be compelled to give in.[79] Wāfi has reached the conclusion, based on the foregoing evidence, that 'Islam permits the expropriation of private property if the owner utilises it in a manner that inflicts harm on another person and no other way can be found to prevent the harm in question.'[80]

The following two articles of the Ottoman *Mejelle* expound the *Sharīʿah* principles on the proper use of proprietary rights:

> Everyone may utilise his property as he wishes, but when the right of another is attached to it, the owner is restricted and his right to the use of his property is no longer an independent right (Art. 1192).

> No one may be prevented from making any disposition as he likes in regard to his own property unless this causes excessive harm to another, in which case the owner may be prevented (Art. 1197).

With reference to the actual evaluation of the harm that might have been inflicted, some jurists, including Abū Yūsuf, the disciple of Imam Abū Ḥanīfa, have considered only the result of, and not the intention behind, the harmful act. This position is upheld in the *Mejelle* to the effect that when an act gives rise to a manifest harm (*ḍarar fāḥish*), it may be obstructed regardless of the owner's intention.[81] Others have held different views. Al-Shāṭibi, who is known for his goal-oriented approach to the *Sharīʿah,* has held the view that the intention must always be given consideration, for the Lawgiver has envisaged a purpose in the use of a right, and it may be obstructed only when that purpose could be violated.[82] The *Mejelle* takes an objective stance with regard to excessive harm (*ḍarar fāḥish*), which is to be removed 'regardless as to how it might have been caused.' The *Mejelle* then gives the following examples: if a forge or a mill is built and adjoins a house, and it might weaken the house by the striking of an iron or the turning of the mill, or when a new factory causes an excessive bad smell or smoke, they may be stopped in any way that seems possible (Art. 1200).

From the viewpoint of the likelihood or otherwise of its occurrence, *ḍarar* has been divided into four types as follow:

(a) *Ḍarar* that is almost certain to cccur (*al-ḍarar al-mu'akkad al-wuquʿ*). There is a near–certainty that the anticipated *ḍarar* will materialise, and cause another person or the community to suffer when the owner exercises his proprietary rights, in which case the owner may be obstructed. The owner's right of use may thus be restricted in advance if the *ḍarar* in question is also excessive (*fāḥish*).[83]

(b) *Ḍarar* that is probable (*al-ḍarar al-ghālib al-wuquʿ*). This is when the anticipated *ḍarar* is excessive and also very likely to materialise if the owner exercises his proprietary rights. The position here is similar to the one above, and the owner may be prevented by judicial intervention.

(c) Excessive *ḍarar* that is uncertain of occurrence (*al-ḍarar al-kathīr ghayr al-ghālib*): When *ḍarar* is excessive but there is doubt as to its occurrence, the ʿulamā' have differed on the question of whether it can be the basis of preventive action. The Mālikīs and Ḥanbalīs apply the legal maxim that the 'Prevention of harm takes priority over the securing of a benefit (*dar' al-mafāsid awlā min jalb al-manāfiʿ*),' and maintain that a likelihood of the occurrence of *ḍarar*, even if not strong, is sufficient to warrant preventive action against it. The Ḥanafis and Shāfiʿīs maintain, on the other hand, that the owner's right over the use of his property takes priority, and as such may not be obstructed on the ground of a mere likelihood of *ḍarar*. The reason given here is that the actual occurrence of harm is not certain, whereas the owner's right to the use of his property is certain; hence the latter takes priority over the former. The Mālikī-Ḥanbalī view has emphasised the excessive nature of the harm that may be inflicted on another, and caution is therefore advisable to prevent its occurrence. This is also the purport of the legal maxim that the prevention of harm takes priority over the attraction of a benefit.

(d) Slight *Ḍarar* (*al-ḍarar al-qalīl*). This is when the anticipated harm is not excessive and it is of rare occurrence, in which case it is ignored, and the owner's right over his property may not be restricted because of it.[84]

As already indicated, this four-fold classification of *ḍarar* enables an evaluation of *ḍarar* in advance, in order to allow preventive action. It would appear that the jurists have used the two terms *al-ḍarar al-fāḥish* and *al-ḍarar al-kathīr* synonymously, and it is basically this variety that provides the basis of preventive action, and also to a large extent, of judicial intervention in any claim for damages after the event.

There is general agreement on the ruling that the owner's right of use must be obstructed in the event where he has no other purpose than to harm another person, and no benefit accrues to him by the exercise of his right either. The owner is in this case deemed to be a transgressor, and he is to be obstructed, even if the harm that is contemplated is not a matter of certainty but seems only probable. This ruling is based on the *ḥadīth*–cum–legal maxim, that 'Harm may neither be inflicted nor reciprocated.' However, in the event where the owner's exercise of his proprietary right contemplates a benefit, which also entails harm to another, and which he can somehow avoid by recourse to an alternative that is available to him, he must follow this latter course and avoid harming another. In the event, however, where the owner cannot avoid inflicting harm to others, and he does need to do what he has to do, then two possibilities arise, one of which is that the anticipated harm is a general one, and the other that it is more limited or specific in its scope and effect. In the former case, the general harm must be avoided, and the owner's right of use is obstructed, but if the expected harm is specific, it is to be tolerated and may not stand in the way of the owner's right of use. This ruling is in accordance with the legal maxim that 'A specific harm is tolerated in order to prevent a general one.' In this comparison and evaluation of the two *ḍarars* (harms), some jurists also seek to determine not only the question of which is greater or more general, but also whether it touches on the question of necessity. The question that is asked here is: which one is avoidable and which is not. This is illustrated as follows: The owner of foodstuffs is normally entitled to use it for his own ordinary needs, but if someone else asks for it in order to prevent death by starvation, which may be certain or probable, then prevention of this harm takes priority over the owner's right of use. A legal maxim that is quoted in support of this ruling states that 'Necessities make the unlawful lawful—*al-ḍarūrāt tubiḥ al-maḥẓūrat*.'[85]

One of the themes in this discussion that acquires some prominence in the Qur'ān and *Sunnah* is good relations with one's neighbours. The Qur'ān enjoins the believers to be good to their 'parents and near kindred and orphans, the needy, and to the neighbour who is kin, and the neighbour who is not kin…'(4:36).

وبالوالدين إحسانا وبذى القربى واليتامى والمساكين والجار ذى القربى .

The Prophet has consistently spoken of the rights of the neighbour, and in one *ḥadīth* he said:

مازال جبريل يوصينى بالجار حتى ظننت أنه ليورثنه .

Gabriel advised me so persistently concerning the neighbour that I almost thought he was going to turn him into a legal heir.[86]

According to another *ḥadīth*:

من كان يؤمن بالله واليوم الآخر فليحسن إلى جاره…فليكرم ضيفه…فليقل خيرا أو ليسكت .

He who believes in God and the Last Day, let him be good to his neighbour…let him honour his guest, and…let him say what is good or remain silent.[87]

If the owner of a house wishes to build a structure that will completely or substantially block light or air from his neighbour's house, or when he digs a well so close to the wall of his neighbour's house that it is likely to cause structural damage, in each case, the situation will need to be evaluated, and the result may be to restrict the owner's right of use.[88] The *Mejelle* provides the following illustrations: A person may not extend over his neighbour's house 'the eaves of a newly-built room. If he does, the projecting part may be demolished' (Art. 1195). If the branches of a tree in someone's garden are extended over the garden or house of his neighbour, the latter has the right 'to cause his own air to be freed, by cutting those branches, or drawing them back and tying them...' (Art. 1196).

The general rule concerning neighbours, whether to the side, or on upper or lower levels, is that the owner is entitled to the use of his property in any way he wishes, provided that he does not inflict a manifest harm on his neighbour, for which he would be liable to pay damages for the harm caused. Having said this, there is some disagreement among jurists in regard to the relative value that they attach to the privileges of ownership on the one hand, and harm to the neighbour on the other. The Ḥanafis and Shāfiʿīs have emphasised the former, and maintain that ownership rights may neither be restricted nor compromised for the sake of one's neighbour. The owner may thus 'open windows whether or not they overlook the neighbour, or expose their women to unsolicited viewing; he is also entitled to build a high-rise that may overshadow the neighbour's house or even block the sun from it, or indeed build a shop or a factory, and dig a water well whether it harms the neighbour or not.'[89] This is also the Shāfiʿī position, and one of the two views of Imam Ibn Ḥanbal, although they all seem to consider it morally reprehensible but legally valid nevertheless. However, the latter-day jurists (*muta'akhirūn*) of the Ḥanafi school, the Mālikīs and the Ḥanbalīs have ruled that it is incumbent on the owner to avoid using his property in such a way as to cause a manifest harm, outside the range of acceptable custom, to the neighbours. They have justified this by saying that shortcomings have been increasingly observed among people in regard to the fair and considerate treatment of neighbours, in line with the teachings of the Qur'ān and the *Sunnah*. The owner may consequently not use his rights in a way that harms the neighbour, such as by opening a bakery next to a perfumery or drug store, or digging a wall so close to his neighbour's house as to draw and divert the water from it, nor can he build a structure that overlooks and exposes the neighbour's household to unsolicited viewing, nor may the owner open a dumping yard for refuse disposal that is harmful to the neighbour, in which cases he could be obstructed or held liable for compensation. The *Mejelle* has preferred this ruling, which now represents the general position of Islamic law.[90]

According to a legal maxim of *fiqh,* which is recorded in the *Mejelle*, 'The elimination of harm takes priority over the realisation of a benefit' (Art. 26). Another useful legal maxim of the *Mejelle* that relates to the evaluation of *ḍarar* proclaims that 'A lesser harm may be tolerated in order to prevent a greater harm' (Art. 30). Other legal maxims on the subject of *ḍarar* that are commonly quoted by the jurists are: 'Harm is to be eliminated (*al-ḍarar yuzāl*);' and 'A particular harm is tolerated in order to prevent a general one (*yutaḥammal al-ḍarar al-khāṣ li-dafʿ al-ḍarar al-ʿāmm*).'

2. Considerations of Public Interest (*Maṣlaḥah*) and Necesssity (*Ḍarūra*)

An owner's exercise of his right of use is restricted in the *Sharīʿah* when it conflicts with the public interest, or when necessity dictates. *Maṣlaḥah* and necessity often co-exist, especially in the area of the five essential values of the *Sharīʿah* (*al-ḍarūriyyāt al-khamsa*). The purpose of *maṣlaḥah* is to protect basic values of religion, life, intellect, family, and property, which constitute the overriding goals of the *Sharīʿah*. When *maṣlaḥah* works towards the protection of these values, and it concerns society at large, it is equated with necessity (*ḍarūrah*). *Maṣlaḥah* in this sense is, according to al-Ghazālī, equivalent to *ḍarūrah*, and the two tend to coincide in regard to the protection of these values. In al-Ghazālī's phrase, 'These five values represent the highest *maṣāliḥ*, and they are in reality identical with necessities.'[91] When an owner's exercise of his right threatens the safety of these values in such a way that one of them has to be given preference in order to protect the other, then the protection of the basic values takes priority over ownership rights. The authorities are therefore within their rights to take measures to ensure that private ownership does not jeopardise considerations of public interest. While this is a legitimate course of action, the authorities must exercise due caution so that prejudice and partisan interests are not projected and advocated in the name of *maṣlaḥah*.

The authority of the Imam in respect of *maṣlaḥah* is articulated in the legal maxim that 'The disposition of the Imam concerning the citizens depends on the public interest (*taṣarruf al-Imām ʿalā al-raʿiyya manūṭ bi'l-maṣlaḥa*).' There is no room for arbitrariness in the evaluation of *maṣlaḥah,* and the *maṣlaḥah* in question must be firm and unmistakeable. This advice of caution was clearly articulated by the Chief Justice Abū Yūsuf who addressed the caliph Hārūn al-Rashid in the following terms: 'No-one may take away anything from anyone unless it is on the basis of a well-known and clearly established right.'[92] (*Laysa li-aḥadin an yakhruja shayʾan min yaddi aḥadin illā bi-ḥaqq thābit maʿrūf*).

In the event where the owner of a house that is close to a public thoroughfare disposes of refuse water onto the street so that it creates a problem for the public, the owner's right may be restricted to the extent needed to remove the threat to public safety. In all eventualities of conflict, however, an attempt at reconciliation and compromise should be made if possible, in such a way that both parties give some ground on their respective claims in order to accommodate the other.

In the event of a conflict arising between private and public interests, the latter often prevails over the former, provided, however, as Shāṭibī has pointed out, that the individual is not made to suffer an irreparable harm.[93] Al-Khafīf has added in this context that public security may sometimes dictate disarming private individuals, and the issuance of a government decree, on grounds of *maṣlaḥah,* that weapons should be surrendered to the police. It is also on grounds of public interest that restrictions are imposed on the operation of factories and commercial and agricultural units.[94]

The *Sharīʿah* also validates the expropriation of private property if this is deemed necessary and that the public interest cannot be realised without it. Examples of this are the extension of a road or a mosque, and the building of new roads and dams and so forth. Public interest considerations of this kind may also amount to necessity (*ḍarūrah*), and a general guideline of the *Sharīʿah* on necessity that relates to such cases of conflict states that 'Necessity renders the unlawful lawful.' This legal maxim actually paraphrases the Qurʾānic verse which declares that:

فمن اضطرّ غير باغ ولاعاد فلا إثم عليه.

The one who is compelled, without being a transgressor or a rebel, commits no sin. (2:173).

But even in cases of necessity, the owner is entitled to a fair compensation, provided that he acquired his property through lawful means. But if he acquired the property unlawfully, such as through usurpation or bribery, he will not be entitled to compensation.[95]

The *Sharīʿah* also authorises the government to expropriate private property, against fair compensation, on the grounds of public interest, such as turning it into a pasture (*ḥimā*) for community use. The Prophet made this a prerogative of the government when he declared that لا حمًى إلا لله ولرسوله 'Pastures are only for God and His Messenger.'[96]

Restrictions on private ownership, whether consisting of expropriation, nationalisation or other restrictions imposed on grounds of *maṣlaḥah,* are subject to certain conditions that are designed to prevent arbitrariness in the name of *maṣlaḥah.* These are as follows:

1) *Maslahah* must be genuine (*haqīqiyyah*) as opposed to specious (*wahmiyyah*) or speculative, i.e., suspected but not genuine. The benefit that is involved, in other words, must be real, and the test here is that it must promote recognised benefits or protect them against harm. The five essential interests recognised by the *Sharīʿah* provide a basic framework by which to ascertain whether the *maslahah* in question is genuine or not.

2) *Maslahah* must be general (*kulliyyah*) as opposed to specific and partisan (*juz'iyyah*), and the test here is that it must bring the greatest benefit to the largest number of people. Personal biases and partisan interests are therefore excluded.

3) And lastly *maslahah* is valid only if it is not in conflict with the clear injunctions (*nusūs*) of the Qur'ān and *Sunnah*.[97]

Government leaders, that is, the Imam and the *ūlu'l-amr*, are authorised to evaluate cases of *maslahah* and necessity (*darūrah*), and make necessary decisions on them provided that they are knowledgeable about the *Sharīʿah* and their decisions are consultative. Since the Qur'ānic reference to *ūlu'l-amr* occurs in the plural, consultation and collective effort become a requirement of decision-making. In matters of a specialised nature, it is the opinion and judgement of the expert that provides the basic frame of reference, and this is understood from the Qur'ānic directive:

$$\text{فاسألوا أهل الذكر إن كنتم لاتعلمون.}$$

'Ask those who know, if you do not know yourselves' (21:7).

Al-Sibāʿī has rightly observed that nationalisation (*al-ta'mīm*) and the decision of whether or not to nationalise, requires both expert and consultative input. This means that the government may not nationalise any industrial unit or private property without first obtaining the opinion of experts in economics and social affairs, and engaging in consultation.[98]

The essentials benefits that relate to the protection of life, religion, property, intellect and honour are called that simply because normal order in society depends on them, and a real threat to their safety threatens a collapse of the social order. When this becomes the issue, *maslahah* and necessity become indistinguishable. But if the benefit in question is not one of the essential benefits for which a 'threat to its safety is likely to cause inconvenience and hardship but not a total collapse of the normal order,' then it falls into the category of complementary interests (*ḥājiyyāt*) or desirabilities (*taḥsīniyyāt*), are not equated with *ḍarūrah*. The only exception here is that of *ḥājiyyāt* which, if they concern the public at large, are automatically elevated to the rank of *ḍarūriyyāt*.

Ḍarūrah, or necessity, is a wide subject, but some of its rules are not relevant to *maṣlaḥah*, especially when necessity relates to urgent situations that require immediate decisions. Necessity of this type is then governed by a different set of rules.

Ḍarūrah and *maṣlaḥah* are not always the same, and there may be issues that fall under one but cannot be covered by the other. Property and ownership issues are not expected to present urgent necessities of the type envisaged in the Qur'ānic verse and legal maxim quoted earlier. For with urgent necessities, recourse to normal methods of consultation may not be feasible, and the Imam or the official in charge may have to make prompt and peremptory decisions whether to comply with the normal rules of *Sharīʿah* or not. It would appear that in the context of ownership, decisions that seek to impose restrictions on private ownership are likely to be covered by the rules of *maṣlaḥah*, and possibly those rules of *ḍarūrah* that fall into the category of *ḍarūriyyāt*, that is the highest class of *maṣlaḥah*. This being the case, restrictions on private ownership, whether consisting of expropriation (*muṣādarah*) or nationalisation (*taʾmīm*), should normally be consultative decisions that are also supported by expert opinion. The basic requirement of fair compensation, which is in harmony with the *Sharīʿah* rules of justice and equality, apply to *muṣādarah* and *taʾmīm*. This is what the caliph ʿUmar b. al-Khaṭṭāb did when he expropriated the private dwellings of some individuals for the expansion of the holy mosque of the *Kaʿba* after the payment of fair compensation to its owners.[99] Al-Sibāʿī comes close to this analysis when he writes that 'When the state resorts to nationalisation on the grounds of social necessity, it must pay fair compensation to the owner, if the latter's ownership is legitimate, especially in cases where the state then sells the nationalised assets to the people, or gives them in exchange for value.' The government position in this case is similar, al-Sibāʿī adds, to the case of hoarding (*iḥtikār*); the *Sharīʿah* permits compelling the hoarders of foodstuffs to sell it at fair price. This is expropriation without the owner's consent, and resembles nationalisation. Nationalisation and hoarding or stockpiling are both subject to the operation of the legal maxim that 'Necessity must be measured in accordance with its true proportions (*al-ḍarūratu tuqdaru bi-qadrihā*).'[100]

This last quotation also implies that necessity (*ḍarūrah*) as a juridical concept is not monolithic, and is open to evaluation and assessment of its proportion and urgency. Thus any decision based on it must be made through consultation by well-informed and qualified persons.

Reports indicate that the Prophet turned al-Naqiʿ (a land area in Madina) into a pasture to provide feeding grounds for horses owned by the people. This was equivalent to what Wahba al-Zuhaylī calls 'nationalisation in contemporary terminology.' The caliph ʿUmar b. al-Khaṭṭāb also assigned two land areas, al-Rabdha and al-Sharf, between Mecca and Madina, as pastures for the benefit of the community. The caliph expropriated that land from its private owners, about which the owners initially protested, but the caliph reasoned with them that the 'horses of *jihād*' needed grazing land, and that the land would also be opened up for the use of the whole community, including the previous owners. The government may accordingly expropriate land for building dams and power plants, as well as parks and recreation grounds, for the public benefit.[101] Zuhaylī adds that the authorities may also impose maximum limits on private ownership in the interests of social justice and a fair distribution of wealth. The right to own property partakes of the *mubāḥ* (permissible), and the head of state may regulate and restrict it in pursuit of the public interest.[102]

The Cairo-based Academy of Islamic Research (*Majmaʿ al-Buḥūth al-Islamiyya*), in its first session in 1964, deliberated on the issue of nationalisation (*al-taʾmīm*) and held that it was permissible, as was imposing restrictions on private ownership within reasonable bounds when this was dictated by the public interest (*maṣlaḥa*). It was stated that the *maṣlaḥah* in question was related to considerations of social justice and economic balance in the community. But the Council added that under the normal conditions of moderation and economic balance, the *maṣlaḥa*-based argument is of little help, as restrictions on ownership under these conditions envisage either of the following two situations:

(1) Where restrictions are imposed after the acquisition of a private property by its owners; this is not likely to be justified since the appropriation of such property in normal situations would most likely amount to usurpation (*ghaṣb*), and the *Sharīʿah* has forbidden this.

(2) Where restrictions are imposed prior to the acquisition of ownership, in which case the authorities would also stand in violation of the rulings of the *Sharīʿah* on the permissibility of private ownership.[103] Unless compelling circumstances require otherwise, people's liberty to own property should not be restricted by unwarranted stipulations.

ʿAlī al-Khafīf, al-Sibāʿi, Zuḥaylī and Ṭubliyya have all concluded that the government is authorised to act in support of the public interest. When necessity and public interest dictate the expropriation of private property, it may be attempted in exchange for a fair price. But if the public interest cannot be protected unless the property is taken away from its owner, and yet the treasury is unable to pay a fair price for it, then expropriation may be attempted even without any payment, and this is equivalent to nationalisation (*al-ta'mīm*). The authors have referred to the authority of the evidence quoted earlier on pasture land (*ḥimā*) that is reported of both the Prophet and the caliph ʿUmar b. al-Khaṭṭāb.[104] A more recent attempt to expropriate property for a fair price in order to expand the holy mosque of the Kaʿba took place under the reign of King Fahd b. ʿAbd al-ʿAzīz. This was a continuation, as Zuḥaylī points out, of the precedent set by the caliphs ʿUmar and ʿUthmān.[105]

Expropriation is also permissible by means of a judicial order in the event where an affluent debtor refuses to pay his debts, in which case the court may expropriate his property and sell it in order to pay his creditors.[106] Furthermore, the *Sharīʿah* forbids hoarding (*al-iḥtikār*), which is a manifest violation of the public interest in that it is manipulative, interferes with normal market prices, and takes advantage of people's need for basic commodities. *Iḥtikār* is defined as the retention of foodstuffs for the purposes of pushing up its price. It is an abuse of the right of ownership because it is harmful to the public, and it is a ground, therefore, of a legal restriction that may be imposed on the rights of the owner. To this effect, it is provided in one *ḥadīth* that:

من احتكر فهو خاطئ .

'The hoarder does not fail to indulge in transgression.'[107]

And in another *ḥadīth* that:

مـن احتكـر حكرة يريد أن يغلى بهـا علـى المسلمين فهـو خاطئ .

The one who hoards with the intention of pushing prices higher for the Muslims is a transgressor.[108]

In yet another *ḥadīth* it is declared that:

من دخل فى شيئ من أسعار المسلمين ليغليه عليهم كان حقا على الله أن يقعده بعظم من النار يوم القيامة.

> The one who interferes with market prices in order to push them up, reserves for himself God's punishment of Hellfire on the Day of Resurrection.[109]

The government is accordingly authorised to order the owner to sell the hoarded goods at a fair market price, failing which the government may compel him to sell the goods at a specified price. The hoarder may also be punished for a violation of the public interest, and the harm that might already have been inflicted on the people.[110]

The *Sharīʿah* may also be said to have validated expropriation on the grounds of the private interest of a co-owner or neighbour, as in the case of the right of pre-emption (*shufʿah*). This is recognised, as discussed below, for a co-owner or partner in real property, according to the majority, and also for neighbours according to the Ḥanafis. Thus when jointly-owned or adjoining land is sold prior to the notification and agreement of the one entitled to *shufʿah* (i.e. the *shafiʿ*), the latter may compel the owner, through judicial action, to revoke the sale to the stranger and observe the pre-emptive right of the *shafiʿ*.[111]

3. Land Utilisation

The *Sharīʿah* encourages the utilisation of land for productive purposes, and authorises the government to encourage property-owners to put their property to productive use. The one who occupies barren land is thus required to reclaim it within three years, failing which the land may be taken away from him and given to someone who will utilise it. The limitation here is reflected in the rulings of the *Sunnah*, which provide, on the one hand, that 'Anyone who reclaims barren land becomes its owner,'[112] and imposes the restriction, on the other hand, that:

ليس لمتحجّر بعد ثلاث سنين حق.

> The one who appropriates land has no right to it after three years.[113]

This was what the caliph ʿUmar b. al-Khaṭṭāb did to a fellow Companion, Bilāl b. al-Ḥārith al-Muzanī, to whom the Prophet himself had assigned a certain amount of land. Years later, the caliph ʿUmar told him that the Prophet did not give the land to him so as to deprive others of it, but so that it could be reclaimed and developed. Bilāl refused and said that the Prophet himself had assigned (*aqṭaʿa*) the land to him. The caliph then ordered Bilāl to 'take of the land what you can reclaim and return the rest.' The caliph then said, 'The one who fails to develop the land he has occupied for three years is no longer entitled to it, and it may be given to anyone who wishes to develop it.'[114] This became a general ruling under the caliph ʿUmar, but it is reported that Ziyād, the caliph ʿAlī's governor in Iraq, and later Muʿāwiya's governor too, reduced this period of grace to two years.[115] It may thus be concluded that the duration of time is a discretionary matter to be determined within the general framework of *maṣlaḥah,* or that of *siyāsah sharʿiyyah.* The basic principle remains that land must be put to productive use and all reasonable measures that promote this objective are deemed to be acceptable.

4. Pre-emption (*Shufʿah*)

This is also a restriction on the right of the owner in that he or she is under an obligation, in the event of wanting to sell a property, to give preference to co-owner or neighbour, according to the Ḥanafīs, or in view of the majority (*jumhūr*), to a co-owner only. The right of pre-emption is established on the authority of the *Sunnah* and in regard only to real property. Bukhārī has recorded a *ḥadīth* from Jābir b. ʿAbd Allāh that:

عـن أبـى هـريرة أن رسـول الله صـلى الله عليـه وسلم قضى بالشفـعـة فـى كـل شركة لم تقسم فإذا وقعت الحدود فلا شفعة.

The Prophet, peace be on him, has determined *shufʿah* in respect of all landed property that is not yet divided, but when it is divided and demarcated, the right to *shufʿah* discontinues.[116]

This *ḥadīth* clearly establishes the right of pre-emption only for a partner or joint owner in an undivided property, and this is the majority position on *shufʿa*. The Ḥanafis have also entitled a neighbouring owner of landed property to the same right, and has quoted the *ḥadīth* cited earlier, which requires every believing Muslim to honour his neighbour and treat him well, as evidence. Since *shufʿah* is predicated on the idea of a prevention of harm to partners and neighbours, the renowned *ḥadīth* of *la-ḍarar wa lā ḍirār* is also quoted in support of *shufʿah*.[117] Neighbouring owners of real property in the Ḥanafi doctrine also include the owners of upper and lower level sections in high-rise buildings. Having said this, the *ḥadīth* that provides direct authority on *shufʿah*, as quoted above, clearly refers to the co-owner of undivided property, who must therefore be given priority over the neighbour in the event of any conflict arising between them. *Shufʿah* is also an indivisible right in that the seller of land is not required to entertain everyone who is entitled to *shufʿa* separately, but can decide to assign to only one party. Should there be more than one individual equally entitled to *shufʿah*, however, they may reach a settlement between them in accordance with the guidelines that are provided in juristic manuals on the subject.

The owner is required to inform his partner and neighbour of his intention before he sells it to a stranger. The majority of jurists maintain that the owner must inform his partner of his intention, and may not sell it until his partner has given permission. If the owner sells his property without the permission of his partner, the latter can take legal action against him. Some jurists, like al-Shāfiʿī, have suggested that the right of pre-emption lasts for only three days following the initial notice to the partner.[118] The right of pre-emption is evidently premised on the idea of promoting fraternity and co-operation in the community, especially among partners and neighbours. Should they wish to buy an adjacent property, their wish is respected and upheld so that it constitutes the basis of a legal right.

5. Inheritance and Bequests

The rules of the *Sharīʿah* on inheritance and bequest are, on the whole, supportive of private ownership in that they entitle the family members of the deceased person to inheritance. Yet at the same time, these rules impose certain restrictions on the liberty of the owner with regard to the disposal of his property. During his lifetime, the owner is entitled to dispose of up to only one-third of his property by way of bequest, and there is a further restriction over the right of the owner in that no bequest may be made to a legal heir.

These are the normal rules, although an exception is granted of bequest to a legal heir in the event when all the existing heirs agree to it. The basic authority for the normal position here is given in a renowned *ḥadīth* which simply declares 'there shall be no bequest to a legal heir—*lā wasiyyata li-warith*.' An alternative rendering of this *ḥadīth*, which is accepted by some Sunnī and the generality of Shīʿite scholars, adds to the standard version, the words '*illā fi'l-thulth* (except in the one-third)'.

With regard to inheritance, the *Sharīʿah* has entitled close relatives, such as sons and daughters, spouses, sisters, parents and grand parents, and some of the descendants thereof, to specified shares in inheritance, and the whole scheme of inheritance operates almost independently of the wishes of the owner. There are causes, conditions and obstacles to inheritance, which the *Sharīʿah* has elaborated so as to realise a fair distribution of wealth in the family. The owner is expected to observe these and avoid interference with the specific shares that the Qur'ān (4:11–12) has allocated to close relatives.

Critics have often said that the *Sharīʿah* scheme of the distribution of inheritance tends to lead to an excessive dismemberment of property, which may prove to be uneconomical. It is thus stated that a plot of land or a family business is likely to be more productive if it is not divided and sub-divided among the generations of heirs. To this one might say that inheritance is a right, which, like all other rights, is enforceable at the request of the right-bearer. Hence the choice is always available to the heirs not to divide the property they own and remain joint owners. It has been widely acknowledged, on the other hand, that the *Sharīʿah* rules on inheritance have been effective in preventing an excessive concentration of wealth in a few hands, an objective that has been explicitly stipulated in the Qur'ān (cf. 59:7), and is eminently conducive to social justice.

The owner is entitled, under Sunni law, to bequeath up to one-third of his assets to anyone who is not a legal heir, and according to Shiʿī law, even to a legal heir, for a good cause, or in some cases, to overcome a possible rigidity that may result from the strict application of the rules of inheritance. Relatives who are not entitled to a share count as outsiders for the purposes of bequest, and may, according to the majority, be made beneficiaries of bequest within the limit of one-third. Only Ibn Ḥazm has inferred the ruling from the Qur'ānic text (2:180) that it is obligatory to make a bequest in favour of such relatives, a view which has been adopted by Egyptian law (no. 71 of 1946).[119]

Whereas the preceding restrictions affect the right of the owner directly, there are also indirect restrictions, which are predicated on considerations of social justice. The *Sharīʿah* thus imposes certain obligations, as already noted, on the owner in respect of the payment of legal alms (*zakāh*) to the poor, and also makes provisions for maintenance (*nafaqa*) within the family. These provisions are legally-enforceable, and the affluent owner who fails to comply with them may be compelled. In most cases, the unpaid sum also constitutes a charge either on the person or property of the owner, or both. If, for example, the owner refuses to pay *zakāh* to the poor or maintenance to his wife, and he becomes an absent or a missing person, the court may order the outstanding sum to be paid out of his assets. Whereas *zakāh* is 'a right of the poor in the property of the rich' (cf., 51:19) and is given on the basis of need, *nafaqa* (to one's wife for example) is not always predicated on need but follows the objective of protecting the family.

The general perspective of the *Sharīʿah* concerning these charges on private property is given in the Qur'ān, which states that:

$$\text{إن الله يأمر بالعدل والاحسان.}$$

God commands justice and the doing of good. (16:90)

And in another place:

$$\text{كي لايكون دولة بين الأغنياء منكم.}$$

So that wealth does not circulate only among the rich. (59:7).

6. Taxation

The *Sharīʿah* permits the state to levy taxes, whether permanent or temporary, on the assets of those who are capable of paying, when this is dictated by necessity and the public interest. It is on the basis of public interest that taxes have been levied, throughout the history of the caliphate, on shops and businesses, imports, and on ships visiting Muslim ports etc. The caliph ʿUmar b. al-Khaṭṭāb introduced the *kharāj* land-tax on fertile land in the conquered territories wherein the land was left with their owners but they were required to pay the *kharāj* tax. Imam Mālik and the renowned Shāfiʿi jurist ʿIzz al-Dīn ʿAbd al-Salām have held that when the *bayt al-māl* is depleted of funds, and money is needed to protect public security and meet the needs of the armed forces, the state may levy taxes in order to meet these needs. These are of course in addition to the *zakāh* and *kharāj*.[121] The general guidelines on taxation that are recorded in the *Kitāb al-Kharāj* of Abū Yūsuf and others specify that no additional tax may be introduced if the existing resources at the disposal of the state can cover the necessary expenditures for the continuation of normal order. Also, any tax levied must be at the minimum level needed, and tax is levied only on those who are capable of paying it.[121]

Concluding Remarks

I would like to conclude this chapter by briefly comparing the Islamic theory of ownership with those of capitalism and Marxism. Contemporary Muslim writers have generally subscribed to the view that ownership in Islam has similarities and differences with both of these systems, but that it tends to strike a middle ground between the two. Capitalism stands for the economic freedom of the individual and imposes minimal restrictions on private ownership, whether of land, capital and means of production, and although it recognises ownership rights for the community and state, these are on the whole subsidiary and subordinate to private ownership. The maximisation of profit and of ownership is the driving force of the capitalist economy, to the extent that it causes an imbalances in the distribution of wealth, and divides society into the two classes of capitalists, who are few in number but dominate the economy with their wealth and power, and the class of the have–nots, including workers and farmers, who constitute the vast majority but who are subjugated and may even be exploited by the powerful minority. Capitalism thus leads to socio-economic imbalances that are inherent in its philosophy and outlook, and tend to be inimical to social harmony.

Marxist socialism entitles the state to own and dominate the means of production and capital, through the ownership and political control of agriculture, industry, the service sector of the economy and natural resources. Private ownership is recognised for assets that are considered to be the essentials of living, such as a house, consumer goods and appliances, but it tends to play a minor role in the economy, and does not in any way command the status of a fundamental right. Communes and co-operatives own the means of production, land and capital. There is thus a degree of imbalance inherent in this theory because it leads to unwarranted restrictions on private ownership, which is a basic right and an important dimension of the human dignity of the individual. The workers and the have-nots are supposed to be engaged in a perpetual struggle to wrench ownership and power from the capitalists and thereby stage the dictatorship of the proletariat. The social classes are pitted against each other in conflict and there is little place in this theory for social cohesion, harmony and co-operation.

Ownership in Islam tends to avoid the excesses of the two systems and seeks to strike a middle ground, which recognises private ownership as a basic right, and yet also incorporates within its fabric a structure of distribution and legal restrictions that aim to realise social justice. The purpose is to nurture social harmony and co-operation (*ukhuwwah, taʿāwun*), and sensitise the rich to the needs of the poor, and also to encourage a sense of responsibility before God and conformity to the *Sharīʿah*. There is an acknowledgement of the rights of both the individual and society in that they are mutually committed to one another and are expected to become the supporters and guarantors of each other's interests. No quantitative limits are imposed on private ownership but the exercise of private ownership is limited by the overriding concern to avoid inflicting harm (*ḍarar*) on other individuals or the community. Private ownership is also subjected to the dictates of public interest (*maṣlaḥah*) that stands for the good of the community, and the state is authorised to judge what it considers to be a *maṣlaḥah,* and which may or may not warrant restrictions on the proprietary rights of individuals. Both the individual and the state are repositories of the trust of vicegerency (*khilāfah*) of God on the earth, and are therefore expected to be conscientious and responsible in the exercise of their proprietary rights in their capacity as trustees. Ownership is not to be used as an instrument of oppression or abuse, and those who do abuse it through indulgence in the pursuit of usurious gain, monopolistic exploitations and profiteering etc., may be restrained and even penalised for their violations.

NOTES

1.   This *ḥadīth* is reported by all the six collections, including Muslim, *Mukhtaṣar Ṣaḥīḥ Muslim*, p. 253, *ḥadīth* no. 982. Ibn ʿAbbās's reading of this *ḥadīth* prompted him to say that bequest should be limited to a quarter as the Prophet considered one-third to be almost excessive.

2.   Muslim, *Mukhtaṣar Ṣaḥīḥ Muslim*, 447, *ḥadīth* 1684; see also Mutawalli, *Mabādi*, 312; al-Sibāʿī, *Ishtirākiyyāt*, 146.

3.   Abu ʿUbayd, *al-Amwāl*, 357: Mutawali, *Mabādi*, 316.

4.   Cf. Ibn Taymiyya, *Naẓariyat al-ʿAqd*, 229.

5.   Muslim, *Mukhtaṣar Ṣaḥīḥ Muslim*, 186, *ḥadīth* no. 707.

6.   Al-Shawkānī, *Nayl al-Awṭār*, vol. V, 355.

7.   Muslim, *Mukhtaṣar Ṣaḥīḥ Muslim*, 473, *ḥadīth* no.1775.

8.   Al-Bayhaqī, *al-Sunan al-Kubrā, Kitāb al-nafaqat, Bāb Nafaqat al-Abawayn*; Mahmassani, *Arkān*, p. 207. This is perhaps a more specific qualifier to another somewhat metaphorical yet equally instructive *ḥadīth*, which provides that 'You and your property belong to your father'.

9.   Muslim, *Ṣaḥīḥ Muslim, K. al-Musāqāt wa'l-muzāra'a, Bāb taḥrim al-ẓulm wa ghaṣb al-arḍ*.

10.   Tabrīzī, *Mishkāt*, vol. II, *ḥadīth* 3512.

11.   Yūsuf Qasim, *Naẓariyya al-Difāʿ*, 118: Wafi, *Ḥimayāh al Islām*, 304.

12.   Wāfi, *Ḥuqūq al-Insān*, p. 304: the quotation is from Kamaluddin b. al-Humām, *Fatḥ al-Qadīr*, vol. IV, 276 (Maṭbaʿa al-Tijariyya al-Kubrā's edn.). Wāfi also quotes the Shāfiʿī jurists Qalyubi and Umayra, (*Ḥāshiya ʿala Sharḥ al-Muḥalla*, IV, 206).

13.   See for details Wāfi, *Ḥimayāh al Islām*, 307–308.

14.   Zuḥaylī, *al-Fiqh al-Islāmī*, vol. VII, 765.

15.   Cf. Shīshānī, *Ḥuqūq al-Insān*, 435–436.

16.   Cf. Shaltut, *Minhāj al-Qur'ān*, 96; Mutawalli, *Mabādi*, 315.

17.   Al-Shawkānī, *Nayl al-Awṭār*, vol. V, 303. Mustafa al-Sibāʿi has held that this *ḥadīth* validates the nationalisation (*ta'mīm*) of water, electricity and certain food items such as salt. *Ḥimā* is the conceptual equivalent of *ta'mīm*. Necessity and public interest are the basic determinants of both, cf. al-Sibāʿi, *al-Takāful al-Ijtimāʿi*, 162.

18.   Wāfi, *Ḥimayāh al Islām*, 61.

19.   *Id.*, 62.

20.   Shāfiʿī, *al-Umm*, III. 266 (Bulaq edn., of Cairo, *bab Iḥyā' al-mawāt*).

21.   Syed Quṭb, *al-ʿAdalah al-Ijtimāʿiyyah*, 108–109, see also Zuḥaylī, *Ḥaqq al-Ḥurriyyah*, 202.

22.   Fathi Osman, *al-Fikr al-Qanūnī*, 71; see also Mutawalli, *Mabādi*, 314.

23.   Khafif, *al-Milkiyyah fi'l-Sharīʿah*, 45; Zuḥaylī, *Ḥaqq al-Ḥurriyyah*, 203.

24. *Id.*, 46.

25. Al-ʿIlī, *Ḥurriyyāt,* 527.

26. Zuḥaylī, *al-Fiqh al-Islāmī,* vol. V, 516.

27. Abu ʿUbayd, *al-Amwāl,* 223; al-ʿIlī, *al-Ḥurriyyāt,* 533, al-Shishānī, *Ḥuqūq al-Insān,* 416.

28. Academy resolution quoted by al-ʿIli, *Ḥurriyyāt,* p.525. Similar views have been recorded by the Ḥanbalī scholars Ibn Taymiyya and his disciple Ibn Qayyim al-Jawziyya.

29. Al-Khafif, *al-Milkiyya fi'l-Sharīʿa,* vol. I, p.111.

30. Cf. al-Bayāti, *al-Niẓām al-Siyāsi,* 135–136.

31. Cf. Wahba al-Zuḥaylī, *al-Fiqh al-Islāmī,* vol. V, 515, Khafif, *al-Milkiyya fi'l-Sharīʿa,* 54, 69.

32. Al-Qarafi, *al-Furuq, farq* no.180, vol. 3, 208. See Badawi, *Daʿā'i'm,* 303; al-Baʿli, *al-Milkiyya wa Ḍawābiyuhā,* 25.

33. Zarqa, *al-Madkhal al-Fiqhi,* vol. I, 220.

34. This definition, which is attributed to Sadr al-Sharīʿa, evidently confines ownership to a tangible object, and is somewhat restrictive. Cf. al-ʿIlī, *Ḥurriyyāt,* 513, Shīshāni, *Ḥuqūq al-Insan* (402–403) has listed six definitions, including those of al-Qarafi and Sadr al-Sharīʿa.

35. Al-Khafif, *al-Milkiyya fi'l-Sharīʿa,* 28.

36. Muhammad Yūsuf Musa, *al-Amwāl wa Naẓariyyat al-ʿAqd fi'l-Fiqh al-Islami,* 165, see also al-ʿIlī, *al-Ḥurriyyāt,* 513.

37. Cf. al-ʿIlī, *Ḥurriyyāt,* 515; al-Zuḥaylī, *al-Fiqh al-Islāmī,* IV, 59 ff.

38. Musa, *al-Fiqh al-Islāmī,* 257 ff; Badawi, *Daʿā'im,* 318; Mawdūdī, *Mas'alah Milkiyyat,* 41.

39. Cf. Kafif, *al-Milkiyyah fi'l-Sharīʿa,* 92.

40. Khafif, *al-Milkiyya fi'l-Sharīʿa,* 98.

41. Ibn ʿĀbidin, *Ḥāshiya,* vol. V, 389; Khafif, *al-Milkiyya fi'l-Sharīʿa,* 73–74.

42. Khafif, *al-Milkiyya fi'l-Sharīʿa,* 424.

43. ʿAlī al-Khafif, *al-Milkiyya fi'l-Sharīʿa al-Islamiyya,* 41; Ṭubliyya, *al-Islam wa Ḥuqūq al-Insān,* 418.

44. See detail Hasanuz Zamam, *Economic Funtions of an Islamic State,* 119 f.

45. Musa, *al-Amwāl,* 167.

46. Abu Zahrah, *Tanẓīm al-Islam li'l Mujtamaʿ,* 26; al-Khafif, *al-Milkiyya fi'l-Sharīʿa,* 76.

47. Tabrīzī, *Mishkāt,* vol. II, *ḥadīth* 2944.

48. Al-Ramlī, *Nihāyat al-Muḥtāj,* VI/87; al-Zuḥaylī, *al-Fiqh,* IV, 70; Abū Zahrah, *Tanẓīm,* 76.

49. Al-Khafif, *al-Milkiyya fi'l-Sharīʿa,* 111.

50. Māwardī, *al-Aḥkām,* 185.

51. *Id.*, see for this and a slight variation of it, Abū Dāwūd, *Sunan Abi Dāwūd*, ed., al-Bughā', 444, *ḥadīth* 3083/4.

52. Cf. Abū Zahrah, *Tanẓīm*, 26; al-ʿĪlī, *Ḥurriyyāt*, 534.

53. Al-ʿĪlī, *Ḥurriyyāt*, 539; Shishani, *Ḥuqūq al-Insān*, 420.

54. See for details, al-Māwardī, *Aḥkām*, 137 ff; al-ʿĪlī, *Ḥurriyyāt*, 536 ff; Ghazawi, *al-Ḥurriyya*, 149 ff.

55. Abū Yūsuf, *Kitab al-Kharāj*, 75.

56. Tabrīzī, *Mishkat*, vol. II, *ḥadīth* 2759.

57. *Ibid.*,

58. Al-Shawkānī, *Nayl al-Awṭār*, V, 255; al-Kāsāni, *Bada'i ʿ*, VI, 200; al-Khafīf, *al-Milkiyya fi'l-Sharīʿa*, 302–304; Shishani, *Ḥuqūq al-Insān*, 429; al-Sibāʿi, *al-Takaful al-Ijtima'i*, 143–147.

59. Cf. Khafīf, *al-Milkiyyah fi'l-Sharīʿah*, 284.

60. ʿAlī al-Khafīf, *al-Milkiyya fi'l-Sharīʿa*, 292; Shishanii, *Ḥuqūq al-Insān*, 430.

61. *Id.*, 292.

62. Shishani, *Ḥuqūq al-Insān*, 430; see also Khafīf, *al-Milkiyyah fi'l-Sharīʿah*, 294.

63. Kāsāni, *Bada'i ʿ al-Sana'i ʿ*, vol. II, 65–68; Zaylaʿi, *Bahr al-Ra'iq*, vol. II, 234; Abū Yūsuf, *K. al-Kharāj*, ch.2.

64. Māwardī, *Aḥkām*, 190.

65. Shawkānī, *Nayl al-Awṭār*, V, 264; Sibāʿi, *al-Takāful al-Ijtimāʿi*, 148–49. In his *Kitab al-Amwāl*, Eng. Trans. by Ghiffari as *The Book of Finance*, Abu ʿUbayd has a chapter on 'Grant of Lands and Estates,' (ch. 42) where he gives details of lands and estates the Prophet and later the Pious Caliphs allotted to individuals.

66. Abū Yūsuf, *Kitab al-Kharāj*, 61; Māwardī, *al-Aḥkām al-Sulṭāniyya*, 190.

67. Sayyid Qutb, *al-ʿAdala al-Ijtimāʿiyya*, 113; Shīshāni, *Ḥuqūq al-Insān*, 431; Sibāʿi, *al-Takāful al-Ijtimāʿi*, 150.

68. Khafīf, *al-Milkiyya fi'l-Sharīʿa*, 321–22.

69. Cf. Niʿmat Mashhur, *'al-Iqṭāʿ' Mawsuʿa al-Mafāhīm al-Islamiyya*, 81–82.

70. Layish, 'Saudi Arabian Legal Reform,' 287.

71. *Id.*, 288.

72. *Id.*, 287.

73. *Id.*, 402.

74. Further details on *zakāh* can be found in a separate volume of this work entitled *Rights to Education, Work and Welfare in Islam* (forthcoming), especially in the last chapter.

75. Al-Khafīf, *al-Milkiyya fi'l-Sharīʿa*, 119; Ṭubliyya, *al-Islam wa Ḥuqūq al-Insān*, 421.

76.   Zuhaylī, *al-Fiqh al-Islāmī*, vol. V, 521 ff; Khafif, *al-Milkiyya*, 100; Badawi, *Daʿāʾim*, 329.

77.   Abū Dāwūd, *Sunan Abū Dāwūd*, II, 283; Zuhaylī, *al-Fiqh al-Islāmī*, vol. V, 519.

78.   Zuhaylī, *al-Fiqh al-Islāmī*, vol. V, 520.

79.   *Id.*, IV, 64.

80.   Wāfi, *Huqūq al-Insān*, 71.

81.   Cf. The *Mejelle*, Eng. Trans. C.S. Tyser at pp. 194–195. There are several articles on this, including Art. 1200, which reads that: Excessive damage in whatever way it may be caused is to be removed.

82.   See for a discussion Mahmassani, *Muqaddima*, 197 ff.

83.   Wahba al-Zuhaylī, *al-Fiqh al-Islāmī*, vol. V, 521; Khafif, *al-Milkiyya fi'l-Sharīʿa*, 122.

84.   *Id.*, V, 522; Khafif, *al-Milkiyya fi'l-Sharīʿa*, 121–22.

85.   Khafif, *al-Milkiyya fi'l-Sharīʿa*, 120.

86.   Muslim, *Mukhtasar Sahīh Muslim*, 474, *hadīth* no. 1780.

87.   Muslim, *Mukhtasar Sahīh Muslim*, 16, *hadīth* no. 32.

88.   Khafif, *al-Milkiyya fi'l-Sharīʿa*, 125; Tubliyya, *al-Islam wa Huqūq*, 421.

89.   Khafif, *al-Milkiyya fi'l-Sharīʿa*, 124.

90.   Id., 125.

91.   Al-Ghazālī, *Mustasfa*, I, 40.

92.   Abū Yūsuf, *Kitab al-Kharāj*, 65; Zuhaylī, *Haqq al-Hurriyya*, 197.

93.   Al-Shātibi, *Muwāfaqāt*, II, 350; al-Khafif, *al-Milkiyya fi'l-Sharīʿa*, 115; Badawi, *Daʿāʾim*, 324, 335; al-Sibāʿi, *Ishtirākiyya*, 100.

94.   Al-Khafif, *al-Milkiyya fi'l-Sharīʿa*, 115.

95.   Al-Shātibi, *Muwāfaqāt*, II, 350; Badawi, *Daʿāʾim*, 324, 335; al-Sibāʿi, *Ishtirākiyya*, 100.

96.   Bukhārī, *Mukhtasar Sahīh al-Bukhārī*, 95, *hadīth* 99; Abū Dāwūd, *Sunan*, ed., al-Bughā', 444, *hadīth* 3083.

97.   See for details Kamali' *Principles of Islamic Jurisprudence*, 350f.

98.   Al-Sibāʿi, *al-Takāful al-Ijtimāʿi*, 164.

99.   Cf. Mutawalli, *Mabādi Nizām al-Hukm* (1966 edn.), 773; al-Sibāʿi *al-Takāful al-Ijtimāʿi*, 164.

100.   Al-Sibāʿi *al-Takāful al-Ijtimāʿi*, 165.

101.   Al-ʿĪlī, *Hurriyyāt*, 542; al-Sibāʿi *al-Takāful*, 161; Shīshāni, *Huqūq al-Insān*, 415; Zuhaylī, *Haqq al-Hurriyya*, 196.

102.   Zuhaylī, *Haqq al-Hurriyya*, 196.

103.   Academy of Islamic Research resolution quoted in al-ʿĪlī, *Hurriyyāt*, 525.

104.   ʿAli al-Khafif, *al-Milkiyyah fi'l-Sharīʿa*, 106; Tubliyya, *al-Islām wa Huqūq al-Insān*, 422, al-Sibāʿi *al-Takāful al-Ijtimāʿi*, 161.

105. Zuḥaylī, *Ḥaqq al-Ḥurriyya*, 197.

106. Cf. Badawi, *Daʿā'im*, 323.

107. Muslim, *Mukhtaṣar Ṣaḥīḥ Muslim*, 251, *ḥadīth* 943.

108. Al-Shawkānī, *Nayl al-Awṭār*, V, 249.

109. Al-Shawkānī, *Nayl al-Awṭār*, V, 249.

110. Cf. Ibn Taymiyya, *al-Ḥisba*, 26; Ibn Qayyim al-Jawziyya, *al-Ṭuruq al-Ḥukmiyya*, p. 244; Khafīf, *al-Milkiyya*, 107; Shīshānī, *Ḥuqūq al-Insān*, 440.

111. Cf. Zuḥaylī, *Ḥaqq al-Ḥurriyya*, 197–98.

112. Al-Tabrīzī, *Mishkāt*, vol. II, *ḥadīth* 2944.

113. Al-Kāsāni, *Badā'iʿ*, VI, 192; al-ʿIli, *Ḥurriyyāt*, 517; Zuḥaylī has noted in his *al-Fiqh al-Islāmī* (vol. IV, 71), however, that this is a statement of the caliph 'Umar b. al-Khaṭṭāb.

114. Abū Yūsuf, *Kitāb al-Kharāj*, 73; see also Badawi, *Daʿā'im*, 323; Shīshāni, *Ḥuqūq al-Insān*, 435.

115. Hasanuz Zaman, *Economic Functions*, 33.

116. Muslim, *Mukhtaṣar Ṣaḥīḥ Muslim*, 256, *ḥadīth* 968.

117. Ibn Maja, *Sunan*, *ḥadīth* no. 2340.

118. Al-Shawkānī, *Nayl al-Awṭār*, V. 280; al-ʿIlī, *al-Ḥurriyyāt*, 518; Zuḥaylī, *al-Fiqh al-Islāmī*, vol. IV, 76.

119. Cf. Wāfi, *Ḥimāyah al-Islām*, 69.

120. Abu Zahrah, *Ibn Taymiyya*, 137; Wāfi, *Ḥimāyah al-Islām*, 76.

121. Cf. Abn Yūsuf, *Kitab al-Kharāj*, 14, 85; Khallāf, *al-Siyāsa*, 108; Kamali, 'Limits of Power,' 343.

Bibliography

ʿAbd Allāh, ʿAbd al-Ghanī Basyūnī, *Naẓariyyat al-Dawla fi'l-Islām*, Beirut: al-Dār al-Jamiʿiyyah, 1986.

Abū Dāwūd, *Sunan Abū Dāwūd*, ed. Muṣṭafā Dib al-Bugha, Damascus: Dār al-ʿUlūm al-Insāniyyah, 1416/1995. I have also used the Eng. Trans. of this work by Aḥmad Ḥasan, 3 vols., Lahore: Ashraf Press., 1984.

Abū Ḥabīb, Saʿdī, *Dirāsah fi Minhāj al-Islām al-Siyāsī*, Beirut: Mu'assasat al-Risālah, 1406/1985.

Abū ʿĪd, ʿArif Khalīl, *Wazifat al-Ḥakim fi'l-Sharīʿat al-Islāmiyyah*, Kuwait: Dār al-Arqam: 1985.

Abū ʿUbayd, al-Qāsim b. Salām, *Kitāb al-Amwāl*, ed. Muḥammad Ḥāmid al-Faqī, Riyad; Maṭbaʿat ʿAbd al-Laṭīf Ḥijāzī, 1353 AH. I have also used the Eng. Trans. of this work by Noor Mohammad Ghiffari, *The Book of Finance*, Islamabad, Pakistan Hijra Council, 1411/1991.

Abū Yūsuf, Yaʿqūb b. Ibrāhīm, *Kitāb al-Kharāj*, 5th edn., Cairo: al-Maṭbaʿah al-Salafiyyah, 1396 AH.

Abū Zahrah, Muḥammad, *Ibn Taymiyya*, Cairo: Dār al-Fikr al-ʿArabī, 1952.

——, *al-Jarīmah wa'l-ʿUqūbah fi'l-Fiqh al-Islāmī*, Cairo: Dār al-Fikr al-ʿArabī, n.d.

——, *al-Mujtamaʿ al-Insānī fi-Ẓill al-Islām*. 2nd ed. Jeddah: Dār al-Suʿūdiyyah, 1401/1981.

——, *Tanẓīm al-Islām li'l-Mujtamaʿ*, Cairo: Dār al-Fikr al-ʿArabī, 1385/1965.

al-ʿAbūdī, Muḥsin, *al-Ḥurriyat al-Ijtimāʿiyyah Bayn al-Nuẓūm al-Muʿāṣirah wa'l-Fikr al-Siyāsī al-Islāmī,* Cairo: Dār al-Nahḍah al-ʿArabiyyah, 1410/1990.

—, *Ra'is al-Dawla Bayn al-Nuzūm al-Muʿāṣir wa'l-Fikr al-Siyāsī al-Islāmī,* Cairo: Dār al-Nahḍah al-ʿArabiyyah, 1410/1990.

Affendi, ʿAbd al-Wahhāb el, "ʾIʿādat al-Naẓar fi-Mafhūm al-Taqlidī li'l-Jamaʿa al-Siyāsiyyah fi'l-Islām: Muslim am Muwatin.', *al-Mustaqbal al-ʿArabī* 22, no. 264 (February 2001), 144-159.

ʿAfifi, Muḥammad al-Ṣādiq, *al-Mujtamaʿ al-Islāmī wa Ḥuquq al-Insān,* Cairo: Idārat al-Sahafa wa'l-Nashr bi-Rabita al-ʿĀlam al-Islāmī, 1407/1987.

Aḥmad, Fu'ād ʿAbd al-Munʿim, *Uṣūl Niẓām al-Ḥukm fi'l-Islām,* Alexandria (Egypt): Mu'assasat Shabāb al-Jāmiʿah, 1991/1411.

Ahmad, Waqar & Charles Husband, 'Religious Identity, Citizenship and Welfare: the Case of Muslims in Britain.', *The American Journal of Islamic Social Sciences* 10 (1993).

ʿAjlānī, Muḥammad Munīr, *ʿAbqariyyāt al-Islām fī Uṣūl al-Ḥukm,* Beirut: Dār al-Nafā'is, 1405/1985.

ʿAlī, ʿAbd al-Jalīl, *Mabda' al-Mashru'iyyah fī Niẓām al-Islāmī wa'l-Anzima al-Qanūniyyah al-Muʿāṣirah, Darāsah Muqārinah,* Cairo: ʿĀlam al-Kutub, 1984.

ʿAlī, Muḥammad Kurd, *Al-Islām wa'l-Ḥaḍara al-ʿArabiyyah.* 2nd edn. Cairo: Majmaʿ Lajnat al-Ta'līf wa'l-Tarjama wa'l-Nashr, 1959.

al-Alūsī, Shihāb al-Dīn Maḥmūd, *Rūḥ al-Maʿānī fī Tafsīr al-Qur'ān al-ʿAẓīm,* Beirut: Dār Iḥyā' al-Turāth al-ʿArabī, n.d.

al-ʿAlwānī, Ṭāhā Jābir, 'The Rights of the Accused in Islam.', *The American Journal of Islamic Social Science* 11 (1994), 348-365.

al-Āmidī, Sayf al-Dīn, *al-Iḥkām fī Uṣūl al-Aḥkām,* 4 vols., ed. ʿAbd al-Razzāq ʿAfifi, 2nd edn., Beirut: al-Maktab al-Islāmī, 1402/1982.

Amīn, Bakri Shaykh, *Adab al-Ḥadīth al-Nabāwī.* 4th edn. Beirut: Dār al-Shurūq, 1399/1979.

Anwarullah, *The Criminal Law of Islam.* Kuala Lumpur: A.S. Nordeen, 1997.

al-ʿAqqad, 'Abbas Mahmud, *ʿAbqariyāt ʿUmar,* Cairo: Kitāb al-Hilāl, 1943.

Asad, Muḥammad, *Principles of State and Government in Islam,* Berkeley: University of California Press, 1966.

—, *The Message of the Qur'an.* Gibraltar: Dār al-Andalus, 1980.

El-Awa, M. Salim, *Punishment in Islamic Law.* Indianapolis: American Trust Publications, 1982.

Awad, M. Awad, 'The Rights of the Accused under Islamic Criminal Procedure', in M. Cherif Bassiouni (ed.), *The Islamic Criminal Justice System*, London and New York: Oceana Publications, 1982.

ʿAwdah, ʿAbd al-Qādir, *al-Tashrīʿ al-Jināʾī al-Islāmī Muqarinan bi'l-Qanūn al-Wadʾi*. 2 vols., Cairo: Maktabah Wahba, 1401/1981.

—, *al-Mawsūʿa al-ʿAsriyyah fi'l-Fiqh al-Jināʾī al-Islāmī*, (being a commentary on ʿAwdah's *al-Tashrīʿ al-Jināʾī*), Commentary and annotations by Ayatullāh al-Syed Ismāʿīl al-Ṣadr and Tawfīq al-Shāwī, 4 vols., Cairo: Dār al-Shurūq, 1421/2001.

al-Badawī, Ismāʿīl, *Daʿāʾim al-Ḥukm fi'l-Sharīʿah al-Islāmiyyah wa'l-Nuẓūm al-Dustūriyyah al-Muʿāṣirah*, Cairo: Dār al-Fikr al-ʿArabī, 1400/1980.

al-Baghawī, Abū Muḥammad al-Ḥusayn b. Masʿūd, *Sharḥ as-Sunna*, Damascus: al-Maktab al-Islāmī, 1974.

al-Bahī, Muḥammad, *al-Dīn wa'l-Dawlah min Tawjīhāt al-Qurʾān al-Karīm*, Beirut: Dār al-Fikr, 1391/1971.

al-Baʾlī, ʿAbd al-Ḥāmid Mahmūd, *al-Milkiyyah wa-Dawabituhā fi'l-Islām: Dirāsah Muqāranah māʾ Aḥdath al-Tatbiqat al-ʿIlmiyyah al-Muʿāṣira*, Cairo: Maktabah Wahbah, 1405/1985.

Bahnasī, Aḥmad Fatḥī, *Naẓariyyat al-Ithbāt*, Cairo: Sharikat al-ʿArabīyyah li'l-Ṭibāʿah, 1962.

al-Bajī, Abū al-Walid Sulaymān b. Khalaf, *al-Muntaqā Sharḥ Muwaṭṭaʾ Mālik*, Cairo: Maṭbaʿah al-Saʿadah, 1332 AH.

al-Bayatī, Munīr Ḥamid, *Al-Niẓām al-Siyāsī al-Islāmī Muqarinan bi'l-Dawala al-Qanūniyyah*, n.p., Dār al-Bashir li'l-Nashr wa'l-Tawzīʿ, n.d.

al-Bayhaqī, Aḥmad b. Ḥusayn b. ʿAlī, *Al-Sunan al-Kubrā*, Beirut: Dār al-Fikr, n.d.

Bassiouni, Cherif M. (ed.), *The Islamic Criminal Justice System*, London & New York: Oceana Publications, 1982.

Beauchamp, Tom L & Childress, J. F., *Principles of Biomedical Ethics*, New York: Oxford University Press, 1979.

al-Buhutī, Manṣūr b. Yūnus al-Ḥanbalī, *Kashshaf al-Qannaʾ ʿala Matn al-Iqnaʾ*, ed. Hilāl Muṣṭafā Hilāl, Beirut: Dār al-Fikr li'l-Ṭibāʿah wa'l-Nashr, 1402/1982.

Bukhārī, Muḥammad b. Ismāʿīl, *Saḥīḥ al-Bukhārī*, Eng. trans. Muḥammad Muḥsin Khan, 9 vols., Lahore: Kazi Publications, 1979.

al-Dughmī, Muḥammad Rākān, *Ḥimāyat al-Ḥayāt al-Khāṣṣah fi'l-Sharīʿa al-Islāmiyyah*, Cairo: Dār al-Salām li'l-Ṭibāʿah wa'l-Nashr, 1405/1985.

—, *Al-Tajassus wa-Aḥkāmuhu fī'l-Sharīʿah al-Islāmiyyah,* 2nd edn., Cairo: Dār al-Salām li'l-Ṭibāʿah wa'l-Nashr, 1406/1985.

Dusūqī, Shams al-Dīn Muḥammad ʿArafa, *Ḥashiyat al-Dusūqī ʿalā al-Sharḥ al-Kabīr li-Abī Barakat Sīdī Aḥmad al-Dardir,* Cairo: ʿĪsā al-Bābī al-Ḥalabī, n.d.

Enayat, Hamid, *Modern Islamic Political Thought,* London: Macmillan Press Ltd, 1982.

al-Farrāʾ, Abū Yaʿlā Muḥammad ibn al-Ḥusayn, *al-Aḥkām al-Sulṭāniyyah,* Cairo: Muṣṭafā al-Bābī al-Ḥalabī, 1357 AH.

al-Ghazālī, Abū Ḥāmid Muḥammad, *Iḥyāʾ ʿUlūm al-Dīn,* Cairo: ʿĪsā al-Bābī al-Ḥalabī, 1957, with a commentary on it by Ḥāfiẓ Zayn al-Dīn al-ʿIraqī entitiled *al-Mughnī ʿan Ḥaml al-Asfār fī'l-Asfār fī Takhrīj mā fī'l-Iḥyāʾ min al-Akhbār.*

—, *al-Mustaṣfa min ʿIlm al-Uṣūl,* Beirut: Dār Iḥyāʾ Turāth al-ʿArabī, n.d.

—, *Shifāʾ al-Ghalīl fī Bayān al-Shabah wa'l-Mukhil wa-Masalik al-Taʾlīl,* Beirut: Dār al-Kutub al-ʿIlmiyyah, 1999/1420.

Ghazāwī, Muḥammad Salim, *al-Ḥurriyat al-ʿĀmmah fī'l-Islām,* Alexandria(Egypt): Muʾassasah Shaba al-Jāmiʿah, n.d.

Hamidullah, Muḥammad, *Muslim Conduct of State,* 3rd edn., Lahore: Shah Muḥammad Ashraf, 1953.

al-Ḥanbali, Ibn Rajab, *Al-Qawāʿid,* Beirut: Dār al-Kutub al-ʿIlmiyah.

al-Haythamī, Nūr al-Dīn ʿAlī b. Abū Bakr b. Ḥajar, *Majmaʿ al-Zawāʾid wa Manbaʾ al-Fawāʾid,* Cairo: Maktabat al-Quds, 1352 AH.

Hepple, B.A and M.H. Matthews, *Tort: Cases and Materials,* London: Butterworths, 1974.

al-Hewesh, Mohammad ibn Ibrahim, 'Murder and Homicide in Islamic Criminal Law: Textual Foundations.', in Mahmood, *Criminal Law,* pp. 151–164.

Ibn ʿĀbidīn, Muḥammad Amīn, *Ḥāshiyah Radd al-Mukhtār ʿalā Durr al-Mukhtār* (known as *Ḥāshiyah Ibn ʿĀbidīn*), Cairo: Dār al-Fikr, 1399/1979; and its 2nd edn., Cairo: Muṣṭafā al-Bābī al-Ḥalabī, 1386/1966.

Ibn Farḥūn, Burhān al-Dīn Ibrāhīm b. ʿAlī, *Tabṣirat al-Ḥukkām fī Uṣūl al-Aqḍiyah wa Manāhij al-Aḥkām,* ed. Ṭāhā ʿAbd al-Raʾūf Saʿd, Cairo: Maktabat al-Kulliyyāt al-Azhariyyāt, 1406/1986.

Ibn Ḥanbal, Imam Aḥmad, *Musnad,* 6 vols., Cairo: al-Maṭbaʿah al-Munayminah, n.d.

Ibn Ḥazm, Muḥammad b. ʿAlī b. Aḥmad b. Saʿīd al-Ẓāhirī, *Al-Muḥallā,* ed. Aḥmad M. Shākir, Cairo: Maṭbaʿah al-Nahḍa, 1347 AH. Also Beirut, Dār al-Kutub al-ʿIlmiyyah, 1408/1988.

Ibn al-Humam, Kamāl al-Dīn Muḥammad b. ʿAbd al-Wāḥid, *Fatḥ al-Qadīr Sharḥ al-Hidāya,* 8 vols., Cairo: al-Maṭbaʿah al-Amiriyyah, 1315 AH.

Ibn Juzay, al-Kalbī, *Qawānin al-Aḥkām al-Sharʿiyyah,* Cairo: ʿĀlam al-Fikr, 1975.

Ibn Kathīr, Ḥāfiẓ Abuʾl-Fidā Ismāʿīl, *Tafsīr al-Qurʾān al-ʿAẓīm* (also known as *Tafsīr Ibn Kathīr*), Cairo: Dār al-Shaʿb, 1393/1973.

Ibn Mājah, Muḥammad b. Yazīd al-Qazwīnī, *Sunan Ibn Mājah,* Istanbul: Cagli Yayinlari, 1401/1981.

Ibn al-Mubārak, Jamīl, *Naẓariyyah al-Ḍarūra al-Sharʿiyyah,* al-Mansura (Egypt): Dār al-Wafa liʾl-Ṭabaʿah waʾl-Nashr, 1988.

Ibn Nujaym, Zayn al-ʿĀbidīn b. Ibrāhīm, *Baḥr al-Rāʾiq Sharḥ Kanz al-Daqāʾiq,* 8 vols., Cairo, 1333.

Ibn Qudāmah, Muwaffaq al-Dīn Abū Muḥammad ʿAbd Allāh, *al-Mughnī,* Cairo: Maṭbaʿat al-Manār, 1367 AH.

Ibn Saʿd, Muḥammad b. Maniʾ, *al-Tabaqāt al-Kubrā,* Beirut: Dār al-Sadir, 1398/1978.

Ibn Taymiyyah, Taqī al-Dīn Aḥmad, *al-Ḥisbah fīʾl-Islām,* Cairo: al-Maṭbaʿah al-Salafiyyah, 1387 AH.

—, *Majmūʿ Fatāwā Shaykh al-Islām Aḥmad Ibn Taymiyyah,* ed. ʿAbd al-Raḥmān b. Qāsim, Riyad: Dār al-Buhuth al-ʿIlmiyyah, 1398 AH.

—, *Naẓariyyāt al-ʿAqd,* Beirut: Dār al-Maʿrifah, 1317 AH.

—, *al-Siyāsah al-Sharʿiyyah fī Iṣlāḥ al-Rāʿī waʾl-Rāʿiyyah,* ed. Abd al-Raḥmān b. Qāsim, Beirut: Muʾassasat al-Risālah, 1398 AH.

Ibrahim, Amad b. Mohamed, *The Administration of Islamic Law in Malaysia,* Kuala Lumpur: Institute of Islamic Understanding, Malaysia, 2000.

al-ʿĪlī, ʿAbd al-Ḥakīm Ḥasan, *al-Ḥurriyyāt al-ʿĀmmah,* Cairo: Dār al-Fikr, 1403/1983.

al-Iṣfahānī, al-Raghib Abuʾl-Qāsim al-Ḥusayn ibn Muḥammad, *al-Mufradat fī Gharib al-Qurʾān,* Cairo: Muṣṭafā al-Bābī al-Ḥalabī, 1961.

Islam, Foridul, ʿAbortion and Euthanasia.ʾ, in The Federation of Students Islamic Societies in U.K and Ireland, *Essays on Islam,* Leicestershire: The Islamic Foundation, 1995, pp. 195–209.

Islamic Fiqh Academy (India), *Important Fiqh Decisions,* New Delhi, 2001.

al-Jābirī, Muḥammad ʿĀbid, *Al-Dimiqratiyyah wa Ḥuqūq al-Insān,* Lebanon: Markaz Darāsat al-Waḥdah al-ʿArabiyyah, 1994.

al-Jawziyya, Ibn Qayyim, *Iʿlām al-Muwaqqiʿīn ʿan Rabb al-ʿĀlamīn*, ed. Muḥammad Munīr al-Dimashqī, Cairo: Idārat al-Ṭibāʿah al-Munīriyyah, n.d. Also Cairo: Maktabah al-Kulliyāt al-Azhariyyah, 1968.

—, *al-Ṭuruq al-Ḥukmiyyah fi'l-Siyāsah al-Sharʿiyyah*, ed. Muḥammad Jamīl Ghāzī, Jeddah: Maṭbaʿat al-Madanī, n.d. See also the Cairo edn. by al-Mu'assasat al-ʿArabiyyah, 1380/1961.

—, *Zād al-Maʿād fī Hudā Khayr al-ʿIbād*, Makka: Maṭbaʿah al-Makkiyyah, n.d.

al-Jundī, Ḥusnī, *Ḍamānāt Ḥurmat al-Ḥayāt al-Khāṣṣah fi'l-Islām*, Cairo: Dār al-Nahḍa al-ʿArabiyyah, 1413/1993.

Kamali, Mohammad Hashim, *The Dignity of Man: An Islamic Perspective*, Cambridge: Islamic Texts Society, 2002.

—, *Freedom of Expression in Islam*, Cambridge: Islamic Texts Society, 1997 & Kuala Lumpur: Ilmiah Publishers, 1998.

—, *Principles of Islamic Jurisprudence*, revised edition, Cambridge: The Islamic Texts Society, 1991; Kuala Lumpur: Ilmiah Publishers, 1998.

—, 'The Limits of Power in an Islamic State.' *Islamic Studies* 28 (1989), 323-353.

—, '*Siyāsah Sharʿiyyah* or the Policies of Islamic Government.', *The American Journal of Islamic Social Science* 6 (1989), 59-81.

Kamar, Fahda Nur Ahmad, 'Exigencies and Right to Privacy.', in *Law Majallah* (2001), 33ff.

al-Kāsānī, ʿAlā al-Dīn, *Badā'iʿ al-Ṣanā'iʿ fī Tartīb al-Sharā'ī*, Cairo: Maṭbaʿat al-Istiqāmah, 1956.

al-Khafīf, Shaykh ʿAlī, *al-Milkiyyah fi'l-Sharīʿah al-Islāmiyyah maʿ al-Muqarana bi'l-Sharāʿī al-Wad'iyyah*, Beirut: Dār al-Nahḍah al-ʿArabiyyah, 1990.

Khallāf, ʿAbd al-Wahhāb, *ʿIlm Uṣūl al-Fiqh*, 12th edn., Kuwait: Dār al-Qalam, 1398/1978.

—, *al-Siyāsa al-Sharʿiyyah*, Cairo: al-Maktabah al-Salafiyyah, 1350 AH.

al-Khulī, Muḥammad b. ʿAbd al-ʿAzīz, *al-Adab al-Nabāwī*, Beirut: Dār al-Maʿrifah, n.d.

al-Kilānī, *ʿUqubat al-iʿdam fī al-sharīʿah al-Islāmiyah wa-al-Qanūn al-Miṣrī: dirāsah muqaranah*, Al-Iskandariyah: Munsha'at al-Maʿārif, 1996.

Layish, Aharon, 'Saudi Arabian Legal Reform as a Mechanism to Moderate Wahhabi Doctrine.', *The American Journal of Oriental Studies* 107: 2 (1987), 279-293.

Madkūr, Muḥammad Salām, *al-Janin wa'l-Aḥkām al-Mutaʿallaqa bihi fi'l-Fiqh al-Islāmī,* Cairo: Dār al-Nahḍah al-ʿArabiyyah, 1389/1969.

—, *al-Qaḍā' fi'l-Islām,* Cairo: Dār al-Nahḍah al-ʿArabiyyah, 1964.

al-Mahdī, Ṣadiq, *al-ʿUqubat al-Sharʿiyyah wa-Mawāqifuha min al-Niẓām al-Ijtimāʿī al-Islāmī,* Cairo: Manshurat al-ʿAṣr al-Ḥadīth, 1983.

Maḥmaṣṣānī, Subḥī Rajab, *Arkān Ḥuqūq al-Insān fi'l-Islām,* Beirut: Dār al-ʿIlm li'l-Malāyīn, 1979.

—, *al-Awzāʿī wa Ta'alimuh al-Qanūniyyah wa'l-Insāniyyah,* Beirut: Dār al-ʿIlm li'l-Malāyīn, 1978.

—, *Muqaddima fī Iḥyā' ʿUlūm al-Sharʿiyyah,* Beirut: Dār al-ʿIlm li'l-Malāyīn, 1962.

Mahmood, Tahir (ed.), *Criminal Law in Islam and the Muslim World: A Comparative Perspective,* Delhi: Institute of Objective Studies, 1996.

—, 'Criminal Procedure at the Shari'ah Law.' in Tahir Mahmood (ed.), *Criminal Law in Islam and the Modern World,* Delhi: Institute of Objective Studies, 1996.

Mālik b. Anas al-Asbahī, *al-Muwaṭṭa',* ed. Muḥammad Fu'ād ʿAbd al-Bāqī, Cairo: ʿĪsā al-Bābī al-Ḥalabī, n.d.

al-Maqdisī, Shams al-Dīn ʿAbd Allāh b. Maflah al-Ḥanbalī, *al-Ādāb al-Sharʿiyyah wa'l-Minaḥ al-Marʿiyyah,* Cairo: Maṭbaʿat al-Manār, 1348 AH.

Mashhūr, Niʿmat. 'al-Iqta'', in Mahmūd Ḥamdi Zaqzuq (ed.), *Mawsūʿah al-Mafāhim al-Islāmiyyah al-ʿAmmah,* Cairo: Ministry of Awqāf, 1421/2000.

Masoodi, Saqlain & Lalita Dhar, 'Euthanasia at Western and Islamic Legal systems: Trends and Developments.', *Islam and the Modern Age* XVI & XVI (1995 & 1996), 1–36.

al-Māwardī, Abū'l-Ḥasan, *Kitāb al-Ahkām al-Sulṭāniyyah,* 2nd edn., Cairo: Muṣṭafā al-Bābī al-Ḥalabī, 1386 AH.

Mawdūdī, Sayyid Abu'l-Aʿla, *Human Rights in Islam,* Leicester: The Islamic Foundation, 1976.

—, *Mas'alah Milkiyyat al-Arḍ fi'l-Islām,* Damascus: al-Maṭbaʿah al-Ta'awuniyyah, 1376/1957.

The Mejelle: Being an English Translation of Majallah el-Akkam el-Adliya, trans. C.R. Tyser, reprint, Lahore: Law Publishing Co., 1967.

Meyers, David W., *The Human Body and The Law,* 2nd edn., Edinburgh: Edinburgh University press, 1990.

Muḥammad, ʿIwad, *Darasat fi'l-Fiqh al-Jinā'ī al-Islāmī,* n.p., Dār al-Maṭbuʿat al-Jamiʿiyyah, n.d.

al-Mundhirī, Zakī al-Dīn ʿAbd al-ʿAẓīm, *al-Targhīb wa'l-Tarhīb,* 2 vols., Cairo: Muṣṭafā al-Bābī al-Ḥalabī, 1373/1954.

Mūsā, Muḥammad Yūsuf, *al-Amwāl wa-Naẓariyyat al-ʿAqd fi'l-Fiqh al-Islāmī ma' Madkhal li-Dirāsat al-Fiqh wa-Falsafatih,* Cairo: Dār al-Kitāb al-ʿArabī, 1958.

—, *al-Fiqh al-Islāmī: Madkhal li-Dirāsatih, Niẓām al-Muʿamalat Fih,* Cairo: Maṭabiʿ Dār al-Kitāb al-ʿArabī, 1374 AH.

al-Musaylihi, Muḥammad al-Ḥusaynī, *Ḥuqūq al-Insān Bayn al-Sharīʿah al-Islāmiyyah wa'l-Qanūn al-Duwalī,* Cairo: Dār al-Nahḍa al-ʿArabiyyah, 1988.

Muslim, Ibn Ḥajjāj al-Nīshāpūrī, *Mukhtaṣar Saḥīḥ Muslim,* edr. Muḥammad Nāṣir al-Dīn al-Albānī, 2nd edn., Beirut: Dār al-Maktab al-Islāmī, 1404/1984.

Mutawallī, ʿAbd al-Ḥamīd, *Mabādī' Niẓām al-Ḥukm fi'l-Islām,* Alexandria (Egypt): Mansha'āt al-Maʿārif, 1974.

al-Nabhān, Muḥammad Fārūq, *Niẓām al-Ḥukm fi'l-Islām,* Kuwait: Jāmiʿat al-Kuwait, 1974.

al-Nawawī, Muḥyī al-Dīn Abī Zakariyā Yaḥyā, *Riyāḍ al-Ṣāliḥīn,* 2nd edn, by Muḥammad Nāsir al-Dīn al-Albānī, Beirut: Dār al-Maktab al-Islāmī, 1404/1984.

Niazi, Liaquat Ali Khan, *Islamic Law of Torts,* Lahore(Pakistan): Dayal Singh Research Cell, 1988.

al-Nīshāpūrī, Abū ʿAbd Allāh al-Ḥakim, *Al-Mustadrak ʿalā'l-Saḥiḥayn,* Aleppo (Syria): Maktab al-Maṭbuʿat al-Islāmiyyah, n.d.

Osborn, D.L., *A Concise Law Dictionary,* 5th edn., London: Sweet & Maxwell, 1964.

Parker, Herbert, *The Limits of the Criminal Sanction,* Stanford: Stanford University Press, 1969.

al-Qaraḍāwī, Yūsuf, *al-Halāl wa'l-Ḥarām fi'l-Islām,* 4th edn., Cairo: Maktabah Wahbah, 1980.

—, *al-Ijtihād al-Muʿāṣir. Bayn al-Indibāt wa'l-Infirāt,* 3rd edn., Beirut: al-Maktab al-Islāmī, 1418/1998.

—, *Min Hudā al-Islām: Fatāwā Muʿāṣira,* 2 vols., Cairo: Dār al-Wafa li'l-Ṭibāʿah wa'l-Nashr, 1993.

—, *al-Shaykh al-Ghazālī Kamā ʿAraftuhu Riḥlata Niṣf Qarn,* Cairo: Dār al-Wafa li'l-Ṭibāʿah wa'l-Nashr wa'l-Tawzīʿ, 1997.

al-Qarāfī, Shihāb al-Dīn, *Kitāb al-Furūq,* Cairo: Maṭbaʿah Dār Iḥyā' al-Kutub al-ʿArabiyyah, 1346 AH.

Qāsim, Yūsuf, *Naẓariyyat al-Difa' al-Sharʿī fi'l-Fiqh al-Jinā'ī al-Islāmī wa'l-Qanūn al-Janā'ī al-Wad'ī,* Cairo: Dār al-Nahḍa al-ʿArabīyya, 1399/1979.

al-Qurshī, Muḥammad ibn Aḥmad, *Maʿalim al-Qurba fi Aḥkām al-Hisbah,* Cambridge edn., Maṭbaʿah Dār al-Funun, 1937.

al-Qurṭubī, Abū ʿAbd Allāh Muḥammad, *al-Jāmiʿ li-Aḥkām al-Qurʾān* (known as *Tafsīr al-Qurṭubī*), Cairo: Maṭbaʿah Dār al-Kutub, 1387/1967.

Quṭb, Sayyid, *al-ʿAdalat al-Ijtimaʿiyyah fiʾl-Islām*, 4th edn., Cairo: ʿĪsā al-Bābī al-Ḥalabī, 1373/1954.

—, *Fī Ẕilāl al-Qurʾān*, Beirut: Dār al-Shuruq, 1397/1977. Also 4th edn., Beirut: Dār al-ʿArabīyyah, n.d.

Rahman, Tanzilur, *Islamization of Law—Pakistan Law,* Karachi (Pakistan): Hamadard Academy, 1978.

al-Ramlī, Shams al-Dīn b. Shihāb Aḥmad, *Nihāyat al-Muhtaj ilā Sharḥ al-Minhaj,* Cairo: ʿĪsā al-Bābī al-Ḥalabī, 1357/1938.

al-Ṣābūnī, Muḥammad ʿAlī, *Safwat al-Tafāsir,* Jakarta (Indonesia): Dār al-Kutub al-Islāmiyyah, n.d.

—, *Mukhtaṣar Tafsīr Ibn Kathīr,* Beirut: Dār al-Qurʾān, 1981.

Sahnūn, al-Tanukhī b. Saʿīd, *al-Mudawwana al-Kubrā liʾl-Imām Mālik b. Anas al-Asbahī,* Cairo: al-Maṭbaʿah al-Khayriyyah, 1324 AH.

al-Sakhawī, Muḥammad ibn Abd al-Raḥmān ibn Muammad Shams al-Dīn, *Al-Iʿlan biʾl-Tawbikh li-man dhamma ahl al-Tarīkh,* Beirut: Mauʾassasa al-Risālah, 1986.

al-Saleh, ʿThe Right of the Individual to Personal Security.ʾ, in ed. Bassiouni, *The Islamic Criminal Justice System,* 55–91.

Salmond & Heuston, *Salmond on Law of Torts,* ed. R.F.V. Heuston, London: Sweet & Maxwell, 1973.

al-Ṣanʿānī, Abū Bakr ʿAbd al Razzāq b. al-Humam, *al-Musannaf,* ed. Ḥabīb al-Raḥmān al-Aʿzamī, Beirut: Dār al-Qalam, 1392.

al-Ṣanʿānī, Muḥammad b. Ismāʿīl al-Kahlanī (known as al-Amīr, d.1182 AH), *Subul as-Salam Sharḥ Bulūgh al-Maram min Jamʿ Adillat al-Aḥkām,* 4th edn., Cairo: Muṣtafā al-Bābī al-Ḥalabī, 1379/1960.

al-Sarakhsī, Shams al-Dīn, *al-Mabsūṭ,* 32 vols., Beirut: Dār al-Maʿrifah, 1406/1986.

al-Sarbinī, Muḥammad al-Khātib, *Mughnī al-Muḥtaj ilā Mcʿrifat al-Alfāẕ al-Minhāj,* Beirut: Dār al-Fikr, n.d.

Sarip Adul, *Kitmān al-Sirr wa Ifshāʾuh fiʾl-Fiqh al-Islāmī,* Amman: Dār al-Nafāʾis liʾl-Nashr waʾl-Tawzīʿ, 1418/1997.

Shāfiʿī, Muḥammad ibn Idrīs, *Kitāb al-Umm,* Bulāq: al-Maṭbaʿah al-Kubrā, 1321/1940.

Shaḥrūr, Muḥammad, *Naḥw Uṣūl Jadīdah liʾl-Fiqh al-Islāmī: Fiqh al-Marʾa,* Damascus: al-Ahali liʾl-Ṭibāʿah waʾl-Tawzīʿ waʾl-Nashr, 2000.

Shaltūt, Maḥmūd, *al-Islām, ʿAqīdah wa Sharīʿah,* Kuwait: Maṭābiʿ Dār al-Qalam, n.d.

—, *al-Fatāwā: Dirāsah li-Mushkilat al-Muslim al-Muᶜāṣir fi Ḥayatihi al-Yawmiyyah al-ᶜĀmmah,* Cairo: Maṭabiᶜ Dār al-Qalam, 1960.

—, *Tafsīr al-Qur'ān al-Karīm,* Cairo: Dār al-Qalam, 1965.

al-Shaᶜrānī, ᶜAbd al-Wahhāb, *Kitāb al-Mizān,* Cairo: al-Maṭbaᶜah al-Ḥusayniyyah, 1329 AH. I have also used Beirut ed.,Dār al-Fikr, 1401/1981.

Sharpe, Sybil, *Judicial Discretion and Criminal Investigation,* London: Sweet & Maxwell, 1998.

al-Shāṭibī, Abū Isḥāq Ibrāhīm, *al-Muwāfaqāt fi Uṣūl al-Sharīᶜah,* ed. Shaykh ᶜAbd Allāh Dirāz, Cairo: al-Maktabah al-Tijāriyyah al-Kubrā, n.d.

—, *Al-Iᶜtiṣām,* Cairo: Maṭbaᶜah al-Manar, 1332/1914, also Beirut: Dār al-Maᶜrifa, 1402.

al-Shawī, Tawfīq, *al-Mawsūᶜa al-ᶜAsriyyah* (see under ᶜAwdah).

al-Shawkānī, Yaḥyā b. ᶜAlī, *Fatḥ al-Qadīr, al-Jamiᶜ Bayn Fannay al-Riwāyah wa'l-Darāyah min ᶜIlm al-Tafsīr,* Beirut: Dār Ibn Ḥazm, 2000.

—, *Nayl al-Awṭār: Sharḥ Muntaqā al-Akhbār,* Cairo: Muṣṭafā al-Bābī al-Ḥalabī, n.d.

al-Shirāzī, Abū Isḥāq Ibrāhīm, *Muhadhdhab fi Fiqh al-Imām al-Shāfiᶜī,* 2nd edn., Beirut: Dār al-Maᶜrifah, 1379 AH.

Shishānī, ᶜAbd al-Wahhāb ᶜAbd al-ᶜAzīz, *Ḥuqūq al-Insān wa Ḥurriya-tuh al-Asasiya fi'l-Niẓām al-Islāmī wa'l-Nuẓum al-Mu'asira,* Amman: Maṭabiᶜ al-Jamᶜiyyah al-Malakiya, 1400/1980.

al-Sibāᶜī, Muṣṭafā, *Ishtirākiyyāt al-Islām,* 2nd edn., Damascus: al-Dār al-Qawmiyyah li'l-Ṭibāᶜah wa'l-Nashr, 1379/1960.

—, *al-Takāful al-Ijtimāᶜī fi'l-Islām,* Beirut: al-Maktab al-Islāmī, 1419/1998.

Siddiqui, Abia Afsar, 'Abortion and Euthanasia.', in *Essays in Islam,* pp.182-194 (cf. entry under Islam).

al-Sūlamī, ᶜIzz al-Dīn ᶜAbd al-Salām, *Qawāᶜid al-Aḥkām fi Masalih al-Anam,* Beirut: Mu'assasah al-Rayyān li'l-Ṭibāᶜah wa'l-Nashr, 1410/1990. Also Cairo: Maṭbaᶜah al-Ḥusayniya, 1934.

Suwaylim, Bandar ibn Fahd, *al-Muttaham: Muᶜāmalatuh wa Ḥuqūquh fi'l-Fiqh al-Islāmī,* Riyad: al-Markaz al-ᶜArabiyyah li'l-Dirāsāt al-Amniyyah, 1408/1978.

al-Suyūṭī, Jalāl al-Dīn, *al-Jāmiᶜ al-Ṣaghīr,* 4th edn., Cairo: Muṣṭafā al-Bābī al-Ḥalabī, 1954.

al-Tabrīzī, ᶜAbd Allāh al-Khaṭīb, *Mishkāt al-Maṣābīḥ,* ed. Muḥammad Nāṣir al-Dīn al-Albānī, 2nd edn., Beirut: al-Maktab al-Islāmī, 1399/1979.

al-Tarablusī, ʿAlā'uddīn Abū al-Ḥasan ʿAlī, *Muʿin al-Ḥukkam fimā Yutridu bayn al-Khasmayn min al-Aḥkām*, 2nd edn., Cairo: Muṣṭafā al-Bābī al-Ḥalabī.

Al-Tirmidhī, Abū ʿĪsā Muḥammad, *Sunan al-Tirmidhī*, Beirut: Dār al-Fikr, 1400/1980.

Ṭubliyah, Muḥammad al-Quṭb, *al-Islām wa Ḥuqūq al-Insān. Dirāsah Muqārinah*, 2nd edn, Cairo: Dār al-Fikr al-ʿArabī, 1404/1984.

ʿUlamā' of India, *Al-Fatāwā al-Hindiyyah* (also known as *al-Fatāwā al-ʿAlamgiriyya*), 6 vols., Cairo: al-Maṭbaʿah al-Munayminah, 1323 AH.

Umri, Jalaluddin, 'Suicide and Euthanasia: Islamic Viewpoint.', in Tahir Mahmood (ed.), *Criminal Law in Islam*.

—, *Ḥuqūq al-Insān fi'l-Islām*, 4th enhanced edn., Cairo: Dār Nahḍa Miṣr, 1387/1967. Also Cairo: Maṭbaʿah al-Risālah, n.d.

ʿUthmān, Muḥammad Fatḥī, *Ḥuqūq al-Insān Bayn al-Sharīʿah al-Islāmiyyah wa'l-Fikr al-Qānūnī al-Gharbī*, Beirut: Dār al-Shurūq, 1401/1982.

—, *al-Fikr al-Qānūnī al-Islāmī: Bayn Uṣūl al-Sharīʿah wa Turāth al-Fiqh*, Cairo: Maktabah Wahbah, n.d.

Wāfi, ʿAbd al-Wāḥid, *Ḥimāyat al-Islām li'l-Anfus wa'l-Aʿrāḍ*, Cairo: Nahḍa Miṣr, 1991.

Warren, S.D & L.D. Brandies, 'The Right to Privacy.', *Harvard Law Review* (1890), 193 ff.

Zaman, Hasanuz. S. M., *Economic Functions of an Islamic State: The Early Experience*, Leicester: The Islamic Foundation, 1991/1411.

al-Zarqā, Muṣṭafā, *Fatāwā Muṣṭafā al-Zarqā*, ed. Majd Aḥmad Makkī, Damascus: Dār al-Qalam, 1420/1999.

—, *al-Madkhal al-Fiqhī al-ʿĀmm*, 3 vols., Damascus: Dār al-Fikr, 1967.

Zuhaylī, Muḥammad, *Ḥuqūq al-Insān fi'l-Islām: Dirāsah Muqārinah maʿ al- Iʿlān al-ʿĀlamī wa'l- Iʿlān al-Islāmī li-Ḥuqūq al-Insān*, 2nd edn., Damascus & Beirut: Dār Ibn Kathīr, 1418/1997.

al-Zuhaylī, Wahbah, *al-Fiqh al-Islāmī wa Adillatuhu*, 3rd edn, 8 vols., Damascus: Dār al-Fikr, 1409/1989.

—, *Ḥaqq al-Ḥurriyyah fi'l-ʿĀlam*, Beirut: Dār al-Fikr al-Muʿāṣir, 1417/1997.

List of Periodicals
All E R (All England Law Reports).
MLJ (Malayan Law Journal).

Index

Abandoned child. See *al-laqīt*.

'Abbās Maḥmūd al-'Aqqād, 192.

'Abd Allāh b. 'Abbās, 173,

'Abd Allāh b. Mas'ūd, 189.

'Abd al-Rahman b. 'Awf

Abortion, 37–47; 'Alī b. Abī Ṭālib on, 42–43; definition of, 37; difference of opinion among *sunni* jurists on, 40–41; *diyyah* as a punishment of, 42; forced, 41; al-Ghazālī on, 40; *ghurra* (compensation), 44–45; Islamic Fiqh Academy of India on, 40; on an AIDS patient, 40; permissible conditions for, 143; punitive criteria of, 44–46; Shī'a Ja'fariyya on, 41; 'Umar b. al-Khaṭṭāb on, 42; valid grounds of, 41.

Abū Bakr, 58, 221, 189.

Abū Dāwūd, 208, 214.

Abū Dharr al-Ghifārī, 257.

Abu Mūsā al-Ash'arī, 176.

Abu Sa'īd al-Khudrī, 176.

Abū 'Ubayda b. al-Jarrāḥ, 189.

adab al-qāḍi (proper conduct of judge), 128.

Affluence, 245; Prophet on, 245.

Agency *(wakālah)*, 123–127.

akl al-māl bi'l-bāṭil (wrongful appopriation of others' properties), 248.

'Alī b. Abī Ṭālib, 13, 42–43, 83, 191.

al-Alūsī, 166.

amāna (trustworthiness), 211; confidential conversation as a token of, 211; al-Ghazālī on, 211; *ḥadīth* on, 213;

'āqilah (legal heir), 12, 19, 45.

arbāb al-bida' (theological innovation and heresy), 228; al-Ghazālī on, 228.

Arrest, see detention.

al-'Awānī, 147.

awqāf khayriyya (charitable endowment), 266.

barā'at al-dhimma al-aṣliyyah. See original non-liability.

bayyinah, 141–4; difference of opinion among jurists on, 142; as a broad criteria of judgment and decision making in court, 141; authenticity of written statement in, 143; concept of, 140; Ibn Qayyim on, 141; Qur'ān on, 141; larger scope of, 141; theological foundation of, 141.

Blood money. See *diyyah*.

Burden of proof, 98.

Charitable endowment *(waqf)*, 261.

Collective duty *(farḍ kifā'ī)* 225.

Court trial. See trial.

Confession *(iqrār)*, 135–138; children and insane precluded from, 136; differences among jurists, 136; non-transient status of, 135; of *ḥudūd* offences, 136; revocability of, 136,138; silence in, 138; sufficient detail as necessary proof in, 135; under duress, 137 (see also duress); valid conditions for, 135.

Credit loan *(dayn)*, 263.

Criminal procedure; no place for tribal councils in, 107; detention as a justifiable part of, 108–109; duration of detention, 107–109; difference of opinion among jurists on, 108–109, 110, 112–113.

D&E, 37. See under abortion and also DNC.

ḍarar fāḥish (exorbitant harm), 203, 256.

dayn (credit loan), 263.

Detention; beating in, 112–115; al-Ghazālī on, 115; differences among jurists on, 107–111; illegality of pre-trial beating, 122; non liability from in absence of reasonable suspicion or evidence, 110. See also habeas